MW00512371

INTRODUCTION TO SOCIOLOGY

This textbook explores the emergence of sociology as a distinct social science. Focusing on the evolution of social theories, movements and ideas through history, it analyses the dynamic relationship between the individual and the larger social forces around them.

This volume examines the definitive aspects of societies, communities and social groups, and their intersections with culture, political and economic movements and religious institutions. It establishes the connections between sociology and other disciplines such as philosophy, history, political science, economics, psychology and anthropology to explore the interdependence between different realms of social life. The chapters in this book explain and highlight the significance of quantitative and qualitative methods of research in understanding the dynamics of social life. Drawing from the works of classical social theorists such as Auguste Comte, Herbert Spencer, Karl Marx, Emile Durkheim and Max Weber, this book traces the development of sociological perspectives and theories and their relevance in the history of ideas.

Lucid and comprehensive, this textbook will be useful for undergraduate and postgraduate students of sociology, development studies, history of ideas, sociological thought, social theory, research methods, political science and anthropology.

Brij Mohan is an Assistant Professor, Department of Sociology, Kamala Nehru College, University of Delhi, India. His areas of specialisation include social theories, research methodology, social stratification, subaltern studies and industrial sociology. He is currently engaged in research on violence against Dalits in India.

INTRODUCTION TO SOCIOLOGY

Concepts and Theories

Brij Mohan

Routledge
Taylor & Francis Group

LONDON AND NEW YORK

Cover image: Getty Images

First published 2022
by Routledge
4 Park Square, Milton Park, Abingdon, Oxon OX14 4RN

and by Routledge
605 Third Avenue, New York, NY 10158

Routledge is an imprint of the Taylor & Francis Group, an informa business

British Library Cataloguing-in-Publication Data
A catalogue record for this book is available from the British Library

Library of Congress Cataloging-in-Publication Data
A catalog record has been requested for this book

ISBN: 978-1-032-04747-8 (hbk)
ISBN: 978-1-032-27037-1 (pbk)
ISBN: 978-1-003-29105-3 (ebk)

DOI: 10.4324/9781003291053

Typeset in Bembo
by Deanta Global Publishing Services, Chennai, India

for
Aditya Mongra

dedicated to
all those noble souls who, despite facing all odds, are still pursuing their
struggle to make this world a better place to live for our future generations

CONTENTS

ILLUSTRATIONS

Figures

Table

PREFACE AND
ACKNOWLEDGEMENTS

Man is a social animal. For ages man has been struggling, striving and experimenting with different forms of social relationships to satisfy his biological, emotional and social needs. The contemporary society, at its present stage of development, is nothing but a story of man's struggle and survival in his pursuit of an ideal social order. Like other social sciences, such as history and anthropology, sociology also attempts to look at this journey of man and his evolving institutions in a rather holistic manner.

As the title suggests, the main objective of this book is to introduce the learner to the most basic and fundamental concepts and theories in sociology, that too in the simplest possible manner. An attempt is made in this work to take the learner along on a journey in time and space, and help them understand the origin and evolution of various concepts and theories related to society, its social structure and social change.

The content and approach of this work go beyond the conventional academic writing. Along with imparting conceptual understanding to the learner, this book aims at facilitating conceptual interlinking and sociological articulation. Given the competitive world we live in, mere sociological knowledge alone is not sufficient for a student of sociology to dream of success. What matters the most in this competitive era is the ability to score better than others in examinations, both academic and competitive. To achieve this, equal emphasis must be placed on making one's argument contemporary as well as sociologically correct. The 'Let's Think' section in each chapter guides the learner to think about the contemporary relevance of the various sociological concepts and theories. The 'Model Answers' section, on the other hand, helps the learner to identify and understand the basic ingredients of a well-structured answer in sociology.

I hope this book will serve the interest of millions of students across the globe who are studying sociology and preparing for various academic and competitive examinations.

Before we begin our journey of learning about society and its related concepts and theories, I wish to express my deepest gratitude to all my teachers and mentors. To begin with, I would like to thank Prof. Upendra Gaur for introducing me to the ABC of sociology. A chance meeting with him was nothing less than a divine intervention in my life which changed the course of my career forever. I gave up Commerce and Accountancy, the subject in my graduation, and opted for Sociology as an optional subject for Civil Services Examination. The simplicity in my thought, in my life and in this book, is nothing but the result of his blessings. However, I am yet to master the art of balancing my professional and personal life, which he lives and demonstrates with such an ease and perfection. I am also grateful to Prof. P.S. Ravindran and Prof. Subas Mohapatra for their continuous guidance and moral support.

My understanding of sociology and society got further refined and became more systematic while pursuing M.Phil. at the Department of Sociology, Delhi School of Economics, University of Delhi. I sincerely thank all my teachers at the Department of Sociology, Delhi School of Economics, particularly Prof. Tulsi Patel, Prof. Abhijit Dasgupta, Prof. Virginius Xaxa, Prof. Satish Deshpande, Prof. Nandini Sundar, Prof. Meena Radhakrishna and Prof. Anuja Agrawal. However, just when I started feeling that I knew enough of sociology and society, I was introduced to myself and reintroduced to sociology and society during my Ph.D. by teachers at the Centre for the Study of Social Systems, School of Social Sciences, Jawaharlal Nehru University. I believe that it was a plan of Mother Nature to bring me in contact with Prof. Harish Naraindas at a very critical juncture in my life. After meeting him, I was no longer the same person, neither as a student nor as a teacher of sociology. He introduced me to myself as an individual and made me realise the importance of academics and its vital role in bringing about social transformation. I am grateful to Prof. Maitrayee Chaudhuri, Prof. Avijit Pathak, Prof. Surinder S. Jodhka, Prof. Amit Kumar Sharma and Prof. Vivek Kumar for sharing their insights on some important aspects of life, society and sociology. I am also thankful to Prof. Gurram Srinivas, Dr. Ratheesh Kumar and Dr. Divya Vaid. I am indebted to my colleagues as well as students at Kamala Nehru College, University of Delhi, for further stimulating my interest in sociology with their intellectual inputs and queries.

I am also thankful to my brothers, Dharmendra and Prakash, for their unconditional love, motivation and support all my life. I wish I could prove myself worthy of their love and affection. Jaiveer, Vikrant and Pranveer, who are not only my friends and colleagues but also my guides, deserve a special mention here for not only motivating me to write this book but also believing in me that I could do it. Most of all, I want to thank my wife, Meenakshi, for putting up with me all along. Truly speaking, it is my wife and son Aditya who paid the real price in terms of their sacrifice of our family time during the period when this book was being written. I am guilty of stealing from our family time to complete this book, especially from the playtime with Aditya. I shall also remain indebted to the blessings of my ancestors, particularly to my grandfather, Late Shri Tungal Ram Ji, for endowing me with a fighting spirit and the virtues of hard work, honesty and perseverance.

My acknowledgements would not be complete without thanking Mr. R.K. Vaid, Mr. Sanjay Gandhi and Prof. D.P. Vajpayee, whose words of wisdom, both in materialistic and spiritual matters, enabled me to sail through critical times in my life. I would also like to thank my friend and teacher of English, Mr. Prabhakar, for bearing with my grammar-related queries which were often raised at short notice. Finally, I wish to express my deepest gratitude to Routledge for promptly recognising the worth of this manuscript and expediting the process of its publication.

To conclude, I wish to state that I am solely responsible for the shortcomings of this book, if any. Remarks and suggestions from readers, to further improve the text, are most welcome.

Brij Mohan
New Delhi, January 2022
Email: bmohan@knc.du.ac.in

PART I

Introduction to Sociology

1

SOCIOLOGY

The Origin

About Sociology

Sociology, in simplest terms, implies a scientific study of society. The word 'sociology' derives its origin from two words: the Latin word *socius* (society) and the Greek word *logos* (study of or science of). The name of our discipline is thus an 'illegitimate' offspring of two languages. The etymological meaning of 'sociology' is 'the science of society,' just as geology (*geos*, earth) is 'the science of earth', biology (*bios*, life) is 'the science of life' and anthropology (*anthropos*, man) is 'the science of man'.

Sociology has a long past but only a short history. Since the dawn of human civilisation, the inquisitive minds of men have been trying to make sense of the reality that they are part of both the physical and the social. And, like nature, society has also been a subject for speculation and enquiry. However, until science appeared on the horizon of human civilisation, as both a systematic body of knowledge and a methodology, our understanding of natural and social worlds was largely based on imaginations, speculations and trial-and-error learnings. In other words, such an understanding about nature and society was often based on non-empirical and non-verifiable common sense assumptions.

In the struggle for survival, man soon realised that for the progress and welfare of mankind, a systematic and comprehensive understanding of the physical and social forces is necessary. In the course of time, man learned to observe carefully and systematically the forces shaping his life, until he reached a point at which he was able to make scientific analyses and generalisations about them. It is worth noting that the progress in man's understanding about the physical aspects of his environment occurred much earlier in comparison to the social aspects. The main reason for this discrepancy in the development of man's understanding of the two distinct environments – the physical and the social – probably

DOI: 10.4324/9781003291053-2

lies in the greater observability and control of physical phenomena, as well as in the impersonal approach that they afford. Physical phenomena are usually more concrete than social phenomena and hence are more observable. Samuel Koenig (1970) states that in his attempt to observe physical phenomena man was able quite early to develop a measure of detachment, but he found it very difficult to do so regarding social phenomena. In the latter case he found himself too close to the object of investigation, too involved in it, to achieve the objectivity which is indispensable to all science.

It is interesting to note that all inquiries were once a part of philosophy, that great mother of the sciences (*mater scientiarum*), and philosophy embraced them all in an undifferentiated and amorphous fashion. However, as Western civilisation developed, various sciences began to pursue separate and independent courses. Astronomy and physics were among the first to break away, and were followed thereafter by chemistry, biology and geology. In the nineteenth century, two new sciences appeared: psychology (the science of human behaviour) and sociology (the science of human society). Thus, what had once been natural philosophy became the science of physics; what had been mental philosophy, or the philosophy of mind, became the science of psychology; and what had once been social philosophy, or the philosophy of history, became the science of sociology. To the ancient mother, philosophy, still belong several important kinds of enquiries – notably metaphysics, epistemology, logic, ethics and aesthetics – but the sciences themselves are no longer studied as subdivisions of philosophy.

As stated earlier, man's observations and analyses of social phenomena during the medieval and early modern periods were almost wholly of a speculative character. They were at best profound reflections, wise observations. While some of these contained a good deal of truth, they were on the whole untrustworthy as guides to living. It is well acknowledged today that in order to attain a real understanding of the laws and principles underlying human association, which alone can enable us to solve effectively the problems arising from it, we must employ methods similar to those used by the natural sciences.

Man's efforts to make use of scientific observation and analysis in understanding social relationships and institutions have resulted in the rise of the social sciences, such as economics, political science, psychology and sociology. While, broadly speaking, all deal with social phenomena and are therefore interrelated and quite interdependent, each, at present, concentrates upon a particular phase of human conduct and specialises in studying it. For example, while economics studies the aspects of production, distribution and exchange, and consumption of goods and services in society, political science centres on the activities whereby man provides himself with the protections and regulations that are afforded by the government or the state. Similarly, while psychology takes a micro-level perspective and studies the individual behaviour, sociology takes a macro-level perspective in its study of human behaviour and focuses its attention on relationships which are definitely *social*. In its larger sense, sociology concerns itself with the entire domain of the social sciences, bringing its own methods and approaches to the study of all group phenomena. This makes sociology an interdisciplinary as well as the most comprehensive social science.

Before proceeding further, it is necessary to understand what we mean by the term *social*, or when an interaction or relationship becomes *social*. Not every relationship of man with man is social. Thus, if two individuals are walking in the same park, independent of each other, their relationship of coexistence, of being at the same time in the same place, or even the circumstance that their attention may be turned to the same object, does not belong to the social order. But as soon as they become aware of each other or exchange greetings, the element of sociality arises. Sociality or society is radically a mental phenomenon. A social relationship, therefore, implies reciprocal awareness between two or more people and the sense of their having something in common. Reciprocal recognition, direct or indirect, and 'commonness' are the characteristic features of every social relationship.

However, if social relationships constitute the essence of society, and if society is the subject matter of sociology, then, can it be assumed that all kinds of social relationships, enduring or unstable, organised or unorganised, constitute the domain of investigation by sociologists? Logically it may appear to be so, but in sociological literature, the term 'social relationship' is generally used for more or less stable and enduring relationships among individuals belonging to a particular group or society. The term 'society' is reserved for 'a collection of individuals held together by certain enduring relationships in the pursuance of common ends' (Gisbert, 2016).

In other words, whatever the scale and scope of a sociological study, to be sociological it must look beyond the individual to understand and explain human behaviour. Rather than explaining human behaviour simply in terms of individual mental states, sociology sees patterns of behaviour as related to the wider social context in which people live. For example, it is highly probable that in a random visit to a school in rural India it may be found that some students are absent in a particular class. Just imagine that one among these absentee students happens to be a female or a Dalit. Now, the absence of this particular student can be attributed to a number of factors such as poor health, fear of punishment for non-completion of homework, some urgent household work, family function, rough weather or just the mood of the student to bunk the class. All these reasons could be personal to that particular absentee student and hence individualistic in nature. This particular case of an absentee student may not appear strange or thought- provoking to an observer. But suppose in a rural survey, it is found that the incidence of absenteeism is very high among the females, and Dalits in particular, then it would definitely invite the attention of social scientists. Because now the reason for such large-scale absenteeism of students belonging to a particular gender or a caste group cannot merely be individualistic, it has to be social. Thus, through sociological research, sociologists may find out some sort of underlying pattern in such large-scale absenteeism, which could be related to socio-economic, cultural and historical factors. A systematic and scientific sociological enquiry would facilitate a deeper insight into gender and caste relations in the Indian society. Hence, research may indicate towards the prevailing patriarchal norms, gender division of labour, marriage practices and property rights as some of the important factors responsible for large-scale absenteeism or high dropout rates of females in the Indian education system. Jean Dreze and Amartya Sen in their famous work *India: Development and Participation* (2002) observed that the progress of female education has been particularly slow in areas of India where the gender division of labour, patrilineal inheritance, patrilocal residence, village exogamy, hypergamous marriage and related patriarchal norms tend to be particularly influential. Similarly, discriminatory attitudes of teachers and classmates, and extreme poverty could be identified as some of the socio-economic factors responsible for large-scale absenteeism or high dropout rates of Dalits in schools in India.

Sociology emerged as a distinct science of society in nineteenth-century Europe. Emerging like other sciences, however, it was preceded by a series of attempts to explain human relations and behaviour, few, if any, of which could be strictly called scientific. 'Social thought' existed, of course, in ancient times and thereafter, consisting now and then of systematic thinking and analysis, but based primarily upon speculation. In fact, this effort to understand the nature of social life may have prepared the ground for the development of sociology as the scientific study of society. Perhaps the earliest attempts at systematic thought regarding social life, at least as far as Western civilisation is concerned, may have begun with the ancient Greek philosophers, particularly the great masters of human thought, Plato (427–347 BC) and Aristotle (384–322 BC).

Social thought of this pre-scientific kind, with few exceptions, advanced very little between the time of Plato and Aristotle and early modern times. The works that could lay claim to any systematic social thought at all – during and immediately preceding the Middle Ages – reflected the teachings of the Church and were for the most part metaphysical speculations regarding the place of man on earth. In any case, none of the thinkers associated with those eras thought of themselves as sociologists, but few of them are now considered the same. However, there was one exception. This refers to one Abdel Rahman Ibn-Khaldun (1332–1406), born in Tunis, North Africa. He challenged the divine theory of kingship. In his book *Muqadimma*, Rahman Ibn-Khaldun presented his ideas, which are quite similar to those of present-day sociology. For example, he was committed to the scientific study of society, empirical research and the search for causes of social phenomena. He devoted considerable attention to various social institutions (for example, politics and economy) and their interrelationships. He stressed the importance of linking sociological thought and historical thought (Ritzer and Stepnisky, 2014). However, barring this one exception, it was not until the sixteenth century that there appeared writers who treated life's problems on a more realistic level.

Perhaps the most notable among these was the Italian Niccolo Machiavelli (1469–1527), in whose work, *The Prince*, published in 1513, we find an attempt at an objective discussion of the state and statecraft. This book, unlike his other works, was devoted chiefly to an exposition of the principles governing the successful state, or rather the successful ruler of a state. It is a practical guide for the ruler who would maintain his power. Insofar as Machiavelli sought to base his theories of the state upon historical data, he may be considered in a sense an objective writer. Another author in this period worth noting was Sir Thomas More (1478–1535). Although his book *Utopia*, published in 1515, represented an approach, virtually the opposite of that found was in Machiavelli's writings, it was nevertheless a step in the direction of dealing with everyday social problems, albeit by means of depicting an ideal social order which presumably was presented for emulation. More's *Utopia* pictured a perfect state where all the problems with which the society, or rather the England of his day, was beset have been solved and where complete justice reigns. This perfect society is made possible by putting into practice the rules of natural law. Considerable strides towards the objective analysis of social forces were made in the writings of the Italian Vico and the Frenchman Montesquieu, who, while primarily political philosophers, had considerable influence upon the consequent rise of a science of society. Giovanni Battista Vico (1668–1744) in his book *The New Science* contended that society was subject to definite laws which can be discovered through objective observation and study. Charles Louis de Secondat Montesquieu (1689–1775) exerted an even greater influence than Vico in the direction of scientific investigation of social phenomena through his brilliant works, particularly his *Esprit des lois (The Spirit of Laws)*, which presents a keen analysis of the role certain external factors, especially climate, play in the life of human societies. To these two writers may be added two more, Condorcet and Saint-Simon, whose contributions towards the development of a science of society were even more direct.

In his *Sketch for a Historical Picture of the Progress of the Human Mind*, Marquis de Condorcet (1743–1794), also known as Nicolas de Condorcet, formulated a theory of social change which had a far-reaching influence upon later sociological theories. In this book he propounded a stage theory of social evolution, according to which civilisation passed through ten developmental stages, each higher than the preceding one, the highest still to be attained in the future. Claude Henri Saint-Simon (1760–1825), though primarily a utopian reformer, insisted that social reform can be achieved only when scientific or 'positive' data have been collected. These four writers, although their contributions were primarily in the field of political thought and philosophy, may be considered among the forerunners of sociology.

It was in the nineteenth century that a French philosopher named Auguste Comte (1798–1857) worked out, in a series of books, a general approach to the study of society. He believed that the sciences follow one another in a definite and logical order and that all enquiry goes through certain stages, arriving finally at the last, scientific stage. He thought that it was time for inquiries into social problems and social phenomena to enter the last stage and so he recommended that the study of society become the science of society. Comte had initially called this new science of society as 'social physics'. Later, however, on finding that a Belgian scientist, Adolphe Quetelet, had used this term to describe simple statistics, Comte reluctantly changed it to 'sociology'. Comte and his ideas about scientific study of society would be discussed in more detail subsequently.

As mentioned earlier, sociology as a science, and particularly as a separate field of study, did not make its appearance until about the middle of the nineteenth century in Europe. Europe then was passing through a period of drastic transformation which had set in on account of a series of revolutions, beginning with the Commercial and Scientific Revolutions (in the fifteenth century), followed by the Agrarian Revolution (in the sixteenth century), Industrial Revolution and the French Revolution (in the eighteenth century). These revolutions revolutionised the socio-economic and political framework of the 'traditional' feudal European society of medieval times and laid the foundations of a new 'modern' industrial society. The social, economic, political and psychological consequences of these revolutions were so great that the French social analyst Alexis de Tocqueville (1805–1859) thought that they amounted to 'nothing short of the regeneration of the whole human race' (Macionis, 2015).

The rise of a factory-based industrial economy, the explosive growth of cities and new ideas about democracy and political rights were considered by some scholars of that time as indicators of progress of human society. In retrospect, contemporary scholars have called these changes 'modern'. However, before we discuss in detail the cause and consequences of these revolutions on the socio-economic and political structure of the feudal European society, let us first try to understand the meaning of the term 'modernity'.

Idea of 'Modernity'

Modernity has often been viewed as being in opposition to and representing a break from tradition. If tradition looked to the past, modernity presumably turned its eye to the future. English language inherits the word 'modern' from ancient Latin, where it has been in use since at least the sixth century of the Christian era. For the first 1,200 years or so of its history, the word was used in a generic sense to characterise the distinctiveness of any contemporary era in order to distinguish it from past eras. Around the eighteenth century, the word acquired a new and more specific sense that referred to the unique social system that emerged in Western Europe between the seventeenth and nineteenth centuries, and the values and institutions associated with this system.

According to Lloyd Rudolph and Susanne Rudolph,

> modernity assumes that local ties and parochial perspectives give way to universal commitments and cosmopolitan attitudes; that the truths of utility, calculation, and science take precedence over those of the emotions, the sacred, and the non-rational; that the individual rather than the group be the primary unit of society and politics; that the associations in which

men live and work be based on choice not birth; that mastery rather than fatalism orient their attitude toward the material and human environment; that identity be chosen and achieved, not ascribed and affirmed; that work be separated from family, residence, and community in bureaucratic organisations.

(Deshpande, 2004)

Eminent Indian sociologist Satish Deshpande argues that by the twentieth century the term 'modernisation' had become increasingly common and was 'normally used to indicate something unquestionably favourable or desirable'. This general connotation of a process of positive change or improvement was inflected by the suggestion of a more predetermined movement towards the European Enlightenment model of modernity.

Deshpande argues that an important aspect of modernity is the fact that it is also a source of the conceptual tools that have been used to understand it. In this sense, therefore, modernity defines our intellectual horizon. The social sciences, as we have known them, are themselves products of and responses to modernity, having emerged in the post-Enlightenment era in Western Europe. The discipline of sociology, in particular, was invented as part of a larger attempt to make sense of this new and historically unprecedented social system. The classical theorists acknowledged as the founders of the discipline – including Auguste Comte, Herbert Spencer, Karl Marx, Emile Durkheim, Max Weber and Ferdinand Tonnies – were all concerned with theorising the Western European experience of modernisation, the process of becoming or being made modern.

Please note that Weber in his writings had suggested that when societies change from agrarian (pre-industrial) to industrial mode of production, this process involves a rational transformation of society. Thus, following the writings of Weber and Durkheim, modernisation may be defined as the process of rational transformation of the psychological, social, economic and political aspects of society.

Before proceeding further, we must understand that if modernity is viewed as being in opposition to and representing a break from tradition, then what was tradition like? In other words, what were the features of traditional feudal society of medieval Europe? In the history of Europe, the medieval period, also sometimes called the Middle Ages, roughly refers to the period from AD 600 to about AD 1500.

Features of Feudal European Society

Historians as well as social theorists generally agree that from the fourteenth century to the sixteenth century AD, Europe had been witnessing changes in its social, economic and political structures, which marked the beginning of what we call the modern period.

Society of medieval Europe (before the fourteenth century) was largely feudal in character. Feudalism was the dominant system of social-economic and political organisation in Western Europe from the tenth to the fifteenth century. It had emerged on account of the downfall and decentralisation of the Roman Empire and the absence of any central authority. The word 'feudal' comes from *feud*, which originally meant a *fief* or land held on condition or service. In a feudal society, land was the source of the power. Thus, feudal system was based on allocation of land in return for service.

Feudalism was based upon a system of land tenure in which land estates of various sizes (fiefs) were given to hold (not to own) by an overlord to his vassals (knights) in return for military service. These fiefs may further be subdivided by a vassal among other knights who would then be his vassals. Such fiefs consisted of one or more *manors*, that is, *estates* with serfs whose agricultural production provided the economic basis for the existence of the feudal class. When receiving a fief, a vassal took an oath of homage and fealty (fidelity) to his lord and owed him loyalty as well as a specified amount of military service. Upon the death of a vassal, the fief would technically revert to the overlord, but it was common practice for the eldest son to take his father's place as vassal of the lord, and thus, in effect, fiefs were passed on through primogeniture.

Medieval European society was primarily divided into feudal 'estates'. Estate system of social stratification was the characteristic feature of feudal European societies. Estates are defined as a system of stratification found in feudal European societies whereby one section or estate is distinguished from the other in terms of status, privileges and restrictions accorded to that estate. The feudal estates of medieval Europe had three important characteristics. First, estates were legally defined. In other words, each estate had a status, in the precise sense of a legal complex of rights and duties, of privileges and obligations. The differences between estates can also be seen in the different penalties imposed for similar offences. Second, the estates represented a broad division of labour and were regarded in the contemporary literature as having definite functions. The nobility were ordained to defend all, the clergy to pray for all and the commons to provide food for all. Third, the feudal estates also acted as political groups.

Thus, the feudal society in Europe was a hierarchical and graded organisation in which every person was allotted a position. At the top stood the king. He bestowed fiefs or estates on a number of lords who were known as dukes and earls. These lords in turn distributed a part of their fiefs among a number of lesser lords, who were called barons and, in return, secured their military support. Thus, the dukes and earls were the king's vassals, that is to say, they owed allegiance directly to the king. The barons were the vassals of the dukes and earls. The knights formed the lowest category of feudal lords. Usually, they were the vassals of barons for whom they performed military service. Knights did not have any vassals of their own. Every feudal lord was expected to pay homage to his overlord and could then be invested with some formal rights. Every feudal lord, except the knight, was first a vassal and then an overlord with a number of vassals under him. The relationship from top to bottom was one of allegiance. No vassal owned any land; he only held the land of his overlord. The vassal was in every way his lord's man. He recognised no other authority than of his overlord. In time of need, for example, when the king fought a war, he could demand military assistance from his vassals; these vassals – the dukes and the earls – demanded the same assistance from their vassals, the barons, and the barons from their vassals, the knights. Every feudal lord contributed a detachment of warriors, and thus a fighting army would be formed (Figure 1.1).

Feudal life, as explained in the previous section, was based on agriculture. The village farm was the *manor*, the size of which varied from place to place. Its centre was the manor house of the lord where he lived or which he visited, for the lords often possessed several manors. The manor included a large farm which supported all those who worked on it, a pasture area where the manor cattle grazed and common woods which supplied fuel and timber. A manor always had a number of cottages where the common people lived, some workshops to provide for manor needs and a chapel.

Manorialism was an essential element of feudal society. It was a system of land tenure and the organising principle of rural economy. It was characterised by the vesting of legal and economic power in a lord, supported economically from his own direct landholding and from the obligatory contributions of a legally subject part of the peasant population under his jurisdiction. These obligations could be payable in several ways: in labour, in kind or in coin, etc. Manor was the lowest unit of territorial organisation in the feudal system in Europe. It may also be referred to as the land tenure unit under manorialism. Country people often lived on a manor. On a manor there was a village, a church, the lord's house or castle and the farmland upon which the people worked.

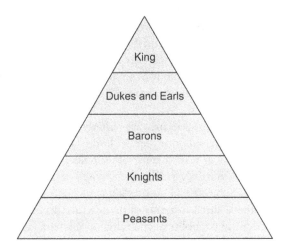

FIGURE 1.1 Feudal Society in Medieval Europe

Let us now briefly discuss the economic, social and political characteristics of the feudal European society. Since feudal estates were based principally on the allotment of large parcels of land to a political aristocracy, they largely constituted autonomous political and legal jurisdictions and were managed by an aristocratic class who used land as a source of economic livelihood. The principal economic activity of the feudal estate was thus confined to agricultural production. Hence, it may be argued that the feudal European society was primarily a stagnant and subsistence type of agrarian economy. The relationship of feudal lords and serfs was both paternalistic and hereditary. Though the relationship was apparently marked by economic exploitation and socio-political subjugation, yet in the times of famine or wars, feudal lords shared a moral obligation to protect and look after its subjects.

Socially, the society was relatively a closed society marked by estate system of social stratification with little opportunity for social mobility. Consequently, feudal society was comprised of village communities with wider and stronger social bonds. Socio-economic and political relations were largely shaped and governed by the Roman Catholic Church, which was a powerful institution in Western Europe during the medieval times. At the head of the Church was the Pope, who was accepted as the vicar of Christ. Many Christian monks – St Francis, St Benedict, St Augustine – laid great stress on purity, resistance to temptation and the pursuit of 'goodness'. Popes were often stronger than the kings and could force them to obey their orders. Gradually, however, corruption crept into the monasteries. They acquired land and amassed wealth, helping to make the Church one of the biggest landowners in medieval times. With cultivation and other work done by serfs, the life of many monks and nuns was no longer frugal and austere. Luxury, good food and drink and idleness became common.

During the early Middle Ages, the Church was the only centre of education and learning. However, the learning fostered by the Church was a narrow type. Subjects that it taught were grammar, logic, arithmetic and theology. The only calling for which this education was suitable was that of a monk or a priest. The language of learning was Latin, which only churchmen could read. Everything was dominated by faith, and anybody who appealed to reason against dogma was punished. Science had come to a standstill. Magic and superstition held the day.

Politically, the system of governance was highly decentralised and unstable, leaving ample scope for any ambitious feudal lord to dream bigger. Such feudal lords were often engaged in wars against other feudal lords or the king itself. Further, the political authority was largely exercised in an arbitrary, autocratic authoritarian manner. Subjects had no fundamental rights, and rule of the king was legitimised by the Church in terms of the 'divine theory of kingship'. The divine theory of kingship is a political and religious doctrine of royal and political legitimacy. It asserts that a monarch is subject to no earthly authority, deriving his right to rule directly from the will of God.

However, during the medieval period, feudalism served its purpose of bringing a measure of social order and stability in European society. It allowed social and economic activity to run its normal course. But feudalism also had another side to it. It developed, and was dependent on, a rigid and hierarchical estate system of social stratification which was deeply marked by socio-economic and political inequality. Man was divided from man, estate from estate, and this stood in the way of political unity. The nobles looked down upon the common man, and their inherited authority brought with it one-man rule and oppression. The lords were often too powerful for the kings to control and fought among themselves for small selfish ends. The king had no contact with the common man, who was left entirely to the mercy of his lord, and the lord was usually irresponsible and unmindful of the welfare of common people. The feudal system also led to economic stagnation. The wealth produced by the peasants and the artisans was wastefully consumed by the feudal lords, in luxurious living and in wars. Individual enterprise and initiative were all but unknown. Further, the desire for the new lands and riches encouraged the lords and leaders of the Church to fight the 'holy wars', or the Crusades.

The medieval period of European society, lasting roughly from the fifth through the thirteenth centuries AD, have often been called the 'Dark Ages', and to some extent it was truly so. This period was marked by the arbitrary rule of the king, helplessness of the common man and absence of national unity. Education was very uncommon and people led miserable lives. The general prevailing European view was that the civilisation during the Dark Ages had stagnated. Scientific and artistic advances were rare and much of the knowledge of the classical period was lost. Cultural activities came to an end with the arrival of invading 'barbarians', and the western Roman Empire disintegrated into thousands of isolated villages where there was little interest in, or time for, study. Memory of the classical period faded, except in a few sequestered monasteries, where ancient texts were stored, and in the Islamic world, where scholars translated Greek texts into Arabic. During the Dark Ages, the overwhelming majority of Europeans were crude illiterates, and even educated people knew less about science, medicine and art than their counterparts in the classical period.

But the character of feudal European society started changing from the fourteenth century onwards. The revival of trade (discussed later under 'Commercial Revolution') was accompanied by the growth of towns. Large towns started emerging mainly as centres of manufacture and trade but gradually freed themselves from feudal control. They had their own governments, militia and courts. Unlike the serfs, there were no restrictions on the movement of people in towns. They could come and go as they pleased and buy and sell property. Towns provided asylum to serfs who escaped from feudal oppression. The towns encouraged the cultivation of cash crops needed for manufactures, and peasants received their payments in money.

Growth of trade was accompanied by the increasing use of money. Money had little use in feudal societies. In traditional feudal society, a feudal manor was more or less self-sufficient for its needs. There was very little of buying and selling, and whatever there was, was done through barter. The use of money indicated far-reaching changes in economy. Land was the indicator of a man's wealth. Some people had wealth, particularly the Church and sometimes the nobles, in the form of gold and silver, but it was idle wealth. It could not be used to make more wealth. With the growth of trade and manufactures, this changed, marking the beginning of the transition from feudal economy to capitalist economy, in which wealth is used to make a profit. This is done by investing money in business, in trade and industry. The profits made are reinvested to make further profits. Such wealth or money is called 'capital'. Money, not the landed property, increasingly became the measure of man's wealth.

Mainly, there were three classes of people in feudal societies: the prayers, that is, the clergy who prayed; the soldiers or the knights who fought; and workers or the peasants who worked for both the prayers and the soldiers. However, with the growth of trade, a new class emerged – the 'middle class' – comprising mainly the merchants. Even though small in number, they began to play an important role in society because of the wealth they possessed. This early phase of capitalism is known as 'mercantile capitalism'. Thus, mercantile capitalism is a system of trading for profit, typically in commodities produced by non-capitalist production methods.

With the growth in trade and commerce, changes also took place in the system of manufacturing goods. In the early medieval period, most of the non-agricultural products required by the peasants were produced in the household of the peasant and by serfs, who were skilled craftsmen, for the lord. However, with the emergence of towns, many of these activities shifted to towns where people skilled in particular crafts organised themselves into 'guilds'. Each craft guild was usually comprised of master craftsmen, journeymen and apprentices. To learn a craft, a person joined a master as an apprentice or learner. After having learned the craft, he worked as a journeyman with the master on a wage, or if he had mastered the craft, he would himself become a master craftsman. However, the guild system was not suited to the requirements of large-scale production required by an expanding market for goods. Soon the system began to decline and was replaced by 'the putting out system'. Under the new system, the merchant would bring the master craftsmen the raw materials, the craftsmen would work with their tools as before in their homes and the produce would be taken away by the merchant who had supplied them with raw materials. Thus, in effect, unlike before, the craftsmen did not own what they produced. They were increasingly reduced to the position of wage earners, except that they still owned the tools used by them and worked at home.

With time, these traditional modes of production gave way to the factory system (discussed later under 'Industrial Revolution'). In the factory system, the production was carried out in a building owned by the capitalist with the help of machines also owned by him. The workers, owing nothing, worked only for wages. In industries, such as mining and metal-working, the new system came into being early. The period saw tremendous expansion of manufactures. This was accompanied by a growing differentiation in towns and the emergence of working class.

These developments struck at the root of the feudal system, and as a result the feudal system broke down. The towns which were free from the control of the lords began to undermine the stability of the feudal society. In course of time, towns became very prosperous. Kings who were quite powerless in the feudal system began to take the help and support of townsmen to increase their power and to enforce their will over the lords. The kings also started having their own armies, and thus freed themselves from their earlier dependence on the lords for soldiers. This led to the emergence of strong nation-states. Thus, feudalism began to decline although it finally ended in most countries only in the eighteenth and nineteenth centuries. In its place, a new system of society (capitalist society) began to emerge.

However, fourteenth century onwards the society in Europe started changing. A number of interrelated developments took place in the period from about the fourteenth century to the seventeenth century, which marked the beginning of modern age. Let us first understand what were these changes that took place from about the fourteenth century to the seventeenth century in Europe and marked the beginning of modern age. How was the new social order, which emerged in Europe from about the seventeenth century onwards, qualitatively different from the previous traditional social orders? In the subsequent sections, we will learn about the various social, economic and political changes that Europe witnessed in the form of Renaissance, Commercial Revolution, Scientific Revolution, Reformation, Enlightenment, Industrial Revolution, French Revolution, etc. We will also try to understand how modernity and social changes in Europe led to the emergence of sociology.

Renaissance

One of the first developments that marked the beginning of a new era was the *Renaissance*. The medieval Dark Ages was followed by the Renaissance, beginning in the fourteenth century and lasting to the end of the sixteenth century. The Renaissance refers, in a literal sense, to the intellectual rebirth of Europe as people tried to recapture the artistic, philosophical, scientific and commercial glory of the 'classical period'. It is important to emphasise that the conventional nineteenth-century assessment was that the Renaissance had been a period of rediscovery. There was a great appreciation for the cultural accomplishments of the Greeks and Romans and a genuine desire to replicate those accomplishments and, hence, to recapture the cultural glory of earlier times.

The 'Classical period' of Western history, the era of Greece and, later, Rome, lasted roughly from the eighth century BC until the fourth century AD. A number of scientific and artistic advances were made during this period, such as geometry was developed, money came into circulation, trade expanded, accounting practices emerged, shipbuilding improved, literature was born, comedies and tragedies were written, amphitheatres and libraries were constructed, great philosophical debates raged, engineers achieved wondrous feats (literally, the 'wonders of the ancient world'), monuments were built, medicine advanced, elements of democratic governmental forms came into being and education expanded. In short, civilisation flowered. Advances were intermittent, to be sure, but over time the total stock of knowledge increased and diffused widely to other parts of the world. At least it was the nineteenth-century European view that the classical period of the Greeks and Romans marked such a flowering of civilisation (Turner et al., 1995).

The term 'Renaissance' literally means rebirth and is, in a narrow sense, used to describe the revival of interest in the learning of the classical civilisations of Greece and Rome. This revival first began in Italy when a number of scholars from Constantinople (Istanbul of today in Turkey) migrated to Italy and a number of Italian scholars went to Constantinople and other cities of the old Byzantine empire in search of Greek classics. The Renaissance emerged in Italy roughly between AD 1300 and AD 1550 and then spread to northern Europe during the first half of the sixteenth century. The Renaissance started in Italy because of several factors. First, due to its strategic geographical location, Italy always had a cultural advantage over the rest of Europe because its geography made it the natural gateway between the East and the West. Several Italian cities like Venice, Genoa, Milan, Pisa and Florence traded uninterruptedly with the Asian countries and maintained a vibrant urban society. The Italian cities had grown up in an atmosphere of freedom from feudal control. Freedom encouraged thinking and a spirit of adventure. The rulers of the Italian states were patrons of learning and the arts.

During the fourteenth and fifteenth centuries, as trade and commerce grew, mercantile cities expanded to become powerful city states dominating the political and economic life of the surrounding countryside. Italian aristocrats largely lived in urban centres rather than in rural castles unlike their counterparts in northern Europe and consequently became fully involved in urban public affairs. The neo-rich mercantile communities, which came to be known as the *bourgeoisie*, tried to gain the status of aristocracy and imitated an aristocratic lifestyle. Their wealth and profession became an important factor for the development of education in Italy. There was an increasing demand for education, not only for the development of skills in reading and accountancy, necessary to become successful merchants, but also because the richest and most prominent families looked for able teachers who would impart to their offspring the knowledge and skills necessary to argue well in the public arena. Consequently, Italy produced a large number of educators, many of whom not only taught students but also demonstrated their learning in the production of political and ethical treaties and works of literature.

Another reason for the birth of an intellectual and artistic renaissance in late medieval Italy was a close association which it shared with the classical past than any other region of Europe. In Italy, the classical past appeared immensely relevant as ancient Roman monuments were present all over the peninsula, and the ancient Latin literature referred to cities and sites that Italians recognised as their own. Further, Italian Renaissance was also facilitated by the patronage that it received from the wealthy cities of Italy, which vied with each other to construct splendid public monuments and support writers whose role was to glorify the urban republic in their writing and speeches. As a result, hundreds of classical writings, unknown to Europeans for centuries, were circulating first in Italy and then in other parts of Europe. The interest in classical learning and in other achievements of the civilisations of Greece and Rome deeply influenced Europeans. However, the Renaissance was not only about a mere revival of ancient learning and knowledge of the achievements of ancient Greece and Rome. It was also marked by a series of new developments in the field of art, literature, religion, philosophy, science and politics.

Some scholars have described the early phase of Renaissance as a period of revival as it concentrated in reviving the old learning which was disseminated through the traditional methods. The latter phase was described as a period of innovation as much new knowledge was generated during this period, which laid the foundation for the growth of modern thought. This new knowledge was spread by a new medium, i.e. print. This meant that a large number of people and countries could share the knowledge and debate the changes. Though the study of classical and Christian antiquity existed before the Renaissance, there was a significant difference between the learning of the middle age scholars and the Renaissance thinkers. The Renaissance thinkers recovered the works of lesser-known scholars and made them popular alongside the more famous ones. The Greek scientific and the philosophical treatises were made available to the Westerners in Latin translations. The Renaissance thinkers used classical texts in new ways such as to reconsider their preconceived notions and alter their mode of expression.

So, rational thinking tempered with a spirit of scientific enquiry about the universe, and the existence of humanity in it, became the important characteristic of the Renaissance outlook. These rational ideas also helped in developing a society that was increasingly non-ecclesiastical in comparison to the culture of the Middle Ages. In the medieval European society, the intellectual and cultural life of people had been dominated by the Catholic Church for centuries. The Renaissance undermined this domination. The revival of pre-Christian classical learning and of interest in the cultural achievements of ancient Greece and Rome were, in themselves, also an important factor in undermining the domination of the Church.

The chief characteristic of the Renaissance way of thinking was *humanism*. It was the heart and soul of the Renaissance. This implied a decisive shift in concern for human as distinct from divine matters. Humanism was a system of views which extolled man, stressed his essential worth and dignity, expressed deep faith in his tremendous creative potential and proclaimed freedom of the individual and inalienable rights of the individual. It was centred on the man of flesh and blood with all his earthly joys and sorrows, opposed to religious asceticism, and defended his right to pleasure and the satisfaction of earthly desires and requirements. It meant the glorification of the human and natural as opposed to the divine and other-worldly. The humanists rejected and even ridiculed religious asceticism, mortification of the flesh and withdrawal from the world. They urged man to seek joy on this earth rather than in an afterlife which the Church advocated. Their works were permeated with the faith that a man with an active mind and body was capable of knowing and controlling the world, of performing miracles and fashioning his own happiness. The proper study of Mankind, it was asserted, is Man, Humanity rather than Divinity. The Renaissance men believed that human life is important, that man is worthy of study and respect and that there should be efforts to improve life on this earth. Because of this interest in human affairs, the study of literature and history became major areas of study. Literature and history came to be called the 'humanities' which were primarily concerned with understanding the affairs of man in his earthly life, not with life after death (Dev, 2002).

Commercial Revolution, Agricultural Revolution and Industrial Revolution

Another development which marked the beginning of the modern age was the 'Commercial Revolution', fostered by a series of 'voyages of discovery'. The Commercial Revolution refers to the expansion of trade and commerce that took place from the fifteenth century onwards. This expansion of trade and commerce was of such a large scale and organised manner that it is called a revolution. It signalled a transition from the largely subsistence and stagnant economy of medieval Europe to a more dynamic and worldwide system. This expansion was as a result of the initiative taken by certain European countries such as Portugal, Spain, Holland and England, to develop and consolidate their economic and political power.

The same spirit of curiosity that led some of Europe's Renaissance men to effect new developments in art, literature, science and religion led others to adventure and the discovery of new lands. The primary motive behind these adventures was the profits that trade with the East would bring. Earlier, Europe's trade with the Oriental or Eastern countries like India and China was transacted by land routes. Italian cities of Venice and Genoa were the major centres of trade. As a result of the Italian monopoly, the prices of goods like spices and silks imported from the East were extremely high. For example, after his first voyage to India, Vasco da Gama found that the price of pepper in Calicut was 1/26 of the price prevailing in Venice. The prosperity of the Italian cities that had grown rich from their trade with eastern countries aroused the envy of the other European nations; they longed to have a share in the trade.

However, after 1453, when the Turks cut off this land route of trade through Asia Minor, search for alternatives routes of trade began. Thus, a shift from land routes to sea routes began. Various scientific inventions such as invention of mariner's compass, astrolabe and newly prepared maps and guidebooks greatly facilitated these voyages. While the compass guided navigators in determining the directions on high seas, the astrolabe helped in determining the latitude of a particular area. Most of these voyages were financed by rulers and merchants who sponsored the costly voyages of the seafarers for the profits that the voyages would bring. These voyages also facilitated greater geographical knowledge about the world, and the older maps which were both inaccurate and incomplete were redrawn.

The voyages and discoveries of Columbus, Vasco da Gama and Magellan changed man's idea of the world, revolutionised trade and started waves of colonisation that have determined the course of world history ever since. Portugal and Spain were among the first European countries which financed these explorations and discoveries. Britain, France and Holland soon followed Spain and Portugal. Soon parts of Asia, Africa, Malacca, the Spice Islands, West Indies, North America and South America came under the control of Spain, Portugal, Britain, France and Holland. The monopoly of the Italian cities was destroyed. European markets were now flooded with new commodities, for example, spices and textiles from the East; tobacco from North America; cocoa, chocolate and quinine from South America; and ivory and, above all, human slaves from Africa. Further, with the discovery of Americas, the range of trade widened, which now included gold and silver along with spices and cloth. However, as the Commercial Revolution progressed, the position of Portugal and Spain declined, and soon Britain, France and Holland came to dominate Europe and eventually the world. This marked the early phase of capitalism known as 'mercantile capitalism'. It was characterised by growth of trade and commerce and generating profits through trade. One of the distinctive characteristics of this period was the rise of the middle class to economic power. The middle class included merchants, bankers, ship owners, investors, etc. Their power, at this stage, was mainly economic. But soon these neo-rich mercantile communities, which later came to be known as the *bourgeoisie*, began asserting their right of political representation and participation. Thus, a power struggle against the feudal nobility and the king became inevitable, which later culminated in the French Revolution.

The enormous wealth or capital that was accumulated by this mercantile class in trade and commerce was further reinvested in land and agriculture (scientific farming and sheep-rearing) to generate further profits. This led to the transformation of agriculture in Europe, called the 'Agricultural Revolution'. The Agrarian Revolution saw the transformation of a system of subsistence into a system of surplus by production of cash crops for the market, the surplus being made possible by reformed and mechanised cultivation. So, mercantile capitalism was followed by the capitalistic transformation of agriculture or agrarian capitalism. The first sign of capitalistic transformation of agriculture manifested itself in England in the form of land enclosures, which began to occur in the rural economy as early as 1560, when landholders began to assert rights of private property over feudal land. It has been called by the historians as 'enclosure movement'.

According to Ken Morrison (2012),

> Essentially, the enclosure movement can be described as a system whereby tenant holdings in feudal land and agriculture became enclosed and made available for the private use of landholder. As a result, peasant families were evicted from their holdings and in many cases thrown off the land.

By 1710, the first Enclosure Bill appeared, which legalised the enclosure of tenant holdings by Parliamentary Acts, and landlords were able to assert rights of modern private property over land to which they previously held only feudal title. Thus, for the first time in the history of mankind, land became a private property which could be bought and sold just like any other commercial commodity. As the pace of economic change began to intensify, the rate of enclosures accelerated to the point where the displaced population of agricultural workers began to increase dramatically, and this began to mobilise a transfer of the population to the centres of industry.

The eviction of the poor peasants from their means of livelihood, their agricultural land, took place at such a massive scale in Europe that it took the form of a society-wide depopulation movement. Under these circumstances, the customary hereditary rights and obligations of peasants in land began to be forcibly dissolved, and soon the historical paternalistic ties between feudal lords and serfs transformed into contractual relationships between the newly emerging class of capitalists and the workers. As soon as money rents replaced labour rent, those peasants who were unable to pay were eventually evicted. Breakdown of feudal obligations in land placed the serf population under new forces of social differentiation and fragmentation. The serf population was now placed at the disposal of the new forces of production, which put into play a massive demographic transfer of the agricultural population into the industrial centres, bringing about a more complete transition to a new category of labour based on wages. At this stage, the flow of population from the old feudal economies to the new economies of industry became a more urgent fact of economic change, and this began to complete the process of transforming the agricultural worker of previous centuries into the wage labourer of the industrial economy (ibid.).

The displacement of the serf population from the rural economies had some serious consequences. First, the massive social displacement of families during enclosure movement disrupted the traditional community ties and regional modes of life. Second, it radically altered the system of economic livelihood by forcing serfs to sell their labour for a wage, and severing the serf's feudal relation to the agricultural means of production. Third, with the shift to an industrial economy, the old class structure of the feudal society was replaced by the formation of a new commercial class that was at the centre of power and industry. This began to bring about the transfer of the ownership of the means of production to the commercial classes and, consequently, as the means of production fell into private hands, it became the property of one class (ibid.).

During much of the eighteenth century, the last remnants of the old economic order were crumbling under the impact of the Industrial Revolution. In historical terminology, Industrial Revolution means primarily the period of British history from the middle of the eighteenth century to the middle of the nineteenth century. England in the eighteenth century was in the most favourable position for an industrial revolution. She had accumulated vast profits through her overseas trade, including trade in slaves, which could provide the necessary capital. In the trade rivalries of European countries, England had emerged as an unrivalled power. England had acquired colonies which ensured a regular supply of raw materials. The term 'Industrial Revolution' was first used in the 1880s to denote the sudden acceleration of technical developments by the application of steam power to machines, which replaced tools. The term got popularised when Arnold Toynbee's *Industrial Revolution* appeared in 1884.

As discussed earlier, the new system of society which had been emerging in Europe from the fifteenth century was called *capitalism*. In the capitalistic mode of production, the instruments and the means by which goods are produced are owned by private individuals and the production is carried out for making profit. The owners of wealth under capitalism, who are called capitalists, do not keep their wealth or consume it or use it for purposes of display but invest it to make profit. Goods are produced for sale in the market with an objective to make profit. The workers under this system do not own anything but work for a wage. This system is in marked contrast with the feudal system in which goods were produced for local use and the investment of wealth for making profit did not take place. Feudal economy was static as goods were produced for local consumption and there was no incentive to produce more by employing better means of producing goods for a bigger market. In contrast, the economy under capitalism was fast-moving with the aim of producing more and more goods for bigger markets so that more profits could be made (Dev, 2002).

The desire to produce more goods at low cost to make higher profits led to the Industrial Revolution and further growth of capitalism. The Industrial Revolution began in England around the 1760s. It brought about great changes in the social and economic life of the people first in England, then in other countries of Europe and later in other continents. During the Industrial Revolution, invention of new tools and techniques facilitated the mass production of goods, and thus gave rise to the factory mode of production. In Europe, especially England, the discovery of new territories, explorations, growth of trade and commerce and the consequent growth of towns and cities had brought about an increase in demand of goods. Increasingly, machines began to take over some of the works of men and animals in the production of goods and commodities, thus marking the beginning of a 'machine age'. Production was now carried on in a factory (in place of workshops in homes), with the help of machines (in place of simple tools). Facilities for production were owned and managed by *capitalists*, the people with money to invest in further production. Everything required for production was provided by the capitalists for the workers who were brought together under one roof. Everything belonged to the owner of the factory, including the finished product, and workers worked for wages. This phase of capitalism is known as industrial capitalism. Industrial capitalism is capitalism's classical or stereotypical form. As capitalism became more and more complex, the development of banks, insurance companies and finance corporations took place. This led to the emergence of new classes of capitalists, managers and industrial workers.

The eighteenth century witnessed the growth of free labour and more competitive manufacturing. Initially, it was the cotton industry to break the hold of the guilds and chartered corporations, but with each decade, other industries too were subjected to the liberating effects of free labour, free trade and free production. Large-scale industrialisation had a profound effect on reorganisation of society. According to Turner et al. (1995),

> Labour was liberated from the land; wealth and capital existed independently of the large noble estates; large-scale industry accelerated urbanisation of the population; the extension of competitive industry hastened the development of new technologies; increased production encouraged the expansion of markets and world trade for securing raw resources and selling finished goods; religious organisations lost much of their authority in the face of secular economic activities; family structure was altered as people moved from rural to urban areas; law became as concerned with regularising the new economic processes as with preserving the privilege of the nobility; and the old political regimes legitimated by 'divine right' successively became less tenable.

The newly emerging capitalist economic system struck at the root of feudal order. These economic changes greatly altered the way people lived, created new social classes (such as the bourgeoisie and urban proletariat) and led not only to a revolution of ideas but also to a series of political revolutions. These changes were less traumatic in England than in France, where the full brunt of these economic forces clashed with the Old Regime. It was in this volatile mixture of economic changes, coupled with the Scientific Revolution of the sixteenth and seventeenth centuries, that political and intellectual revolutions were to be spawned. And out of these combined revolutions, sociology emerged (ibid.).

Scientific Revolution and Religious Reformation

The Renaissance period also saw the beginning of the 'Scientific Revolution'. It is an undeniable fact that if we want to seek out the causes of the Scientific Revolution, we must look for them among the wider changes taking place in that period of sea change in European history known as the Renaissance. The Scientific Revolution cannot be explained without reference to the Renaissance. The Scientific Revolution, like the Protestant Reformation, can and should be seen as one of the outcomes of the Renaissance. The Scientific Revolution marked an era of description and criticism in the field of science. It was a clear break from the past, a challenge to old authority. The impact of the Scientific Revolution was crucial not just in changing material life, but also man's ideas about nature and society. It is worth noting that science does not develop independent of society; rather it develops in response to human needs. For example, various vaccines were developed out of the necessity to cure diseases. Apart from influencing the physical or material life of society, science is intimately connected with ideas. The general intellectual atmosphere existing in society influences the development of science. Similarly, new developments in science can also change the attitudes and beliefs of people about nature and society. New scientific ideas influenced scholars to think about society in new ways. The emergence of sociology in Europe owes a great deal to the ideas and discoveries contributed by science.

In the medieval feudal society of Europe, the Church was the epicentre of authority and learning. Knowledge was largely religious in nature. Nothing could challenge the 'dogmas' or rigid beliefs of the Church. New, daring ideas could not flower in such an atmosphere. Thus, the development of science was restricted mainly to improvement in the techniques of production. However, the Renaissance thinkers rejected the blind acceptance of authority. They asserted that knowledge could be gained 'by going out and studying mentally and manually the Book of Nature', and not by speculation (Dev, 2002). This new outlook marked a break with the past and prepared the way for the advancement of science. It was summed up by Francis Bacon (1561–1626), an English philosopher, who said that knowledge could be gained only by observation and experimentation. According to Bacon,

> he who seeks knowledge should first look at things that happen in the world around him. He should then ask himself what causes these things to happen and, after he has formed a theory or belief, as to the possible cause, he should experiment. The experiment is to test his belief and see whether the assumed cause does, in fact, produce the result he has observed.
>
> *(Dev, 2002)*

Bacon believed that the 'true and lawful end of the sciences is that human life be enriched by new discoveries and powers'. One of the first achievements of the Renaissance in science was in astronomy. The year 1543 marked the development of modern astronomical studies with the publication of Copernicus' *Six Books Concerning the Revolutions of the Heavenly Spheres*. Copernicus (1473–1543) was a Polish scholar who lived in Italy for many years. His work in mathematics and astronomy demolished the hypothesis of the geocentric (Earth-centred) universe derived from Ptolemy and other astronomers of the past. In its place, he advanced the revolutionary new hypothesis of the heliocentric (sun-centred) universe. This meant that the earth moved round a fixed sun and not the other way round. The Copernican hypothesis had radical implications. It destroyed the idea of the earth's uniqueness by suggesting that it acted like other heavenly bodies. More importantly, his theory contradicted the earlier notions about the centrality of the earth to the cosmic order. The very idea of an open universe, of which the earth was but a small part, shattered the earlier view of a closed universe created and maintained in motion by God. This was an important break with the ancient system of thought. For over a thousand years it was believed that the earth was the centre of the universe. It was one of the basic dogmas of the philosophers of the time. Its refutation was an attack on the conception of the universe held by the Church. This was, therefore, condemned as a heresy. Copernicus' book was published in 1543, the year in which he died. He had hesitated from publishing it for fear of the hostility of the Church. About half a century after the publication of Copernicus' book, in 1600, Giordano Bruno was burnt at the stake on the charge of heresy. He had advocated ideas which were based on Copernicus' view of the universe (ibid.).

The next major steps towards the conception of a heliocentric system were taken by the Danish astronomer Tycho Brahe (1546–1601) and the German astronomer Johannes Kepler (1571–1630). Tycho Brahe constructed the most accurate tables of astronomical observations. After his death, these observations came into the possession of Kepler, who after much work agreed to the heliocentric theory, though he abandoned the Copernican concept of circular orbits. The mathematical relationship that emerged from a consideration of Brahe's observations suggested that the orbits of the planets were elliptical. Kepler published his findings in 1609 in a book entitled *On the Motion of Mars*. Thus, he solved the problems of planetary orbits by using the Copernican theory and Brahe's empirical data.

However, in the same year when Kepler published his book, an Italian scientist, Galileo Galilei (1564–1642), first turned a telescope invented by him towards the sky. Through this instrument he saw stars where none had been known to exist, mountains on the moon, spots moving across the sun and the moon and the orbiting Jupiter. Some of Galileo's colleagues at the University of Padua were so unnerved that they refused to look through the telescope because it revealed the heaven to be different from the teachings of the Church and the Ptolemaic theories. Galileo published his findings in numerous works, the most famous of which is his *Dialogues on the Two Chief Systems of the World* (1632). This book brought down on him the condemnation of the Roman Catholic Church. His life was spared only after he agreed to withdraw his views. He spent the rest of his life virtually under house arrest.

Isaac Newton was born in England in 1642, the year Galileo died. He solved the major remaining problems on the planetary motions and established a base for the modern physics. Much of the researches of Newton were based on the work of Galileo and other predecessors. In 1687, he published his treatise, *The Mathematical Principles of Natural Philosophy*. In this work, he proposed that the planets and, in fact, all other particles in the universe moved through the force of mutual attraction, a law which came to be known as the Law of Gravitation. In this way, Newton combined mathematics and physics for the study of astronomy. Incidentally, he was preceded in this by Varahamihira and Aryabhatta in the fifth and sixth centuries AD in India.

The modern age of science that began with these Renaissance scientists not only increased man's knowledge but also established a method of study that could be applied to other branches of knowledge. For example, significant discoveries were made in the study of the human body and circulation of the blood, which helped to fight many superstitions. In 1543, the year in which Copernicus' book was published, Vesalius, a Belgian, published his profusely illustrated *De Humani Corporis Fabrica*. Based on his study of the dissections of the human body, this book provided the first complete description of the anatomy of the human body. Similarly, a Spaniard named Servetus published a book explaining the circulation of blood. He was condemned to death for questioning the Church's belief in Trinity. Later, Harvey, an Englishman, gave a complete account of the constant process of circulation of blood, from the heart to all parts of the body and back to the heart, in about 1610. This new knowledge changed the perspective to the study of the problems of health and disease (ibid.).

It is important to remember that what the Renaissance scientists began learning by questioning, observation and experimentation is the method that scientists continue to use even today. This is the scientific method. It is by applying this method that our knowledge has grown so greatly. The knowledge produced during the Scientific Revolution deeply influenced the attitudes and beliefs of people about nature and society. New scientific ideas influenced scholars to think about society in new ways.

As mentioned earlier, in medieval Europe, the Roman Catholic Church was the epicentre of authority and learning. Knowledge was largely religious in nature. Nothing could challenge the 'dogmas' or rigid beliefs of the Church. Any idea or action which challenged the authority of the Church was, therefore, condemned as a heresy. This newly emerging scientific knowledge, which was based on empirical observation and experimentation, was not only different but also contradictory to the many teachings of the Church. This stimulated the process of 'reformation' in the religious sphere of the European society. Thus, European people with new spirit of enquiry and thought started questioning the superstitious beliefs and malpractices of the Catholic Church. From the fourteenth century, opposition to some of the Church practices and doctrines began to grow.

The term 'Reformation' refers to two major developments in the history of Europe towards the later part of the Renaissance. The first was the Protestant Reformation, which resulted in a split in Christianity and the secession of a large number of countries from the Roman Catholic Church and establishment of separate Churches in those countries, generally on national lines. The second development concerned reforms within the Roman Catholic Church, generally referred to as Catholic Reformation or Counter-Reformation. But Reformation was not merely a religious movement. It was intimately connected with, and was in fact a part of, the social and political movement of the period which brought about the end of the medieval period and the emergence of the modern world.

The Catholic Church, during the early medieval period, had become a vast hierarchical organisation headed by the Pope in Rome. Reformation is often described as a revolt against moral degeneration and corruption which had grown in the Catholic Church. Abuse of sacraments and the institution of priesthood were the primary reasons for the resentment against the Church. A sacrament was defined as an instrument by which divine grace was communicated to men. The sacraments were regarded as indispensable for securing God's grace, and there was no salvation without them. Likewise, it was held that the priest had the power to cooperate with God in performing certain miracles and in releasing sinners from the consequences of their sins. Religious offices were sold to the highest bidder, and many priests and higher-ups in the Church hierarchy received their appointments through corrupt means. Many such appointees were utterly ignorant. They led lives of luxury and immorality.

A new abuse was the sale of letters which remitted punishments of the sinners who bought them, both in this life and after their death in purgatory. Normally, if a person committed any sin, the priests used to impose a penance or punishment on that person. In some cases, he was also required to perform a special service or make a pilgrimage to a holy place. But increasingly, sinners with enough money could be exempted from doing penance for their sins by paying the clergy for a 'Letter of Indulgence'. The sale of indulgences, which began to be considered as passports to heaven, became one of the major immediate issues which caused the Protestant Reformation. Besides the sale of indulgences, one could now gain salvation in exchange for fees (ibid.).

The Protestant Reformation was largely a response to the degeneration of moral and ethical order which the Roman Church symbolised. It was in 1517 when Martin Luther, a monk of the Order of St Augustine, protested against the corruption prevalent in the religious and administrative practices of the Church. Luther nailed his 95 theses or statements, which attacked the sale of indulgences, on the door of the Church in Wittenberg in Germany. Being aware of the fact that his doctrines could not be reconciled with those of the Catholic Church, he had no alternative but to break with the Catholic Church. In 1520, the Pope ordered him to recant within 60 days or be condemned as a heretic. Luther burnt the proclamation of the Pope in public. He introduced German as the language of Church services. He also rejected the entire system of the hierarchy of the Catholic Church, abolished the special status of priests as representatives of God on earth, eliminated most of the sacraments and emphasised faith rather than pilgrimages. He gave the highest priority to the supreme authority of the scriptures. Another important change was the abandonment of the view of the

Catholic Church that the Church was supreme over the state. The German rulers and common people of Germany supported Luther. There were political reasons for the support of the rulers. They wanted to be free from the authority of Popes and get possession of the wealth in German monasteries for themselves. The common people liked Luther's teaching because it gave them an opportunity to demand more freedom from their rulers. Many rulers in Germany were hostile to the Church, and when Luther was excommunicated, he remained unharmed. During the next 25 years, he occupied himself with the task of building an independent German Church, and in expounding his doctrine.

John Calvin and Ulrich Zwingli were other prominent leaders of the Protestant movement in Switzerland. During their time, the Swiss cities became a refuge for Protestants fleeing to other countries in Western Europe due to religious persecution. Calvin established an academy for the training of Protestant missionaries, who in return would spread the true word of God in other lands. As part of the work of propagating his version of Protestantism, Calvin composed a treatise, entitled *The Institutes of the Christian Religion*, wherein he gave a more concise and logical definition of the Protestant doctrines than what had been given by any other leader of this movement.

In England, the Protestant movement was led by political leaders, particularly King Henry VIII and Queen Elizabeth I. However, their reforms were not driven by the ideas of religious or social reforms but by the interests of the state, and more practically, the personal ambition of Henry VIII. The King of England, Henry VIII, wanted to divorce his wife Catherine of Aragon and marry his beloved Anne Boleyn. But the Pope refused to grant the divorce on the ground that Henry, before marrying Catherine, had asked for and had received a special papal dispensation declaring his marriage with Catherine as valid and indissoluble. Rebuffed by the Pope, Henry promptly declared himself the 'sole protector and supreme head of the Church and the Clergy of England'. After that he married Anne Boleyn. From this marriage was born Elizabeth I, who later became the Queen of England. England's final break with the Pope came in 1529, when in a special session of the British Parliament a series of laws were passed to make the English Church completely free from the jurisdiction of the Pope. The King of England was also declared as the head of the English Church, which hereafter came to be known as the Anglican Church.

The Roman Catholic Church had been shaken to its very root by the movements started by Luther, Zwingli and Calvin. To counter the damage caused by the Protestant Movements, a series of reforms began within the Catholic Church, which came to be known as the 'Counter-Reformation'. During Counter-Reformation efforts were made to restore the Catholic Church's universal authority. One of these efforts took place in the Council of Trent (1545) summoned by Pope Paul III. The Council was to consider the ways and means to combat Protestantism. So, it decided to settle the doctrinal disputes between the Catholics and the Protestants, clean up moral and administrative abuses within the Catholic Church and organise a new crusade against the Muslims. The next step was the organisation of an order of missionaries, known as the Jesuits, with the dedicated purpose of spreading the message of Christ. The above measures adopted by the Catholic Church were not sufficient to bring the whole of Europe under the authority of the Pope. The campaign, however, did achieve a considerable measure of success in checking the further spread of Protestantism. Though much of Europe remained Protestant, new lands overseas were being won to the Catholic Church.

Enlightenment

Reacting to economic and political changes, the concomitant reorganisation of social life, much of the eighteenth century was consumed by intellectual ferment. The intellectual revolution of the eighteenth century is commonly referred to as the *Enlightenment*. In England and Scotland, the Enlightenment was dominated by a group of thinkers who argued for a vision of human beings and society that both reflected and justified the industrial capitalism that first emerged in the British Isles. For scholars such as Adam Smith, individuals are to be free of external constraint and allowed to compete, thereby creating a better society. In France, the Enlightenment is often termed the *Age of Reason*, and it was dominated by a group of scholars known as the *philosophes*. It is out of the intellectual ferment generated by the French philosophes that sociology was born (Turner et al., 1995).

The term 'Enlightenment' is used in academic and technical senses to indicate the intellectual movement in eighteenth-century Western and Central Europe, especially in England and France. Its historical significance lay in breaking the shackles of ideas imposed by tradition or authority, whether of the state or of the Church. For a long period in history up to that time, the standard method of arriving at the truth lay in an appeal to authority. It meant in practice that truth was determined by one's superiors and one was not expected to doubt or question their wisdom. To buttress their claim, both state and Church would base their authority on supernatural sanction rather than on popular sovereignty. This had been the basis of absolutism and absolute monarchs ruled in nearly all parts of Europe. Conflicts between Church and state were not infrequent, but these rarely concerned the common man in an age when communications were poor and his struggle for existence much harder.

Things in the meantime had changed fast during the sixteenth and seventeenth centuries. Significant advances had been made in discoveries of new lands and routes; technologies as applied to agriculture and industries had increased production, and that possibly accounts for the rapid increase of population that took place both in England and France. Urban areas expanded and a middle class emerged to avail itself of the new opportunities in sectors like banking, industry, trade, journalism and, above all, education, which served as a catalyst in the movement of ideas.

The essence of the Enlightenment lay in its challenge to absolutism, the questioning of authority through a new conception of truth. In the course of the

Enlightenment, reason supplanted authority as the accepted method of arriving at the truth. All who took part in this movement of ideas were convinced that human understanding is capable by its own power and without recourse to supernatural assistance, of comprehending the system of the world. A new optimism was breathed about man's capacity to usher in a happier social order. The basic difference between the Absolutist view and Enlightened view centred around the individual. Under absolutism, the individual had to submit to the authority which was supposed to possess the monopoly of the truth; but under the Enlightenment the individual acquired a new importance, dignity and self-respect. Any man's opinion was potentially worth something. One no longer had to be a bishop or prince to claim access to truth.

The Enlightenment stood for the classic trilogy – liberty, equality, and fraternity – and as such represented the fight against oppression imposed by the old social hierarchy that had developed a vested interest in keeping people ignorant and superstitious. A challenge was thrown to religious education since it was believed that such education sapped a young person's courage and killed initiative by training him to fear and obey. Thus, the Enlightenment was a period of remarkable intellectual development and change in the philosophical thought. A number of long-standing ideas and beliefs – many of which related to social life – were overthrown and replaced during the Enlightenment. The most prominent thinkers associated with the Enlightenment were the French philosophers Charles Montesquieu (1689–1755) and Jean-Jacques Rousseau (1712–1778).

Montesquieu in his book *The Spirit of the Law* held that there should not be concentration of authority, such as executive, legislative and judicial, at one place. He believed in the theory of separation of powers and the liberty of the individual. Similarly, Rousseau argued that people can develop their personalities best only under a government which is of their own choice. In his book *The Social Contract*, Rousseau argued that the people of a country have the right to choose their sovereign. For Rousseau, the social contract is the sole foundation of the political community. By virtue of this social contract, individuals lose their natural liberties (limited merely by their ability to exercise force over one another). However, man's natural liberty promoted unlimited acquisitiveness and avarice and thus encouraged individuals to destroy the freedom of others weaker than them. By submitting to a law vested in a social contract – a mandate that can be withdrawn at any time – individuals find in the laws to which they consent a pure expression of their being as civilised human entities.

Although the Enlightenment was fuelled by the political, social and economic changes of the eighteenth century, it derived considerable inspiration from the Scientific Revolution of the sixteenth and seventeenth centuries. As noted earlier, the Scientific Revolution reached a symbolic peak, at least in the eye of eighteenth-century thinkers, with Newtonian physics. In the light of various revolutionary developments in science, particularly physics, the universe (physical world) came to be viewed as orderly or patterned. It was argued that with scientific enquiry (based on empirical observation and application of reason), the underlying natural laws governing the universe could be discovered. Further, the knowledge of these laws would facilitate better prediction and greater control over the physical world. Thus, physics was to become the vision of how scientific enquiry and theory should be conducted. And both the individual and the society were increasingly drawn into the orbit of the new view of science. This gradual inclusion of the individual and the society into the realm of science represented a startling break with the past, because heretofore these phenomena had been considered the domain of morals, ethics and religion.

So, the Enlightenment thinkers argued that just as the physical world was governed by the natural laws, it was likely that social world was, too. Thus, it was up to the philosopher, using reason and research, to discover these social laws. And once such social laws are discovered, then with the knowledge of those laws we can control and create a better society (social engineering).

It is important to note that almost all Enlightenment thinkers also shared 'a vision of human progress'. Humanity was seen to be marching in a direction and was considered to be governed by a 'law of progress' that was as fundamental as the law of gravitation in the physical world. For example, with economic modernisation and advancement of technology, agricultural and industrial revolution took place, leading to a phenomenal increase in the agricultural and industrial outputs. With the Commercial Revolution (trade and commerce), unprecedented wealth or capital was generated. Further, the Scientific Revolution demolished the traditionally held superstitious beliefs (sanctified by Church) and ushered in the age of reason. With its emphasis on empirical observation and application of reason, it significantly changed the social outlook of man and brought about social modernisation.

At the psychological level, modernity was reflected in terms of reflexivity. Reflexivity refers to the reflexive monitoring of action, that is, the way in which humans think about and reflect upon what they are doing in order to consider acting differently in future. Humans have always been reflexive up to a point, but in pre-industrial societies, the importance of tradition limited reflexivity. Humans would do some things simply because they were the traditional things to do. However, with modernity, tradition loses much of its importance and reflexivity becomes the norm (psychological modernisation). Social reflexivity implies that social practices are constantly examined and reformed in the light of incoming information about those very practices, thus continuously altering their character.

Further, with the rise of various social and political movements, demands for greater individual freedom and democratisation were being made. For the first time in human history, the idea of fundamental rights of the individuals was being entertained in the public discourse. Traditional authoritarian and autocratic systems of governance were being challenged. The Enlightenment thinkers argued that all humans had certain inalienable 'natural rights' which must be respected, such as right to freedom of speech and expression, right of participation in the decision-making process, etc. This marked a significant step towards political modernisation.

Thus, in brief, the Enlightenment may be described as an eighteenth-century philosophical movement based on notions of progress through the application of reason and rationality. Enlightenment philosophers foresaw a world free from religious dogma, under human control and leading ultimately to emancipation for all humankind. They saw these developments as the sign of progress, and the Enlightenment period was marked by a new optimism or hope about the man's capacity to usher in a happier social order.

French Revolution

The French Revolution was a period of far-reaching social and political upheaval in France. It is important to note that for a revolution to occur, revolutionary ideas must emerge first. The underlying revolutionary ideology of the French Revolution could be traced to ideas of Enlightenment thinkers. Now let us briefly discuss the developments taking place in France, the birthplace of sociology.

Europeans in the Middle Ages viewed society as an expression of God's will. From the royalty to the serfs, each person up and down the social ladder played a part in the holy plan. This theological view of society is captured in the lines from the old Anglican hymn 'All Things Bright and Beautiful':

> The rich man in his castle,
> The poor man at his gate,
> God made them high and lowly
> And ordered their estate.

(Macionis, 2015)

In the years preceding the revolution, France retained the political and economic characteristics of a feudal society: rigid social hierarchy, social and economic inequality, monarchy, etc. The French society was divided into feudal 'estates'. The structure of the feudal French society comprised the 'three estates'. Estates are defined as a system of stratification found in feudal European societies whereby one section or estate is distinguished from the other in terms of status, privileges and restrictions accorded to that estate.

The first estate (the Church) consisted of the clergy, which was in itself stratified into higher clergy, such as the cardinal, the archbishops, the bishops, etc. Those who occupied higher positions in the hierarchical structure of the Church lived a life of luxury and gave very little attention to religion. Often the members of higher clergy took keen interest in politics and actively participated in the political affairs. Most of them preferred the life of politics to religion. The Church owned approximately one-fifth of the cultivated lands in France and enjoyed great influence with the government. Like the feudal nobility, the higher clergy was also exempt from paying most of the taxes. With the nobles they supported absolute monarchy.

The second estate consisted of the nobility. There were two kinds of nobles: the nobles of the sword and the nobles of the robe. The nobles of the sword primarily referred to the big feudal landlords. Though in principle they were considered to be the protectors of the people, in reality they led the life of a parasite, living off the hard work of the peasants. They spent extravagantly and did not work themselves. They can be compared to the erstwhile zamindars in India. On the other hand, the nobles of the robe were nobles not by birth but by title. This category of nobles was largely constituted of the magistrates and judges. Among these nobles, some were very progressive and liberal as they had moved in their positions from common citizens who belonged to the third estate. However, these noble families continued to enjoy all the privileges such as non-payment of most of the taxes, avenues to higher positions in the French administration and income from various feudal dues of the peasants.

The third estate comprised the rest of the society and included the peasants, the merchants, the artisans and others. There was a vast difference between the condition of the peasants and that of the clergy and the nobility. It was the peasant community that worked day and night, and produced food on which the whole society depended. Yet they could barely survive due to failure of any kind of protection from the government. Peasants were overloaded with so many taxes that they lived a hand-to-mouth existence. The king, along with the clergy and the nobility, continued to exploit the poor. The poor peasants had no power against him.

Land ownership was largely concentrated in the hands of the first two estates. Approximately, 35 per cent of the land was owned by the clergy and the nobility, who together constituted only 2 per cent of the population. The peasants who formed 80 per cent of the population owned only 30 per cent of the land. The first two estates paid almost no taxes to the government, but the peasantry was burdened with taxes of various kinds. It paid taxes to the Church, the feudal lord, taxed in the form of income tax, poll tax and land tax to the state. They were virtually carrying the burden of the first two estates on their shoulders. Thus, the French system of taxation was both unjust and unfair.

For about 200 years, the kings of the Bourbon dynasty ruled France. Following its imperial policy, France established colonies in Africa and Asia through French East India company. As a result, France came into conflict with many European countries and fought several wars. Under Louis XVI, France also helped the 13 American colonies to gain their independence from the common enemy, Britain. As a result, France incurred heavy economic losses. Further, the increasing population led to a rapid increase in the demand for food grains. Production of grains could not keep pace with the demand; as a result, the price of bread, which was the staple diet of the majority, rose rapidly. But wages did not keep pace with the rise in prices. So, the gap between the poor and the rich widened. Things became worse whenever drought or hail reduced the harvest. As a cumulative effect, the prices in France rose by about 65 per cent during the period 1720–1789.

Relatively, in comparison to the peasants, the condition of the middle class was much better. The middle classes, also known as the bourgeoisie, included the merchants, bankers, lawyers, manufacturers, etc. These classes too belonged to the third estate. But the poverty of the state, which led to a price rise during 1720–1789, instead of adversely affecting them, helped them. They derived profit from this rise, and the fact that French trade had improved enormously also helped the commercial classes to a great extent. Thus, this class was rich and secure. But it had no social prestige as compared with the high prestige of the members of the first and the second estates. In spite of controlling trade, industries, banking, etc., the bourgeoisie had no power to influence the court or administration. They were looked down upon by the other two estates, and the king paid very little attention to them. Thus, gaining political power became a necessity for them.

Like in all absolute monarchies, the theory of the Divine Right of the King was followed in France too. Under the rule of the king, the ordinary people had no personal rights. They only served the king and his nobles in various capacities. The king's word was law and no trials were required to arrest a person on the king's orders. Laws too were different in different regions giving rise to confusion and arbitrariness. There was no distinction between the income of the state and the income of the king. The kings of France, from Louis XIV onwards, fought costly wars, which ruined the country, and when Louis XIV died in 1715, France had become bankrupt. Louis XV instead of recovering from this ruin kept on borrowing money from bankers. His famous sentence, 'After me the deluge', describes the kind of financial crisis that France was facing. Louis XVI, a very weak and ineffective king, inherited the ruin of a bankrupt government. His wife, Queen Marie Antoinette, known for her expensive habits, is famous for her reply, which she gave to the poor, hungry people of France who came to her asking for bread. She told the people that 'if you don't have bread, eat cake'.

Now let us examine the intellectual developments in France, which proved to be the igniting force in bringing about the French Revolution. France, like some other European countries during the eighteenth century, had entered the age of reason and rationalism. Some of the major philosophers, whose ideas influenced the French people, were rationalists who believed that all true things could be proved by reason. Some of these thinkers were John Locke (1632–1704), Montesquieu (1689–1755), Voltaire (1694–1778) and Rousseau (1712–1778).

Locke is among the most influential political philosophers of the modern period. He was an English philosopher and physician, widely regarded as one of the most influential of Enlightenment thinkers and commonly known as the 'Father of Liberalism'. His writings influenced Voltaire and Jean-Jacques Rousseau and many Scottish Enlightenment thinkers. In his work *Two Treatises of Government*, Locke defended the claim that men are by nature free and equal against claims that God had made all people naturally subject to a monarch. He advocated that every individual has certain fundamental rights, which cannot be taken away by any authority, such as the right to live, the right to property, the right to personal freedom, etc. He also believed that any ruler who took away these rights from his people should be removed from the seat of power and replaced by another ruler who is able to protect these rights.

Montesquieu in his book *The Spirit of the Law* argued in favour of a democratic government based on the principle of separation of powers. He held that there should not be concentration of authority, such as executive, legislative and juridical, at one place. He stood for the liberty of the individual.

Voltaire became internationally famous as a great writer and critic whose style and pungent criticism were inimitable. It was through his plays and writings that he launched his bitter attacks against the existing institutions like the Church and the state. He made fun of the eccentricities of the nobles. He advocated religious toleration and freedom of speech. He also stood for the rights of individuals, for freedom of speech and expression.

Probably the greatest French philosopher of the age was Jean-Jacques Rousseau. In his book *The Social Contract*, Rousseau argued that the people of a country have the right to choose their sovereign. He believed that people can develop their personalities best only under a government which is of their own choice. He further explained that the king and his subjects are parties to a contract, and therefore if the king does not rule the people according to their general will, he loses their loyalty. Rousseau was advocating popular sovereignty theory. His writings cast such a spell on his admirers that they were ready to revolt against the oppressive monarchy.

The major ideas of these, and several other intellectuals, struck the imagination of the French people. Many of those who had served in the French army, which was sent to assist the Americans in their War of Independence from British imperialism, also came back with the ideas of equality of individuals and their right to choose their own government. Barred from political power and denied the rights and privileges of the aristocracy, the emerging middle classes were receptive to the ideas of social change and deeply affected by these ideas of liberty and equality.

So far, we have learnt about the basic picture of the French society just before the Revolution. Now let us discuss some of the major events that took place during the Revolution. It is worth noting that when the American colonists revolted against the oppressive rule of the mother country and won a resounding victory at Saratoga, the French government decided to help them with men, money and materials. It caused a serious strain on the finances of the country and cast a heavy burden on the poor peasants. Turgot was appointed as the Minister of Finance to suggest remedies. He advised the king to tax the privileged class. He was summarily dismissed at the instance of the queen. Unfortunately, France witnessed near-famine conditions in 1788 with the result that there was a serious food shortage. It was at this critical juncture that the king was advised by his courtiers to summon the Estates-General (French Parliament) to get approval for further dose of taxation.

When the Estates-General was summoned, the king ignored the importance of the third estate (600 representatives elected by the common people) and tried to consult the representatives of the three estates separately. However, the representatives of the third estate advised the king to bring together the representatives of all the three estates at one place for discussion of state problems. The king discarded their advice. Subsequently, it led to a quarrel between the king and the representatives of the third estate. This led to the formation of the National Assembly. The meeting of the National Assembly led by middle-class leaders and some liberal-minded nobles was met with stiff resistance. On 20 June 1789, when a meeting was to be held in the Hall at Versailles near Paris, the members found that it was closed and guarded by the king's men. Therefore, the National Assembly members led by their leader, Bailey, went to the next building, which was an indoor tennis court. It was here that they took an oath to draw a new constitution for France. This oath, which marks the beginning of the French Revolution, is popularly known as the Oath of the Tennis Court.

Next, one of the most important events of the French Revolution took place on 14 July 1789. It was the storming of the Bastille, an ancient royal prison that stood as a symbol of oppression. On this date, the mobs of Paris, led by some middle-class leaders, broke open this prison and set its inmates free. The causes for this event were the shortage of food, on the one hand, and the dismissal of a very popular minister called Necker, on the other. The mobs of Paris rebelled against the ruling class, especially the king. This day is celebrated in France as its Independence Day.

Shortly after these events, the National Assembly drafted the 'Declaration of the Rights of Man', which was a central political document defining human rights and setting out demands for reform. The political rights and freedoms proclaimed by the 'Declaration' were so wide-ranging in their human emancipation that it set the standard for social and political thinking, and formed the central rallying point of the revolution. The 'Declaration' stated at the outset that all human beings were born free and equal in their political rights, regardless of their class position, and this proceeded to set up a system of constitutional principles based on liberty, security and resistance to oppression. With philosophical authority, the 'Declaration' proclaimed that all individuals had the prerogative to exercise their 'natural right' and that the law rather than the monarch was the expression of the common interest. This led to the elimination of all social distinctions, on the one hand, and the right to resist oppression, on the other. Thus, the ideas of liberty, equality and fraternity were enshrined in this declaration. Liberty and equality put an end to the age of serfdom, despotism and hereditary privileges found in the old feudal society.

By August, the National Assembly began to deal directly with political and legal reforms, first by eliminating feudal dues and then by abolishing serfdom. Second, by compelling the Church to give up the right to tithes, the National Assembly altered the authority and class position of the clergy. Third, in declaring that 'all citizens, without distinction, can be admitted to ecclesiastical, civil and military posts and dignities', it proclaimed an end to all feudal social distinctions. As the criticism of social and political inequalities spread throughout society, there was a widespread critique of economic inequality altogether, and this led to putting into question all other forms of subordination. With this came the idea that human beings, without distinctions, were the bearers of natural rights – a concept which had a corrosive effect on all other forms of inequality. Finally, from the assertions inherent in the 'Declarations of Rights', a new category of social person came into being, which came fundamentally to rest in the concept of the 'citizen', whose social and political rights were brought within the framework of the state.

As the political changes began to take effect, there were abrupt social changes in the form of altered politics and in the form of the political reorganisation of the feudal way of life. This brought with it two central historical shifts. First, it transformed the existing class structure of feudal society and led to the decline of class privilege and a change in the relations of subordination which had existed up until that time. Second, it set loose political and legal reforms which brought about a change from a political aristocracy based on sovereign authority to a democratic republic based on the rights of the citizen. Thus, the French Revolution of 1789 marked the phase of political modernisation.

Society of 'Hope' and 'Despair': An Intellectual Debate

The newly emerging modern industrial society, however, was a society of paradox. It was a society of hope as well as despair. In socio-economic terms, surplus production and enormous capital accumulation coincided with mass dislocation of the population (enclosure movement), disruption of traditional community bonds, extreme economic exploitation and inequalities. Further, the orthodox religious ideology of the Catholic Church was being challenged by scientific temper and secular outlook, leading to increasing desacralisation of social life. Similarly, on the political front, new liberal ideologies propagating the values of equality, liberty and freedom challenged the divine theory of kingship, and gave rise to the demands for greater political rights, often leading to civil wars and political movements like the French Revolution.

Let us once again return to our discussion on the Enlightenment. As we had discussed earlier, the Enlightenment thinkers saw these socio-economic and political developments as the sign of progress. The Enlightenment period was marked by a new optimism or hope about the man's capacity to usher in a happier social order. So, Enlightenment thinkers represented intellectual modernity. But, at the same time, there were also some other philosophers who viewed these changes otherwise. These philosophers were not only sceptic about these changes taking place in European society but even condemned these changes. We can call these philosophers as counter-Enlightenment or conservative philosophers and their views as a conservative reaction to the Enlightenment thought. The ideas of Comte Joseph de Maistre (1753–1821) and Vicomte Louis de Bonald (1754–1840) represent the most extreme form of opposition to the Enlightenment thought, unlike the Enlightenment thinkers, who emphasised

individualism, rationality, empiricism and change, the conservative philoso-
phers instead reflected a strong anti-modernity sentiment. In Seidman's words,
'The ideology of the counter-Enlightenment represented a virtual inversion of
Enlightenment liberalism' (Ritzer and Stepnisky, 2014).

Conservative philosophers glorified the traditional customs and institutions
such as patriarchy, the family, the monarchy and the Catholic Church in maintaining social order and harmony. They looked at human society as a divine
creation. They believed that since God had created society, people should not
tamper with it and should not try to change a holy creation. They looked at the
whole society as a unit and something more than simply an aggregate of individuals. Society was viewed as having an independent existence of its own with
its own laws of development. Thus, society was seen as more important than the
individual. It was society that produced the individual, primarily through the
process of socialisation. Hence, conservative philosophers believed that society,
through its institutions, exercised a powerful and necessary constraint over free
individual actions. They held that the Enlightenment had undermined the traditional customs and institutions that produced social order and thus made the
French Revolution inevitable. They highlighted the cohesive power of religion
and lamented the decline in Catholic belief and practice (Scott, 2006). They were
disturbed by the revolutionary changes unleashed by the Industrial Revolution
and French Revolution, which they saw as disruptive forces. They sought to
retain the existing order and yearned for a return to the peace and harmony of
the Middle Ages (Ritzer and Stepnisky, 2014).

In general, these scholars deplored the disruption of the socio-economic
and political fabric of the traditional medieval society caused by the Industrial
Revolution and French Revolution. As mentioned earlier, there was massive
dislocation of rural population due to enclosure movement. The newly emerging social life in towns and cities was bereft of close-knit community and kinship bonds, we-feeling, stability and harmonic social order. Since these cities
had emerged spontaneously, without any proper planning, they lacked even the
basic amenities such as proper sewage and sanitation. As a result, due to such
unhygienic living conditions, epidemics were a common phenomenon. Further,
these newly emerging industrial cities were marked by gross socio-economic
disparities. Workers, including women and children, were forced to work for
long hours in the factories marked by inhuman working conditions. In this new
mode of production, worker had lost control over both the process of production
and his product. He was simply reduced to a wage labourer. In Marxist terms,
the worker became alienated from the product of his labour.

Further, demand for political rights fuelled by the writings of Enlightenment
thinkers often led to civil wars, leading to political anomie. Furthermore, religion too, which until now regulated the social order, started declining. Religion,
as the source of solace and meaning of life, started losing its appeal with the
advances in science. Conservative philosophers saw these changes, i.e. decline
of family and community life, decline of religion, economic exploitation of

workers in factories, rising socio-economic disparities and political turmoil, as a sign of social decay and not as progress. Hence, they were preoccupied with their concerns for peace and harmony, and stability in the society. So, while Enlightenment thinkers glorified change, conservative philosophers deplored such changes and emphasised stability, peace and harmony. However, the idea that there must be peace and harmony in social life came to be generally accepted by the proponents of both intellectual traditions.

Emergence of Sociology

According to Irving Zeitlin, 'Early sociology emerged as a reaction to the Enlightenment' (Ritzer and Stepnisky, 2014). The Enlightenment, as discussed earlier, was an intellectual revolution of the eighteenth century rooted in the socio-economic and political developments unfolding in western Europe. Zeitlin's arguments could be best understood in the context of the concerns of both Enlightenment thinkers and conservative philosophers. As stated earlier, conservative philosophers like Maistre and Bonald were reacting against not only the Enlightenment but also the socio-economic and political disruptions caused by Industrial Revolution and French Revolution. These scholars were disturbed by these revolutionary changes and were preoccupied with concerns of social order and stability in the society. They yearned for a return to the peace and harmony of the Middle Ages.

Early social theorists in Europe, particularly in France, too were concerned with the disruption of socio-economic and political fabric of the traditional medieval society caused by the Industrial Revolution and French Revolution. They wanted to make sure that revolutionary ideas do not spread to the working class and society in general. Probably, they did not want the revolutionary ideology as well as the methodology to become popular and to be regarded as a legitimate form of protest to articulate and address grievances. Hence, they shared the concerns of the conservative philosophers who emphasised the need for social order and stability in society.

However, social theorists like Saint-Simon, Comte, etc. realised that it was impossible to return to the old discredited feudal order, as hoped by the conservative philosophers. Instead, they proposed a new doctrine that would justify itself by appealing to science. In other words, this new doctrine or knowledge was to be based on empirical observation and reason. Here, we can see the influence of the Enlightenment ideas on these social theorists. Inspired by the success of natural sciences, particularly Newtonian physics, in discovering the laws which govern natural or physical reality, these early social theorists (also known as positivists) advocated the application of the scientific method to social issues. They argued that through scientific study of society, social scientists can discover social laws that govern social order and thus, through corrective social legislation, can create a harmonic society. Their conservative paradigm soon received support from the government, first in France in the latter part of the nineteenth century and soon after in other Western European countries.

Thus, the social conditions prevalent in Europe in the eighteenth and nineteenth centuries, generated by social changes such as Renaissance, Commercial Revolution, Scientific Revolution, Reformation, Counter-Reformation, Industrial Revolution and French Revolution, created the need for a distinct discipline to understand and analyse these changes. We know that the then existing knowledge was predominantly religious in nature, largely propagated by the Church. But such knowledge had no solution to the newly emerging socio-economic and political challenges. Further, with the growth of science, religion itself was under attack, and religious ideas were losing their plausibility. So, there was a need for a new body of knowledge. A new body of knowledge was needed to understand and explain social change and also help people to find solutions to the newly emerging problems. That is how the social changes triggered by the forces of modernity in Europe in the late eighteenth and early nineteenth centuries created the need for a new knowledge. Thus, while social conditions created the need for sociology, intellectual conditions provided the means for building sociology as a distinct discipline. It was a synthesis of both the Enlightenment and conservative intellectual traditions, achieved by early social scientists, that gave birth to the new knowledge called sociology. How?

The emergence of sociology out of the intellectual synthesis of both the Enlightenment and conservative thought can be understood at three levels: objectives of sociology, theoretical perspective and methodological orientation of early sociology.

In terms of objectives of sociology, as discussed earlier, the early social theorists, though influenced by Enlightenment thought, shared the concerns of the conservative philosophers who emphasised the need for social order and stability in society. They believed that the scientific knowledge of society and social processes can facilitate social reformation and, thus, the establishment of an orderly and harmonic society. With regard to the theoretical perspective, we can notice an inclination among early social theorists towards macro-sociological analysis and functional explanation. Here we can see how strongly the ideas of conservative philosophers influenced the theoretical perspective of early sociology. As discussed earlier, contrary to the Enlightenment thinkers, who emphasised the individual, the conservative reaction led to a major sociological interest in society as a unit of analysis. Society was seen as more important than the individual and shaping the individual through the process of socialisation. Further, parts (social institutions) of society were seen as interrelated and interdependent, and fulfilling some vital functions is necessary for maintaining social order and stability in society. This led to a conservative or status-quoist orientation in early sociology in contrast to the change-oriented Enlightenment thought. Therefore, at times, it is argued that the early sociology developed as a reaction to the Enlightenment.

But, as far as methodological orientations are concerned, early sociology was largely influenced by the ideas of the Enlightenment thinkers. Unlike conservative philosophers, who yearned for a return to the peace and harmony of the Middle Ages, early social theorists emphasised the need for a scientific study of society based on empirical observation and reason – an idea of the Enlightenment thinkers. They argued that through scientific study of society, social scientists can discover social laws that govern social order, and thus through corrective social legislation can create a harmonic society. That is how the intellectual conditions helped in creating a new discipline that would use the scientific method to study society, discover the laws that govern society and use that knowledge of laws to create a peaceful and harmonic society.

So, it may be said that while social conditions created the need for sociology, intellectual conditions provided the means for building sociology. That is how modernity and social changes in Europe led to the emergence of sociology.

Sociology and Common Sense

Sociology is one of the youngest among social sciences. It emerged in the early nineteenth century as a synthesis of conflicting intellectual traditions which were in itself a response to the rapid and drastic transformation that was taking place in the Western European society in the post-Renaissance period. Sociology, in simplest terms, is defined as the scientific study of society. Even though sociology as a distinct science may be relatively new, human attempts to understand society, its organisation and the process of social change are as old as the human society itself.

In the past, most of the ideas, concepts and theories related to society and its ideal form were largely based on common sense. Common sense beliefs are often based on traditional customs and values, religious beliefs and practices. Common sense may also consist of a group's accumulation of collective guesses, speculations and trial-and-error learnings. Since common sense beliefs are not always supported by a systematic and scientific body of evidence, there is a possibility that some common sense conclusions could be based on ignorance, prejudice and mistaken interpretation. Hence, there is high possibility for some common sense beliefs to be mutually conflicting and contradictory. When facing such conflicting common sense ideas, how can we tell which ones are correct and which ones are false? We can get the answer from sociological research. Common sense thus preserves both folk wisdom and folk nonsense, and to sort out one from the other is a task for science. Thus, sociology is more than common sense because it is based largely on scientific evidence. Today, science is replacing common sense as a source of dependable knowledge. Even though science has become a source of knowledge about our *social* world only recently, yet in the brief period since we began to use the scientific method, we have learned more about our world than had been learned in the preceding 10,000 years. The spectacular explosion of knowledge in the modern world parallels our use of the scientific method (Horton and Hunt, 2004).

To many people, sociology appears to be a laborious study of the obvious, an expensive way to discover what everybody already knows. To these people, sociology is merely common sense. But this is not true. Common sense to a large extent tends to be speculative and intuitive. It is contextual and subjective. One person's common sense could be nonsense for another. Most importantly, common sense is non-reflexive in nature. That is, it does not question its own origins. As a result, it tends to be conservative in outlook and status quoist in nature. When we do not know where our ideas come from or on what they are based, we sometimes call them 'common sense'. The term 'common sense' puts a respectable front on all sorts of ideas for which there is no systematic body of evidence that can be cited. Common sense requires only a willingness to believe what it tells us. It cannot tell us whether those beliefs have any basis in fact. But sociology can. This is one of the reasons why sociology is exciting.

Not all common sense propositions are false. Some are sound, logical and useful bits of knowledge. But many common sense conclusions are based on ignorance, prejudice and mistaken interpretation. By systematically checking common sense ideas against reliable facts, sociology can tell us which popular beliefs are myths and which are realities. For example, it is commonly known that there is more poverty and joblessness among Dalits and Muslims in India than among other caste groups and minorities, or that there are more poor people than rich people in prisons. This is common sense. So, when sociological research arrives at similar conclusions on the basis of empirical data, you are not surprised because it has only verified and validated what was already known.

But now, just consider another scenario. For thousands of years, people's common sense told them that the earth was flat, that big objects fell faster than small ones and that character was revealed in facial features; yet today we know none of these is true. Similarly, in most of patriarchal societies, it is commonly believed that women, in comparison to men, are biologically, psychologically and intellectually inferior and hence remain the weaker section of society. However, various sociological and social anthropological researches have demystified this commonly held belief. Margaret Mead, a distinguished American anthropologist, made a comparative study of the respective gender roles of men and women in three primitive societies in New Guinea. She found that in each of these cultures, gender roles were radically different from those of the Western culture. For example, in the Tchambuli tribe, women are masculine and men feminine, in terms of Western cultural standards. Women are dominant, responsible and are engaged in aesthetic matters, besides being charming. Among the Arapesh, both men and women show feminine traits; they do not indulge in aggressive behaviour. Among the Mundugumor, both men and women exhibit masculine traits. Their behaviour reflects violence and aggressiveness. Mead, therefore, concluded that the gender roles are culturally conditioned. Such scientific findings have radically altered the dominant common sense notions with regard to women and their position in society, leading to demands for gender equality, and later triggered feminist movement. The same holds true for various prejudices and discriminatory attitudes towards lower castes and minorities in India. Thus, sociological findings play a critical role in demystifying various commonly held

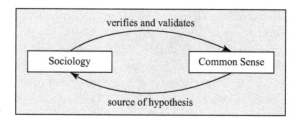

FIGURE 1.2 Relationship between Sociology and Common Sense

beliefs which support and legitimise the existing social structure, and consequently altering it.

So, it is not true that sociology is only common sense. If it were, we wouldn't bother to study sociology. Why would sociologists spend their time and energy in learning something that was already known? The fact is that while common sense gives us familiar and untested ideas, sociology offers factually supported ideas as well as the excitement of discovering something new about ourselves (Thio, 2003). To conclude, it may be said that both sociology and common sense share a complementary relationship with each other. While common sense acts as a source of ideas which facilitates the formulation of hypothesis to carry out sociological research, sociology, on the other hand, serves to verify and validate various commonly held beliefs (Figure 1.2).

Sociological Imagination

Charles Wright Mills (1916–1962) was an American sociologist who introduced the idea of sociological imagination. Mills in his famous book *The Sociological Imagination* (1959) helps us explore the connections between our individual experiences and the larger social world. He argued that most of us see the world around us through our individual experiences. Seldom are we aware of the intricate connection between the patterns of our personal lives (biography) and the historical evolution of social institutions (history). In other words, often we don't see the connections between the personal events in our everyday lives and the larger society in which we live. For example, when someone faces difficulty in finding employment or gets divorced, he has problem imagining that these experiences are somehow related to the wider socio-economic, political and historical processes. This is exactly what Mills emphasises through his concept of *sociological imagination*. Sociological imagination, according to Mills, refers to the quality of mind which enables an individual to acknowledge and understand the intricate relationship between his personal experiences (biography) and the wider social and historical context (history). To Mills, the sociological imagination enables us to grasp the connection between history and biography. Because of its history, a society has certain broad characteristics, for example, its commonly accepted ideas of gender roles. By biography Mills meant the individual's unique and specific experiences in society. This intersection of history and biography results in individuals emphasising particular values, goals and aspirations. Thus, in the sociological view, people don't do what they do because of some innate tendencies, such as instinct. Rather, external influences – people's social experiences – become internalised, become part of an individual's thinking, motivation and self-concept. Mills argues that neither the life of an individual nor the history of a society can be understood without understanding both.

> We have come to know that every individual lives, from one generation to the next, in some society; that he lives out a biography, and that he lives it out within some historical sequence. By the fact of his living he contributes, however minutely, to the shaping of this society and to the course of its history, even as he is made by society and by its historical push and shove. ... The sociological imagination enables us to grasp history and biography and the relations between the two within society. That is its task and its promise.
>
> *(Mills, 1959)*

According to Mills, the task of sociology is to help us view our lives as an intersection between personal biography and societal history, and thereby to provide a means for us to interpret our lives and social circumstances. If you do not examine your personal problem in relation to social forces, you miss an opportunity to address the problem in an effective way. If you do not reflect on the problems of others, even if you don't experience them yourself, you also miss an important component of sociological thinking. It is important to understand that everything you experience personally has a social context that is bigger than you, and sociology can help you gain that perspective (Figure 1.3).

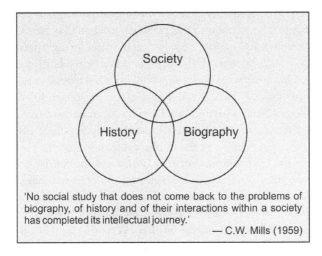

FIGURE 1.3 Sociological Imagination

Unlike any other discipline, sociology provides us with a form of self-consciousness, an awareness that our personal experiences are deeply connected with social forces. Mills challenges our tendency to see our lives as purely psychological experiences overwhelmed by forces out of our control. Sociology enables us to step out of our personal cocoons and connect our personal lives to larger social structures and historical trends. This process helps us understand that individuals alone are not entirely responsible for the circumstances of their lives. When we understand the role that social forces play in our lives, we get closer to being able to influence those social forces in the hope of bettering our own lives and those of others. From a sociological perspective, problems and their solutions don't just involve individuals; they also have a great deal to do with the social structures in our society.

According to Mills, the sociological imagination can help us distinguish between *personal troubles* and *public issues*. Mills describes how personal troubles occur within the 'character of the individual and within the range of his immediate relationships with others', whereas public issues are a 'public matter: some value cherished by publics is felt to be threatened' (Mills, 1959). As a result, the individual, or those in contact with that individual, can resolve a problem, but the resolution of an issue requires public debate about what values are being threatened and the source of such a threat. In other words, according to Mills, an individual may be able to solve a personal trouble, but a public issue can only be resolved by society and its social structures. Thus, sociological imagination allows us to recognise that the solutions to many of our serious social problems lie not in changing the personal situations and characteristics of individual people but in changing the social institutions. Social problems, such as unemployment, divorce, drug addiction, sexual violence, suicide and communal riots, will not go away simply by treating or punishing a person who is suffering from or engaging in a behaviour (Newman, 2016).

Let's consider unemployment. When an individual is unemployed, it is his personal problem. The solution to this personal problem may lie either in applying afresh for new employment opportunities, considering alternative career opportunities or learning new skills. Once he has a new job, his personal problem is solved. However, what happens when a society overall experiences high rates of unemployment? This affects not just one person, rather thousands or millions of people. Now, a personal problem has been transformed into a public issue. This is the case not just because of how many people it affects; a problem becomes an issue because of the public values it threatens. Unemployment threatens our sense of economic security. Economic insecurity in turn affects our life chances, that is, chances or possibilities of an individual for obtaining those things that are considered desirable in a given society, such as access to higher education, better medical facilities, good quality housing, etc. The issue of unemployment challenges our belief that everyone can work hard and succeed. Unemployment raises questions about society's obligation to help those without a job. Now the solutions need to be sought at societal level in terms of structural inconsistencies between demographic, educational, economic and political systems. In India, for example, low expenditure on primary and vocational education in comparison to the continuously increasing population, imbalanced regional development and economic growth without job opportunities could be cited as some of the structural factors responsible for high rates of unemployment. Hence, a purely personal and psychological explanation for the failure of an individual to secure a respectable job and career would be inadequate.

Similar observations can be made regarding increasing divorce rates, threatening the stability of the institution of marriage. A couple may experience personal problems in continuing with their marriage. These personal problems could range from petty household issues to serious emotional and temperamental incompatibility. But when we look at the problem of divorce from the societal perspective, and find a very high divorce rate, then divorce becomes a public issue. As a public issue, it threatens the values of the institutions of marriage and family, which are the building blocks of any society.

The sociological imagination challenges the claim that the problem is 'natural' or based on individual failures, instead reminding us how the problem is rooted in society, in our social structures themselves. The sociological imagination emphasises the structural bases of social problems, making us aware of the economic, political and social structures that govern employment and unemployment trends. Individuals may have *agency*, the ability to make their own choices, but their actions and even their choices may be constrained by the realities of the social structure. Sociology, thus, is uniquely able to connect personal experiences to larger social issues by applying the sociological imagination.

According to Jeanne Ballantine and Keith Roberts,

> sociologists examine the software and hardware of society. A society consists of individuals who live together in a specific geographic area, who interact with each other, and who cooperate for the attainment of common goals. The software is our culture. Each society has a culture that serves as a system of guidelines for living. A culture includes *norms* (rules of behaviour shared by members of society and rooted in a value system), *values* (shared judgments about what is desirable or undesirable, right or wrong, good or bad), and *beliefs* (ideas about life, the way society works, and where one fits in). The hardware comprises the enduring social structures that bring order to our lives. This includes the positions or *statuses* that we occupy in society (student, employee) and the social *groups* to which we belong and identify with (our family, our community, our workplace). *Social institutions* are the most complex hardware. Social institutions such as the family, religion, or education, are relatively permanent social units of roles, rules, relationships, and organised activities devoted to meeting human needs and to directing and controlling human behaviour.
>
> *(Leon-Guerrero, 2016)*

LET'S THINK

- Dear Learner, in this chapter, you have learned how social conditions in a given society serve as a womb for new ideas to emerge and consequently trigger social change. Think about some contemporary developments in your society in the form of new ideas, debates, laws or policies. Try to explain these new developments in terms of socio-economic and political conditions prevalent in society. Also think about the functional and dysfunctional consequences of these developments for the different sections of society.

- How can we develop a sociological perspective? You can develop a sociological perspective for a phenomenon when you look at it in terms of wider socio-economic, political and historical context. Try to look at some of the personal problems that people often experience, like challenges in securing a good career, identity crises, discrimination, etc. Although individuals may have various ways of dealing with these problems, there is a social context to each that takes them out of the purely personal into the larger social world. It is important to understand that everything you experience personally has a social context that is bigger than you, and sociology can help you gain that perspective.

The Art of Answer Writing

Dear Learner, the first and the most important thing in writing a correct as well as a good answer is to understand the question correctly. All you have to do for this is to follow a very simple process. First, read the question carefully and underline the keywords. Second, try to understand from which dimension the question has been framed on the topic. This is very important because questions can be framed from multiple dimensions on the same topic. Third, divide the question into some logical sub-questions. When you do this, it will not only keep you focused on the main theme of the question but also help complete the paper in time.

Further, while answering any question, I generally suggest candidates preparing for various academic and competitive examinations to apply the 'Dialectical Approach'. I have borrowed the idea of *dialectics* from the famous German philosopher G.W.F. Hegel. In this approach, the structure of the answer is divided into four sections, viz. introduction, thesis, anti-thesis and synthesis (Figure 1.4). The 'Introduction' section is the most important section of your answer as it introduces you as a candidate to the examiner. The examiner forms an image about you and your understanding of the concept just by reading the introduction. Hence, you must start by directly addressing the question, without beating around the bush. By this, I mean that given the limitations of time and word limit, please avoid developing the background and glorifying the thinkers. In the introduction, briefly explain the key concept asked in the question. The introduction section should constitute nearly 20 per cent of the total length of your answer.

The next section is 'Thesis'. In this section, you need to elaborate on the concept or theme asked in the question. Here, you must enrich and substantiate your

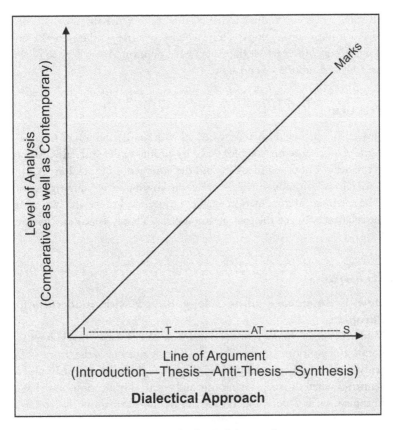

FIGURE 1.4 Dialectical Approach

answer by highlighting the works of some scholars, and case studies in support of your argument. Depending upon the demand of the question, this section could be either detailed or brief. For example, if the question has keywords like 'Discuss', 'Describe', 'Explain', 'Elaborate', etc., then the thesis part must be in detail and anti-thesis in brief. On the other hand, if the question has keywords like 'Critically Examine', 'Critically Analyse', etc., then the thesis part should be in brief, while the anti-thesis part should be discussed in detail.

In the 'Anti-thesis' section, try to present a critique of the main argument asked in the question. By incorporating this in your answer, you can convince the examiner that there are other alternative explanations as well on the topic on which the question has been asked. I am sure that the examiner will be impressed by your holistic understanding of the debate and will reward you accordingly. Please note that the length of the thesis and anti-thesis sections would depend on the demand of the question.

Last, but not the least, is the 'Synthesis' section or the concluding remarks. Please remember that the concluding remarks in your answer reflect your overall understanding of the subject. Also note that the concluding remarks are not supposed to be your personal opinion about the theme or issue asked in the question. Rather, your concluding remarks must reflect the insight that you have gained as a student of sociology. Thus, when you write synthesis, make sure it is an academic conclusion rather than a personal opinion. Always try to make your synthesis as contemporary as possible.

For Practice

Q1. How is emergence of sociology linked with modernisation of Europe?
Q2. Write a short note on 'sociology as a by-product of Industrial Revolution'.
Q3. Write a short note on 'ideology and the emergence of sociology'.
Q4. Is sociology common sense? Give reasons in support of your arguments.
Q5. 'The sociological imagination enables us to grasp history and biography and the relation between the two within society. That is its task and its promise'. Explain.

Model Answers

Q. How is emergence of sociology linked with modernisation of Europe?

A. Modernity refers to the rational transformation of social, psychological, economic and political aspects of society. The beginning of the process of modernisation could be traced back to the late eighteenth and early nineteenth centuries when the socio-economic and political institutions in the Western European society were undergoing drastic transformations due to Industrial Revolution and French Revolution.

The newly emerging modern industrial society, however, was a society of paradox. It was a society of hope as well as despair. In socio-economic terms, surplus production and enormous capital accumulation coincided with mass dislocation of the population (enclosure movement), disruption of traditional community bonds, extreme economic exploitation and inequalities. Further, the orthodox religious ideology of the Catholic Church was being challenged by scientific temper and secular outlook, leading to increasing desacralisation of social life. Similarly, on the political front, new liberal ideologies propagating the values of equality, liberty and freedom challenged the divine theory of kingship, and gave rise to the demands for greater political rights, often leading to civil wars and political movements like the French Revolution.

Intellectuals responding to these profound changes were divided in their opinions with regard to the nature, impact and direction of such changes. Enlightenment scholars like Rousseau, Montesquieu, Adam Smith, Saint-Simon and Auguste Comte had a positive view of the newly emerging social order. They considered such changes as progressive, and hence desirable. Conservative philosophers like Joseph de Maistre and Louis de Bonald had a rather sceptic view of these profound and far-reaching institutional changes that were taking place in society. They were preoccupied with the concern for social stability and order in the society as the new social order was marked by violent political revolutions, class wars, extreme economic inequalities and widespread misery and poverty.

Thus, while social conditions created the need for sociology, intellectual conditions provided the means for building sociology as a distinct discipline. It may be said that while the goals of sociology (i.e. to restore social order and harmony) were influenced by the conservative reaction, the means to discover such social laws that govern social order (i.e. through scientific methodology) were largely dictated by Enlightenment scholars.

Q. Is sociology common sense? Give reasons in support of your arguments.

A. Sociology as a discipline basically implies a systematic and scientific study of society. It emerged in the early nineteenth century, and is one of the youngest among social sciences. Common sense beliefs, on the other hand, are often based on traditional customs and values, religious beliefs and practices. Common sense may also consist of a group's accumulation of collective guesses, speculations and trial-and-error learnings. Prior to the emergence of sociology, most of the ideas, concepts and theories related to society and its ideal form were largely based on common sense.

To many people, sociology appears to be a laborious study of the obvious, an expensive way to discover what everybody already knows. To these people, sociology is merely common sense. But this is not true. Common sense to a large extent tends to be speculative and intuitive. It is contextual and subjective. One person's common sense could be nonsense for another. Most importantly, common sense is non-reflexive in nature. That is, it does not question its own origins. As a result, it tends to be conservative in outlook, and status quoist in nature. Since common sense beliefs are not always supported by a systematic and scientific body of evidence, there is a possibility that some common sense conclusions could be based on ignorance, prejudice and mistaken interpretation. Hence, there is high possibility for some common sense beliefs to be mutually conflicting and contradictory. When facing such conflicting common sense ideas, how can we tell which are correct and which are false? We can get the answer from sociological research. Common sense thus preserves both folk wisdom and folk nonsense, and to sort out one from the other is a task for science.

Thus, sociology is more than common sense, because it is based largely on scientific evidence. Today, science is replacing common sense as a source of dependable knowledge. Early sociologists distinguished the subject matter of sociology from that of common sense. For example, positivists like Emile Durkheim (Structural Approach) focused on the study of only those aspects of social reality that could be empirically observed and quantified. Their primary objective was to discover universal laws of human behaviour, in other words, to arrive at universal generalisations. Hence, they completely ignored the subjective dimension of human behaviour (unique meanings and values) for the simple reason that it could not be subjected to empirical observation and quantification. As stated earlier, common sense is contextual and subjective. However, other sociologists belonging to non-positivist or anti-positivist tradition like Max Weber (Social Action Approach) also focussed on the study of subjective or contextual aspect of social reality. These scholars suggested that at best only limited generalisations are possible in social sciences. (You will learn about positivist and anti-positivist approaches in later chapters.)

To conclude, it may be said that both sociology and common sense share a complementary relationship with each other. While common sense acts as a source of ideas that facilitates the formulation of hypothesis to carry out sociological research, sociology serves to verify and validate various commonly held beliefs.

References

Deshpande, Satish. *Contemporary India: A Sociological View.* New Delhi: Penguin, 2004.

Dev, Arjun. *The Story of Civilization (Vol. I).* New Delhi: National Council of Educational Research and Training, 2002.

Dreze, Jean and Amartya Sen. *India: Development and Participation.* New Delhi: Oxford University Press, 2002.

Gisbert, P. *Fundamentals of Sociology.* New Delhi: Orient BlackSwan, 2016.

Horton, Paul B. and Chester L. Hunt. *Sociology.* 6th Edition. New Delhi: Tata McGraw-Hill, 2004.

Koenig, Samuel. *Sociology: An Introduction to the Science of Society.* New York: Barnes & Noble, 1970.

Leon-Guerrero, Anna. *Social Problems: Community, Policy, and Social Action.* 5th Edition. New Delhi: SAGE Publications, 2016.

Macionis, John J. *Sociology.* 15th Edition. England: Pearson Education, 2015.

Mills, C.W. *The Sociological Imagination.* London: Oxford University Press, 1959.

Morrison, Ken. *Marx, Durkheim, Weber: Formations of Modern Social Thought.* 2nd Edition. New Delhi: SAGE Publications, 2012.

Newman, David M. *Sociology: Exploring the Architecture of Everyday Life.* 11th Edition. New Delhi: SAGE Publications, 2016.

Ritzer, George and Jeffrey Stepnisky. *Sociological Theory.* 9th Edition. New York: McGraw-Hill Education, 2014.

Scott, John. *Social Theory: Central Issues in Sociology.* New Delhi: SAGE Publications, 2006.

Thio, Alex. *Sociology: A Brief Introduction.* Boston: Pearson Education, 2003.

Turner, Jonathan H., Leonard Beeghley and Charles H. Powers. *The Emergence of Sociological Theory.* 3rd Edition. California: Wadsworth Publishing Company, 1995.

2
BASIC CONCEPTS IN SOCIOLOGY

Society

The concept of society constitutes the core of the discipline of sociology. It is the very subject matter of sociology. Sociology is nothing but a scientific study of society and the variety of interactions that unfold within and between individuals and groups. Social beings express their nature by creating and recreating an organisation which guides and controls their behaviour in various ways. This organisation, society, liberates and limits the activities of men, and sets up standards for them to follow and maintain. Society is a necessary condition of every fulfilment of life. According to MacIver and Page (2007),

> Society is a system of usages and procedures, authority and mutual aid, of many groupings and divisions, of controls of human behaviour and of liberties. This ever-changing, complex system we call society. It is the web of social relationships. And it is always changing.

Prof. Wright states that 'Society is not a group of people, it is the system of relationships that exists between the individuals of the group' (Bhushan and Sachdeva, 2019).

However, society is not limited to human beings. There are animal societies of many degrees. For example, the remarkable social organisations of insects, such as the ant, the bee, etc., are well known. However, in the lowest stages of life, social awareness, if it exists, is extremely dim and social contact is often extremely fleeting. Whereas, among all higher animals at least there is a very definite society, arising out of the requirements of their nature and the conditions involved in the perpetuation of their species (ibid.). Kingsley Davis, an American sociologist, argues that irrespective of their types, all societies have

DOI: 10.4324/9781003291053-3

certain common needs which must be fulfilled. These needs, which Davis called 'primary needs', define the necessary conditions for the existence of any society. Davis classified these societal needs into four major categories: the need for population (which includes needs for nutrition, protection and reproduction), specialisation, solidarity and continuity. To meet these minimum requirements for survival, animals largely depend upon their instinctual learning and communication. According to Davis, the fulfilment of these basic conditions of continued existence by means of learnt, normative behaviour (i.e. culture), rather than primarily by hereditary mechanisms, constitutes the major difference between human and animal societies (Rao, 2017).

According to MacIver and Page (2007),

> Society involves both likeness and difference … Without likeness and the sense of likeness there could be no mutual recognition of 'belonging together' and therefore no society. Society exists among those who resemble one another in some degree, in body and in mind, and who are near enough or intelligent enough to appreciate the fact. Society, as F.H. Giddings expressed it, rests on 'consciousness of kind' … Society, however, also depends on difference. If people were all exactly alike, merely alike, their social relationships would be as limited, perhaps, as those of ant or bee. There would be little give-and-take, little reciprocity … For example, the family rests upon the biological difference between the sexes. There are other natural differences, of aptitude, of capacity, of interest. Further differences are developed in the process of specialization. These differences, natural and developed, show themselves in society in the social division of labour.

MacIver and Page further state that society means likeness, and in a society, difference is subordinate to likeness. They argue that the division of labour in society is cooperation before it is division. For it is because people have *like* wants that they associate in the performance of unlike functions. It may also be borne in mind that while society means likeness, the converse of the statement is not true. Likeness may exist without giving birth to society. Similarly, while difference is necessary to society, difference by itself does not create society. The likeness of men's wants is necessarily prior to the differentiation of social organisation. As MacIver and Page observe, 'Primary likeness and secondary difference create the greatest of all social institutions – the division of labour' (Bhushan and Sachdeva, 2019).

Society, however, is not just a group of people. It is the system of relationships that exists between the individuals of the group. According to MacIver and Page (2007), 'Society is a web of social relationships'. But what do we mean by social relationship? Can the relationship existing between fire and smoke or pen and ink be called a social relationship? Obviously not, because psychical awareness of the presence of one another is lacking. Without this awareness, there can be no social relationship, and therefore no society. On the other hand, the relationship between mother and child, teacher and student or employer and employee qualify as social relationship since it is marked by mutual awareness. Without mutual or reciprocal awareness, there is no social relationship, no society. Society, as F.H. Giddings expressed it, rests on 'consciousness of the kind'. This reciprocal recognition may be the 'we-feeling' of Cooley or a 'common propensity' of W.I. Thomas (Bhushan and Sachdeva, 2019).

Harry M. Johnson (2007) lists four characteristics of a society, viz. definite territory, sexual reproduction, comprehensive culture and independence. A society is a territorial group. In other words, territoriality is one of the distinctive features of any society. Further, members of a society are recruited, in large part, by means of human reproduction within the group. For social stability and sustenance, a clearly defined normative order is essential for a society. This normative order constituting of a set of patterned social norms and social sanctions is culture. In a plural society like India, it is possible that more than one culture may coexist at the same time. Last but not the least, a society has its own independent identity. It is not a subgroup of any other social entity. Rather, it is a self-contained and integrated group.

After having discussed the concept of society in detail, let us now analyse whether society should be viewed as a process or as a structure. It should be noted, however, that there is really no conflict between the two views of society. As a matter of fact, these two views complement each other.

From the functional point of view, society is understood as a complex network of reciprocal relationships among the members of a society, with individual members helping each other to fulfil their respective interests. When we view society from a functional perspective, it appears as a process – a process involving 'mutual recognition' or 'reciprocal awareness' of the interacting individuals on the one hand, and a 'sense of belongingness', on the other. In the case of physical relationship, such as the relationship between a typist and the typewriter, there is no such mutual recognition. Similarly, if two individuals are walking in the same garden independent of each other, their relationship of coexistence, of being at the same time in the same place, cannot be called a social relationship. The psychical condition, a characteristic feature of social relationship, is lacking here. Reciprocal recognition, direct or indirect, is one of the characteristic features of every social relationship. The second feature is a sense of belonging together or a 'consciousness of kind', as Giddings puts it. A society consists of people who share attitudes, beliefs and ideals in common. There might, of course, be feuds and mutual hostility among members of a society. But these are, in the nature of things, transitory and occasional. In the words of MacIver and Page (2007): 'Co-operation crossed by conflict marks society wherever it is revealed'.

From the structural point of view, society is the total social heritage of folkways, mores and institutions; of habits, sentiments and ideals. The structure of human society can be understood as similar to the structure of a building. A building has mainly three structural components: (i) the building material (bricks, stones, mortar, pillars, beams, etc.); (ii) the definite arrangement of these material components in relationship to each other; and (iii) all these put together make a building one unit. Similarly, a human society consists of (i) individual members (such as males and females, adults and children) as well as social groups (such as various occupational and religious groups and so on); (ii) a relatively patterned relationship between various individuals occupying different social statuses (such as relationship between husband and wife, between parents and children and between various groups); and (iii) all the parts of the society are put together to work as a unit. Thus, the term 'social structure' refers to the way the various parts of society are organised and follow stable patterns of collective rules, roles and activities. In simple words, social structure refers to the pattern of social relations among members of a society (in terms of interrelated statuses and roles) at a particular point of time. Thus, constituting a relatively stable set of social relations. Although the structure itself remains invisible, it silently shapes our actions. The basic elements of social structure which guide our actions are social statuses, social roles, norms and values.

The concepts of status and role are integral to the understanding of society as a process as well as a structure. While status refers to a position occupied by an individual in a group or society, role is the expected behaviour of an individual who holds a certain status. Ralph Linton, in his famous work *The Study of Man*, has described status as a set of rights and duties. Since a status refers to a social position in a given society, it is socially defined in terms of certain rights and duties. For example, an individual who occupies the status of father has certain rights over his children as well as certain responsibilities towards them. The same is true for the statuses of a son, daughter, teacher, leader, etc. However, a status may either be ascribed or achieved. Ascribed status is assigned to an individual either on the basis of his birth and biological characteristics such as sex, age and race or the status of his/her parents. In India, caste plays a significant role in determining the social status of an individual, which is an example of ascribed status. Achieved status is a position which an individual attains through personal efforts. For instance, one can become a doctor, engineer or lawyer by one's own efforts. It is important to note that while persons occupying the status (or social position) may be replaced but the social positions will continue to exist in the social structure. This stability in patterns of relations among individuals or groups occupying different statuses over a period of time gives rise to social structure in a society.

Role may be defined as the normatively expected behaviour from an individual who holds a particular status. Each distinctive status, whether ascribed or achieved, has certain role expectations. Role is the expected behaviour of an individual who holds a certain status. While status is the positional aspect of behaviour, role is the behavioural aspect of a given status or position. A person's role in any situation is defined by the set of expectations for his behaviour held by others and by the person himself. However, actual performance may vary from individual to individual. For example, two individuals, occupying a similar status, like that of a teacher, may perform their respective roles differently. Therefore, Ralph Linton calls role as the dynamic aspect of the status (Scott, 1999).

It is important to understand that if we consider just a point of time, then both status and role would appear to be static concepts. Status is fixed and unchanging. So is role. Viewed in this context, the society is a structure. However, if we consider a period of time, then both status and role would appear to be dynamic concepts. Status changes in relation to other statuses from time to time. There is a corresponding change in role also. Viewed in the context of period of time, it would thus appear that society is a process and that social relationships are in a state of flux. For example, the relations between traditional upper caste and lower caste groups have significantly transformed in post-independent India with the constitution coming into effect. The same is true of gender roles as well. Thus, if there is any equilibrium in society, it is a moving equilibrium. The society is thus viewed as both a process and a structure. One who studies society must take into account both of these views (Figure 2.1).

As MacIver and Page (2007) have also stated 'Society exists only as a time-sequence. It is a becoming, not a product'. This is the essence of society. Thus, society is to be interpreted in a wider sense. It is both a structural and functional organisation. It consists in the mutual interactions and mutual interrelations of the individuals but it is also a structure formed by these relations.

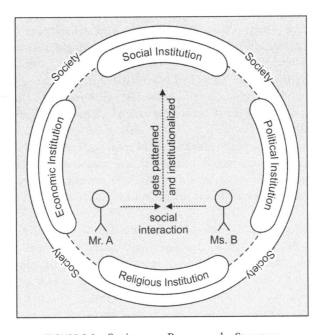

FIGURE 2.1 Society as a Process and a Structure

Community

According to MacIver and Page (2007), 'wherever the members of any group, small or large, live together in such a way that they share the basic conditions of a common life, then, such a group may be called a community'. Thus, the distinctive feature of a community is that one's life may be lived wholly within it. In other words, the basic criterion of community then is that all of one's social relationships may be found within it. However, communities need not always be self-sufficient. Some communities are all-inclusive and independent of others. But modern communities, even very large ones, are much less self-contained. Economic and, increasingly so, political interdependence is a major characteristic of our great modern communities. Communities may exist within greater communities: the town within a region, the region within a nation and the nation within the world community which, perhaps, is in the process of development.

MacIver and Page further state that community is 'an area of social living marked by some degree of social coherence'. The bases of community are *locality* and *community sentiment*. A community always occupies a territorial area. Most communities are settled and derive from the conditions of their locality a strong bond of solidarity. To some extent, this local bond has been weakened in the modern world by the extending facilities of communications. But the extension of communication is itself the condition of a larger community. Locality, though a necessary condition, is not enough to create a community. A community, to repeat, is an area of common living. There must be the common living with its awareness of sharing a way of life as well as the common earth. Some scholars argue that a community always occupies a territorial area. The area need not be fixed forever. The people may change their area of habitation from time to time just as the nomadic community does. Further, with globalisation, when we talk about a global village or global community, this indicates that the concept of community is no more limited to a limited geographical area. Community sentiment is another key feature of a community. However, such sentiment need not always be particularistic in nature, for example, based on religion, language, region or caste, etc. In modern times, the basis of community sentiment could also be secular in character. Modern means of communications and various social media platforms have facilitated the formation of virtual social groups based on common interests and concerns, for example, to protect the natural environment, to promote nuclear disarmament and to protest against cruelty against animals.

Other scholars have also offered their respective definitions of community. For example, Bogardus defines community as 'a social group with some degree of "we-feeling" and "living in given area"'. According to Kingsley Davis, 'Community is the smallest territorial group that can embrace all aspects of social life'. For Manheim, Community is any circle of people who live together and belong together in such a way that they do not share this or that particular interest only, but a whole set of interests (Bhushan and Sachdeva, 2019).

Let's now try to understand the differences in the concepts of society and community. While society may be defined as a web of social relationships, community, on the other hand, consists of a group of individuals living in a particular area with some degree of 'we-feeling'. A definite geographic area is not an essential aspect of society but community always denotes a definite locality or geographic area. While society is abstract, community is concrete. Community sentiment or a sense of 'we-feeling' may or may not be present in society but community sentiment is an essential element of community. There can be no community in its absence. Society is wider, as there can be more than one community in a society. The objectives and interests of society are more extensive and varied as compared to that of a community. Society involves both likeness and difference. Common interests as well as diverse interests are present in society. But likeness is more important than difference in community. There is common agreement of interests and objectives on the part of members.

Association

An association is a group of people organised for a particular purpose or a limited number of purposes. According to some scholars, to constitute an association there must be, first, a group of people. Second, these people must be organised ones, i.e. there must be certain rules for their conduct in the group. Third, they must have a common purpose of specific nature to pursue. Thus, family, church, trade union, music club are all instances of association. Associations may be formed on several bases, for example, on the basis of duration, i.e. temporary or permanent, like a Flood Relief Association, which is temporary, and state which is permanent. On the basis of power, i.e. sovereign, like state, and semi-sovereign, like university, etc. On the basis of function, i.e. biological, like family, and vocational, like trade union, recreational, like music club, etc.

An association, according to MacIver and Page (2007), may be defined as 'a group organised for the pursuit of an interest or group of interests in common'. An association is different from a community. While an association is organised for particular purposes, the mark a community is that one's life may be lived wholly within it, or, in other words, its members share the very basic conditions of a common life. Membership of an association is voluntary, i.e. individuals are at liberty to join them, while on the other hand, by birth itself individuals become members of a community. An association does not necessarily imply the spatial aspects, while a community is marked by a locality. An association may or may not be stable and long-lasting, but a community is relatively more stable and permanent. Further, associations may have their legal status, but a community has no legal status. Associations may have their own rules and regulations to regulate the relations of their members. They may have written or unwritten rules. A community regulates the behaviour of its members by means of customs, traditions and social norms, etc. Association is partial and it may be regarded as a part of the community; while community, on the other hand, is integral as it may have within its boundary several associations.

Thus, an association is not a community but an organisation within a community, and a community is more than any specific organisations that rise within it. However, associations may become communities at least temporarily over a period of time; for example, the military units may create their own communities when isolated for a period of time. The qualification, expressly organised, enables us to distinguish between association and other social groups. As we shall see, there are many forms and types of social groups: class and crowd, primary and secondary groups, face-to-face groups and great associations. But a social class, for example, is not an association. Organisations established on class lines such as certain political parties are associations, but a class itself is not a group expressly organised to pursue certain ends or to fulfil certain functions. Nor is the group we term a crowd an association, though certain crowds in some situations may acquire the characteristics of temporary associations (MacIver and Page, 2007).

Institution

Institutions are the forms of procedure which are recognised and accepted by society and govern the relations between individuals and groups. In other words, a social institution refers to an interrelated system of social roles and norms organised for the satisfaction of an important social need or perform a vital function. The social roles and norms comprising the social institution define proper and expected behaviour oriented to the fulfilment of the particular social, economic, political or physical needs. Marriage, education, property, religion, etc. are some of the main institutions in any given society. The concept of institution is one of the most important in the entire field of sociology. In fact, Durkheim has gone to the extent of defining sociology as the science of social institutions.

According to MacIver and Page, institutions may be defined as the 'established forms or conditions of procedure characteristic of group activity'. H.E. Barnes describes social institutions as 'the social structure and machinery through which human society organises, directs and executes the multifarious activities required to satisfy human needs'. According to Bogardus, a social institution is 'a structure of society that is organised to meet the needs of people chiefly through well established procedures' (Bhushan and Sachdeva, 2019).

> When men create associations they must also create rules and procedures for the dispatch of the common business and for the regulation of the members to one another. Such *forms* are distinctively institutions. Every association has, with respect to its particular interest, its characteristic institutions. The church, for example, has its sacraments, its modes of worship, its rituals. The family has marriage, that is, the institution of the mating relationship; it has the home, the family meal, and so forth. The state has

its own peculiar institutions, such as representative government and legislative procedures … We belong to associations but not to institutions …
the church is an association and communion an institution, that the trade-
union is an association and collective bargaining an institution, that the
family is an association and monogamy an institution.

(MacIver and Page, 2007)

In the following section, some of the key characteristics of institution are discussed. Essentially, institutions are social in nature. Institutions come into being
due to the collective activities of the people. Another important feature is their
universality. They exist in all societies and existed at all stages of social development. The basic institutions like family, religion, property and some kinds of
political institutions are observed even in tribal or primitive societies. Further,
it is important to note that institutions are nothing but standardised norms and
procedures. They prescribe certain ways of doing things. They prescribe rules
and regulations that are to be followed, for example, marriage as an institution
governs the relations between the husband and the wife. Institutions are formed
to satisfy some of the most basic and vital needs of man, such as need for self-
preservation, the need for self-perpetuation, the need for self-expression, etc.

Institutions also act as the controlling mechanisms in a society. Institutions
like religion, morality, state, government, law, legislation, etc. control the behaviour of men. These mechanisms preserve the social order and give stability to
it. Further, institutions are relatively permanent. Institutions normally do not
undergo sudden or rapid changes. Changes take place slowly and gradually in
them. Institutions are abstract in nature. They are not external, visible or tangible
things. Institutions may have their own symbols, material or non-material, for
example, the state has flag, emblem, etc. as its symbols, while religion may have
its own symbols like crucifix, crescent, star, swastika, etc. Institutions, though
diverse, are interrelated. The social, economic, political, religious, educational
and other types of institutions are essentially interlinked with each other.

Related to the concept of institution are the concepts of custom, folkways and
mores. This section deals with the concept of custom and its interrelationship
with the concept of institution. The concepts of folkways and mores are discussed subsequently. Underlying and sustaining the more formal order of institutions and associations, there exists an intricate complex of usages or modes
of behaviour. Thus, there are accepted procedures of eating, conversing, meeting folks, wooing, training the young, caring for the aged, etc. These socially
accredited ways of acting are the customs of society. We conform to the customs
of our own society, in a sense, 'unconsciously', for they are a strongly imbedded
part of our group life. They are so strongly imbedded, indeed, that we frequently
make the error of identifying our particular customs with the only correct ways
of doing this or that, or even with human nature itself.

The difference between a social usage or custom, on the one hand, and an
institution, on the other, is essentially one of degree. Institution implies a more

definite recognition. For example, we would call the marriage feast an institution, but various courtship practices are better-named customs. Marriage itself is an institution and not a custom. Institutions have external insignia, marks of public recognition, which customs as such do not require. The term 'institution' stresses the impersonal factor in social relationships. When we speak of customs, we think of the accepted ways in which people do things together, in personal contacts. When we speak of institutions, we think rather of the system of controls that extends beyond personal relations (MacIver and Page, 2007).

Institutions are often classified into (i) *primary institutions* and (ii) *secondary institutions*. The most basic institutions like religion, family, marriage, property and some kinds of political systems, which are found even in primitive societies, are primary in character. As societies grew in size and complexity, institutions became progressive and more differentiated. Accordingly, a large number of institutions are evolved to cater to the secondary needs of people. They may be called secondary institutions. For example, education, examination, law, legislation, constitution, parliamentary procedure, business, etc.

William Graham Sumner, an American sociologist, viewed man as pitted against nature, on the one hand, and against other men with a competing economic interest, on the other. The cooperation and conflict are the basic processes among the members of the society. In their attempt to conquer nature, individuals engage in cooperation with each other. Similarly, individuals having common or compatible economic interests join hands and form groups in their struggle against other groups and individuals having conflicting economic interest. In their struggle for survival, the social groups spontaneously develop various ways of acting. The best and fittest under the particular conditions are selected. These methods are repeated and their repetition produces habits in the individual and custom in the group. These persisting ways of doing things that develop in the spontaneous and unconscious manners are called *folkways*. They arise, no one knows when and how, and grow as if by the play of internal life and energy.

> The folkways, then, are the recognised or accepted ways of behaving in society. They include conventions, forms of etiquette, and the myriad modes of behaviour men have evolved and continue to evolve with which to go about the business of social living. They vary, of course, from society to society and from time to time. Wearing a necktie is a folkway of adornment in our community; no less so is the filing of teeth among the Philippine Negritos. Such are the ways of the folk.
>
> *(MacIver and Page, 2007)*

Sumner further argued that some folkways are considered crucial for the survival of the group. The special significance attached to these folkways is manifested in the form of special sanctions which existed against their violation. Such folkways were called by Sumner as 'mores'. Thus, according to Sumner, folkways are simply the customary, normal, habitual ways a group does things. Mores are those strong ideas of right and wrong which require certain acts and forbid others. Mores are time and space bound. They keep changing according to time and situations.

According to Sumner, folkways also form the basis of group cohesion. Thus, members of a group having similar folkways develop a strong 'we-feeling'. Such a group is called an 'in-group'. On the other hand, members of a group having different folkways are termed as 'out-group'. Members of an in-group may display a sense of distrust and hostility towards members of an out-group. Each group, therefore, nourishes its pride and vanity, boasts of its own superiority and looks with contempt towards outsiders. To this attitude of superiority, concerning the folkways of one's 'in-group' and of judging others in terms of these folkways, Sumner gave the name *ethnocentrism*. The term 'ethnocentrism' was introduced by Sumner in his book *Folkways*.

Sumner argued that the subject matter of sociology was the study of evolution, nature and functions of *social institutions*, both crescive and enacted. The *crescive institutions* are those which develop spontaneously in an unplanned manner like folkways and mores. While *enacted institutions* consist of the laws that are the result of conscious and deliberate human efforts. The crescive ones are more akin to primary institutions, whereas the enacted ones resemble secondary institutions (Scott, 1999).

Social Groups

The concept of group is central to sociology. While in normal discourse we regard any collection of two or more individuals to be group, but sociologically, individuals constituting a group must be conscious of a common belongingness, of sharing some common understandings, as well as of accepting certain rights and obligations. In this sense, a family or a class can be called a group.

According to Horton and Hunt (2004), a social group may be defined as 'any number of people who share consciousness of membership together and of interaction'. By this definition, two persons waiting for a bus would not be a group but would become a group if they started a conversation, a fight or any other interaction. A number of people waiting at a stop light would be an *aggregation* or a *collectivity*, not a group, unless something – a street orator, an accident, a suicide – caught their attention and held their interest, converting them into an audience, which is one kind of group. A busload of passengers would not ordinarily be a group, because they have no consciousness of interaction with each other. It is possible that interaction may develop and groups may form in the course of the trip.

Thus, the essence of a social group is not physical closeness but a consciousness of interactions. A stimulus incident may change an aggregation into a group. For example, let a bus driver announce that he is stopping for fuel, and the aggregation of passengers promptly becomes a group, sharing their annoyance and protesting this delay. This consciousness of interaction is necessary for them to be a group, while mere physical presence is not necessary at all. Many groups meet rarely, if at all, but they interact by telephone, letters, bulletins and magazines. The term 'group' covers many kinds of human interactions. H.M. Johnson

(2007) defines a social group as 'a system of social interaction'. For MacIver and Page (2007), social group is 'any collection of human beings who are brought into social relationships with one another'.

Man is a social animal. It is often said that man becomes man only among men. For his all-round personality development, exposure to a human environment is essential for a man. In the absence of a human environment, man fails to develop human qualities. Few instances can be cited to corroborate this point. The first example is the case of Wolf Children. In 1920, two feral girls, Amala (18 months) and Kamala (8 years old), were discovered in a wolf den in Bengal, India. The younger child died within a few months of discovery, but the elder one, named Kamala, survived until 1929. As reported, the children had developed no human qualities when they were discovered. The girls enjoyed the taste of raw meat and would eat out of a bowl on the ground. They seemed to be insensitive to cold and heat and appeared to show no human emotions of any kind, apart from fear. At night they would howl like wolves, calling out to their 'family'. They did not speak. They could walk only on 'fours' and were shy to meet or face people. After some sympathetic training, Kamala was taught basic social habits. Before her death Kamala had slowly learnt some simple speech, human eating and dressing habits and the like. This wolf child has no 'sense of human selfhood', when she was discovered, but it emerged gradually. However, there is some controversy as to the authenticity of the story.

In yet another case, Anna, an illegitimate American child, was kept in complete social isolation since her birth until her discovery five years later in 1938. Though Anna was regularly fed during her confinement, she neither received any training nor had any social contact with other human beings. After her discovery, it was found that Anna could neither walk nor speak. She was completely indifferent to people around her. As in the case of Kamala, Anna was given some training to which she responded. She became 'humanised' much more rapidly before she died in 1942. Here, improvement showed that socialisation could do a great deal towards making her a 'person'. These instances convincingly prove that man becomes social only in social groups (Rao, 2017).

In every society, there exists a wide variety of groups, but the most fundamental division which sociologists make is that of primary and secondary groups. The term 'primary group' was first coined by the sociologist C.H. Cooley. According to Cooley, a primary group is relatively small (though, not all small groups are primary); its members generally have face-to-face contact, and thus, have intimate and cooperative relationships as well as strong loyalty. The relationships between the members are ends in themselves. That is, members derive pleasure and enjoyment merely by associating with one another. They have no other particular ends or goals in view. The primary group is an end in itself. The primary group comes to an end, when one or more members leave it; they cannot be substituted by others. The best example of a primary group is the family or the 'peer' group.

On the other hand, secondary groups, in several respects, are the opposite of primary groups. These are generally large size groups, though not always so. Members of the secondary group maintain relatively limited, formal and impersonal relationships with one another. Unlike primary groups, secondary groups are specific or specialised interest groups. Generally, a well-defined division of labour characterises these groups. Members of secondary groups can be substituted and replaced. Hence, a secondary group may continue irrespective of whether its original members continue to be its members or not. A cricket team, a music club, an army or a factory, etc. are examples of secondary groups. It is possible that within secondary groups, some members may come close to one another and develop primary relations and form a group of peers. Several sociological studies have shown that the presence of primary groups in armies, factories and other secondary groups have contributed to high level of morale, and more effective functioning.

Various other sociologists have also classified groups on the basis of their own criteria. For example, W.G. Summer in his *Folkways* differentiates between 'in-group' and 'out-group'. An 'in-group' is simply the 'we-group', and an 'out-group' the 'they group'. The classification is more subjective in the sense that it depends on the tendency for a particular individual to identify himself with a particular group in a particular situation for a particular reason. For example, for an individual belonging to a particular caste, his own caste group members constitute his 'in-group', while those belonging to other castes would constitute an 'out-group' for him. The best manifestation of this tendency is the widely prevalent practice of caste endogamy in India.

Another important classification of groups has been developed by the German sociologist Ferdinand Tonnies in terms of Gemeinschaft and Gesellschaft. These two terms translate roughly as 'community' and 'society'. The Gemeinschaft is a social system in which most relationships are personal or traditional, and often both. A good example is the Jajmani system, in which the rural community was held together by a combination of personal relationships and mutual obligations on the part of various caste groups. In the Gesellschaft, the society of tradition is replaced with the society of contract. In this society, neither personal attachment nor traditional rights and duties are important. The relationships between people are determined by bargaining and defined in written agreements. In other words, the relationships in Gemeinschaft are personal, informal, traditional, sentimental and general in nature, while those in Gesellschaft are impersonal, formal, contractual, utilitarian, realistic and specialised. Thus, it may be argued that in the Gemeinschaft, primary group relationships are dominant, while in the Gesellschaft, secondary group relationships are more dominant.

Charles A. Ellwood in his *Psychology of Human Society* has mentioned a three-fold classification of social groups. These are 'involuntary and voluntary groups', 'institutional and non-institutional groups' and 'temporary and permanent groups'. Membership to involuntary groups is largely ascribed in nature, and it may include groups such as family, caste, race, state, etc., and the voluntary groups may include political parties, trade unions, youth associations, religious associations, culture associations and so on. Institutional groups are mostly permanent in nature and include church, state, caste, the school and so on, while the non-institutional groups are temporary in nature and include groups such as crowds, mobs, public, audience and so on.

Another eminent sociologist, P.A. Sorokin, has divided groups into two major types: horizontal and vertical. The former are large, inclusive groups such as nations, religious organisations and political parties. The latter are smaller divisions, such as economic classes, which give the individual his status in society. Park and Burgess have distinguished between territorial groups, such as communities, states, etc., and non-territorial groups such as classes, castes, crowds and public, etc. Other scholars like Leopold Von Wiese and Howard Becker have also classified human groups into three categories, viz. crowds, groups and collectivities.

F.H. Giddings has introduced the classification of genetic groups and congregate groups. Genetic groups are involuntary in nature and the individuals are born in them. Congregate groups are voluntary in nature and the individuals are at liberty to join or not. Family groups, racial groups, ethnic groups are genetic groups, while parties, trade unions, etc. are congregate. George C. Homans, an American social theorist, put forward his exchange theory which states that individual assessments of costs and benefits are the basis of such social phenomena as competition and cooperation, authority and conformity. Homans maintained a lifelong interest in the study of small groups and also wrote the book *The Human Group*. Another scholar Newcomb classified groups in terms of positive and negative groups. According to him, the individual tends to be more favourable towards some groups. He easily adopts the values and patterns of such groups, which he calls the positive group. While on the other hand, there are some groups which the individual does not like. These are the negative groups for that individual. Thus, these two groups depend on the subjective desire of the individual (Bhushan and Sachdeva, 2019).

However, it is important to note that we are not equally involved in all our in-groups, nor do we feel equally distant from all our out-groups. Bogardus developed Bogardus Social Distance Scale to measure the degree of closeness or acceptance that members of one group feel towards other groups. Social distance is measured either by direct observation of people interacting or more often by questionnaires in which people are asked what kind of people they would accept in a particular relationship. In these questionnaires, a number of groups may be listed and the informants are asked to check whether they would accept a member of each group as a neighbour, as a fellow worker, as a marriage partner and so on through a series of relationships. Please note that the term 'social distance' was first used by Georg Simmel and refers to the feeling of separation or actual social separation between individuals or groups. The greater the social distance between two groups of different status or culture, the less sympathy, understanding, intimacy and interaction between them (Marshall, 1998).

Culture

The classic definition of culture, framed by E.B. Tylor in his book *Primitive Culture* (1871), reads, 'Culture ... is that complex whole which includes knowledge, belief, art, morals, law, custom and any other capabilities and habits acquired by man as a member of society'.

Stated more simply, culture is everything which is socially learnt and shared by the members of a society. In other words, culture is the totality of learnt and socially transmitted behaviour from one generation to the next. It includes symbols, signs and languages, besides religion, rituals, beliefs and artefacts. In fact, culture is a guiding force in everyday life. It is culture that distinguishes one society from the other. Each society has a culture of its own that is historically derived and passed on from one generation to the next and constantly enriched by those who live it.

According to MacIver and Page, 'Culture is the expression of our nature in our modes of living and our thinking, intercourse, in our literature, in religion, in recreation and enjoyment'. For Spencer, culture is 'the super-organic environment as distinguished from the organic or physical, the world of plants and animals'. Mazumdar states that culture is 'the sum total of human achievements, material as well as non-material, capable of transmission, sociologically, i.e., by tradition and communication vertically as well as horizontally' (Bhushan and Sachdeva, 2019).

Thus, on the basis of various viewpoints mentioned above from various sociologists and anthropologists, some of the chief characteristics of culture have been summarised in this section. First, culture is shared in common by the members of a given society or community. Culture, therefore, refers not to the beliefs and activities of individuals but to those of groups or people who are organised in communities. It is fundamentally a social phenomenon. Second, culture is learnt and acquired by human beings in interaction with others. An individual acquires the characteristics of his parents and his group in two ways. On the one hand, he acquires the physical characteristics and features of his parents, such as skin colour, stature, texture of hair and colour of the eyes, through genetic transmission, over which he has no control. On the other hand, he learns and acquires the thoughts, attitudes, language and habits of his parents, and through them, of his group, by way of cultural transmission. Third, culture is not only learnt and acquired by individuals in a social context, but it is also accumulated and transmitted from generation to generation, through the mechanism of symbolic communication or language.

Herskovits, an American anthropologist, has also identified certain characteristics of culture in his book *Man and His Works*. He argues that culture consists of man-made part of the environment, in other words, it is socially created. He states that culture is learnt, thus implying that it is an acquired behaviour. He further argues that culture derives from the biological, environmental, psychological and historical components of human experience. Culture is structured;

it consists of organised patterns of thinking, feeling and behaving. Culture is dynamic. Culture is variable, it is relative. Culture exhibits regularities that permit its analysis by the methods of science.

There is consensus among a large body of scholars that culture constitutes a structural unity, in that its various elements or constituent parts are mutually interrelated and interdependent. Thus, it is possible, for the purposes of analysis and understanding, to delineate the major components or divisions of culture. The major components of culture, which are universal in nature, can be summarised as follows: technology, economic organisation, social organisation, political organisation, ideology, arts and language. Technology refers to the system of tools, implements and artefacts, made and used by people to meet their basic needs. Economic organisation includes the techniques that are employed by a people in organising the production and distribution of goods and services. Social organisation refers to the framework of social and interpersonal relations. A political organisation refers to the ways and methods of controlling conflict, and deals with the maintenance of the social order. Ideology includes a guiding set of beliefs, values and ideals. Arts include the forms which ensure the fulfilment of man's aesthetic urges. Language is the medium through which all the above operate.

Robert Bierstedt, in his book *The Social Order*, has classified the contents of culture into three categories: *ideas*, *norms* and *material*. In other words, the components of culture may be classified into three dimensions: cognitive, normative and material. Ideas refer to the cognitive dimension of culture, which includes beliefs and knowledge. Cognition is the process that enables humans to comprehend and to relate to their surroundings. Thus, the first and the most important component of culture is idea, which consists of myth, superstitions, scientific facts, art and religion. The normative dimension is the second large component of culture. It includes rules, expectations and standardised procedures; in short, ways of behaving in almost all the situations that we confront and in which people participate. The normative dimension of culture is of critical importance in promoting recurrence and predictability in human interaction. Norms can be classified as folkways, mores, customs and laws, etc., which guide individual conduct.

The third major component of culture is the material culture, referring to what we have or possess as members of society. The culture provides knowledge, rules for organising work and tools for human survival. Material culture refers mainly to basic conditions, which generally include material items that the members of a society have and use, and also to science, technology and instruments of production, transport and communication. Material culture is often counterposed with non-material culture, under which the cognitive and normative dimensions of culture are classified, and refers to the intangible product of human creation. In simpler terms, culture may be divided into material and non-material cultures. Non-material culture (implying cognitive and normative dimension) consists of the words people use; the ideas, norms, customs and beliefs they hold; and the habits they follow. Material culture consists of manufactured objects such as tools, furniture automobiles, buildings, roads, bridges and, in fact, any physical substance that has been changed and used by people. Such manufactured objects are called artefacts (Bierstedt, 1963).

Culture is often confused with society, but the two words have different meanings. Whereas culture is a system of norms and values, society is a relatively independent, self-perpetuating human group that occupies a territory, shares a culture and has most of its associations within this group. A society is an organisation of people whose association are with one another. A culture is an organised system of norms and values which people hold. In other words, society may be perceived as a chain of social relations among groups of individuals who are held together by commonly shared institutions and processes. All processes of the human life cycle are carried out and regulated in society. Thus, there is an integral reality of the individual, culture and society. All these are mutually interdependent, so that any one of them cannot be adequately understood without reference to the other. Culture depends for its existence and continuity on groups of individuals whose social relations form society.

Further, though man is generally defined as a social animal, man's social nature is not particularly unique to him. A society can exist even at the subhuman level. Ants and bees, for example, have genuine societies. The chimpanzees in the wild live in their society much like human beings: they form stable relationships; they move about and hunt in groups. Culture exists only in human societies. In other words, there can be an animal society without culture. Consequently, what differentiates man qualitatively from other species of animals is not his social nature, but his culture. Man is essentially a cultural or symbolic animal. Man's capacity for symbolic communication or language sharply differentiates him from other animals. Language plays a crucial role in the process of enculturation, whereby the individual acquires and imbibes the value, beliefs, customs and habits of his society. Language facilitates the sharing and accumulation of experiences and skills; it is also instrumental in the transmission of cultural traditions from one generation to another. It is worth noting that while among the animals the basic needs are satisfied through the mechanism of instincts, in man they are fulfilled and regulated through culture. Thus, in actual life, society and culture cannot be separated. Even though culture is a broader category, it cannot exist and function without society. Society, in other words, is a necessary precondition for culture. Similarly, neither society nor culture can exist independent of human beings.

Culture also needs to be distinguished from race. Race may be defined as a human population whose members share some hereditary biological characteristics that separate them from other groups. It must be noted that racial features are largely determined by genetic and biological factors, whereas cultures and language are learnt, acquired and transmitted through training and education. In this context, it is worth highlighting the role of culture in determining the sex roles in society. In human societies, men and women differ not only in anatomical and physical features, but also in respect of behaviour, role and attitude. It is generally held that men and women behave differently because of their biological differences as nature has prescribed different roles and behaviour patterns for them. This is a mistaken view. The differences between the roles and behaviour patterns of men and women, though related to certain anatomical and physical processes, are not entirely determined by them. Sex roles and traits, in other words, are not biologically given, they are conditioned by culture.

Margaret Mead, a distinguished American anthropologist, made a comparative study of the respective role of men and women in three primitive societies in New Guinea. She found that in each of these cultures, sex roles were radically different from those in Western culture. For example, in the Tchambuli tribe, women are masculine and men feminine, in terms of Western cultural standards. Women are dominant, responsible and engaged in aesthetic matters, besides being charming. Among the Arapesh, both men and women show feminine traits; they do not indulge in aggressive behaviour. Among the Mundugumor, both men and women exhibit masculine traits. Their behaviour reflects violence and aggressiveness. Mead, therefore, concluded the sex roles are culturally conditioned.

Another distinction of significance is that of culture and civilisation. Alfred Weber is well known for his cultural sociology and the analysis of the distinction between the concepts of culture and civilisation. Culture and civilisation are closely related terms. Civilisation refers to a historical phase of culture. A civilisation is characterised by certain distinctive features, such as cities and urbanisation, occupational specialisation, monumental structures, such as temples, palaces and tombs, classes and hierarchies and, above all, the art of writing. For example, civilisation emerged for the first time in human history as early as fourth millennium BC in ancient Mesopotamia. Some of the important points of difference between culture and civilisation may be summarised as follows: First, civilisation has a precise standard of measurement, but not culture. Second, civilisation is always advancing, but not culture. Civilisation is unilinear and cumulative and tends to advance indefinitely. Culture, on the other hand, advances slowly and is often subject to retrogression. In the contemporary scenario, the rise in religious fundamentalism in some societies can be cited as an example of this. Third, civilisation is borrowed without change or loss, but not culture. Further, civilisation is external and mechanical, while culture is internal and organic. In this context, MacIver appropriately remarks, 'Civilisation is what we have, culture is what we are'. Some of the important concepts and terms related to culture are discussed next.

Real and ideal culture: The ideal culture includes the formally approved folkways and mores which people are supposed to follow (the cultural norms); the real culture consists of those that they actually practise. In most societies, some behaviour patterns are generally condemned yet widely practised. In some places, these illicit behaviour patterns have existed for centuries side by side with the cultural norms that are supposed to outlaw them. Malinowski cites as an example of this type of behaviour among Trobriand Islanders, a group whose incest taboos extend to third and fourth cousins. Similarly, selling cigarettes and other tobacco products to children may be banned and declared illegal as a norm but yet widely practised in reality.

Diffusion: It is the process by which cultural traits or complexes spread from one society to another or one part of a society to another (Scott, 1999).

Acculturation: It is the modification of the culture of a group or an individual through contact with one or more other cultures and the acquiring or exchanging of cultural traits. In other words, it refers to the process whereby an individual or a group acquires the cultural characteristics of another through direct contact and interaction. From an individual point of view, this is a process of social learning. From a social point of view, acculturation implies the diffusion of particular values, techniques and institutions and their modification under different conditions. It may give rise to culture conflict and to adaptation, leading to a modification of group identity. Some scholars defined acculturation as 'those phenomena which result when groups of individuals having different cultures come into first hand contact, with subsequent change in the original cultural patterns of both groups' (ibid.).

It is worth highlighting here the distinction between diffusion and acculturation. Diffusion generally refers to the spread of specific cultural traits or elements, whereas acculturation refers to the changes brought about in whole cultures. When groups of individuals, having different cultural traditions, come into contact, changes take place in their original cultural patterns. This is referred to as acculturation or culture contact. Diffusion, on the other hand, refers to the spread of cultural traits and patterns from major centres of civilisation to smaller cultures and occasionally the other way round. Some scholars argue that when cultural traits or complexes have been diffused, we talk about diffusion, but when a whole way of life is in process of change under the influence of another culture, we call it acculturation. The processes of acculturation and diffusion have been going on in human society since very ancient times. Thus, as far back as the third millennium BC, we find trade and cultural relations between the Mesopotamian civilisation and the Indus civilisation. An interesting illustration of the diffusion of cultural traits is provided by the mathematical symbol of zero. The zero was invented, along with the system of numerals, for the first time in India. This system of numerals was adopted by the Arabs during the fifth century. The Arabs, in turn, transmitted the Indian system of numerals to Europe. Similarly, paper, gun powder, compass, etc. were invented in China, which later spread through the Muslim world from Samarkand and reached Europe.

Culture shock: It is the often rather severe psychological and social maladjustment many individuals experience when they visit or live in a society different from their own. Culture shock involves bewilderment due to new customs, unknown expectations, a feeling of being conspicuous, 'different' and foreign, and often a foreign language (ibid.).

Ethnocentrism: It is an attitude of regarding one's own culture or group as inherently superior. The ethnocentric attitude judges the worth of other cultures in terms of its own cultural standards, and, since other cultures are, of course, different, they are held to be inferior. Ethnocentrism reflects an inability to appreciate the viewpoint of others whose cultures have, for example, a different morality, religion or language. The term was introduced by William G. Summer in his work *Folkways*. Ethnocentric view is seen as a threat to the intergroup solidarity and communal harmony in a complex society where diverse groups belonging to different cultural backgrounds live together. However, for an individual ethnocentrism may be appealing because it reaffirms the individual's 'belongingness' to the group. It is also considered functional for intragroup solidarity. It is argued that ethnocentric groups seem to survive better than tolerant groups because ethnocentrism reinforces nationalism and patriotism. Without ethnocentrism, a vigorous national consciousness is probably impossible. Nationalism is but another level of group loyalty (ibid.).

Xenocentrism: This word means a preference for the foreign. It is exact opposite of ethnocentrism. It is the belief that our own products, styles or ideas are necessarily inferior to those that originate elsewhere. For example, there are many occasions when people seem happy to pay more for imported goods on the assumption that anything from abroad is better.

Cultural relativism: Cultural relativism refers to the view that the values, ideas and behaviour patterns of people are not to be evaluated and judged in terms of our own values and ideas but must be understood and appreciated in their cultural context. For example, premarital pregnancy is bad in our society, where the mores do not approve it and where there are no entirely comfortable arrangements for the care of illegitimate children. Premarital pregnancy is good in a society such as that of the Bontocs of the Philippines, who consider a woman more marriageable when her fertility has been established and who have a set of customs and values which make a secure place for the children. Similarly, adolescent girls in the United States are advised that they will improve their marital bargaining power by avoiding pregnancy until marriage, while adolescent girls in New Guinea are given the opposite advice, and in each setting the advice is probably correct.

Subculture: The culture of an identifiable segment of a society. A subculture is part of the total culture of society but it differs from the larger culture in certain respects, for example, in language, customs, values or social norms. It is agreed that ethnic groups have subcultures, but writers also refer to the subcultures of occupations, adolescents, criminals, social classes, etc.

Contraculture: It is a subculture that stands in opposition to important aspects of the dominant culture of the society. The term was introduced by J. Milton Yinger to designate a particular type of subculture, in which certain values and social norms of the dominant culture are specifically rejected, and contrary values and norms deliberately accepted. In fact, the value and normative system of the contraculture can really by understood only in terms of its theme of opposition to the dominant culture. However, it should be remembered that a contraculture rejects some, but not all, of the norms of the dominant culture. For example, delinquency and drug addiction often have a contracultural aspect. The terms contraculture and counterculture are often used interchangeably in sociological literature (ibid.).

Culture lag: This concept was introduced by William F. Ogburn, who applied it especially to modern industrial societies in which the material culture, through rapid advances in technology and science, has developed at a much faster rate than that part of the non-material culture (ideas, values, norms, etc.) which regulates man's adjustment to the material culture. Cultural lag as a concept and theory was developed by Ogburn as part of a wider theory of technological evolutionism. It suggests that there is a gap between the technical development of a society and its moral and legal institutions. The failure of the latter to keep pace with the former in certain societies is cited as the basic factor to explain (at least some) social conflict and problems (ibid.).

Scope of Sociology

Sociology is the youngest of the recognised social sciences. Sociology emerged in the nineteenth century as an attempt towards scientific study of social life. Auguste Comte in France coined the word 'sociology' in his book *Positive Philosophy*, published in 1838. He believed that sociology, being a science of society, should be based on empirical observation and verification, not on authority and speculation. This was relatively a new idea at that time. In England, Herbert Spencer too reiterated a similar idea. In his book *Principles of Sociology*, published in 1876, Spencer applied the theory of organic evolution to human society and developed a grand theory of 'social evolution'. Similarly, Lester F. Ward, an American, in his book *Dynamic Sociology*, published in 1883, called for social progress through intelligent social action that sociologists should guide. All these founders of sociology believed that sociologists should derive social theories on the basis of empirical observation, systematic classification and verification of facts (Horton and Hunt, 2004).

Sociology is a scientific study of society and a variety of interactions that unfold within and between individuals and groups. In other words, sociology is the science of human society and of social relations, social groups and social change. Samuel Koenig in his book *Sociology: An Introduction to the Science of Society* (1970) states that:

> The principal task of sociology is to obtain and interpret the facts regarding human association, not to solve social problems. Its ultimate aim, however, is to improve man's adjustment to life by developing objective knowledge concerning social phenomena which can be used to deal effectively with social problems. In this respect sociology bears the same relation to the solution of social problems as, say, biology and bacteriology bear to medicine, or mathematics and physics to engineering. Without the research done in the theoretical and experimental sciences, modern techniques for

curing disease or those for bridge-building would be impossible. Similarly, without the investigations carried on by sociology and the other social sciences, no really effective social planning or lasting solutions to social problems would be possible.

The subject matter of sociology is society itself rather than the individual. However, given the reciprocal relationship between the individual and society, most sociologists regard the study of the individual as essential to an understanding of society. Furthermore, although sociology deals with problems involving subjective values, beliefs, sentiments and interests very close to man's heart, it endeavours to keep aloof, to refrain from passing judgement as to the goodness or badness of a thing, its propriety or impropriety, its desirability or undesirability. This makes sociology ethically neutral and hence enhances its scientific stature. Sociology takes this attitude because of the conviction, long accepted in all science, that the true nature of any phenomenon cannot be discovered or cannot be adequately understood (and, hence, that the problems connected with it cannot be effectively solved) if the investigator makes up his mind in advance about the subject being investigated. In other words, if the investigator has predilections, he will tend to see the phenomenon or problem not as it actually is, but rather as he wishes it to be. Thus, only an objective study can reveal the real nature and purpose of the phenomenon. Otherwise, in the absence of an objective approach, many erroneous conclusions regarding social phenomena have been made. Of course, it is impossible to achieve complete objectivity in anything, particularly when dealing with human values, but a large measure of it can be attained with the proper effort and training (Koenig, 1970).

As stated earlier, for a comprehensive understanding of a given social phenomenon, sociology is often obliged to draw upon findings of various other disciplines such as biology, psychology, anthropology, geography and history. Furthermore, since man's social life cannot be divorced from his economic and political activities, the sociologist has to utilise the data made available by economics and political science. This dependence upon other disciplines might give one the impression that sociology is a kind of parasite, living off the efforts of other sciences. But this is not true. As a matter of fact, these contributing sciences (particularly psychology, economics, and political science) are just as dependent, if not more so, upon the data and conclusions of sociology, for their special problems cannot be fully or satisfactorily understood apart from the more general social aspects of life with which sociology is chiefly concerned.

Sociology includes within its scope all of man's behaviour which may be called social. Since many different aspects of social life have to be studied, the science of sociology can be subdivided into specialised areas of enquiry, each of which may employ techniques of its own. This subdivision was inevitable since no individual could possibly become expert in every phase of this ramified subject. Sociology is thus divided into several major fields. *Sociological theory*, for example, as a field is primarily concerned with deriving theoretical generalisations about a given social phenomenon on the basis of empirical observation and validation. Sociologists develop theories to explain social phenomena. A theory is a proposed relationship between two or more concepts. In other words, a theory is explanation for why or how a phenomenon occurs. *Historical sociology* is a branch of sociology that focuses on how societies develop through history. It looks at how social structures that many regard as natural are in fact shaped by complex social processes.

Political sociology is another major field of sociology. The basic subject matter of political sociology is the relation between politics and society. Political sociology is the study of power and the relationship between the individual, civil society and the state. It also involves sociological investigation on topics such as citizenship, social movements, the sources of social power and the causes of political conflict. *Economic sociology*, in simplest terms, is the study of the social cause and effect of various economic phenomena. It implies the application of sociological concepts and methods to the analysis of production, distribution, exchange and consumption of goods and services in society. *Sociology of religion*, on the other hand, is the study of the beliefs, practices and organisational forms of religion using the tools and methods of the discipline of sociology. It seeks to understand humanly constructed aspects of religion in their social context and deals with what religion is, how it works and what effects it has. *Sociology of marriage, kinship and family* studies the origin, evolution and forms of institutions of marriage, kinship and family in various periods of history and in different societies, as well as the contemporary issues related to them. *Sociology of education* is a diverse and vibrant subfield that focuses on how education as a social institution affects and gets affected by other social institutions in a society. It studies how various social forces shape the policies, practices and outcomes of schooling.

Sociology also analyses the organisation and problems of both rural and urban types of communities. Since the problems of city and country are in many respects quite distinct, this field of study is subdivided into rural and urban sociology. *Sociology of work* is concerned with the nature of social relations, normative codes and organisational structures that inform the behaviour, experience and identities of people during the course of their working lives. It primarily explores contemporary transformations in work and employment, and their impact on social relations. *Industrial sociology*, until recently a crucial research area within the field of sociology of work, examines the trends in technological change and globalisation, and their implications on labour markets, work organisation, managerial practices and employment relations. It also examines the extent to which these trends are intimately related to changing patterns of inequality in modern societies. *Agrarian sociology*, on the other hand, is concerned with the study of societies whose economy depends on the production of food crops and maintaining farmlands. The word agrarian means agriculture related. It includes the study of the pattern of land distribution, socio-economic inequality, agrarian unrest and peasant movements. *Environmental sociology*, a newly emerging field, examines the complex relationship between people and nature. It explores the reciprocal relationship between societies and their environments. It may focus on the social dimensions of either the natural environment or the human-built environment.

The other two fields of sociology worth mentioning here are sociology of deviance and sociology of law. *Sociology of deviance* primarily examines the way a society defines deviance, the societal reaction and its consequences. It explores the causes of the 'abnormal' social behaviour and its consequences, both for the individual and the society. *Sociology of law* concerns itself with the study of formalised methods and agencies of social control. It enquires into the factors that bring about the formation of regulatory systems, as well as into the reasons for their adequacies and inadequacies as a means of social control. *Sociology of population* is yet another important field of sociology. Demography is the statistical study of populations, especially human beings. It encompasses the study of the size, structure, and distribution of human populations, and spatial or temporal changes in them in response to birth, migration, ageing and death. While formal demography limits its object of study to the measurement of population processes, social demography or population studies also analyses the relationships between economic, social, cultural and biological processes influencing a population.

Although the foregoing are the main divisions of sociology, new areas and subareas are evolved as the problems coming within the scope of this science are explored more thoroughly and systematically, and as new techniques are devised and developed for dealing with them. Thus, in addition to the areas listed above, there are a number of others such as *sociology of art, sociology of health and medicine, folk sociology, military sociology, development sociology* and such special topics as social stratification, mass media and communication, public opinion and bureaucracy. Sociology, therefore, is the study of social life as a whole. It has a wide range of concerns and interests. It seeks to provide classifications and forms of social relationships, institutions and associations, relating to economic, political, moral, religious and social aspects of human life. Let us now look at the relationship of sociology with other social sciences.

Given the importance of interdisciplinary nature of studies in contemporary times, this section would greatly help us to understand society and its various social processes in a comprehensive manner. Since a social phenomenon does not occur in vacuum, it is necessary to study and understand it in terms of its various correlates such as social, economic, political, psychological, historical, etc. (Figure 2.2).

Sociology and Anthropology

Anthropology is a broad scientific discipline dedicated to the comparative study of mankind, from its first appearance to its present stage of development (Scott, 1999). It is a scientific study of man in all its dimensions, both biological and sociocultural. The branch of anthropology that studies the biological aspects of humankind is called physical or biological anthropology, while the study of social and cultural aspects is known as social anthropology. In the United States,

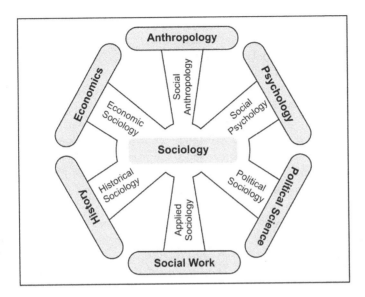

FIGURE 2.2   Sociology and Its Relationship with Other Social Sciences

this branch is, however, known as cultural anthropology. The third branch of anthropology is the study of languages in a comparative perspective. It is known as linguistic anthropology or anthropological linguistics. The branch of anthropology that studies the pre-historic past of mankind, before writing began, is called archaeological anthropology or pre-historic archaeology. Of the four branches of anthropology, sociology is most closely related to social anthropology.

It is often said that although sociology and social anthropology had quite different origins, but in contemporary times, they are practically indistinguishable. Sociology originated from philosophy of history, political thought and positive sciences. Philosophy of history is the philosophical study of history and the past. It became an important intellectual influence in the early part of the nineteenth century. The basic assumption of this philosophy was that human society has progressed through a series of stages, from a simple to complex one. Social anthropology, on the other hand, traces its origin in physical anthropology and ultimately in biology (Bottomore, 1986). Sociology as a subject came into existence during the late eighteenth and early nineteenth centuries. Social anthropology had its beginnings as a discipline during the second half of the nineteenth century but it came to occupy a respectable place in the first half of the twentieth century.

In the earlier periods of their growth, both the disciplines grew up in close cooperation with each other, in terms of the concepts used, areas of interest and their methods of study. This can be seen in the works of founders, which cannot easily be assigned exclusively to either one of the disciplines (e.g. Tylor, Spencer) However, the initial phase of convergence between the two disciplines was followed by a phase of extreme divergence in terms of their subject matter, objective and methodology. Some scholars are of the opinion that such divergence between the two disciplines was more of an accidental phenomenon. They argue that during the phase of colonial expansion, social anthropologists increasingly became more interested in the study of newly found or conquered societies (colonies). These newly found societies were of a very different character than those which social anthropologists belonged to. These were small-scale societies, relatively unchanging and lacking historical records.

To summarise, it may be stated that the division of labour that traditionally developed was that sociology concentrated on the study of complex, modern and urban-industrial societies, whereas social anthropology studied tribal, peasant and pre-literate societies of the world, those societies that were largely untouched by the forces of civilisation. In other words, sociologists studied the societies which were their own, while anthropologists studied societies that were different from theirs. This was the reason why sociology came to be regarded as the study of one's own society, while anthropology earned the reputation of being the study of 'other cultures'. Thus, the broad differences between sociology and social anthropology that emerged during the period of divergence can easily be related to their different subject matter.

Differences in the subject matter soon translated into differences in the objectives of the two disciplines. Social, political and historical conditions of the time also played a significant role in shaping the objectives of social anthropology. Colonial rule inevitably projects the view that the institutions and customs of the ruling country are fundamentally different from those of the colonies. Hence, in order to better govern the colonised societies, a holistic understanding of their beliefs, customs and institutions was necessary. Since these societies were relatively unchanging, social anthropologists could study them in totality, as functioning wholes. Thus, the functional approach was generally adopted in social anthropology, while sociology continued to be historically oriented and concerned with problems of development. Sociologists largely remained preoccupied with the problems of industrial societies. The primary objective of sociology as a scientific discipline was to study social problems in a systematic manner and derive some generalisations based on the cause-and-effect relationship of the phenomena involved. Such generalisations could then serve as a guide for social policy formulation.

During this phase of divergence, sociology and social anthropology also differed in terms of their respective methodologies. Since these small-scale primitive societies changed little and had no records of past changes, a historical approach was unnecessary and more or less impossible. Hence, social anthropologists largely relied on fieldwork and used qualitative research methods for data collection, such as participant observation. In its early phase, Malinowski and Radcliffe-Brown laid the foundations of intensive fieldwork among anthropologists in Britain. Radcliffe-Brown's study of Andaman Islands and Malinowski's study of Trobriand Islands are classic examples of early fieldwork and participant observation in social anthropology. In Indian context, it was M.N. Srinivas who strongly advocated for the 'field-view' of Indian society in place of the 'book-view'. In simple words, participant observation is a method in which the investigator becomes a part of the situation he is studying. He involves himself in the setting and group life of the research subjects. He shares the activities of the community observing what is going on around him, supplementing this by conversations and interview. One of the pioneering uses of participant observation by sociologists in a modern setting is recorded in William Foote Whyte's *Street Corner Society: The Social Structure of an Italian Slum.*

Given the size and complexity of modern industrial societies, which was its subject matter, sociology largely relied on quantitative techniques of data collection such as survey in its formative years. Study of modern society in totality was not possible given its complexity as well as due to time and economy constraints of sociological research. Hence, sociological research proceeded with a clearly formulated hypothesis seeking to explore the relationship between two or more variables. This was best demonstrated in the works of Emile Durkheim such as *Suicide*. Even Max Weber, who strongly advocated the use of both quantitative and qualitative research methods in sociological enquiry, believed that at a given point of time social reality should be studied from a specific point of view. This was popularly known as *ideal type* approach. It must be noted that the above-stated distinction between sociology and social anthropology could be applied without much problem, where the difference between the 'our' and 'their' societies, i.e. between 'civilised' and 'primitive' societies, was huge and perceptible. For example, it was the case in America, Australia, New Zealand and Africa, where the native population was totally different from its white colonisers. However, due to forces of industrialisation, urbanisation and globalisation, this situation has now radically altered. Most of the traditional simple societies are undergoing a similar process of socio-economic and political modernisation, which Western societies once witnessed in the eighteenth and nineteenth centuries. As a result, these societies too are characterised with various social and political movements which involve the social anthropologist in the same kind of value problems which the sociologist has had to face in studying his own society. For example, both sociologist and anthropologists have to face the fact of revolutionary movements in the Third World. Thus, it is often argued that in recent years, there has been a new convergence between sociology and social anthropology.

In one sense, we can see the convergence between sociology and social anthropology in terms of their subject matter. Primitive societies, which were once regarded as the preserve of the social anthropologist, are on the verge of disappearance. As a result, societies undergoing socio-economic and political transition such as in Asia and Africa have now become a common object of study for both the sociologist and the social anthropologist. Thus, with the passage of time, social anthropologists have included within their orbit of study societies, such as urban and industrial, that were supposed to be studied by sociologists. It all happened because tribal societies were on their way to transformation because of urbanisation and industrialisation. At the same time, sociology has increased its scope to include tribal and peasant societies. The outcome of all this is that, as far as the subject matters of sociology and social anthropology are concerned, there is hardly any distinction. Furthermore, the convergence can also be witnessed in terms of the research methodologies of the two disciplines. For example, in post-Weberian sociological thought, an emphasis has been placed on the combination of both quantitative and qualitative research methodologies to ensure greater reliability and validity. Similarly, since social anthropologists now operate in a large and complex social setting, they too have to rely on quantitative methods for their research along with qualitative methods.

It is important to understand that the division of labour between sociology and social anthropology emerged in Britain or the United States under specific historical conditions, and was then transmitted to other countries where conditions were different. There is no ground to believe that what appeared reasonable and appropriate under certain conditions will always appear to be so (Béteille, 1985). Among contemporary societies there is a category of those which are neither primitive nor industrially advanced. In such societies, for example India, the distinction between sociology and social anthropology has little meaning. Sociological research in India, whether it is concerned with the caste system, village communities or the process of industrialisation and its effects, is and should be carried out by sociologists and social anthropologists (Bottomore, 1986).

In their early years, sociology and social anthropology specialised in the study of different types of societies and hence contributed to the development of different theoretical interests. While sociologists have made significant contribution to survey methods of data collection, anthropologists' contribution has been to fieldwork methodology. Similarly, anthropologists have contributed immensely to the understanding of institutions of crucial importance in simple societies such as marriage, family, kinship and religion. To the understanding of social stratification, education and urban industrial society, the contribution of sociologists is unparalleled, because these institutions are of primary importance in modern societies. These specialisations apart, there are more similarities between sociology and social anthropology than are between either of them and other social sciences. Both disciplines attempt to study human society in a holistic manner and generalise about social phenomena. Both are also comparative in nature. In fact, French sociologist Emile Durkheim called anthropology as 'comparative sociology'. Social anthropology was considered a branch of sociology, or better, as a 'sociology of primitive societies'. A.L. Kroeber succinctly regards sociology and anthropology as twin sisters. Radcliffe-Brown often used the term 'comparative sociology' as a synonym for social anthropology.

Sociology and History

Both sociology and history are social science disciplines, and both are concerned with human activities and events. Though both the disciplines share the same subject matter, yet they differ in terms of their approach, objective and methodology. What is common between sociology and history is the society. But, while sociology is primarily concerned with the present and to some extent with the study of recent past and future, history studies only the past. Since the present society cannot be analysed without reference to the past society, it is here that these are related to each other. Highlighting this close relationship between the two disciplines, G.E. Howard remarked 'History is the past sociology and sociology is the present history'.

History is the study of the past. In simpler terms, it is a chronological and descriptive account of people and events of the past. Historians are concerned with specific societies. They tell about the system that prevailed in a society at a particular time. Data for historians come in the form of records from archives, museums, libraries and personal collections of people. Historians of ancient times also study inscriptions. Historical data may not be complete. Some might have been destroyed, lost, stolen or inaccessible. Therefore, historians have to build up their interpretations of the past on the limitations of the material. Further, whatever comparisons historians make are of limited scale. They may compare societies inhabiting the same area, but vast comparisons of societies different in scale and time are beyond the scope of history. Therefore, historians rarely attempt to generalise about human society as a whole. They provide a detailed account of a specific social situation.

By comparison, sociology is principally concerned with the study of contemporary societies. As stated earlier, for a comprehensive understanding of the present, knowledge of past is equally necessary. Sociologists must hold up the past to understand the present. Thus, in this sense, history supplies the material in the form of historical data to sociology for analysing the factors responsible for the continuity and change in social customs and institutions. For example, Marx has used historical data in his works to explain the changing nature of the mode of production in human societies overtime. Similarly, Durkheim and Weber too have relied on historical data to develop their theories. However, sociology too contributes to history by providing the social background for various historical events. Sociology enables history to explain historical events in terms of cause-and-effect relationship vis-à-vis several socio-economic and political factors. Commenting on this close relationship between history and sociology, Sir John Robert Seeley (1834–1895), an English historian, stated that 'History without sociology has no fruit, sociology without history has no root'.

The other significant difference is that the historian interests himself in the particular character of events over a period of time. The sociologist, on the other hand, is interested in the regular and the recurrent social phenomena. *It is often said that history occupies itself with the differences in similar events and sociology deals with the similarities in different events.* History seeks to establish the sequence in which events occur; it is the chronological arrangement of social events in time. The sociologist is concerned with relationship between events occurring more or less at the same time. He seeks to know the interrelations between events with a view to propose causal sequences. The historian prides himself on the explicitness and concreteness of details. The sociologist abstracts from concrete reality, and then categorises and generalises about the observed phenomena. Hence, it is often said that while history only gives the actual account of the past, sociology is capable of indicating future. History is concrete and sociology is abstract (Nagla and Singh, 2002).

Further, it is also worth noting that sociologists not only refer to the historical data but they also generate their own data by studying various contemporary societies, for which the term 'primary data' is used. Primary data can be collected through various methods of sociological research such as survey, questionnaire, interview, schedule, fieldwork (including both participant and non-participant observation), focus group discussion, etc. As a result, the data collected by sociologists are more comprehensive than that by historians, who have to content themselves with whatever is available.

To conclude, it may be argued that while sociology is an observational, comparative and generalising science, history, on the other hand, is a particularising or individualising discipline. Sociology is an analytical discipline, whereas history is a descriptive discipline. Sociology emphasises on the regular and the recurrent, whereas history investigates the unique and the individual. An event that has occurred only once in the human past is of no sociological significance unless it can be related to a pattern of events that repeats itself generation after generation, historical period after historical period and human group after human group. According to Radcliffe-Brown, 'sociology is nomothetic, while history is idiographic'. In other words, sociologists produce generalisations while historians describe unique events. This distinction holds true for traditional narrative history, but is only partly true for modern historiography. There are works of some serious historians which abound in generalisations such as English historian R.H. Tawney's *Religion and the Rise of Capitalism* (Bottomore, 1986). The intimate relationship between history and sociology has given rise to hybrid disciplines of social history in history and historical sociology in sociology.

Sociology and Political Science

Political science is also known as the 'science of government' or the 'science of polity or politics'. Political science studies political institutions such as the state, government, political parties, executive, legislative and judicial institutions. Political science also studies behaviour of the people in power. The concept of power is important. Thus, political science can also be defined as a study of power.

Eminent sociologist Max Weber has defined power as 'the chance of a man or a number of men to realise their own will in a communal action even against the resistance of others who are participating in the action'. Sociologists often distinguish between two forms of power: authority and coercion. Authority is that form of power that is accepted as legitimate – that is, right and just – and therefore obeyed on that basis. For example, citizens consider the action of levying taxes by the government as legitimate and hence voluntarily comply with it. Coercion, on the other hand, is that form of power which is not regarded as legitimate by those subject to it. Thus, though a thief or a robber may be able to extort money at gun point, his action is not considered as legitimate by people (Haralambos and Heald, 2006). Sociology also studies power in terms of its social contexts. For example, the processes which enable an individual or a social group to wield power and exercise dominance in society are the focal points of study in sociology. Thus, the stratification of society in terms of power by different classes, castes and religious groups becomes the basis of sociological analysis (Nagla and Singh, 2002).

Political science is generally concerned with larger systems, i.e. those societies that have the machinery of state and written law. Sociology, however, studies all types of societies such as 'tribal', 'peasant' or 'urban-industrial'. It is comparative in nature and studies the distribution of power and nature of political institutions in different types of societies. Sociologists and social anthropologists also study those societies that were without the institution of state. Such societies were called the stateless societies, for example, Nuer of the Sudan. Several anthropological researches have described how in stateless societies order was maintained. Sociology supplements the understanding of political scientists by providing information about the mechanisms of socialisation and social control in simple societies.

Sociology is devoted to the study of diverse aspects of society, be it social, religious, cultural, economic or political. Political science, however, restricts itself mainly to the study of power as embodied in formal organizations. Historically speaking, the influence of sociology in the field of political studies began to be felt at an early stage in the development of sociology, particularly through the writings of Marx. Marx, for the first time, systematically explained the origin and nature of political institutions and linked it with the economic and the general social context. It was the Marxist thought which provoked, in the late nineteenth and early twentieth century, the political sociology of Michels, Weber and Pareto, and thus led directly to the modern studies of political parties, elites, voting behaviour, social protest, agitation and social movements (Bottomore, 1986).

The growing interface between sociology and political science has led to the emergence of political sociology. Political sociology seeks to investigate and explain the interrelationship of various political phenomena with the respective social structure, ideology and culture of society. For example, the functioning of democracy, electoral politics and voting behaviour of people in India cannot be completely understood without taking into account the social realities of caste, religious and linguistic identities.

Sociology and Economics

Economics studies the aspects of production, distribution and exchange, and consumption in society. It begins with the observation that resources are scarce and limited, whereas human needs are unlimited. Hence, there is a need to strike a balance between limited resources and unlimited needs and wants. The strategy human beings adopt is to make the best use to the resources available with them, and at the same time put a check on one's needs. The process of striking a balance between the two, resources and needs, is called economisation, and the science of economics studies this.

Like political science, the scope of economics in comparison to sociology is relatively narrow. This is because economics studies only the economic aspect of social life, whereas sociology is concerned with the whole of 'social life – the legal, political, educational, philosophical, economic, etc.' All these aspects are covered up by the term 'social'. Sociologists look at the social aspects of economic phenomena. In this term, their work is different from that of the economist, who is mainly concerned with the economic consequences of people's actions. For instance, Adam Smith, a foremost economist, explained division of labour in society purely in terms of its economic consequences. He argued that increase in population in a given society leads to increase in demand for goods and services.

Division of labour, thus, becomes inevitable to cater to the increasing demands of goods and services in society. Thus, Smith explained division of labour largely in terms of its effect on increasing the efficiency of production process and accelerating the rate of production of goods and services.

Eminent sociologist Emile Durkheim, however, explained division of labour in terms of its overall social consequences. For example, division of labour also has its implications on the structure of family, communities, legal and political institutions, etc. In general, Durkheim argued that the nature of social division of labour in a given society is directly linked to the nature of social cohesion or social solidarity in that society. Durkheim developed a classificatory typology of societies based on different degrees of division of labour. For example, he argued that societies based on low division of labour are marked by mechanical solidarity (which results due to likeness or similarity of attributes among people and hence low interdependence), while those with high division of labour are marked by organic solidarity (which is based on differences or specialisation in attributes among people and hence high interdependence). As such, the scope of sociology is much broader than that of economics. Sociology has a comprehensive viewpoint. Sociology is a general social science, while economics is a special social science.

Further, classical economics largely explained man's economic behaviour purely in rational or utilitarian terms. It believed that the ultimate objective of man is to maximise the gains out of the economic transactions. Although it recognises the role of social factors such as religious beliefs and values in influencing economic behaviour of man, it considers them as essentially 'irrational', which tend to slow, or even retard, the growth of economy. It asserts that for developing an economy, one has to take rational decisions because they will lead to gains and profits. Each economic system is based on the principle of maximisation of gains and returns. Thus, economics is primarily concerned with the relationship between demands and supply in a society, the rational use of resources for fulfilling one's needs and the issues of economic development. However, for the sociologist, economic institution is one of the several institutions of human society. He examines the functioning of the economic institution in relationship with other institutions of society such as social, political, religious and cultural institutions. Sociologists believe that social factors exercise a tremendous impact on the decisions people make with respect to resources, their use and distribution. The factors that seem irrational to economists are, in fact, quite meaningful from the perspective of people. From various tribal and peasant studies, sociologists have confirmed that what appears to be a 'wasteful expenditure' for outsiders is actually very rational, meaningful and important from the native's point of view since it enhances one's prestige and honour in the respective society. Similarly, Max Weber in his work *The Protestant Ethic and the Spirit of Capitalism* demonstrated how an inner-worldly protestant religious ideology contributed to the rise of capitalism in Western Europe. India and China, which were far advanced from Europe in materialistic terms until the seventeenth century, did not witness capitalistic transformation as Europe did. Weber explained this in terms of other-worldly religious ideologies prevalent in India and China.

Despite these differences, both sociology and economics are coming closer together in recent times. One of the reasons for this convergence is the shift in modern economics. Economists today are no longer interested only in market mechanisms. They are increasingly focusing on the social factors influencing economic growth. It is apparent in recent works on problems of economic development in underdeveloped regions, where the economist has either to collaborate with the sociologist or to become a sociologist himself (Bottomore, 1986). Nobel Laureate Amartya Sen's contributions to welfare economics and social choice theory, and his interest in the problems of society's poorest members, are worth mentioning in this regard. One manifestation of the convergence between sociology and economics is the emergence of economic sociology as a distinct field of sociological enquiry. Economic sociology focuses on the study of social causes and consequences of various economic phenomena. Industrial sociology is another emerging field indicating this convergence.

Sociology and Psychology

Sociology is the scientific study of modern society. According to Emile Durkheim, sociology is a science of social institutions. It takes a macro-level perspective in its study of social behaviour of man. Psychology, on the other hand, is the scientific study of the mind and behaviour. It includes the study of conscious and unconscious phenomena, as well as feeling and thought. It takes a micro-level perspective and primarily focuses on the study of the individual behaviour.

The individual and society are the two main concepts in social sciences. No doubt that society is made up of individuals but an individual too depends on society for his various social and emotional needs. Both sociology and psychology study this interface between the individual and society from their respective perspectives. It is often said that while sociology is the study of social systems, psychology studies mental systems. A sociologist, in his observation of social phenomena, attempts to figure out at a general similarity or enduring patterns (if any) and tries to formulate a cause-and-effect relationship between different social phenomena. This can only be done if the sociologist focuses on the study of commonly shared attributes or facts. Hence, Durkheim had argued that sociology is the study of social facts. Social facts, in general, are the socially shared and institutionalised norms and values that are external to individual actors and also constrain them to act in a particular way. According to Durkheim, 'conscience collective' is the ultimate social fact. In other words, according to Durkheim, a given social phenomenon must be studied in its collective manifestation, independent of its individual manifestations.

Psychology, on the other hand, focuses upon the individual behaviour and his mental structure. It investigates various aspects of the individual behaviour such as memory, intelligence, deep-rooted complexes, psychological problems, etc. Psychology tries to understand why an individual behaves in the manner he does. Hence, it is also called the study of psychic (or mental) facts. Unlike sociology, which is keen in identifying the general similarities or patterns in

beliefs and practices of people within and between societies, psychology, on the other hand, is interested in highlighting individual differences in the personality characteristics among people within and between societies. Further, in terms of methodology, psychology has maintained its closeness with the natural sciences, and there is more scope of carrying out psychological experiments in relatively controlled conditions. In addition to a qualitative assessment, psychology makes a lot of use of quantitative techniques, for it measures phenomena in precise terms. For understanding certain psychological phenomena, knowledge of the human biological system is also required. Thus, psychology pays a lot of attention to the understanding of human body, especially the nervous system. Sociology, however, has moved far from its early association with natural science methodology and is increasingly using both qualitative and comparative methods in its enquiry to ensure greater reliability and validity.

The difference between the approaches of the two disciplines can be best highlighted with Durkheim's work on suicide. In his study *Suicide* (1897), Durkheim established that how the very act of committing suicide, which was until then largely explained in terms of psychological states of individuals, was actually triggered by the social structure. At the time Durkheim began his study, suicide was largely treated as a nervous disorder. Many believed that suicide was the result of mental illness, depression, sudden tragedy, reversal of fortune and even personal setbacks and bankruptcy. In this light, suicide was seen by many as the result of a weak disposition and a psychological response to the burdens of life. Durkheim, however, called these views into question by shifting the focus from individual motives and psychological states to social causes. He not only established suicide as a social fact by calculating *social rates of suicide* but also explained its causes in terms of social conditions such as lack of integration or solidarity in society.

However, in later years, various sociologists and social psychologists like Max Weber, G.H. Mead, Anthony Giddens, etc. have highlighted the significance of mutual interdependence between individual and society. Unlike the extreme stance of Durkheim, Weber instead believed that sociological explanations can be further enriched if an attempt is made to understand social behaviour in terms of underlying meanings. This debate between individual and society is popularly known as agency-structure debate in sociology. Anthony Giddens has tried to resolve the agency-structure debate with his concept of *structuration*, which implies the mutual and reciprocal relationship between the two. The intimate interaction between sociology and psychology has given birth to a hybrid discipline 'social psychology'. In general, social psychology studies how people's thoughts, feelings and behaviour are influenced by the actual, imagined or implied presence of others. In other words, it attempts to understand the sociopsychological causes and motives of human behaviour in groups.

Sociology and Philosophy

Sociology and philosophy are very closely related disciplines. Philosophy, in literal sense, implies enquiry or search for knowledge about life and the universe. Sociology too traces its origin to philosophy of history. Sociology originated with the ambition to account for the course of human history and to explain the social crisis of nineteenth-century Europe. The intimate interconnection between the two is evident from the fact that Auguste Comte, a French philosopher, who laid the foundations of positivistic philosophy, is also the founder of sociology. It was Comte who coined the term 'sociology' in 1839. Likewise, Karl Marx, who was a philosopher, also provided many contributions to sociology in terms of a new perspective and methodology.

Though both disciplines are concerned with the study of human society, yet they differ in their scope, approach and methodology. The scope of philosophy is much broader than that of sociology. Philosophy is the study of general and fundamental questions about existence, knowledge, values, reason, mind and language. Philosophy encompasses the study of human moral values, spirit, metaphysics, epistemology, logic and ethics. Sociology, however, is restricted to the scientific study of social institutions, their structure and change. Sociological research is largely based on empirical observation, correlation and verification. Thus, metaphysical aspects and speculative assumptions lie beyond the purview of sociology. Though sociology is a daughter of philosophy, but it is often said that philosophy is more about *what ought to be*, while sociology focuses on *what is*. Sociology was created during great French Revolution in France by positivists as positive or applied philosophy. In other words, it is still philosophy but without mysticism.

The difference between the methodological orientations of the two disciplines can be illustrated with a comparison of Hegel and Marx. According to Hegel, the great German philosopher, the entire process of human history was the progress of the human *Geist* towards self-realization. Geist is a German term which translates literally as 'spirit', or 'mind', or 'consciousness'. Marx rejects the priority Hegel gives to ideas, mind or consciousness. Rejecting Hegel's idealistic approach, Marx proposed the materialist approach. According to Marx, a proper understanding of the social structure and change can be acquired only through an investigation into the materialistic (primarily economic) conditions of a given society. Marx remarked that '*the philosophers have interpreted the world, the point however is to change it*' (Ransome, 2011). Though Marx was not a sociologist, yet his ideas were of great sociological relevance. Similarly, sociologists like Durkheim and Weber too have explained social structure and change in empirical terms.

Commenting upon the interrelationship between the two disciplines, T.B. Bottomore argues that sociology raises philosophical problems to a much greater extent than other social sciences. According to Bottomore, it is not at all harmful to sociological theory or research that the sociologist should interest himself in such problems and should seek to acquire a philosophical education which will equip him to deal with them. Study of human social behaviour, morals and values is common to sociology and social and moral philosophy (Bottomore, 1986).

Sociology and Social Work

While both draw on a similar body of knowledge, sociology generally focuses on research and study, while social workers are more directly involved with applying knowledge about society to assisting individuals and families. The relation between sociology and social work is like the relation between a 'pure science' and an 'applied science'. Social work is concerned with the 'technology of application' of ideas for improving social conditions.

Social work essentially grew out of a concern for human welfare. The drastic transformation of the European society in the nineteenth century and the resulting economic inequalities and social disruption and political instability compelled the philosophers and scholars of that time to contemplate about the nature of these changes. The social scientists were mainly concerned with acquiring knowledge about the working of society and discovering certain laws for social stability and order. Philosophers and scholars also discussed and debated about the nature of ideal society. However, what technology should be adopted for building it up was not given a serious thought. Knowledge is of no significance unless it is put to use. The field of social work emerged in this background and attempted to chart out suitable technology for human welfare and upliftment of the unprivileged. For example, sociologists study poverty as a social problem from multiple perspectives and explore its relationship with various other social variables such as caste, religion, migration, unemployment, etc. Social workers, with the help of this sociological insight, formulate practically possible social welfare programmes to address the target group.

However, for any action, it is essential to have a complete knowledge of the social situation, and sociology provided such knowledge. Social work, thus, is dependent upon sociological insights. Sociology generates holistic knowledge about society. The branch of sociology that takes up the areas of application is called applied sociology. Between sociology and social work lies applied sociology. Sociologists themselves do not carry out the action. Through research they try to arrive at certain generalisations or cause-and-effect relationship between two or more social variables. Social workers, on the other hand, use this sociological knowledge to plan their action and they also carry out the action. Therefore, social work is also often called as the 'technology of action'. Thus, the contribution of sociology in the development of social work theories and their plan of action cannot be denied.

Sociology and Ethics

Ethics and sociology share a close and intimate relationship. Ethics, or moral philosophy, is a branch of philosophy that deals with moral principles, i.e. concepts of right and wrong conduct. However, what is defined as morally right or wrong cannot be understood without its social context. Since the definition of right and wrong is largely socially defined, this brings ethics and sociology closer to each other.

Man cannot even be imagined outside society. He acquires his thoughts of good and bad, virtue and vice from society. Thus, the mental and ethical development of the individual depends very much upon society. Social scientists argue that man does not do good acts because God wants such acts or that they are essential for living in society but rather because society accepts them as good and the ethical thoughts related to such conduct are inherent in social institutions. Further, the evolution of society is also judged in terms of the development of its ethics. Various philosophers and social scientists such as Hegel, Comte, Spencer, etc. have emphasised on this relationship.

According to Gisbert (2010),

> Ethics is concerned with the moral rightness or depravity of human actions. It investigates the laws of morality and formulates the principles and rules of morally desirable actions. It cannot be said that ethics is concerned with ends only to the exclusion of means, because every human action is capable of morality, not only in itself as an end, but also in relation to other ends which it may subserve. A peaceful strike directed to improve the condition of the working class, when all other legal means have proved futile, is

morally good, or at least not wrong; whereas the same strike, when used as a piece of revolutionary strategy, with the object of spreading unrest in the population, is ethically wrong.

However, despite the close association between the two disciplines, there are some differences as well. First, their fields do not totally coincide, for not everything that is social is ethical; nor is everything, that is ethical, social. Second, the viewpoint from which they may envisage the same problem is different. On the other hand, though the moral life of man is developed in society, the influence of ethical behaviour on social and political life can hardly be exaggerated. To conclude, one may say, 'What is ethically wrong cannot be socially right' (Gisbert, 2010).

LET'S THINK

Dear Learner, in this chapter you have learnt about some basic concepts that are often used in sociology. In order to understand them better, try to observe social interactions in society more closely. In any given interaction situation, try to figure out the quality or nature of social interaction that you had with other individuals or social actors. For example, what is the nature of your interaction with your family members? Most likely, it would be personal and intimate. Isn't it? But what about your interaction with a shopkeeper or a state official. It is more likely to be formal and contractual. That's it. This way you will understand not only the meaning of these concepts but also similarities and differences between them.

For Practice

Q1. Is society a process or a structure? Explain.
Q2. Write a short note on comparison between sociology and anthropology.
Q3. 'Sociology without history is rootless and history without sociology is fruitless'. Elaborate.
Q4. Write a short note on comparison between sociology and economics.
Q5. Discuss the significance of multidisciplinary approach in social sciences.

Model Answers

Q. Is society a process or a structure? Explain.

A. The concept of society constitutes the core of the discipline of sociology. Sociology is nothing but a scientific study of society and a variety of interactions that unfold within and between individuals and groups. According to MacIver and Page, society is the web of social relationships and it is always changing.

Society can be looked at from both functional and structural perspectives. When looked from the functional perspective, society is understood as a complex network of constantly evolving reciprocal relationships among the members of a society, with individual members helping each other to fulfil their respective interests. From this perspective, society appears as a process – a process involving 'mutual recognition' or 'reciprocal awareness' of the interacting individuals on the one hand, and, a 'sense of belonging-ness', on the other. However, when looked from the structural perspective, society appears as a structure – a structure of relatively patterned social rela-tionships and institutionalised social norms in the form of social statuses and roles. The term 'social structure' refers to the pattern of interrelated statuses and roles found in a society at a particular point of time and constituting a relatively stable set of social relations. Although the social structure itself remains invisible, it silently shapes our actions.

It is important to understand that if we consider just a point of time, then society appears to be a structure. For example, in pre-British period, the Indian society was characterised by a rigid caste hierarchy. Each caste was defined in terms of purity and pollution, and identified in terms of certain privileges and prescriptions. Thus, to an extent, a hierarchical and inegali-tarian social structure of traditional Indian society could be identified. The same holds true for gender roles as well. However, when we look at society over a period of time, then it appears to be a process. For example, we can notice significant changes in the caste system as well as gender roles. These changes are basically the changes that occur in the rights and duties asso-ciated with a particular social status in society. This subsequently leads to overall social change in society.

The society is thus viewed as both a process and a structure. One who studies society must take into account both these views. MacIver and Page have also stated that 'Society exists only as a time-sequence. It is a becoming, not a product'. This is the essence of society. Thus, society is to be inter-preted in a wider sense. It is both a structural and functional organisation. It consists of the mutual interactions and mutual interrelations of the individu-als but it is also a structure formed by these relations.

Q. 'Sociology without history is rootless, and history without sociol-ogy is fruitless'. Elaborate.

A. Both sociology and history are social science disciplines and are concerned with human activities and events. Though both the disciplines share the same subject matter, i.e. society, yet they differ in terms of their approaches, objec-tives and methodologies. While sociology is primarily concerned with the present and to some extent with the study of the recent past and future, history studies only the past. Since the present society cannot be analysed without reference to the past society, it is here that these are related to each other. Commenting on this close relationship between history and sociology, Sir John Robert Seeley (1834–1895), an English historian, stated that 'History without sociology has no fruit, sociology without history has no root'.

Sociology without history is rootless in the sense that for a comprehensive understanding of the present, knowledge of past is essential. Sociologists must hold up the past to understand the present. Thus, in this sense, history supplies the material in the form of historical data to sociology for analysing the factors responsible for the continuity and change in social customs and institutions. For example, Marx has used historical data in his works to explain the changing nature of the mode of production in human societies over time. Likewise, Durkheim and Weber too have relied on historical data to develop their theories.

Similarly, a mere chronological and descriptive account of events of the past would be fruitless if a certain cause-and-effect relationship between historical events vis-à-vis several socio-economic and political factors is not established. Such generalisations not only facilitate a comprehensive understanding of historical phenomena but also enable the social scientists to predict and caution about future developments. For example, historical social practices of *sati* and child marriage in India, which were largely described in religious terms, could be better understood when explained from a patriarchal and socio-economic perspective. Likewise, though India's struggle for independence is a historical event, Indian sociologist A.R. Desai in his famous book *Social Background of Indian Nationalism* has explained the emergence of nationalism in India in Marxist terms. Desai explains how the convergence of economic interest of various social groups laid the foundation of early nationalism in India.

Thus, it is rightly said that 'sociology without history is rootless, and history without sociology is fruitless'.

References

Béteille, André. *Six Essays in Comparative Sociology*. New Delhi: Oxford University Press, 1985.

Bhushan, Vidya and D.R. Sachdeva. *An Introduction to Sociology*. Allahabad: Kitab Mahal, 2019.

Bierstedt, Robert. *The Social Order: An Introduction to Sociology*. 2nd Edition. New York: McGraw-Hill Book Company, 1963.

Bottomore, T.B. *Sociology: A Guide to Problems and Literature*. 5th Edition. India: Blackie & Son (India), 1986.

Gisbert, P. *Fundamentals of Sociology*. New Delhi: Orient BlackSwan, 2010.

Haralambos, M. and R.M. Heald. *Sociology: Themes and Perspectives*. New Delhi: Oxford University Press, 2006.

Horton, Paul B. and Chester L. Hunt. *Sociology*. 6th Edition. New Delhi: Tata McGraw-Hill, 2004.

Johnson, Harry M. *Sociology: A Systematic Introduction*. New Delhi: Allied Publishers Pvt. Ltd., 2007.

Koenig, Samuel. *Sociology: An Introduction to the Science of Society*. New York: Barnes & Noble, 1970.

MacIver, R.M. and Charles H. Page. *Society: An Introductory Analysis*. New Delhi: Macmillan India, 2007.

Marshall, Gordon. *Oxford Dictionary of Sociology*. New York: Oxford University Press, 1998.

Nagla, Bhupendra K. and Sheobahal Singh. *Introducing Sociology*. New Delhi: National Council of Educational Research and Training, 2002.

Ransome, Paul. *Social Theory*. Jaipur: Rawat Publications, 2011.

Rao, C.N. Shankar. *Sociology: Principles of Sociology with an Introduction to Social Thought*. New Delhi: S. Chand & Company, 2017.

Scott, William P. *Dictionary of Sociology*. New Delhi: GOYLSaaB, 1999.

3

SOCIOLOGY AS A SCIENCE

Is Sociology a Science?

Science refers to the application of objective methods of investigation, reasoning and logic to develop a body of knowledge about a given phenomenon. There are three goals of science. The first is to explain why something happens. The second is to make generalisations, that is, to go beyond the individual cases and make statements that apply to a collective group. The third is to predict, to specify, what will happen in future, in the light of the available knowledge. Thus, science refers to a systematic body of certified and changing knowledge which is based upon observable and verifiable facts and the methods used to acquire this knowledge. So, the term 'science' is used for both the knowledge and the methods that are used to acquire that knowledge.

Like all scientists, sociologists must study the specific in order to understand the general. The true concern of the geologist is not the peculiarity of the rock he holds in his hands, the concern of the botanist is not the fate of the flower he finds in the field and the concern of the sociologist is not the specific event he observes and records. All sciences are concerned with the order and pattern of their subject matter – what is it that rocks or flowers or persons or societies have in common. One of the ways scientists move from the specific to the general is through statistical averaging. A chemist who observes the reactions of millions of atoms cannot predict with certainty the behaviour of any single hydrogen atom, but he can say with assurance that most hydrogen atoms behave in a certain way. Similarly, although a sociologist can never predict the political opinion of any particular blue-collar worker, he can say that most members of a given socio-economic class have political opinions of a certain kind.

Sociology is a scientific discipline. It is a science in the sense that it involves objective and systematic methods of investigation and evaluation of social reality

DOI: 10.4324/9781003291053-4

in the light of empirical evidence and interpretation. But it cannot be directly modelled on the patterns of natural sciences because human behaviour is different from the world of nature. Among other differences, the subject matter of natural sciences is relatively static and unchanging, whereas human behaviour as the subject matter of sociology is flexible and dynamic. Moreover, the natural phenomena can be put under controlled observation; it may not be possible to do the same regarding the subject matter of sociology. This is because all social phenomena and social institutions like family, marriage, caste, etc. are constantly changing even while they are being studied. In sociological research, it is difficult to be completely value-free. Moreover, the research situation itself becomes a social situation where the researcher confronts another human being and gets involved in a process of interaction. This makes it difficult to be objective. Good social scientists keep these limitations in mind and try to be as objective as possible. For that purpose, different research tools are used and data are checked and crosschecked.

To sum up, it may be said that any discipline is considered to be scientific when it is *empirical, theoretical, cumulative* and *value neutral*. Please note that these characteristics are also considered as the basic postulates of scientific method. Against this yardstick, let us examine the status of sociology as a science:

1. *Sociology is empirical*: It is based on observation and reasoning, not on supernatural revelations, and its results are not speculative. In the early stages of their creative work, all scientists speculate, of course, but, ideally at least, they submit their speculations to the test of fact before announcing them as scientific discoveries. All aspects of sociological knowledge are subject to evaluations made about social behaviour or can be put to test for empirical evidence.

2. *Sociology is theoretical*: It attempts to summarise complex observations in abstract logically related propositions which purport to explain causal relationships in the subject matter. Its main aim is to interpret and interrelate sociological data in order to explain the nature of social phenomena and to produce hypotheses whose final validity can be checked by further empirical research.

3. *Sociology is cumulative*: Sociological theories are built upon one another, extending and refining the older ones and producing new ones. As such, theoretical integration becomes a goal in the construction of sociological formulations. Thus, sociology is cumulative.

4. *Sociology is non-ethical or value neutral*: Sociologists do not ask whether particular social actions are good or bad; they seek merely to explain them. Sociology addresses issues. The study of human relations is the prime consideration in sociology. In this context, Morris Ginsberg observes that ethical problems should be dealt with neutrality. Objectivity and rationality based on thorough knowledge of a situation alone can ensure scientific status to the discipline of sociology (Nagla and Singh, 2002).

Thus, sociology is a science of its own kind. It is a social science. The subject matter of sociology is fundamentally different from that of natural sciences. Sociology studies social phenomena (society, its institutions and patterns of interactions among people), while natural sciences study physical or natural phenomena. Given its distinct, diverse and dynamic subject matter, sociology can at best aspire to arrive at limited generalisations in comparison to natural sciences that claim universality of their generalisations.

Scientific Method and Sociological Research

As discussed earlier, science is a body of verified knowledge about physical or social reality. The method used to acquire this kind of knowledge is called scientific method. The general guideline for all scientific research is the scientific method. Although it is possible to outline the series of steps that comprise this method, its real importance is not as a body of rules but as an attitude towards the work of observation and generalisation. It has often been said that many scientific discoveries have been due to lucky accidents; Galvani, for example, discovered that nerves transmit electrical impulses when one of his assistants left a freshly dissected frog on the lab table near an unrelated experiment in electrical conduction. But it is not the element of chance that should be stressed in such an occurrence; the key element was Galvani's trained powers of observation, his ability to derive a possible explanation for what he saw, his knowledge of the way to test that explanation. While Galvani's assistant, who also observed this lucky accident, dismissed this as a curious coincidence, Galvani the scientist saw the implications of the coincidence.

How can one learn to observe and generalise in a scientific manner? The following steps serve as general guidelines when applying the scientific method in sociological research.

First, make a careful statement of the problem to be investigated and frame a hypothesis. A sociologist begins by defining precisely what it is that he wants to know. He generally states the problem so that it fits into existing theoretical frameworks and is related to the relevant findings of previous research. Stating the problem in this manner ensures that knowledge will be cumulative and that one researcher's findings can be easily utilised by others. The problem must also be formulated as a verifiable hypothesis, one that can be tested before it is accepted or rejected. Many provocative hypotheses can never be tested. For example, one might hypothesise that God exists, but no one has found a way to test this hypothesis. Scientists must modify the original hypothesis to one they can test, such as the majority of adult Americans believe that God exists. Please note that a hypothesis is nothing but a tentative statement asserting a relationship between certain facts (or variables). You will learn more about hypothesis in the next chapter.

In sociological research, the application of this first step in the scientific method can be illustrated by the case of a researcher who suspects an association between urban residence and mental illness. The researcher would begin by identifying certain defining qualities of a city: How big is it? What are its social characteristics? How does it differ from a nearby suburb? With a definition in mind, he looks for the aspects of a city that might be associated with mental illness: population size and density, quality of housing, prevalence of low-income groups, availability of recreational facilities. After examining existing theories and research findings in this area, he would frame a hypothesis stating a suspected or tentative relationship between some specific urban characteristic and mental illness. For example, he might hypothesise that the incidence of mental illness increases in proportion to the size of the city, with the largest cities having the highest rates of mental illness.

In the search for ways that these variables (characteristics that are present in varying amounts or degrees) could be measured, the hypothesis might be further refined. The researcher might choose to limit his study to those patients actually hospitalised with a diagnosis of mental illness, thus eliminating all those mentally ill urban residents who have not been diagnosed and are not being treated. Although this refinement makes the hypothesis easier to test, it also introduces an additional problem: the number of institutions that can diagnose and treat mental illness. Thus, the rates of mental illness might appear higher in some cities simply because they have more facilities to treat the mentally ill, whereas in other cities a large percentage of the mentally ill population go untreated. Each choice of a specific measure brings with it new possibilities of error and bias, yet the general hypothesis must be reduced to specifics if it is to be tested at all.

Second, develop a research design. A research design is a plan for the collection, analysis and evaluation of data; it involves deciding how facts are to be selected, how they are to be evaluated and classified and how they are to be analysed to uncover relationships and patterns that bear on the original hypothesis. The major goal of the research design is to ensure that the evidence gathered to test a hypothesis will be trustworthy, and that extraneous factors that might falsify the results will be controlled. Please note that extraneous variables are undesirable variables that influence the relationship between the variables that an experimenter is examining. In other words, extraneous variables are the variables which, though not a part of the study yet, are capable of influencing the outcome of the study. These variables are undesirable because they add error to an experiment. A major goal in research design is to decrease or control the influence of extraneous variables as much as possible.

The classic controlled experiment in a laboratory is the ideal scientific research design. It is an experiment designed in advance and conducted under conditions in which it is possible to control all relevant factors while measuring the effect on an experimentally induced variable. In a controlled experiment, the subjects are divided into two groups. The variable whose effect is to be tested (independent variable) is then introduced into one group called the *experimental group*, while it is withheld from the other group called the *control group*. The two groups are subsequently compared to determine whether there are any significant differences between them regarding the variable that is expected to change, or the dependent variable. On the basis of this comparison, the original hypothesis, which proposes a specific relationship between the independent and dependent variables, can be confirmed or rejected.

The use of the controlled experiment can best be illustrated by cancer research. Suppose one wishes to test the hypothesis that nicotine causes cancer in mice. A number of mice can be randomly assigned to experimental and control groups. Those in the experimental group are then given a dose of nicotine (the independent variable), while those in the control group are not. Everything else about the two groups is held constant. If the incidence of cancer (the dependent variable) is subsequently found to be higher in the experimental than in the control group, a cause-and-effect relationship between nicotine and cancer in mice may be assumed. It is seldom possible to test sociological hypotheses under controlled laboratory conditions. The typical social research design is therefore developed with this limitation in mind.

Third, collect data in accordance with the research design. One way of obtaining information about human behaviour and social life is to observe the way people actually behave: how they act in a given situation, what they do on a daily and regular basis. This constitutes the *objective reality*. Accurate and objective observation by trained observers is a fundamental distinguishing feature of all the sciences. Another way is to ask people about their actions, attitudes and beliefs. Their answers help to reveal the *subjective reality* – the meanings and thoughts, or 'reasons' that lie behind a person's behaviour. Subjective reality distinguishes the social sciences from the natural sciences, which deals only with objective reality, that which can be seen to happen.

Some sociologists, however, question whether subjective reality can be accurately analysed scientifically and prefer to concentrate exclusively on the observation of objective reality. They maintain that the only valid evidence for scientific purposes is what they can observe about human behaviour, not what people tell them. Such scholars are called '*positivists*'. In sociology, positivism is generally associated with the view that there is an objective world which is capable of being understood in objective and scientific terms. The founders of sociology, be it Comte, Spencer or Durkheim, all advocated positivist approach to study social life, though this approach had its own limitations and was later criticised by the scholars belonging to the anti-positivist tradition. You will read about this in more detail in our subsequent discussion on 'Positivism and its critique'.

The fourth step in the scientific method is to analyse the data and draw conclusions. It is at this step that the initial hypothesis is accepted or rejected and the conclusions of the research are related to the existing body of theory, perhaps modifying it to take account of the new findings. The findings are usually presented as articles in scholarly journals, monographs or books. The accuracy and significance of scientific findings are assessed in terms of their validity and reliability. Validity refers to the correspondence between what a scientific investigation or technique purports to measure and what it actually measures. An example of this kind of assessment is the current challenge by many social scientists of the validity of IQ tests. These scientists question whether the tests really measure innate human intelligence or something else. Reliability refers to the degree to which a scientific test or measurement is consistent and accurate. There is less doubt about the reliability of IQ tests; although the IQ tests may not measure intelligence, they seem to measure some particular characteristic consistently. To determine reliability, replication, the repetition of an experiment a number of times, is done to see if the same results are obtained.

By no means do all, or even most, sociological research investigations closely follow this outline of the scientific method. Many sociologists are simply interested in accurate descriptions, others do not develop precise hypotheses or elaborate research designs and most do not formally go through the step of either accepting or rejecting a hypothesis. Nevertheless, this model of the scientific method is highly influential as a guideline for both planning research and evaluating research findings. It represents the ideal that all scientists seek to attain.

What Is Theory?

The desire to translate observations into understanding brings us to the important aspect of sociology known as *theory*. However, before we begin to look at the importance of social theory, we should ask the question: 'What are we theorising about?' Though it is obvious that sociologists theorise about society and social issues, it is necessary to pay attention to some features of society that are important when looking at social theory. In earlier chapters, we have discussed that society basically consists of social relationships and social institutions. However, we must understand that these relationships and institutions are both concrete and abstract at the same time.

For example, let us consider the institution of the monarchy. Some people may interact with the monarch of their country on a daily basis such as nobles, courtiers, personal attendants, etc. Others may have only an abstract relationship with their monarch. That is, they are subjects of the monarch but may have had no direct interaction with him or her. The relationships, though abstract, is nonetheless real in its effects – for example, the taxes given by the subjects support the monarch in his or her duties. Thus, the monarch is a person but monarchy is an institution. While individual kings and queens come and go, the institution of monarchy persists in the form of the functions it performs. Thus, the institution of the monarchy exists as an abstract concept, fulfilling constitutional and emotional elements of society. So, it is the abstract nature of much of society and our experiences of it that leads to the need for social theory.

A second feature of society that is important for theorising is that it is patterned. Stable and patterned social relationships are essential for the survival and social order of any society. It is these regularities of social behaviour that enable and facilitate sociologists to theorise about society. Sociologists do not study those aspects of social life which are random or spontaneous. However, regularities also appear beyond the surface level of human activity. For example, it can be shown that lower caste groups in India have consistently lagged behind in terms of educational attainment or their representation in white-collar professions. Sociological theory seeks to explain both the surface and the deep patterns of social behaviour.

Having discussed some of the important aspects of society that are essential to understand the significance of theorising, let us now try to understand the meaning and some important features of a theory. A theory is a set of ideas which provides an explanation for something. A sociological theory is, therefore, a set of ideas which provides an explanation for human society.

The first most important feature of a theory is that it is 'a generalised statement about a social phenomenon'. This means that sociologists seek to go beyond the simple description of single events to a different level of analysis. Theoretical statements, therefore, cover a number of similar events and describe the similarities between them and why any differences might occur. For example, sociologists may theorise about the low educational attainment of lower castes in contemporary India in terms of their historical socio-economic, educational and political exclusion. Similarly, low educational attainment and poor representation of women in the economic and political sphere may be explained in terms of religious prescriptions and proscriptions prevalent in the past as well as the institution of patriarchy.

This leads to a second feature of theory that is important, namely that theory seeks to explain social phenomena. With the help of statistical evidence, a theory attempts to explain the causes of a phenomenon. This facilitates prediction of future patterns and influence social policies. As in the case of the above-mentioned example, if we know why some social groups underperform in terms of educational attainment, then suitable policy measures could be implemented. It is worth noting at this point that this is not necessarily an easy thing to do, and this is because society differs from natural circumstances in two important respects. First, human beings have free will and change their behaviour according to their preferences, ideologies or even whims. Second, societies do not remain static, but change over time and in unpredictable ways, and hence establishing universal laws that would hold true for all societies and for all times is impossible.

A third aspect of theory is that theoretical statements should be verifiable by others who are not responsible for developing them. This is because sociologists, as human beings, are affected by their own values, assumptions and biases. In developing their theories, sociologists exhibit systematic ways of thinking that constitute perspectives, which inform and shape their theoretical work. Therefore, it is important that the evidence that sociologists use to support their theoretical statements can be verified independently, and this is where methodology comes into play (Churton and Brown, 2017).

Thus, in essence, theory is nothing more than sociologists' generalisations about 'real' social interactions and the everyday practices of social life. For example, the fact that women, rather than men, do the bulk of housework and child care in our society is explained, in part, by the concept of patriarchy, meaning the rule of the father or oldest male, and the cultural assumption that housework is not real work. Taken together, the concept and the assumption provide a basis for a theory about gender relations. Theorising is and always has been a part of everyone's way of thinking. Every time you try to guess why a group of people act in a particular way, you are theorising about a social phenomenon on the basis of your own knowledge of reality. Sociologists do much the same thing, with a bit more formality.

Major Theoretical Strands of Research Methodology

Sociologists approach the study of human society in different ways. They can look at the 'big picture' of society to see how it operates. This is a macro view focusing on the large social phenomena of society such as social institutions and inequality. Sociologists can also take a micro view, zeroing in on the immediate social situations in which people interact with one another. From these two views, sociologists have developed various theoretical perspectives, each a set of general assumptions about the nature of society (Thio, 2003).

To help understand the beginners, these major theoretical strands of research methodology could broadly be classified into two major approaches in sociology. These are the *structural approach* (also called macro-sociology and identified with positivist methodology) and the *social action approach* (also called the interpretive or micro-sociology and identified with non-positivist and anti-positivist methodology). Structural and social action approaches to the study and research of society exhibit two major differences. One involves how they conceive of society, the social world itself. In other words, they completely disagree on the question of what society is. The second question follows from the first. It concerns the question of how we are to conduct our research into the social world. That is, because structural and social action sociologies have very different ideas of what society in fact is, they also have very different ideas about the research methods which are most appropriate to the conduct of research into social life. This is why we can say that how we conceive of society cannot be separated from the question of how we should proceed in our study of it. A student of sociology must understand this point very clearly, because this links the theoretical perspectives with the research methodology. It will become clearer as we proceed with our discussion.

Let us now discuss these two major theoretical strands and the various sociological perspectives and approaches that fall under their respective domain.

Structural Approach

Structural approach (also called systems approach) is a macro-sociological analysis, with a broad focus on social structures that shape society as a whole. Structural approach analyses the way society as a whole fits together. As discussed earlier, the term 'social structure' refers to the pattern of social relations among members of a society (in terms of interrelated statuses and roles). Structural theory sees society as a system of relationships that creates the structure of the society in which we live. It is this structure that determines our lives and characters. Structured sets of social relationships are the 'reality' that lie below the appearance of 'the free individual'.

Philip Jones in his *Theory and Method in Sociology* (1987) argues that the structuralist sociologists look at society as 'a structure of (cultural) rules', guiding our behaviour and telling us how to behave appropriately in any given situation and what to expect in terms of the behaviour of others. Thus, structural sociology is based on the premise that society comes before individuals. This general idea – that sociologists should study the way society impacts on individual behaviour – represents the main way structuralist sociologists differ from social action sociologists.

Further, with these assumptions about the social reality, the structural theorists argue that there can be a sociology which is a science. In other words, sociology can be a science of society just as, for example, nuclear physics is the science of the structure of matter – of atoms, neutrons, electrons and so on. Structural theorists conceive society as an objective phenomenon, a 'thing'. In other words, just as natural sciences study the structure and composition of matter, sociology too can identify and objectively study the social structure and its various constituents such as shared norms, values, attitudes and beliefs, etc. Hence, structural theorists argue that the study of the social world can be modelled on the study of natural phenomena, and the scientific methodology of natural (or positive) sciences can be adopted to study the social phenomena. Thus, we can conclude that structural approaches (also called systems approaches) are positivist in nature.

Once behaviour is seen as a response to some external stimulus, such as economic forces or the requirements of the social system, the methods and assumptions of the natural sciences appear appropriate to the study of humans. Marxism has often been regarded as a positivist approach since it can be argued that it sees human behaviour as a reaction to the stimulus of the economic infrastructure. Functionalism has been viewed in a similar light. The behaviour of members of society can be seen as a response to the functional prerequisites of the social system. These views of the structural or systems theory represent a considerable oversimplification. However, it is probably fair to say that the structural or systems theory is closer to a positivist approach.

In sociology, there are two main structural or system approaches:

1. Consensus approach (functionalism)
2. Conflict approach (Marxism and feminism)

Consensus Approach: Functionalism

Functional analysis, also known as functionalism and structural functionalism, is rooted in the origin of sociology. It is prominent in the works of Auguste

Comte (1798–1857) and Herbert Spencer (1820–1903), two of the founding fathers of the discipline. Functional analysis was developed by Emile Durkheim (1858–1917) and refined by Talcott Parsons (1902–1979). Functionalism was the dominant theoretical perspective in sociology during the 1940s and 1950s. From the mid-1960s onwards, its popularity steadily declined due partly to damaging criticism and partly to competing perspectives which appeared to provide superior explanations.

Functionalism views society as a system, that is, as a set of interrelated parts which form a whole. The basic unit of analysis is society, and its various parts are understood primarily in terms of their relationship to the whole. For example, various institutions of society such as marriage, family, politics and religion are analysed as a part of the social system rather than as isolated units. In particular, they are understood with reference to the contribution they make to the system as a whole. Functionalism, thus, conceptualises society as a whole, which is more than the sum of its constituent parts (Figure 3.1).

Early functionalists like Auguste Comte, Herbert Spencer and Emile Durkheim often drew an analogy between society and an organism such as the human body. The key points of the functionalist perspective may be summarised by a comparison drawn from biology. If a biologist wanted to know how an organism such as the human body worked, he might begin by examining the various parts such as the brain, lungs, heart and liver. However, if he simply analysed the parts in isolation from each other, he would be unable to explain how life was maintained. To do this, he would have to examine the parts in relation to each other since they work together to maintain the organism. Thus, he would analyse the relationship between the heart, lungs, brain and so on to understand how they operate and appreciate their importance. From this viewpoint, any part of the organism must be seen in terms of the organism as a whole.

Functionalism adopts a similar perspective. The various parts of society are seen to be interrelated, and taken together they form a complete system. To

FIGURE 3.1 Functionalists' View of Society

understand any part of society, such as the family or religion, the part must be seen in relation to society as a whole. Thus, where a biologist will examine a part of the body, such as the heart, in terms of its contribution to the maintenance of the human organism, the functionalist will examine a part of society, such as the family, in terms of its contribution to the maintenance of the social system. Continuing this analogy, functionalists argued that just as an organism has certain basic needs which must be satisfied if it is to survive, so has society the basic needs which must be met if it is to continue to exist. These basic needs or necessary conditions of existence are sometimes known as functional prerequisites of society. Various sociologists have identified different sets of functional prerequisites on the basis of their respective researches. However, the more important point to note here is that functionalists tend to analyse and evaluate different parts of society in terms of fulfilling certain functional prerequisites. Thus, each part of society is understood and explained in terms of its contribution (function) to the maintenance of equilibrium in society as a whole. For example, a major function of the economic system is the production of food and shelter. An important function of the family is the socialisation of new members of society.

The concept of 'function' in functionalist analysis refers to the contribution of the part to the whole. More specifically, the function of any part of society is the contribution it makes to meet the functional prerequisites of the social system. Parts of society are functional insofar as they maintain the system and contribute to its survival. For example, the function of a family is to ensure the continuity of society by reproducing and socialising new members. Similarly, the function of religion is to integrate the social system by reinforcing common values (Haralambos and Holborn, 2014).

Further, functionalism begins with the observation that behaviour in society is structured. As discussed earlier, the concepts of status and role are integral to the understanding of social structure of a given society. This means that relationships between members of society are organised in terms of rules that stipulate how people are expected to behave. Rules can be formal (for example, laws) or informal (for example, norms). Norms refer to the commonly accepted standards of behaviour in a social group or society. Norms are specific guides to action, which tell you, for example, how you are expected to dress and behave at a party or at a funeral. Norms are associated with particular roles in society. Thus, one's roles and obligations in a social group are defined by that group's social norms. Social relationships are patterned and recurrent because of the existence of rules which are ultimately based on cultural values.

Values are socially accepted standards of desirability. In other words, a value is a belief that something is good and desirable. It defines what is important and worthwhile. Values differ from society to society and culture to culture. For example, in the West, the dominant values are individualism and materialism, which are this-worldly in nature, while in India, *moksha* had been a long-cherished goal of human life and is other-worldly in nature. Values provide general guidelines for behaviour. Values are translated into more specific directives in terms of norms. The value of privacy produces a range of norms, such as those that stipulate that you should knock before entering a room and that you should ask people's permission before photographing them. The structure of society, thus, can be understood as the totality of normative behaviour, i.e. the complex of social relationships governed by norms. The main parts of society, its institutions, such as family, economy, educational and political systems, are major aspects of social structure. Thus, an institution can be seen as a structure made up of interconnected roles or interrelated norms. For example, the family is made up of the interconnected roles of husband, father, wife, mother, son and daughter. Social relationships within the family are structured in terms of a set of related norms.

From a functionalist perspective, society is regarded as a system and as a system it has certain functional prerequisites. One of the important functional prerequisites of society is a minimal degree of integration between the parts. Many functionalists argue that this integration is based largely on *value consensus* among members of a society. Thus, value consensus integrates the various parts of society. It forms the basis of social unity or social solidarity since individuals will tend to identify and feel kinship with those who share the same values as themselves. Value consensus provides the foundation for cooperation since common values produce common goals. Members of society will tend to cooperate in pursuit of goals which they share. Having attributed such importance to value consensus, many functionalists then focus on the question of how this consensus is maintained. An investigation of the source of value consensus is, therefore, a major concern of functionalist analysis. Indeed, the American sociologist Talcott Parsons has stated that the main task of sociology is to examine 'the institutionalisation of patterns of value orientation in the social system'. Emphasis is therefore placed on the process of socialisation whereby values are internalised and transmitted from one generation to the next. In this respect, the family is regarded as a vital part of the social structure. Once learned, values must be maintained. In particular, those who deviate from society's values must be brought back into line. Thus, the mechanisms of social control are seen as essential to the maintenance of social order.

Thus, if the major values of society are expressed in the various parts of the social structure, those parts will be integrated. For example, it can be argued that the value of materialism integrates many parts of the social structure in Western industrial society. The economic system produces a large range of goods, and ever-increasing productivity is regarded as an important goal. The educational system is partly concerned with producing the skills and expertise to expand production and increase its efficiency. The family is an important unit of consumption with its steadily increasing demand for consumer durables such as washing machines, televisions and three-piece suits. The political system is partly concerned with improving material living standards and raising productivity. To the extent that these parts of the social structure are based on the same value, they may be said to be integrated.

However, with their concern for investigating how functional prerequisites are met, functionalists have concentrated on functions rather than dysfunctions. According to the functionalist perspective, many institutions are seen as not only beneficial but indispensable, such as the family, religion, social stratification, etc. This view has led critics to argue that functionalism has a built-in conservative bias which supports the status quo. The argument that certain social arrangements are beneficial or indispensable provides support for their retention and rejects proposals for radical change (Haralambos and Holborn, 2014).

Conflict Approach

Although functionalists emphasise the importance of value consensus in society, they do recognise that conflict can occur. However, they see conflict as being the result of temporary disturbances in the social system. These disturbances are usually quickly corrected as society evolves. Functionalists accept that social groups can have differences of interest, but believe that these are of minor importance compared to the interests that all social groups share in common. They believe that all social groups benefit if their society runs smoothly and prospers. The conflict perspective, however, produces a portrait of society strikingly different from that offered by functionalism. Whereas functionalism emphasises society's stability, the conflict perspective portrays society as always changing and always marked by conflict. As stated earlier, due to its emphasis on social order, functionalism was criticised for having a built-in conservative bias which supports the status quo. Functionalists tend to view social change as harmful. Instead, they assume that the social order is based largely on people's willing cooperation. In contrast, proponents of the conflict perspective are inclined to concentrate on social conflict, to see social change as beneficial and to assume that the social order is forcibly imposed by the powerful on the weak. They criticise the status quo and advocate radical and revolutionary change (Thio, 2003).

There are many varieties of conflict perspectives within sociology. But, despite their differences, all have a model of society as a whole, and all adopt a structural approach. In other words, conflict theorists focus on the macro level. Further, all conflict perspectives share the notion that there are groups in society that have different and often conflicting interests. As a result, the possibility of conflict is always present. Conflict theories differ from functionalism in stressing the existence of competing groups, while functionalists stress cooperation between social groups. As discussed earlier, functionalists consider value consensus as one of the fundamental prerequisites for the maintenance of integration and order in society.

The conflict perspective originated largely from Karl Marx's writings on class conflict between capitalists and the proletariat. In America, sociologists tended to ignore Marx and the conflict perspective for a long time because functionalism was the dominant theoretical perspective in sociology during the 1940s and 1950s. However, since the turbulent 1960s, the conflict perspective has gained popularity. Karl Marx (1818–83) primarily emphasised on the conflict between social groups (*Classes* as per Marx) resulting out of their mutually incompatible and conflicting economic interests. However, conflict is now defined more broadly. Conflict theorists today define social conflict to mean conflict between any *unequal* groups or societies. Thus, they examine conflict between whites and blacks, men and women, one religious group and another, one society and another and so on. Conflict theorists emphasise that different groups in societies have conflicting interests and values and compete with each other for scarce resources. The more powerful groups gain more than the less powerful, but the former continue to seek more wealth and power, while the latter continue to struggle for more resources. Because of this perpetual competition, society, or the world, is always changing.

The conflict perspective raises several critical questions, such as: which groups are socially, economically and politically more powerful and which are weaker? What is the source of dominance of powerful groups in a given society? How can an egalitarian society be established? For example, according to the conflict perspective, prostitution reflects the unequal social positions of men and women. In prostitution, members of a dominant group, men, benefit from the exploitation of a weaker group, women. This exploitation is made possible by the existence of a social order in which women are subordinate to men. If both sexes were treated equally – with women having full access to and being equally paid for more respectable types of work as men – women would be unlikely to become prostitutes. Prostitution further reinforces the general dominance of men over women because it helps perpetuate the sexist idea that women are inferior beings who can be used as mere objects for pleasure. In short, prostitution reflects and reinforces the power of one group over another (Thio, 2003). There are a number of different conflict perspectives, and their supporters tend to disagree about the precise nature, causes and extent of conflict. For the sake of simplicity, in this section we will concentrate upon two conflict theories: Marxism and Feminism (Figure 3.2).

Marxism

Conflict theory in sociology is the creation of Karl Marx. Indeed, Marxism and conflict theory are sometimes discussed as though the two were synonymous. Marx analysed both historical and contemporary society in terms of conflicts between social groups, which he called *classes*, with different economic interests. Marx emphasised the primacy of technology and of patterns of property ownership in determining the nature of people's lives and course of social conflict. At the time when most scholars believed that society generally functioned smoothly and that social change, when it happened, evolved slowly and peacefully, Marx contrarily argued that social changes resulted from harsh conflicts between groups with opposing economic interests (Wallace and Wolf, 2012).

According to Marx, '*The history of all hitherto existing society is the history of class struggles*'. Marx argued that at the dawn of human history, when man supposedly

Structural Approaches	Perspective (assumptions about social reality)	Subject Matter	Methodology*	Level of Analysis
Functionalism	• views society as a system made up of interrelated parts • focuses on social order and believes in evolutionary social change • functionalists believe that social order results from value consensus among members of a society and consider value consensus essential for maintaining equilibrium in society • assumes social action to be recurrent and patterned in nature, and consider it being largely influenced and shaped by shared values	• to explore the interrelationship between various parts of society and their respective functions for the maintenance of equilibrium in society	• mainly quantitative research methodology (positivist) e.g. Durkheim's *Suicide*	• mainly macro-sociological analysis • early functionalists believed in formulation of universal generalization • however, later functionalists, like Merton, advocated middle-range theories (i.e. limited generalizations)
Marxism	• views society as a system primarily constituting of two parts: superstructure and economic infrastructure • gives primacy to economic infrastructure in shaping superstructure • focuses on social conflict and believes in evolutionary as well as revolutionary change • Marxists believe that social order is maintained through coercion and imposed by the powerful on the weak • explains patterned social action resulting from unequal and exploitative relations of production and sustained by false class consciousness generated by ruling class ideology	• to explore the nature of class conflict	• mainly quantitative research methodology (positivist) e.g. historical or dialectical materialism as advocated by Karl Marx	• mainly macro-sociological analysis
Feminism	• views society as characterized by exploitation of women by men • feminists believe that sex roles are culturally conditioned	• analysis of unequal and exploitative gender relations	• combination of both quantitative as well as qualitative research methodology	• both macro as well as micro-sociological analysis

* In contemporary sociology, many scholars advocate a combination of both quantitative (positivist) as well as qualitative (interpretive) research methods to ensure greater reliability and validity of sociological research.

FIGURE 3.2 Structural Approaches

lived in a state of primitive communism, the forces of production and the products of labour were communally owned. During the era of primitive communism, i.e. the earliest form of human society, each member of society produced both for himself and for society as a whole. Hence, there were no conflicts of interest between individuals and groups. However, with surplus production and emergence of private property, the fundamental contradiction of human society was created. Some were able to acquire the forces of production and others were, therefore, obliged to work for them. The result was a class of non-producers who owned the forces of production and a class of producers who owned only the labour power. Through its ownership of the forces of production, a minority is able to control, command and enjoy the fruits of the labour of the majority. Since one group gains at the expense of the other, a conflict of interest exists between the minority group that owns the forces of production (ownership class) and the majority group that performs productive labour (non-ownership class). Marx uses the concept of 'class' to highlight the mutually conflicting economic interests of these groups.

Marx used the term 'class' to refer to the main strata in all stratification systems, though most modern sociologists would reserve the term for strata in capitalist society. From the Marxian view, a class is a social group whose members share the same relationship to the forces of production, and as a result share common economic interests. According to Marx, Western society had developed through four main epochs: primitive communism, ancient society, feudal society and capitalist society. Primitive communism provides the only example of a classless society. Except primitive communism, all societies are divided into two major classes: a *ruling class* and a *subject class*. For example, masters and slaves in ancient society, lords and serfs in feudal society and capitalists (*bourgeoisie*) and wage labourers (*proletariat*) in capitalist society. The power of the ruling class derives from its ownership and control of the forces of production. Thus, the ruling class is the ownership class, and the subject class is the non-ownership class. Marx maintained that in all class societies, the ruling class exploits and oppresses the subject class. As a result, there is a basic conflict of interest between the two classes. Since Marx is analysing social structure and social change in terms of relations of production and conflict between distinct classes, his theory is classified as a structural approach.

Marx's theory primarily analyses the changing nature of industrial capitalism in the nineteenth century – a period in which there was a shift in the nature of economic and social relations, from a society based on feudal principles to one that was based on the notion of waged labour. In capitalist economy, the capitalists are motivated by maximisation of profit, and this profit is primarily accumulated by paying the workers less than the value of the goods they produce. According to Marx, the difference between the value of wages and commodities is known as 'surplus value'. This surplus value is appropriated in the form of profit by the capitalists. This is how Marx explains the exploitation of the working class at the hands of capitalists.

Marx believed that as capitalism advances, certain conditions and developments would transform the proletariat into a revolutionary force. Subsequently, the proletariat would overthrow the bourgeoisie and seize the forces of production, the source of power. Property would be communally owned and, since all members of society would now share the same relationship to the forces of production, a classless society would result. Since history is the history of the class struggle, history would now end. The communist society which replaces capitalism will contain no contradictions, no conflicts of interest and, therefore, be unchanging. Industrial manufacture would remain as the basic technique of production in the socialist or communist society which would replace capitalism.

Although functionalism and Marxism provide very different perspectives on society, they have a number of factors in common. First, they offer a general explanation of society as a whole and as a result are also known as macro-theories. Second, they regard society as a system, hence they are sometimes referred to as systems theories. Third, they tend to see man's behaviour as shaped by the system. For example, according to Durkheim, human behaviour is largely shaped by social facts, i.e. institutionalised norms and values of society. From a Marxian viewpoint, behaviour is ultimately determined by the economic infrastructure. Some versions of feminism have similar characteristics in that they explain how society works in terms of the existence of a patriarchal system and explain the behaviour of males and females in terms of that system.

Feminism

There are several different versions of feminism, but most share a number of features that are common. Like Marxists, feminists tend to see society as divided into different social groups. Unlike Marxists, they see the major division as being between men and women rather than between different classes. Like Marxists, they tend to see society as characterised by exploitation. Unlike Marxists, they see the exploitation of women by men as the most important kind of exploitation, rather than that of the working class by the ruling class. Since feminist scholars are largely occupied with the analysis of unequal and often exploitative gender relations, which are relatively patterned across societies, feminist theory can be seen as yet another example of structural approach.

Many feminists characterise contemporary societies as patriarchal, that is, men dominate them. For example, feminists have argued that men have most of the power in families, that they tend to be employed in better-paid and higher-status jobs than women and that they tend to monopolise positions of political power. The ultimate aim of these types of feminism is to end men's domination and to rid society of the exploitation of women. Such feminists advance a range of explanations for, and solutions to, the exploitation of women. However, they all believe that the development of society can be explained and that progress towards an improved future is possible.

Some feminist writers (sometimes called difference feminists) disagree that all women are equally oppressed and disadvantaged in contemporary societies. They believe that it is important to recognise the different experiences and problems faced by various groups of women. For example, they do not believe that all husbands oppress their wives, that women are equally disadvantaged in all types of work or that looking after children is necessarily oppressive to women. They emphasise the differences between women of different ages, class backgrounds and ethnic groups. Like other feminists, they believe that the oppression of women exists, but they do not see it as affecting all women to the same extent and in the same way. For example, a wealthy white woman in a rich capitalist country is in a very different position from a poor black woman living in an impoverished part of Africa. Since their problems are different, they would require very different solutions.

Despite their disagreements, feminists tend to agree that, at least until recently, sociology has neglected women. Certainly, until the 1970s, men largely wrote sociology about men. There were relatively few studies of women, and issues of particular concern to women (such as housework and women's health) were rarely studied. A number of feminists criticise what they call 'malestream sociology'. By this they mean mainstream, male-dominated sociology. They have attacked not just what male sociologists study, but also how they carry out their studies. For example, they have suggested that feminist sociology should get away from rigid 'scientific' methods and should adopt more sympathetic approaches. These can involve working in partnership with those being studied rather than treating them as simply the passive providers of data. As feminist scholarship has developed, it has started to examine numerous aspects of social life from feminist viewpoints.3.2

Social Action Approach

Till now we have discussed the structural approach (also called systems approach), one of the two major theoretical strands of research methodology. While discussing structural approach, we have discussed two main structural approaches in sociology, viz. consensus theory (functionalism) and conflict theory (Marxism and feminism). We have also discussed how these structural approaches are largely positivist in nature and oriented for macro-sociological analysis. Now, let us discuss the other major theoretical strand of research methodology, that is, the social action approach.

As a student of sociology, you must remember that not all sociological perspectives base their analysis upon an examination of the structure of society as a whole. Rather than seeing human behaviour as being largely determined by society, they see society as being the product of human activity. They stress the meaningfulness of human behaviour, denying that it is primarily determined by the structure of society. These approaches are known as social action theory. Max Weber (1864–1920), a German sociologist, was the first to advocate a social action approach. In contemporary sociology, there are two main varieties of this type of sociology.

These are symbolic interactionism and ethnomethodology. However, before we discuss these approaches in detail, let us first try to understand the general assumptions about social reality that underlie the social action approach.

Social action approach (also called the interpretive, phenomenological or micro-sociology) in sociology rejects many of the assumptions of positivism. Social action theorists argue that the subject matter of the social and natural sciences is fundamentally different. While natural sciences deal with matter, social sciences deal with man and his behaviour. Matter, for example, atoms and molecules, does not have consciousness. It does not have meanings and purposes which direct its behaviour. Matter simply reacts 'unconsciously' to external stimuli; in scientific language, it behaves. As a result, the natural scientist is able to observe, measure and impose an external logic on that behaviour in order to explain it. He need not explore the internal logic of the consciousness of matter simply because it does not exist. Hence, to understand and explain the behaviour of matter, it is sufficient to observe it from the outside.

However, unlike matter, humans have consciousness – thoughts, feelings, meanings, intentions and an awareness of being. Because of this, humans' actions are meaningful: humans define situations and give meaning to their actions and those of others. As a result, they do not merely react to external stimuli, they do not simply behave – they act. Hence, the methods and assumptions of the natural sciences are inappropriate to the study of man. Unlike positivists, social action theorists argue that a mere statistical correlation based on direct observation would be inadequate for a comprehensive understanding of man's social behaviour. Instead, they emphasise on the interpretative understanding of man's social behaviour. In other words, since social action is meaningful, it must be understood from the subjective viewpoint of the social actors involved. For example, imagine the response of early humans to fire caused by volcanoes or spontaneous combustion. They did not simply react in a uniform manner to the experience of fire. Instead, they attached a range of meanings to it and these meanings directed their actions. Some defined fire as a means of warmth and used it to ward off wild animals, while others employed it for cooking and as a means of transforming substances, for example, hardening the points of wooden spears. Humans do not just react to fire, they act upon it in terms of the meanings they give to it. If action stems from subjective meanings, it follows that the sociologist must discover those meanings in order to understand action. Sociologists cannot simply observe action from the outside and impose an external logic upon it. They must interpret the internal logic which directs the actions of the actor (Haralambos and Holborn, 2014).

Social action approach and interpretive sociology are often seen as umbrella terms which include within themselves multiple schools of thought, which share the basic assumptions of social action approach and yet differ from each other in certain aspects. The prominent ones are Weberianism, symbolic interactionism, phenomenology and ethnomethodology. In the following section, we will learn about these schools of thought and their similarities and differences with each other (Figure 3.3).

Social Action Approaches	Perspective (assumptions about social reality)	Subject Matter	Methodology	Level of Analysis
Weberianism	• behaviour of man is qualitatively different from that of physical objects and biological organisms • considers social action as meaningful • social action is the basic unit of social life	• Weber conceived of sociology as a comprehensive science of 'social action'	• alongwith positive science methods, Weber also emphasized on the interpretation of subjective meanings that underlie social action • advocated formulation of *ideal types* of social phenomena and application of the *Verstehen* approach	• useful for both macro as well as micro sociological analysis • limited generalizations
Symbolic Interactionism	• like Weber, interactionists too consider social action as meaningful • society is composed of individuals whose actions depend on interpreting each other's behaviour • social order is a 'negotiated order'. Social order is maintained through constant negotiations between individuals trying to understand each other's actions and reactions	• studies the symbolic (subjective) meaning of human interaction	• like Weber, interactionists too supplemented positivist methodology with interpretation of social action	• micro sociological analysis • limited generalizations
Phenomenology	• humans can know the outside world only through their senses. In order to make sense of infinite sensory experiences, humans tend to classify them into categories. Such categorization, however, is purely subjective • social order is not an objective reality. It is an illusion, a subjective perception, held by members of a given society	• phenomenologists try to understand the meaning of phenomena, rather than explaining how they came into existence	• it is impossible to objectively measure any aspect of human behaviour • interpretive methods	• micro sociological analysis • rejects the possibility of any kind of causal explanation of human behaviour
Ethnomethodology	• like phenomenologists, ethnomethodologists abandon the belief that an actual or objective social order exists • ethnomethodologists argue that social life appears orderly because the members of a society perceive and interpret social reality as such	• to study the methods used by people to comprehend their social world	• interpretive methods	• micro sociological analysis • rejects the possibility of any kind of causal explanation of human behaviour

FIGURE 3.3   Social Action Approaches

Weberianism

Max Weber (1864–1920) was one of the first sociologists to advocate and highlight the significance of social action approach in sociology. Weber conceived of sociology as a comprehensive science of 'social action' which constitutes the basic unit of social life. According to Weber, social action is 'the meaningful behaviour oriented towards other individuals'. He argued that behaviour of man in society is qualitatively different from that of physical objects and biological organisms. What accounts for these differences is the presence of meanings and motives which underlie the social behaviour of man. Thus, any study of human behaviour in society must take cognisance of these meanings to understand this behaviour. The cognitive aims or objectives of sociological studies are, therefore, different from those of positive sciences. While positive sciences seek to discover the underlying patterns of interactions between various aspects of physical and natural phenomena, the social sciences, on the other hand, seek to understand the meanings and motives to explain the social phenomena. Hence, positive science methods alone would prove inadequate to study the social behaviour. However, Weber was not opposed to building generalisation in social sciences, but he pointed out that given the variable nature of social phenomena, only limited generalisation can be made. According to Weber, since the cognitive aim of sociology is to understand human behaviour, therefore, a sociological explanation should be adequate both at the level of meanings as well as at the level of causality. Therefore, Weber suggests the *Verstehen* method for sociological enquiry. This expression is taken from Dilthey, but Weber used it in a somewhat different sense. The *Verstehen* approach is usually translated as 'interpretive understanding'.

Here we can see that Weber partly agreed and partly disagreed with the claims of positivist scholars. For example, he accepted the positivists' argument for the scientific study of social phenomena and acknowledged the need for arriving at generalisations if sociology has to be a social science. But he criticised the positivists for not taking into account the unique meanings and motives of the social actors into consideration. Further, he argued that sociology, given the variable nature of the social phenomena, could only aspire for limited generalisations, not universal generalisations as advocated by the positivists. Because of these reasons, some scholars prefer to consider Weber as a non-positivist rather than an anti-positivist. However, such strict demarcation between non-positivism and anti-positivism is not a universally established practice in sociological literature. Scholars also freely identify Weber with anti-positivist tradition because he was the first one to question the basic assumptions of structural approach and positivist tradition in sociology and lay the foundation of social action approach and anti-positivist tradition.

Interactionism shares basic assumptions of social action approach. Like Weberianism, interactionism too considers social action as a meaningful action. Interactionism differs from functionalism, Marxism and most feminist theories in that it focuses on small-scale interaction rather than society as a whole. It usually rejects the notion of a social system. As a result, it does not regard human action as a response or reaction to the system. Interactionists believe that it is possible to analyse society systematically and that it is possible to improve society. However, improvements have to be made on a smaller scale and in a more piecemeal way than implied by macro or system theories. Thus, like Weberianism, interactionists too partly acknowledge the usefulness of scientific methodology and possibility for arriving at limited generalisation. However, interactionists supplemented positivist methodology with insight and understanding. For interactionists, social action is meaningful. Since it is not possible to get inside the heads of actors, the discovery of meaning must be based on interpretation and intuition. Since meanings are constantly negotiated in ongoing interaction process, it is not possible to establish simple cause-and-effect relationships. Thus, some sociologists argue that sociology is limited to an interpretation of social action, and hence, the social action approaches are also sometimes referred to as 'interpretive sociology'.

Nevertheless, both Weber and the interactionists did think it was possible to produce causal explanations of human behaviour, so long as an understanding of meanings formed part of those explanations. For these reasons, interactionism or symbolic interactionism is also sometimes categorised as non-positivist sociological tradition, like Weberianism. Again, such categorization is not a universal practice. In general, all social action approaches are identified with anti-positivist tradition.

However, some sociologists, particularly phenomenologists (like Alfred Schutz) and ethnomethodologists (like Harold Garfinkel), take the argument further and claim that it is impossible for sociologists to study human behaviour through scientific method and arrive at any kind of cause-and-effect relationship about it. Thus, those sociologists who classify Weberianism and symbolic interactionism as non-positivist approaches tend to identify phenomenological and ethnomethodological approaches as anti-positivist approaches because of their extreme stance.

Interactionism

As its name suggests, interactionism is concerned with social interaction among individual members of a society in a given situation. Social interaction involves reciprocal social action between individuals. Since interactionists consider social action as meaningful, they argue that an understanding of social action requires an interpretation of the meanings that the actors give to their activities. Interactionism is also called symbolic interactionism because it studies the symbolic (subjective) meaning of human interaction.

Let us imagine a situation with a couple in a room and the man lighting a candle. Now this action is open to a number of interpretations. For example, the couple may simply require light because a fuse has blown out or a power cut has occurred. Or they may be planning a candle light dinner. Alternatively, they may be trying to create a more intimate atmosphere as a prelude to a sexual encounter. Or the couple may be celebrating a birthday or a wedding anniversary. In each case, a different meaning is attached to the act of lighting a candle. To understand the act, it is therefore necessary to discover the meaning held by the actors.

Meanings are not fixed entities. As the above example shows, they depend in part on the context of the interaction. Meanings are also created, developed, modified and changed within the actual process of interaction. For example, a student entering a new class may initially define the situation as threatening and even hostile. This definition may be confirmed, modified or changed depending on the student's perception of the interaction that takes place in the classroom. The student may come to perceive the teacher and fellow students as friendly and understanding, and so change his assessment of the situation. The way in which actors define situations has important consequences. It represents their reality in terms of which they structure their actions. For example, if the student maintains a definition of the classroom as threatening and hostile, he may say little and speak only when spoken to. Conversely, if the definition changed, there would probably be a corresponding change in the student's actions in that context (ibid.).

In the example mentioned above, the actions of the student will depend in part on his interpretation of the way others see him. For this reason, many interactionists place particular emphasis on the idea of the self. They suggest that individuals develop a self-concept, a picture of themselves, which has an important influence on their actions. Charles Horton Cooley (1864–1929) and his colleague George Herbert Mead (1863–1931) were two American sociologists who formulated the original interactionist theories based on the finding that the self is the result of a learning process that occurs when individuals interact with those around them. A self-concept develops from interaction processes, since it is in large part a reflection of the reactions of others towards the individual. Hence, the term 'looking glass self' coined by Cooley. Actors tend to act in terms of their self-concept. Thus, if they are consistently defined as disreputable or respectable, servile or arrogant, they will tend to see themselves in this light and act accordingly.

Since interactionists are concerned with definitions of situation and self, they are also concerned with the process by which those definitions are constructed. For example, how does an individual come to be defined in a certain way? The answer to this question involves an investigation of the construction of meaning in the interaction processes. This requires an analysis of the way actors interpret the language, gestures, appearance and manner of others and their interpretation of the context in which the interaction takes place. The definition of an individual as a delinquent is an example. Various researches have shown that law enforcement agencies are more likely to perceive an act as delinquent if it occurs in a low-income area or a slum. Interactionist perspective could also be useful in partly explaining why a majority of undertrial prisoners languishing in Indian jails happen to be from poor and underprivileged sections of society. This fact has been acknowledged even by National Human Rights Commission and Supreme Court of India.

From an interactionist perspective, an individual from a lower caste or lower class is more likely to be defined as a juvenile delinquent for a petty offence if his appearance and manners are interpreted as aggressive by police officials and if his posture gives the impression of disrespect for authority. However, an educated middle-class youth may be let off merely with a warning for a similar offence. Definitions of individuals as certain kinds of persons are not, however, simply based on preconceptions that actors bring to interaction situations. A process of negotiation occurs from which the definition emerges. Often negotiations will reinforce preconceptions, but not necessarily. For example, a group of young lads from a slum may be able to convince the police office that the fight was a friendly brawl that did not involve intent to injure or steal. In this way, they may successfully promote images of themselves as high-spirited teenagers rather than as malicious delinquents. Definitions and meanings are therefore constructed in interaction situations by a process of negotiation.

The idea of negotiation is also applied to the concept of role. Like functionalists, interactionists employ the concept of role, but they adopt a somewhat different perspective. Functionalists, like all other structural approaches, tend to give primacy to the social structure over the individual. They view individual behaviour as being largely shaped by the norms, values and institutions of the society. Functionalists imply that roles are provided by the social system and individuals enact their roles accordingly with little or no scope for deviation from the prescribed role. Interactionists, however, argue that roles are often unclear, ambiguous and vague. This lack of clarity provides actors with considerable room for negotiation, manoeuvre, improvisation and creative action. At most, roles provide very general guidelines for action. What matters is how they are employed in interaction situations. For example, two individuals enter marriage with a vague idea about the roles of husband and wife. Their interaction will not be constrained by these roles. Their definition of what constitutes a husband, a wife and a marital relationship will be negotiated and continually renegotiated. It will be fluid rather than fixed, changeable rather than static. Thus, from an interactionist perspective, roles, like meanings and definitions of the situation, are negotiated in interaction processes. While interactionists admit the existence of roles, they regard them as vague and imprecise and, therefore, as open to negotiation. From an interactionist perspective, action proceeds from negotiated meanings that are constructed in ongoing interaction situations (ibid.).

The symbolic interactionist perspective has been criticised, however, for ignoring the larger issues of national and international order and change. It has also been faulted for ignoring the influence of larger social forces, such as social institutions, groups, cultures and societies, on individual interactions. In other words, symbolic interactionism has been largely criticised for its failure to take into account the role of macro-structures in shaping the human behaviour. Interactionists have often been accused of examining human interaction in a vacuum. They have tended to focus on small-scale face-to-face interaction with little concern for its historical or social setting. While symbolic interactionism provides a corrective to the excesses of societal determinism, many critics have argued that it has gone too far in this direction. Though they claim that action is not determined by structural norms, interactionists do admit the presence of such norms. However, they tend to take them as given rather than explaining their origin.

Similar criticisms have been made with reference to what many see as the failure of interactionists to explain the source of the meanings to which they attach such importance. Interactionism provides little indication of the origins of the meanings in terms of which individuals are labelled by teachers, police, etc. Critics argue that such meanings are not spontaneously created in interaction situations. Instead, they are systematically generated by the social structure. For example, for functionalists, meanings are largely culturally determined. Similarly, for Marxists, meanings are largely the product of class relationships. Thus, from this view point, interactionists have failed to explain the most significant thing about meanings: the source of their origin (ibid.).

Phenomenology

The word 'phenomenon' derives from Greek, meaning 'appearance'. *The Encyclopedia of Sociology* defines phenomenology as 'a method in philosophy that begins with the individual and his own conscious experience and tries to avoid prior assumptions, prejudices, and philosophical dogmas. Phenomenology, thus, examines phenomena as they are apprehended in their "immediacy" by the social actor' (Wallace and Wolf, 2012). The roots of phenomenological sociology are primarily in European phenomenological philosophy, especially in the work of the German philosopher Edmund Husserl (1859–1938), who was the first to use the term 'phenomenology'. Husserl defined phenomenology as interest in those things that can be directly apprehended by one's senses. This is the essential point about phenomenology: it denies that we can ever know more about things than what we experience directly through our senses. According to Husserl, all our knowledge comes directly from these sensory phenomena. Anything else is speculation, and Husserl argued that we should not even try to speculate. In other words, according to phenomenologists, individuals come into contact with the outside world only through their senses: touch, sight, smell, hear and taste. It is not possible to know about the outside world except through these senses (Wallace and Wolf, 2012).

However, simply possessing senses, though, is not enough for a person to be able to make any sense out of the world. If humans took their sense experiences at face value, they would be confronted by an infinite and unintelligible mass of sensory impressions. Hence, in order to make sense of infinite sensory experiences, humans begin to organise the world around them into phenomena; they classify their sense experiences into things that appear to have common characteristics. For example, the infinite variety of physical objects in the universe may be classified in terms of animate and inanimate objects. Animate objects may further be classified into mammals and non-mammals. Mammals may be subdivided into different species and species subdivided into different breeds. Thus, humans have a series of shorthand ways of classifying and understanding the world external to their own consciousness. However,

> Husserl did not believe that this process was in any sense objective. According to him, the classification of phenomena was entirely a product of the human mind, and could not be evaluated in terms of whether it was true or false. He did not deny the existence of physical objects beyond and outside the human mind, but he argued that, since people could only come into contact with them through their senses, they could never be sure about their true nature. Thus, in trying to secure knowledge, humans had to 'bracket' reality and common sense beliefs: that is, put them, as it were, inside brackets and forget about whether they were true or false. Once they had done this, they could turn their attention to a phenomenological understanding of the world. Husserl argued that, in order to understand social life, phenomenologists should study the way that humans placed the external world into categories by distinguishing particular phenomena. In doing so, it would be possible to understand the meaning of a phenomenon by discovering its essence.
>
> *(Haralambos and Holborn, 2014)*

Actually, what Husserl meant by this was that the researcher could find the distinguishing features (the essence) of a group of things (or phenomena) that humans classed together. Thus, for example, it might be found that a distinguishing feature – part of the essence – of a category of objects like a boat, canoe or ship was that they could float. Similarly, Atkinson's work on suicide shows how he tried to understand the nature of the phenomenon suicide by investigating how coroners distinguished it from other types of death.

Phenomenology, thus, differs from the social action approaches that have been examined so far in that it denies the possibility of explaining social action as such. Its emphasis is upon sensory experiences, internal workings of the human mind and the way that humans classify and make sense of the world around them. It is not concerned with the causal explanation of human behaviour in the same way as other perspectives. Phenomenologists try to understand the meaning of phenomena or things, rather than explaining how they came into existence (ibid.).

Further, phenomenology asks us not to take for granted the notions we have learnt but to question them instead, to question our way of looking at and our way of being in the world. Phenomenological sociologists study how people define their social situations once they have suspended or 'bracketed' their learned cultural notions. The basic proposition states that everyday reality is a socially constructed system of ideas that has accumulated over time and is taken for granted by its group members. This perspective takes a critical stance with regard to the social order, and, in contrast to functionalism, it challenges our culturally learned ideas. For example, phenomenological sociologists could question the prevailing gender relations in society by asking questions like, 'Is it natural for women to bear children and take the sole responsibility for nurturing and rearing them?', 'Are women biologically and intellectually inferior to men?', 'Why majority of women are restricted to household work?', etc. Contemporary feminists not only challenge these taken-for-granted ideas but also interject alternative definitions of female identity and propose other 'realities' for women. Similar questions could be raised by the members of various weaker and marginalised sections of society such as the poor, ethnic and religious minorities, gays and lesbians, etc. Phenomenological perspective would not only help them acquire a new insight into their situation but could possibly trigger social transformation. Thus, phenomenology also teaches us to question the way our world is ordered (Wallace and Wolf, 2012).

What precipitated the emergence of phenomenology? Wallace states that the rise of fascism in Europe and a period of social unrest in the 1960s in the wake of American civil rights movement, the anti-war movement and the feminist movement created conditions for the emergence of a new perspective. While Edmund Husserl wrote in the shadow of Nazism in Germany, his student, Alfred Schutz, moved to the United States in order to escape the Nazi regime. Various other contemporary writers such as Harold Garfinkel, Peter Berger, etc. wrote their major works during this period of social unrest. Phenomenology was developed along more sociological lines by Alfred Schutz (1899–1959).

In his attempt to adapt Husserl's philosophy to sociology, Schutz incorporated Weber's concept of *Verstehen* (subjective understanding). For Schutz, the meaning that the individual imparts to situations in everyday life is of prime importance; he puts the spotlight on the individual's own definition of the situation. For Schutz, the definition of the situation includes the assumption that individuals draw on a common *stock of knowledge*, that is, social recipes of conceptions of appropriate behaviour that enable them to think of the world as made up of 'types' of things like books, cars, houses, clothing and so on. Schutz's idea of the stock of knowledge is similar to Mead's *generalised other*. Schutz, thus, views individuals as constructing a world by using the typifications (or ideal types) passed on to them by their social group (Wallace, 2012).

The general approach adopted by phenomenology is a type of philosophy of knowledge, rather than a sociological perspective. Alfred Schutz was the first to try to explain how phenomenology could be applied to develop insights into the social world. Schutz's work stemmed from an interest in social life, but instead of focusing on meaning, for Schutz the central concept is *inter-subjectivity*. Schutz used this term to refer to a network of common influences and understandings that characterise the social world and individual experiences. For Schutz, the analysis of this intersubjective social world is the key to understand society.

Schutz developed a number of concepts to explain social world. He coined the term 'typifications' to explain the way in which individual's behaviour is structured or organised. According to Schutz,

> Typifications are prestructured constructs (schemas or pattern of ideas) that are used to communicate and to make sense of the world. Schutz saw language as potentially the most versatile mechanism for typifying: 'the typifying medium par excellence'. Typifications exist in all aspects of social life and are generally derived from and approved by society. People develop and use typifications in daily life to help them to understand their experiences. For example, when people meet others for the first time they may compare them with similar people they have met before and use this to guide their behaviour. People may also use typifications to make sense of a particular individual's behaviour – for example, 'that's typical of him – always late!' Typifications can also be used to group similar individuals into conceptual clusters. All individuals who fit a particular 'type' become members of that group.
>
> *(Churton and Brown, 2017)*

Schutz's main contribution was to insist that the way that humans classified and attached meaning to the outside world was not a purely individual process. Humans developed what he called 'typifications' – the concepts attached to classes of things that are experienced. According to Schutz, these typifications are not unique to each person, but are shared by members of a society. They are passed on from one generation to another through the process of socialisation, through learning a language, reading books or speaking to other people. Schutz argues that by the use of typifications, people are able to communicate with one another on the basis of the assumption that they see the world in the same way. Gradually, a member of society builds up a stock of what Schutz called 'common sense knowledge', which is shared with other members of society and allows humans to live and communicate together. Schutz believed such knowledge was essential to accomplish practical tasks in everyday life.

For example, he described the way in which a simple act such as posting a letter rests upon common sense knowledge and the existence of shared typifications. The person posting the letter assumes another person (a postal worker whom they may never have met) will be able to recognise the piece of paper with writing on it as a letter, and will deliver it to the address on the envelope. The person also assumes the recipient of the letter – again someone they might not have met – will have common sense knowledge similar to their own, and will therefore be able to understand the message, and react in an appropriate way (Haralambos and Holborn, 2014).

As typifications refer to people, Schutz coined the term 'recipes' to refer to situations. According to Schutz, recipes are the unnoticed rules that determine our response to routine situations. It is these rules that prevent us from making social faux pas.

For example, when someone asks you how you are, your response is determined by who is asking the question. If it is a friend or a colleague, you may say 'OK. Thanks – and you?', but if a doctor asks you during a consultation, you will provide him with details about your physical condition and probably will not enquire about the health of the doctor. It is these social conventions (recipes) that shape the way we respond in social situations (Churton and Brown, 2017).

It is worth mentioning here that although Schutz stresses that knowledge is shared, he does not think it is fixed and unchanging. Indeed, common sense knowledge is constantly modified in the course of human interaction. Schutz acknowledged that each individual has a unique biography and, thus, interprets and experiences the world in a slightly different way. However, the existence of a stock of common sense knowledge allows humans to understand, at least partly, each other's actions. In doing so, they convince themselves that there are regular and ordered patterns in the world, and in social life. From this point of view, humans create between themselves the illusion that there is stability and order in society, when in reality there is simply a jumble of individual experiences that have no clear shape or form (Haralambos and Holborn, 2014).

Thus, for phenomenologists, it is impossible to measure objectively any aspect of human behaviour. Humans make sense of the world by categorising it. Through language they distinguish between different types of objects, events, actions and people. For instance, some actions are defined as criminal and others are not; similarly, some people are defined as criminals while others are seen as law-abiding. The process of categorisation is subjective: it depends upon the opinions of the observer. Statistics are simply the product of the opinions of those who produce them. Thus, the police and the courts produce crime statistics, and they represent no more than the opinions of the individuals involved. If sociologists produce their own statistics, these too are the result of subjective opinions – in this case the opinions of sociologists.

Phenomenologists believe that it is impossible to produce factual data and that it is, therefore, impossible to produce and check causal explanations. The most that sociologists can hope to do is to understand the meaning that individuals give to particular phenomena. Phenomenologists do not try to establish what causes crime; instead they try to discover how certain events come to be defined as crimes and how certain people come to be defined as criminals. Phenomenologists therefore examine the way that police officers reach decisions about whether to arrest and charge suspects. In doing so, they hope to establish the meanings attached to the words 'crime' and 'criminal' by the police. The end product of phenomenological research is an understanding of the meanings employed by members of society in their everyday life.

Despite emphasising on a subjective understanding of social reality, phenomenological perspective has also been subjected to criticism. For example, the work of phenomenologist scholars is seen by critics as nothing more than a subjective characterisation of the social world. The theory and its various interpretations lack empirical validity. Phenomenological perspective is criticised for being a mere collection of abstract concepts than a coherent theory.

Ethnomethodology

Ethnomethodology is the most recent of all the theoretical perspectives discussed so far. The term was coined by the American sociologist Harold Garfinkel (1917–2011), who is generally regarded as its founder. Garfinkel's book *Studies in Ethnomethodology*, which provided the initial framework for the perspective, was published in 1967. Taken from Greek, *ethno* means 'folk' or 'people' and *methodology* means 'a systematic or standard method'. So, ethnomethodology literally means 'folk method', implying that the method is popular, traditional, conventional and widely shared. Roughly translated ethnomethodology means the study of the methods used by people to comprehend their social world. It is concerned with examining the methods and procedures employed by members of society to construct, account for and give meaning to their social world. Ethnomethodologists draw heavily on the European tradition of phenomenological philosophy and in particular acknowledge a debt to the ideas of the philosopher–sociologist Alfred Schutz (ibid.).

Many ethnomethodologists begin with the assumption that society exists only insofar as members perceive its existence. In ethnomethodology, the term 'member' replaces the interactionist term 'actor'. With this emphasis on members' views of social reality, ethnomethodology is generally regarded as a phenomenological approach. Ethnomethodology is a developing perspective which contains a diversity of viewpoints. The following account provides a brief and partial introduction. In order to study the methods that people use to define their world in everyday interaction situations, Garfinkel asked his students to interact with their friends, relatives and others in an anti-folk, anti-traditional, anti-conventional manner. On the basis of such experiments, Garfinkel discovered that the folk method generally involves defining the world in a vague and ambiguous manner, leaving out a lot of specific details. Consider the following two interactions: one involving a wife and her husband; the other, a student and his friend.

Interaction 1

On Friday my husband remarked that he was tired.

I asked, 'How are you tired? Physically, mentally or just bored?'
'I don't know, I guess physically, mainly', he responded.
'You mean that your muscles ache or your bones?' I asked.
A little irritated, he said, 'I guess so. Don't be so technical'.

Interaction 2

> *Friend:* How are you?
> *Student:* How am I in regard to what? You mean my health, my finances, my school work, my sex life, my peace of mind, my …
> *Friend:* Look, I was just trying to be polite. Frankly, I don't give a damn how you are (Thio, 2003).

Why do people interacting with one another define things vaguely and leave out the specific details? Garfinkel concluded that the prime reason is the popular assumption that *people understand one another without specific details.* However, this assumption of shared understanding, or the folk method based on it, is so often employed, widely shared and taken for granted that most people are not aware that it exists. Only when such assumption is questioned, as in examples given above, people come to realise that they have not only held it for a long time but also that it can be incorrect. As a consequence, they may become irritated, angry or embarrassed. Such negative reactions show the discomfort of having their cherished and taken-for-granted assumption taken away (ibid.).

This insight was later applied by Garfinkel to explain social order. Since one of the major concerns of sociology is the explanation of social order, various schools of sociology have explained social life as ordered and regular. Structural approaches, in particular, view social action as systematic and patterned. For example, from a functionalist perspective, social order derives ultimately from the functional prerequisites of social systems which require its presence as a necessary condition of their existence. Social action assumes its systematic and regular nature from the fact that it is governed by values and norms which guide and direct behaviour. From a conflict (Marxian) perspective, social order is seen as precarious, but its existence is recognised. It results from the constraints imposed on members of society by their position in the relations of production and from the reinforcement of these constraints by the superstructure. From an interactionist perspective, social order results from interpretive procedures it, therefore, employed by actors in interactions. It is a 'negotiated order' in that it derives from meanings which are negotiated in the process of interaction and involves the mutual adjustment of the actors concerned. The net result is the establishment of social order, of an orderly, regular and patterned process of interaction. Although the above perspectives provide very different explanations for social order, they nevertheless agree that some form of order actually exists and that has an objective reality (Haralambos and Holborn, 2014).

Unlike the above discussed perspectives, ethnomethodologists either suspend or abandon the belief that an actual or objective social order exists. Instead, they proceed from the assumption that social life appears orderly to members of society. For ethnomethodologists, social life appears orderly because the members of a society perceive and interpret social reality as such. Thus, in the eyes of the members, their everyday activities seem ordered and systematic, but this order is not necessarily due to the intrinsic nature or inherent qualities of the social world. In other words, it may not actually exist. As explained earlier, shared understanding or common sense knowledge enables the members to describe and explain social world in systematic and orderly terms. Social order therefore becomes a convenient fiction, an appearance of order constructed by members of society. Thus, in Atkinson's study of suicide, coroners (investigating officers) were able to justify and explain their actions to themselves and to others in terms of the common sense ways they went about reaching a verdict. Atkinson argues that coroners have a 'common sense theory' of suicide. If information about the deceased fits the theory, they are likely to categorise the death as suicide. Thus, the methods and accounting procedures used by members for creating a sense of order form the subject matter of ethnomethodological enquiry. Zimmerman and Wieder state that the ethnomethodologist is concerned with how members of society go about the task of seeing, describing, and explaining order in the world in which they live (ibid.)

Ethnomethodologists are highly critical of other perspectives in sociology. They argue that 'conventional' sociologists have misunderstood the nature of social reality. They have treated the social world as if it had an objective reality which is independent of members' accounts and interpretations. By contrast, ethnomethodologists argue that the social world consists of nothing more than the constructs, interpretations and accounts of its members. The job of the sociologist is, therefore, to explain the methods and accounting procedures which members employ to construct their social world. According to ethnomethodologists, this is the very job that mainstream sociology has failed to do. There is little doubt that the ideas and research of ethnomethodologists are innovative and interesting. The research appears to have a number of practical applications. Businesses and other institutions can use ethnomethodological techniques to improve the quality of relationships and working practices. However, critics argue that the ethnomethodological research can at best be carried out at a small scale and it lacks a historical and social setting. In other words, it lacks the sweeping power of a grand theory and offers little explanation of society at large. It has also been criticised for being highly unscientific, being nothing more than the subjective interpretation of individual sociologists studying a particular social situation (Churton and Brown, 2017).

Although there are some differences between the various variants of social action approaches, they all agree that the positivist approach has produced a distorted picture of social life. The distinction between positivist and anti-positivist (or phenomenological) approaches is not as clear-cut as this section has implied. There is considerable debate over whether or not a particular theory should be labelled positivist or anti-positivist. Often, it is a matter of degree since many theories lie somewhere between the two extremes. After reading about these different perspectives, you might be wondering: Which one is right? The answer can be found in the following story from sociologist Elliot Liebow (Thio, 2003):

Mr. Shapiro and Mr. Goldberg had an argument they were unable to resolve. It was agreed that Mr. Shapiro would present the case to a rabbi.

The rabbi said to Mr. Shapiro, 'You are right'.

When Mr. Goldberg learned of this, he ran to the rabbi with his version of the argument. The rabbi said to him, 'You are right'.

Then the rabbi's wife said to the rabbi, 'You told Mr. Shapiro he was right and you told Mr. Goldberg he was right. They can't both be right!'

The rabbi said to his wife, 'You are right too'.

As the rabbi would say, each of the above discussed perspectives in sociology is right in its own way. Each perspective looks and explains our social world from a certain angle. While structural approaches give us a macro view of society, social action approaches offer us a micro view of society. In other words, for structural approaches, society comes first. They primarily look at and explain individual's behaviour as largely being shaped by the social structure of a society comprising of patterned and institutionalised norms and values. Social action approaches, on the other hand, focus on the ability of individual actors to interpret a given situation and act accordingly, in their own subjective ways. Thus, each perspective is useful because we cannot take everything about the complex social world into account at once. We need some vantage point. Each perspective tells us what to look for, and each brings some aspect of society and human behaviour into sharper focus. Brought together, these diverse perspectives can enrich our sociological knowledge of the world (Thio, 2003).

Uniting Structural and Social Action Approaches

In the preceding section on major theoretical strands of research methodology, we broadly discussed two major types of approaches in sociology. Structural approaches, both consensus and conflict, emphasise the way in which the structure of society directs human behaviour. Social action approaches, also called interpretive approaches, instead assume humans as capable of attributing meanings and interpreting situations. Hence, these approaches argue that humans create society through their actions. As stated earlier, such a division of sociological approaches into structural and social action approaches is not neat and clear-cut. Most approaches in sociology show some concern with both social structure and social action. And most approaches emphasise one aspect of social life at the expense of another.

As a result, some sociologists in recent times have argued that it would be desirable to produce a sociological theory that combined an understanding of both social structure and social action. This insight could be traced back to C. Wright Mills' idea of sociological imagination. Charles Wright Mills (1916–1962) was an American sociologist who introduced the idea of sociological imagination. Mills in his famous book *The Sociological Imagination* (1959) helps us explore the connections between our individual experiences and the larger social world. He emphasised on the fact that we must try to look at our seemingly *personal troubles* from a social context. The sociological imagination emphasises the structural bases of social problems. Individuals may have *agency*, the ability to make their own choices, but their actions and even their choices may be constrained by the realities of the social structure. Sociology, thus, is uniquely able to connect personal experiences to larger social issues by applying the sociological imagination.

More recently, Anthony Giddens, a British sociologist, has attempted to overcome the division between structure and action. Giddens claims that structure and action are two sides of the same coin. Neither structure nor action can exist independently; both are intimately related (Haralambos and Holborn, 2014). Giddens uses the term 'structuration' to highlight both the intimate and the intricate relationship between social structure and social action. Giddens argues that:

> While we are all influenced by social context, our behaviour is never determined entirely by that context. Sociology investigates the connections between what society makes of us and what we make of society and ourselves. Our activities both structure – or give shape to – the social world around us and, at the same time, are structured by that world. The social contexts of our lives are not a mass of completely random events or actions; they are structured, or patterned, in distinct ways. There are regularities in the ways we behave and in the relationships we have with one another.
>
> *(Giddens, 2017)*

Giddens further argues that social structure is not like a physical structure, such as a building, which once built exists independent of human actions. Human societies are always in the process of structuration. They are reconstructed at every moment by the very 'building blocks' that compose them, that is, human beings (and their actions). Giddens explains this with an example of coffee producers. For example, it is an individual's choice to have a cup of coffee. A cup of coffee, however, does not automatically arrive in his hands. To have a cup of coffee, the individual may choose to go to a particular coffee shop and decide to have a particular coffee out of choices available, such as a latte or an espresso, etc. When the individual takes this decision, then, along with millions of other such people, he is shaping the market for coffee and affecting the lives of coffee producers living perhaps thousands of miles away on the other side of the world (Giddens, 2017).

Positivism and Its Critique

Many of the founders of sociology believed it would be possible to create a science of society based upon the same principles and procedures as the natural sciences like chemistry and biology, even though the natural sciences often deal with inanimate matter and so are not concerned with feelings, emotions and other subjective states. The most influential attempt to apply natural science methodology to sociology is known as positivism.

Auguste Comte (1798–1857), who is credited with coining the term 'sociology' and regarded as one of the founders of the discipline, maintained that the application of the methods and assumptions of the natural sciences produce a 'positive science of society'. He believed that this reveals the evolution of society followed 'invariable laws'. It shows that the behaviour of man was governed by the principles of cause and effect, which were just as invariable as the behaviour of matter, the subject of the natural sciences (Haralambos and Holborn, 2014).

In sociological terms, the positivist approach makes the following assumptions. First, the behaviour of man, like the behaviour of matter, can be objectively measured. In other words, just as the behaviour of matter can be quantified by measures such as weight, temperature and pressure, methods of objective measurement can be devised for human behaviour. Such measurement is essential to explain behaviour. Theories may then be devised to explain observed behaviour. This emphasis on the objective measurement of human social behaviour forces the positivist scholars to rely more on the quantitative methods while conducting research. You will read more on quantitative methods in the next chapter.

Second, the positivist approach in sociology places particular emphasis on behaviour that can be directly observed. It argues that those aspects of behaviour which are not directly observable, such as meanings, feelings and purposes, are not particularly important and can be misleading. For example, crime in a given society can be observed and quantified with the help of data from police records. In other words, the amount of different types of crime or the rate of crime in a given society can be objectively measured. These observable facts on crime, therefore, form reliable data. However, the reasons that people may give for their criminal act could be infinite. These reasons are neither directly observable nor their validity could be established beyond doubt due to their highly subjective nature. While one person may say that he committed crime because he needed money for medical treatment, the other may justify his act in the name of social justice and so on.

As mentioned earlier, positivists, in order to make sociology a scientific discipline, wanted to mould sociology along the line of natural sciences. The positivists' emphasis on observable 'facts' is due largely to the belief that human behaviour can be explained in much the same way as the behaviour of matter. Natural scientists do not inquire into the meanings and purposes of matter for the obvious reason of their absence. Atoms and molecules do not act in terms of meanings, they simply react to external stimuli. Thus, if heat, an external stimulus, is applied to matter, that matter will react. The job of the natural scientist is to observe, measure and then explain that reaction. The positivist approach to human behaviour applies a similar logic. People react to external stimuli, and their behaviour can be explained in terms of this reaction. Thus, people commit crime in response to social stimuli which could either be poverty, injustice or ineffective law and order. The meanings and purposes they attach to their behaviour and action are largely inconsequential.

Thus, it has often been argued that the structural theory (also called systems theory) in sociology adopts a positivist approach. Once behaviour is seen as a response to some external stimulus, such as economic forces or the requirements of the social system, the methods and assumptions of the natural sciences appear appropriate to the study of humans. Marxism has often been regarded as a positivist approach since it can be argued that it sees human behaviour as a reaction to the stimulus of the economic infrastructure. Functionalism has been viewed in a similar light. The behaviour of members of society can be seen as a response to the functional prerequisites of the social system. These views of the structural or systems theory represent a considerable oversimplification of complex theories. However, it is probably fair to say that the structural or systems theory is closer to a positivist approach (ibid.).

However, the assumptions of positivism came under severe criticism. Some scholars argued that in order to have a complete understanding of man's social behaviour, it is not only important but also necessary to take into account the unique meanings, motives and values that underlie such behaviour. Initially this view was advocated by anti-positivist scholars (also known as neo-Kantian scholars in Germany) like Wilhelm Dilthey (1833–1911), Wilhelm Windelband (1848–1915) and Heinrich Rickert (1863–1936). Later, Weber also argued that behaviour of man in society is qualitatively different from that of physical objects and biological organisms. He argued that unlike matter, man has consciousness – thoughts, feelings, meanings, intentions and an awareness of being. Because of this, his actions are meaningful. He defines situations and gives meaning to his actions and those of others. As a result, he does not merely react to external stimuli, he does not simply behave, he acts. Thus, if action stems from subjective meanings, it follows that the sociologist must discover those meanings in order to understand action. He cannot simply observe action from the outside and impose an external logic upon it. He must interpret the internal logic which directs the actions of the actor. These views constitute basic assumptions of social action approaches. Some of the important social action approaches, like Weberianism, symbolic interactionism, phenomenology and ethnomethodology, have been discussed above. Further, anti-positivist scholars also question the positivists' view with regard to the possibility of arriving at universal generalisation about human behaviour. Some anti-positivist scholars argue that given the diversity and dynamism of human behaviour at best, only limited generalisations may be possible. However, scholars belonging to phenomenological and ethnomethodological traditions deny even this possibility.

Fact, Value and Objectivity

The word fact derives from the Latin term *factum*. A fact is something that has really occurred or is actually the case. The usual test for a statement of fact is its verifiability, that is, whether it can be proven to correspond to experience. Scientific facts are verified by repeatable experiments. Thus, a fact is regarded as an empirically verifiable observation. A theory, on the other hand, is a set of ideas which provides an explanation for something. It is an abstract and generalised statement which tends to establish a logical interrelationship between facts (concepts or variables). Theories involve constructing abstract interpretations that can be used to explain a wide variety of empirical situations.

Thus, in sociology, we can say that a sociological theory is a set of ideas which provides an explanation for human society. As discussed earlier, sociology is a scientific study of society, and we know that scientific research is a guided search for facts based on the formulated hypothesis. A hypothesis is a tentative statement asserting a relationship between certain facts. It is the hypothesis that guides the researcher what data to look for. A social scientist or researcher conducts a field research and collects data (facts) in order to test the hypothesis. After data are collected, they are processed. Thereafter, the researcher tests the hypothesis against the processed data. If the hypothesis is proved (i.e. supported by data), then it becomes a thesis. If it is repeatedly proved, it becomes a theory. However, if the hypothesis is held to be universally true, then it becomes the law.

Thesis → Theory → Law

Thesis, theory and law, they are all generalisations. They represent different degrees of generalisations. In natural sciences, we hear about several laws, but in social sciences we only have theories. Social sciences study social behaviour of man, which is guided by unique meanings and motives, values and beliefs, etc. Hence, given the diversity and dynamism of human society in general, it is nearly impossible to arrive at a universally valid generalisation or law of human society.

Let us now discuss the interrelationship of theory and facts (empirical research). Robert K. Merton, the American sociologist, has elaborated on this aspect in detail in his essays. Merton's two classic essays on the relationship between sociological theory and empirical research appear as chapters in his best-known book, *Social Theory and Social Structure*, first published in 1949. In his essay 'The Bearing of Sociological Theory on Empirical Research', Merton argues that without a theoretical approach, we would not know what facts to look for at the beginning of a study or in interpreting the results of research. Often, existing theories serve as a source for hypothesis formulation and, thus, stimulate and guide further research resulting in discovery of new facts. For example, Marxian theory suggests that increasing economic inequalities is the primary cause of alienation and class conflict in modern capitalist societies. This theory can serve as a source for our hypothesis to understand the rising discontentment among masses in the contemporary Indian society. Thus, you may start exploring to what extent the existing economic inequality is a factor in the rise of naxalism or caste conflicts in rural India, etc. Thus, theory helps to define which kinds of facts are relevant. Second, theory establishes a rational link between two or more variables and, thus, can act as a tool for prediction and control. For example, various theories have highlighted female education as a critical factor in the overall social development. Thus, in order to improve their ranking on the social development index, countries with low female education can initiate female education programmes at the national level because we now know that female education has direct bearing on the social development of a society. Third, as stated earlier, theory is an abstract and generalised statement which tends to establish a logical interrelationship between facts (concepts or variables). Theories involve constructing abstract interpretations and, thus, making the knowledge cross-culturally useful. For example, Weber's ideal type of bureaucracy is nothing but an abstraction which can serve as tool for a comparative study of bureaucratic models across societies.

In another essay, 'The Bearing of Empirical Research on Sociological Theory', Merton argues that empirical research is generally assigned a rather passive role: the testing or verification of hypotheses. Merton argues that empirical research goes far beyond the passive role of verifying and testing theory. It does more than confirm or refute hypotheses. According to Merton, research plays an active role: it performs at least four major functions which help shape the development of theory. It initiates, it reformulates, it deflects and it clarifies theory. Merton explains in his essay that how under certain conditions a research finding gives rise to social theory. He calls it 'serendipity pattern'. Merton argues that fruitful empirical research not only tests theoretically derived hypothesis, it also originates a new hypothesis. This might be termed the 'serendipity' component of research, i.e. the discovery, by chance or sagacity, of valid results which were not sought for. In simpler words, it implies that during the course of research some unanticipated but strategic data may come to light, which may initiate a new theory altogether. For example, Elton Mayo, a professor at the Harvard Business School, in his investigation at the Hawthorne plant of Western Electric Company in Chicago conducted a series of experiments designed to investigate the relationship between working conditions and productivity. Mayo began with the assumptions of scientific management, believing that the physical conditions of the work environment, the aptitude of the worker and the financial incentives were the main determinants of productivity. However, during the course of his research, Mayo struck upon the role of informal groups and group norms in determining the productivity. From the Hawthorne studies developed the human relations school, which challenged and led to the reformulation of the conventional scientific management approach. It stated that scientific management provided too narrow a view of man and that financial incentives alone were insufficient to motivate workers and ensure their cooperation. The Hawthorne studies moved the emphasis from the individual worker to the worker as a member of a social group. The behaviour of the worker was seen as a response to group norms rather than simply being directed by economic incentives and management-designed work schemes. It was found that the informal work groups develop their own norms and values, which are enforced by the application of group sanctions. The power of such sanctions derives from the dependence of the individual upon the group. He has a basic need to belong, to feel part of a social group. He needs approval, recognition and status, needs which cannot be satisfied if he fails to conform to group norms (Merton, 1972).

Thus, there is an intricate relation between theory and fact. Facts (i.e. empirical research) and theories are inherently dependent on each other. Factual research and theories can never be completely separated. We can only develop valid theoretical approaches if we are able to test them out by means of factual research.

Now we will discuss the role of values in sociological enquiry and associated with it is the problem of objectivity.

As stated earlier, the subject matter of sociology is the study of human behaviour in society. All human behaviour is guided by values. Moreover, social research is in itself a type of social behaviour guided by the value of 'search for true knowledge'. Values are socially accepted standards of desirability. In other words, a value is a belief that something is good and desirable. It defines what is important and worthwhile. Values differ from society to society and culture to culture. For example, in the West, the dominant values are individualism and materialism, which are this-worldly in nature. While in India, *moksha* had been a long-cherished goal of human life and is other-worldly in nature.

In order to have a complete understanding of man's social behaviour, it is not only important but also necessary to take into account the unique meanings, motives and values that underlie such a behaviour. Initially, this view was advocated by anti-positivists scholars (also known as neo-Kantian scholars in Germany) like Wilhelm Dilthey (1833–1911), Wilhelm Windelband (1848–1915) and Heinrich Rickert (1863–1936). Later, Weber also argued that behaviour of man in society is qualitatively different from that of physical objects and biological organisms. He argued that unlike matter, man has consciousness – thoughts, feelings, meanings, intentions and an awareness of being. Because of this, his actions are meaningful. He defines situations and gives meaning to his actions and those of others. As a result, he does not merely react to external stimuli, he does not simply behave, he acts. Thus, if action stems from subjective meanings, it follows that the sociologist must discover those meanings in order to understand action. He cannot simply observe action from the outside and impose an external logic upon it. He must interpret the internal logic which directs the actions of the actor.

However, the views mentioned above are quite antithetical to the propositions of positivist tradition in sociology. Auguste Comte, who is credited with coining the term 'sociology' and regarded as one of the founders of the discipline, maintained that the application of the methods and assumptions of the natural sciences would produce a 'positive science of society'. In terms of sociology, the positivist approach makes the following assumptions. The behaviour of man, like the behaviour of matter, can be objectively measured. Just as the behaviour of matter can be quantified by measures such as weight, temperature and pressure, methods of objective measurement can also be devised for human behaviour. The positivist approach in sociology places particular emphasis on behaviour that can be directly observed. It argues that factors which are not directly observable such as meanings, feelings, motives, etc. are not particularly important and can be misleading. This is best manifested in the works of Durkheim. Durkheim in his book *The Rules of Sociological Method* (1895) states that social facts must be treated as 'things' and all the preconceived notions about the social facts must be abandoned.

On the basis of the above discussed ideas of both positivist and anti-positivist scholars, one thing is clear that without taking into account the values that underlie human behaviour, a comprehensive understanding of man's social behaviour would not be possible. Our reliance on positivist approach alone would produce a partial picture of social reality. But if we undertake study of values as well in the course of sociological research, then the problem of objectivity raises its head (because we know that values are subjective). Let us now discuss what objectivity means, and how different scholars have tried to address the problem of objectivity in sociology.

Objectivity is a 'frame of mind' so that the personal prejudices or preferences of the social scientists do not contaminate the collection and analysis of data. Objectivity is the goal of scientific investigation. Sociology, also being a science, aspires for the goal of objectivity. Thus, scientific investigations should be free from the prejudices of race, colour, religion, sex or ideological biases. The need of objectivity in sociological research has been emphasised by all important sociologists. For example, Durkheim, in his book *The Rules of the Sociological Method* (1895), stated that 'social facts' must be treated as 'things' and all preconceived notions about the social facts must be abandoned. Even Max Weber emphasised the need of objectivity when he said that sociology must be free from any kind of value biases on the part of the researcher. According to Radcliffe-Brown, the social scientist must abandon or transcend his ethnocentric and egocentric biases while carrying out researches. Similarly, Malinowski advocated 'cultural relativism' while conducting anthropological fieldwork in order to ensure objectivity.

However, objectivity continues to be an elusive goal at the practical level. In fact, one school of thought represented by Gunnar Myrdal (1898–1987) states that complete objectivity in social sciences is a myth. Gunnar Myrdal in his book *Objectivity in Social Research* (1970) argues that total objectivity is an illusion which can never be achieved, because all research is always guided by certain viewpoints, and viewpoints involve subjectivity. Myrdal argues that subjectivity creeps in at various stages in the course of sociological research. For example, the very choice of topic of research is influenced by personal preferences and ideological biases of the researcher. How personal preferences influence the choice of the topic of research can be illustrated from a study made by Professor Schwab. In his study, Schwab analysed 4,000 scientific papers produced over a span of centuries. He found that the choice made by scientists in pursuing their research was based on their personal preferences as determined by personality factors and social circumstances.

Besides personal preferences, the ideological biases acquired in the course of education and training also have a bearing on the choice of the topic of research.

The impact of ideological biases on social research can be very far-reaching as can be seen from the study of Tepoztlán village in Mexico. Robert Redfield (1897–1958), an American anthropologist, studied the village in 1930 with a functionalist perspective and concluded that there exists total harmony between various groups in the village, while another American anthropologist, Oscar Lewis (1914–1970), studied this village at almost the same time from Marxist perspective, and found that the society was conflict-ridden. Here we can see how the differences of ideological perspectives had a bearing on the research findings even though the society studied was the same.

Subjectivity can also creep in at the time of formulation of hypothesis. Normally, hypotheses are deducted from existing body of theory. Now all sociological theories are produced by and limited to particular groups whose view points and interests they represent. Thus, the formulation of a hypothesis will automatically introduce a bias in the sociological research.

The fourth stage at which subjectivity creeps in the course of research is that of collection of empirical data. No technique of data collection is perfect. Each technique may lead to subjectivity in one way or the other. For example, in case of participant observation, the observer as a result of 'nativisation' acquires a bias in favour of the group he is studying. While in non-participant observation, the sociologist belongs to a different group than that under study. He is likely to impose his values and prejudices. In all societies, there are certain prejudices. For example, in America, people have prejudices against the blacks, and in India, people have prejudices against untouchables or women. Such prejudices of the observer may influence his observation. Further, in case of interview as a technique of data collection, the data may be influenced by (i) the context of the interview; (ii) the interaction of the participants; (iii) the participants' definition of the situation; and (iv) adequate rapport not being established between them, which can create communication barriers. Thus, according to P.V. Young, interview sometimes carries a double dose of subjectivity.

Finally, subjectivity can also creep in due to field limitations, as was found in the case of André Béteille's study of Sripuram village in Tanjore, where the Brahmins did not allow him to visit the untouchable locality and study their point of view.

Thus, complete objectivity continues to be an elusive goal. Myrdal argues that sociology at best could aspire for the goal of value neutrality on the part of the researcher. This could be attained by either of the following ways:

1. The researcher should exclude all ideological or non-scientific assumptions from his research.
2. The researcher should make his value preference clear in the research monograph. As Weber has also stated that the researcher should be value-frank.
3. The researcher should not make any evaluative judgement about empirical evidence.

4. The researcher should remain indifferent to the moral implication of his research.
5. Highly trained and skilled research workers should be employed.
6. Various methods of data collection should be used and the result obtained from one should be cross checked with those from the other.
7. Field limitations must be clearly stated in the research monograph.

Eminent sociologist T.K. Oommen in his book *Knowledge and Society* emphasises the importance of 'contextualisation' in sociological enquiry. Oommen argues that while objectivity in natural sciences is *generalising objectivity*, in social sciences it is *particularising objectivity*. He suggests that objectivity in social sciences has to be *contextual objectivity*. Contextual objectivity, according to Oommen, can be determined by intra-subjectivity and inter-subjectivity. Intra-subjectivity is one where the same researcher (with his given value orientation) studies the same object (the social group) at two different points of time using same method and arrives at similar conclusions. Inter-subjectivity, on the other hand, is one when two researchers (with similar value orientations) study the same object at the same time using same method and arrive at similar conclusions (Oommen, 2013).

Of late, a group of American sociologists who have come to be known as 'radical sociologists' have advocated that total value neutrality is not desirable. Commitment to total political neutrality reduces the sociologist to the status of a mere spectator, and sociologists can play no creative role in the society. After all, the basic purpose of sociological knowledge is social welfare. But, given such excessive preoccupation with value neutrality, the role of sociologists has been like, to use W.H. Auden's phrase, 'Lecturing on navigation while the ship is going down'. C. Wright Mills has also complained that sociology has lost its 'reforming push'.

Alvin W. Gouldner, most remembered for his work *The Coming Crisis of Western Sociology* (1970), argued that sociology must turn away from producing objective truths and understand the subjective nature of sociology and knowledge in general and how it is bound up with the context of the times. He called for a reflexive sociology in which there would be no forgetting of the idea that the sociologist was part of society and played a social role. As the commonplace has it, sociology cannot be practised outside its historical and social context. Thus, according to C. Wright Mills, Alvin W. Gouldner and others, sociology must have commitment to certain basic human values, and sociologists should be ready to defend human freedom and the pursuit of reason.

Reflexive Sociology

Reflexive sociology is the newly emerging perspective in sociology. Reflexivity refers to the 'reflexive monitoring of action', that is, the way in which humans think about and reflect upon what they are doing in order to consider acting differently in future. Humans have always been reflexive up to a point, but in pre-industrial societies, the importance of tradition limited reflexivity. Humans would do some things simply because they were the traditional things to do. However, with modernity, tradition loses much of its importance and reflexivity becomes the norm. Social reflexivity implies that social practices are constantly examined and reformed in the light of incoming information about those very practices, thus continuously altering their character.

Contemporary sociologists want sociology to be a reflexive discipline. They try to understand society, and to feed the knowledge they gain back into social life. Social change is informed by our understanding of how society works and what the consequences of various actions might be. Anthony Giddens summed up this idea in his book *The Consequences of Modernity* (1990):

> The practical impact of social sciences is both profound and inescapable. Modern societies together with the organizations that compose and straddle them are like learning machines, imbibing information in order to regularize their mastery of themselves. ... Only societies reflexively capable of modifying their institutions in the face of accelerated social change will be able to confront the future with any confidence. Sociology is the prime medium of such reflexivity.
>
> *(Bilton et al., 2016)*

This concept of a reflexive sociology is nothing new, but it can help us to grasp the place of sociological understanding today. It is important to note what Giddens is *not* saying in this passage. He is not suggesting here that social scientists know best. This means they cannot plan social development from above. Sociologists do not write the script for the future. They cannot tell people what values they should believe in or what their goals should be. Those who are capable of taking action against and change society are not social scientists but members of society with varying amounts of power. Social science knowledge is a resource that people can draw upon when planning social change. However, social science knowledge is necessary for not only policymakers but also for people like us. All of us need frameworks to interpret our world and act upon it. Social science knowledge is one important source (among others) of frameworks to guide our action.

However, there is inevitably a critical dimension if sociology is offering people an understanding of their social position. Alvin Gouldner emphasised this in his book *The Coming Crisis of Western Sociology* (1970). The solution he offered then – a liberating, reflexive sociology – is extremely relevant today. Gouldner was one of the first modern sociologists to reject the focus of the 1950s on social order and continuity in favour of studying change, conflict and social renewal through action. His work expressed the mood of radicalism in sociology in the 1960s and 1970s.

Alvin W. Gouldner (1920–1980), an American sociologist, in his most influential work *The Coming Crisis of Western Sociology* (1970) offered a substantial and exhaustive argument for 'reflexive sociology'. Reflexive sociology, as put forward by Alvin W. Gouldner, is a meaningful alternative to positivism. Gouldner, an American sociologist, wrote with a high degree of moral sensitivity, and critiqued positivism. Against the view that science in general and sociology in particular is concerned with producing objective truths, Gouldner argued that knowledge is not independent of the knower and that sociology is intimately bound up with the socio-economic and political context in which it exists.

Gouldner advocated 'reflexive sociology' in response to methodological dualism (implicit in positivism), which was the dominant methodological assumption in early twentieth century in American sociology. Methodological dualism was based on the elementary distinction of subject and object. Natural sciences in general were based on this premise. Since the subject matter of natural sciences was physical reality or matter, their prime concern was to discover the underlying pattern in nature and arrive at certain universal laws which can help in predicting and controlling natural phenomenon. In sociology, methodological dualism was emphasised by scholars belonging to the positivist tradition in France and America. They argued that like natural sciences, social sciences can also study social reality in an objective manner, and the information thus arrived at could be used to predict and control man's social behaviour and social change. Methodological dualism in sociology implied a clear distinction between the *inquiring subject* (social scientist) and the *studied object* (the social group whom he observes). Methodological dualism enjoins the sociologist to be detached from the world he studies. It sees his involvement with his object of study primarily from the standpoint of its contaminating effect upon the information system.

Gouldner warned social scientists of the methodological dualism which was implicit in positivism. This dualism separates the knower from the known, subject from object, fact from value. Not only that, it takes the view that if the sociologist engages politically, emotionally and aesthetically with the object of his study, the 'scientific nature' of the discipline would suffer. This cold objectivity, as Gouldner would argue, is essentially an expression of alienation, that is, the alienation of the sociologist from his own self. It is like looking at sociological knowledge as just a piece of amoral technique.

> Methodological dualism is based upon a fear; but this is a fear not so much of those being studied as of the sociologist's own self. Methodological dualism is, at bottom, concerned to constitute a strategy for coping with the feared vulnerability of the scholar's self. It strives to free him from disgust, pity, anger, from egoism or moral outrage, from his passions and interest, on the supposition that it is a bloodless and disembodied mind that works best. It also seeks to insulate the scholar from the values and interests of his other roles and commitments on the dubious assumption that these can be

anything but blinders. It assumes that feeling is the blood enemy of intelligence, and that there can be an unfeeling, unsentimental knower.

(Gouldner, 1970)

Gouldner rejects the assumption of methodological dualism in sociology. He argues
that positivists who emphasise on methodological dualism in sociology do so primarily because they conceive of knowledge only as information. But, according to
Gouldner, the ultimate goal of sociology is not to seek neutral information about
social reality but rather such knowledge which facilitates a better understanding
of social reality in terms of men's changing interests, expectations, values, etc. In
this regard, Gouldner cites the example of Weber's *Verstehen* method. In contrast
to positivists, Weber had emphasised the need for the interpretative understanding
of social action. He argued that in order to have a better understanding of social
action, it is necessary to take into account the unique meanings and motives that
underlie such action. Weber suggests that this can be done by the sociologist by
establishing empathetic liaison with the actor. In other words, it implies that the
sociologist should imaginatively place himself in the actor's position and then try
to understand the motives of the actor which guided his action.

Gouldner, however, pleads for methodological monism and asserts that the
separation between the knower and the known must be overcome, because you
cannot know others without knowing yourself. That is why, self-reflexivity is
absolutely important. To know others, a sociologist cannot simply study them
but must also listen to and confront himself. Knowing is not an impersonal effort
but 'a personalised effort by whole, embodied men'. Reflexive sociology invites
methodological monism, and, therefore, alters the very meaning of knowledge.
It does not remain merely a piece of information. Instead, it becomes an awareness. It generates self-awareness and new sensitivity. Reflexive sociology, you
would appreciate, is heavily demanding. Unlike positivist sociology in which
you can remain 'neutral' and 'apolitical', reflexive sociology demands your moral
commitment and ethical engagement. You cannot separate your life from your
work. Gouldner wrote,

> Reflexive Sociology, then, is not characterized by what it studies. It is
> distinguished neither by the persons and the problems studied nor even by
> the techniques and instruments used in studying them. It is characterised,
> rather, by a relationship it establishes between being a sociologist and being
> a person, between the role and the man performing it. Reflexive sociology
> embodies a critique of the conventional conception of segregated scholarly
> roles and has a vision of an alternative. It aims at transforming the sociolo-
> gist's relation to his work.
>
> *(Gouldner, 1970)*

In other words, Gouldner argues that the knowledge of the world cannot be
advanced apart from the sociologist's knowledge of himself and his position in

the social world. He argues that to know others a sociologist cannot simply study them but must also listen to and confront himself. Awareness of the self is seen as an indispensable avenue to awareness of the social world. Reflexive sociology aims at transforming the sociologist's relation to his work. It is characterised by the relationship it establishes between being a sociologist and being a person, between the role and the man performing it.

Reflexive sociology rejects the subject/object dichotomy, that is, the sociologist who studies and those whom he studies or observes. Rather, the historical mission of sociology, according to Gouldner, is to raise the sociologist's awareness of himself and his position in the social world. Thus, a reflexive sociologist must become aware of himself as both *knower* and as *agent of change*. He cannot know others unless he also knows his intentions towards and his effects upon them. He cannot know others without knowing himself, his place in the social world, and the forces – in society and in himself – to which he is subjected.

Gouldner argues that reflexive sociology is radical sociology. It is radical because in contrast to positivism, it rejects the assumption of methodological dualism, i.e. subject/object dichotomy. It is radical because it is a historically sensitive sociology as it seeks to deepen the awareness of sociologists about themselves, of their own historically evolving character and of their place in a historically evolving society. It is radical because it embodies and advances certain specific values. As a work ethic, it affirms the creative potential of the sociologist and encourages him to take an independent stand of his own and resist the demands for conformity by the established authorities and institutions. Hence, according to Gouldner, a reflexive sociology would be a moral sociology.

Take an example. Suppose you wish to study the phenomenon called 'slum culture'. The way of studying this is, of course, a highly positivistic/technical research. You hire research assistants, send them to a particular slum with a questionnaire and instruct them to distribute copies of it after random sampling. The data you gather get classified and quantified, and you make your conclusions. These are the conclusions derived from 'hard' facts. And never do you feel the need to engage yourself as a person with the slum. In other words, your dispassionate exercise is not different from the way a mathematician solves a puzzle or a scientist works in a lab.

Now, Gouldner's reflexive sociology would oppose this kind of research. Instead, it would make you reflect on your own self and your politics and morality. Possibly you are urban, upper class, English speaking and relatively privileged. What does it mean for you to understand the slum culture? Isn't it the fact that their suffering cannot be separated from your privilege? Can you understand them without questioning this asymmetrical power? These questions born out of self-reflexivity would possibly create a new sociology, which far from objectifying the world tries to create a new one. Possibly new trends in sociological research emanating from feminist and Dalit movements resemble this sort of reflexive sociology, because in these research trends one sees not just technical objectivity, but essentially a high degree of empathy, an urge to understand suffering and a striving for an alternative praxis (process).

LET'S THINK

Dear Learner, I hope you have enjoyed learning about some of the technical aspects of sociology. It is these technicalities that set apart sociological knowledge from our common sense beliefs and help make sociology a scientific discipline. Sociology is a scientific discipline of its own kind. Various theoretical and methodological perspectives comment about the scientific nature of the discipline in their own respective ways. You must remember that though these perspectives differ from each other, they must not be seen as contradictory. Rather, these different perspectives must be seen as complementary to each other, and thus enable us to develop a comprehensive understanding of society and its various social processes. You have also learned in this chapter about reflexive sociology. Do you agree that reflexive sociology offers a refreshing break from the classical sociological approaches? Can you think of some examples from contemporary sociological traditions that are reflexive in nature?

For Practice

Q1. Is sociology a science? Give reasons for your answer.

Q2. Examine the basic postulates of positivism and post-positivism.

Q3. Is non-positivistic methodology scientific? Illustrate.

Q4. Examine the notion that 'complete objectivity is a myth' in social science research.

Q5. Examine ethnomethodological and phenomenological perspectives as critique of positivism.

Q6. Examine the problems of maintaining objectivity and value neutrality in social science research.

Q7. Reflexive sociology is a radical sociology. Comment.

Model Answers

Q. Examine the notion that 'complete objectivity is a myth' in social science research.

A. Objectivity is a 'frame of mind' so that the personal prejudices or preferences of the social scientists do not contaminate the collection and analysis of data. Sociology too being a scientific discipline aspires for the goal of objectivity. However, sociologists belonging to different sociological traditions differ in their opinion with regard to the degree of objectivity that could be achieved in sociological research.

Early sociologists like Comte, Spencer and Durkheim maintained that the application of the methods and assumptions of the natural sciences would produce a 'positive science of society'. They were called positivists and emphasised on the study of only those aspects of social behaviour that can be directly observed. However, scholars belonging to the anti-positivist tradition argued that social action is meaningful and asserted for interpretive understanding of social action. Some of the major interpretative approaches, also called social action approaches, are Weberianism, symbolic interactionism, phenomenology and ethnomethodology. They all share the view that complete objectivity, like in natural sciences, is not possible in sociology. But Weber, in particular, believed that sociology can at best aspire for value neutrality.

Taking the argument of Weber even further, Gunnar Myrdal argued that complete objectivity in social sciences is a myth. In his book *Objectivity in Social Research* (1970), Myrdal argued that total objectivity is an illusion which can never be achieved, because all research is always guided by certain viewpoints, and viewpoints involve subjectivity. Myrdal argues that subjectivity creeps in at various stages in the course of sociological research such as at the time of choosing the topic of research, during the course of education and training, at the time of formulation of hypothesis and identification of field, during the selection of techniques of data collection, etc. These views of Myrdal could be substantiated from conclusions of two different studies of Tepoztlan village in Mexico conducted by Robert Redfield and Oscar Lewis, respectively.

Further, a group of American sociologists, who have come to be known as 'radical sociologists', have questioned the possibility as well as the desirability of objectivity (as advocated by positivists) and value neutrality (as suggested by Weber) in sociology. More recently, eminent Indian sociologist T.K. Oommen has tried to address the debate on objectivity in social sciences. In his book *Knowledge and Society*, Oommen emphasises the importance of 'contextualisation' in sociological enquiry. Oommen argues that while objectivity in natural sciences is *generalising objectivity*, in social sciences it is *particularising objectivity*. He suggests that objectivity in social sciences has to be *contextual objectivity*.

Q. Reflexive sociology is a radical sociology. Comment.

A. Reflexive sociology emerged as a critique to positivist approach and expressed the mood of radicalism in sociology in the 1960s and 1970s. American sociologist Alvin W. Gouldner (1920–1980) in his most influential work, *The Coming Crisis of Western Sociology* (1970), offered a substantial and exhaustive argument for 'reflexive sociology'.

Gouldner advocated 'reflexive sociology' in response to methodological dualism (implicit in positivism), which was the dominant methodological assumption in the early twentieth century in American sociology. Methodological dualism was based on the elementary distinction of *subject* and *object*, with objectivity as its primary concern. In sociology, methodological dualism was emphasised by scholars belonging to the positivist tradition in France and America. They argued that like natural sciences, social sciences can also study social reality in an objective manner, and information thus arrived at could be used to predict and control man's social behaviour and social change.

Gouldner rejected the assumption of methodological dualism in sociology and instead pleaded for methodological monism. He asserted that the separation between the knower and the known must be overcome, because you cannot know others without knowing yourself. The historical mission of sociology, according to Gouldner, is to raise the sociologist's awareness of himself and his position in the social world. Thus, a reflexive sociologist must become aware of himself as both *knower* and as *agent of change*. Reflexive sociology alters the very meaning of knowledge. It does not remain merely a piece of information. Instead, it generates self-awareness and new sensitivity. Unlike positivist sociology, in which you can remain 'neutral' and 'apolitical', reflexive sociology demands your moral commitment and ethical engagement. As a work ethic, it affirms the creative potential of the sociologist and encourages him to take an independent stand of his own and resist the demands for conformity by the established authorities and institutions. Hence, reflexive sociology is both radical and moral.

Reflexive sociology, in contemporary times, has provided a refreshing break from the classical approaches. It has further intensified the debate centring around the theoretical orientations and methodological issues in sociological enquiry. Marxist sociology, subaltern sociology, feminist sociology, environmental sociology, etc. can be cited as some of the examples of reflexive sociology.

References

Bilton, Tony, Kevin Bonnet, Pip Jones, Tony Lawson, David Skinner, Michelle Stanworth and Andrew Webster. *Introductory Sociology*. 4th Edition. Hampshire: Palgrave Macmillan, 2016.

Churton, Mel and Anne Brown. *Theory & Method*. 2nd Edition. Hampshire: Palgrave Macmillan, 2017.

Giddens, Anthony and Philip W. Sutton. *Sociology*. 8th Edition. New Delhi: Wiley India, 2017.

Gouldner, Alvin. *The Coming Crisis of Western Sociology*. New York: Basic Books, 1970.

Haralambos, Michael, Martin Holborn, Steve Chapman and Stephen Moore. *Sociology: Themes and Perspectives*. 8th Edition. London: Collins, 2014.

Merton, R.K. *Social Theory and Social Structure*. New Delhi: Arvind Publishing House, 1972.

Myrdal, Gunnar. *Objectivity in Social Research*. London: Gerald Duckworth, 1970.

Nagla, Bhupendra K. and Sheo Bahal Singh. *Introducing Sociology*. New Delhi: National Council of Educational Research and Training, 2002.

Oommen, T.K. *Knowledge and Society: Situating Sociology and Social Anthropology*, 2nd Edition. New Delhi: Oxford University Press, 2013.

Thio, Alex. *Sociology: A Brief Introduction*. Boston: Pearson Education, 2003.

Wallace, Ruth A. and Alison Wolf. *Contemporary Sociological Theory: Expanding the Classical Tradition*. 6th Edition. New Delhi: PHI Learning, 2012.

4

RESEARCH METHODS AND ANALYSIS

Field

A systematic and scientific research is essential for sociology to claim itself as a scientific discipline. However, whatsoever be the theoretical perspective or methodological orientation of the researcher, ultimately, he has to carry out his research in the field. So, let's try to understand what 'field' implies in a sociological enquiry and what are the problems or challenges associated with the fieldwork.

In the context of sociological research, the term 'field' refers to the members of a social group which is the prime object of study for a social scientist. In its early phase, Malinowski and Radcliffe-Brown laid the foundations of intensive fieldwork among anthropologists in Britain. However, in the Indian context, it was M.N. Srinivas who strongly advocated for the 'field-view' of Indian society in place of the 'book-view'. The book-view of Indian society was largely championed by Indologists like B.K. Sarkar, G.S. Ghurye, Radhakamal Mukerjee and Irawati Karve. Indologists have claimed that the Indian society could be understood only through the concepts, theories and frameworks of Indian civilisation. They believed that an examination of the classical texts, manuscripts, archaeological artefacts, etc. should be the starting point for the study of the present (Beteille, 2009).

Srinivas was critical of the 'book-view' of Indian society. He argued that the book-view gave a distorted picture of society by dwelling on the ideals of the past from which the present reality departed considerably. The book-view of Indian society presented an idealised picture of its institutions – marriage, family, kinship, caste and religion – dwelling more on what they were supposed to be than on how they actually worked. For example, the book-view had represented caste in terms of the invariant and immutable scheme of the four *varnas*. Field studies

DOI: 10.4324/9781003291053-5

shifted attention away from the fourfold scheme of the *varnas* to the operative units of the system, namely the innumerable *jatis*. They also drew attention to the ambiguities of caste ranking and the very distinctive process of caste mobility. Thus, the field-view revealed the gap everywhere between the ideal and the actual. By bringing to attention ambiguities, contradictions and conflicts, it paved the way for a better understanding of the dynamics of social change. Thus, the idea of an unchanging and immutable society began to give way, and the field-view changed not only the perception of India's present, but to some extent also the perception of its past (Beteille, 2009).

However, like every other method, fieldwork too is marked by its own set of challenges and problems in conducting genuine sociological research. First and foremost, the researcher faces the problem of the choice of the 'field' to carry out his fieldwork as no typical field exists in reality. As stated earlier, unlike natural sciences, sociology cannot study any particular social phenomena in a laboratory by the experimental method due to certain moral and ethical reasons. As a result, social research takes place in the open, where, unlike a scientific experiment, it is extremely difficult to control the extraneous variables. Hence, it becomes increasingly challenging for the social scientist to establish a cause–effect relationship between the variables stated under the hypothesis. After having identified the field for his research, the researcher faces the challenge of entry into the field. This implies that unless the researcher is able to establish a good rapport with the natives, he would find it hard to carry out his research. Thus, in order to seek the cooperation of the native population for his data collection, the researcher must gain their acceptability. In this, the social background of the researcher also plays an important role.

Further, since the researcher can carry out only a limited study of any given social phenomenon, the problem of holism looms large. Since holistic study appears to be impractical in the study of complex societies, the researcher should keep in mind that the segment he is studying is a part of the larger and complex whole and should look for interrelationships. A researcher may also face problems in the formulation of hypothesis and might have to reformulate or modify his hypothesis because hypotheses cannot be formulated in vacuum, without the knowledge of the field. Further, the issues of objectivity and ethical neutrality also need to be addressed. The researcher should be aware of his biases and prejudices and try to make certain that they do not influence his collection and interpretation of data. Though some of these challenges are endemic to any social science enquiry, yet they can be dealt with a cautious and informed approach on the part of the researcher. Since the fieldwork basically involves dealing with people, the researcher must be empathetic and flexible in his approach and employ the services of well-trained field workers.

In the ultimate analysis, it may be argued that in any field research, the sociologist is an integral part of the research process. The data so collected have no existence independent of the researcher. His data are 'constructions, not reflections of facts or relationships alone. In the process of knowing, external facts are sensorily perceived and transformed into conceptual knowledge'. Thus, the sociologist as a researcher is an active factor in the creation of knowledge and is not just a mere passive recipient. The importance of his perception makes a sociologist as integral part of the research process as the data he observes (Srinivas et al., 2002).

Reflexivity and the Changing Notion of Field and Fieldwork Practices

You now know that reflexivity offers an alternate perspective to study social reality. Reflexivity in social anthropological research implies that the ideas about 'field' and 'practices' of fieldwork are constantly examined and reformed in the light of new developments, thus continuously altering their character. Reflexivity challenges the conventional notions of anthropological research with regard to field and practices of fieldwork. Early social anthropological research was largely concerned with the study of small-scale societies in their natural state or surroundings. Hence, the term 'field' came to denote a distinct social group which was to be studied in its unique sociocultural and geographical setting. Early anthropological research was largely based on the dichotomy of subject and object. In other words, it was based on the separation of the social scientist (subject) from those 'others' whom he observes (object). It was based on the assumption that over-involvement of the social scientist with his object of study (social group) may contaminate the research findings. The idea about 'otherness' remained remarkably central to the fieldwork practices of Malinowski, A.R. Radcliffe-Brown, etc.

Amory shows how these ideas about 'otherness' and taking for granted of a white subject have shaped the field of African studies in the United States. She shows that African American scholars were discouraged from working in Africa, on the grounds that they were 'too close' and would not manage to be 'objective', while white scholars were judged to have the appropriate distance from the black 'other'. This helps to explain why the contemporary field of African studies contains remarkably few black American scholars. Kath Weston too in her study of gay and lesbian communities in United States arrived at a similar conclusion. She argued that her position as a native ethnographer itself blurs the subject/object distinction on which ethnography is conventionally founded. She calls native ethnographer a 'virtual anthropologist'.

Akhil Gupta and James Ferguson also question the conventional notion of field and argue that in the light of new developments, there is a need for reconstruction of field and fieldwork practices. They argue that processes such as decolonisation and globalisation, accompanied by processes of diffusion and acculturation, have challenged the traditional definition of field and the very idea of a clearly demarcated space of 'otherness'. They argue that the conventional notion about the 'field' in terms of a homogenous social group with its unique culture and geographical surroundings has come to be questioned in the wake of globalisation. Social groups are no longer tightly territorialised or spatially bounded. Further, the processes of diffusion and acculturation have significantly altered the homogenous character of social groups, and today cultural heterogeneity is more common.

Gupta and Ferguson further question the 'field/home dichotomy' in social anthropological research. They question the traditional notion of field which rested on the idea that different cultures exist in discrete and separate places. They argued that the 'location' of the field should not merely be seen in geographical sense alone. They advocated retheorising of fieldwork from spatial sites to social and political locations in terms of unequal power relations. For example, subaltern approach in sociology has significantly contributed towards a better understanding of various socio-economic and political processes in India, which were until now largely studied from an elitist perspective. Gupta and Ferguson argue that with decolonisation, there is proliferation of domestic research led by the natives. As a result, today, the very idea of 'otherness', which was central to the early anthropological fieldwork, is subjected to review. Hence, there is a need to modify the practices of fieldwork accordingly.

Further, Gupta and Ferguson also question the fundamental premise of early anthropological fieldwork practices that only professionally trained observers could be trusted to collect ethnographic data. Paul Radin in his study found that his untrained native research assistants proved to be better than the academically and professionally qualified observers in terms of gathering valuable data. This is because, as Radin argues, such professionals are socially separated from those whom they study by their very training. The training of the professional observers erects an undesirable barrier between themselves and the persons to be interrogated. It may lead to difficulty in establishing direct and immediate contact and building rapport with their sources of information. On the other hand, the native research assistants or local intellectuals are better positioned at least for certain sorts of data collection (Gupta and Fergusson, 1997).

Thus, reflexivity has significantly contributed in reconstruction of the ideas about field and fieldwork practices in social anthropology. Such a rethinking of the idea of the 'field' coupled with an explicit attentiveness to 'location' might open the way for a different kind of anthropological knowledge and a different kind of anthropological subject.

Let us now discuss some of the fundamental characteristics of quantitative as well as qualitative research methods.

Quantitative and Qualitative Research Methods

Methodology is an integral aspect of any scientific discipline. Every discipline requires a methodology to reach its conclusions. In other words, it must have ways of producing and analysing data so that theories can be tested, accepted or rejected. In the absence of a systematic way of producing knowledge, the findings of a subject can be dismissed as guesswork or mere common sense assumptions.

You know that sociology first developed in Europe in the nineteenth century when industrialisation resulted in massive social changes. Accompanying these social changes were intellectual changes during which science started to enjoy a higher reputation than ever before. Many of the founders of sociology believed it would be possible to create a science of society based upon the same principles and procedures as that of the natural sciences.

However, not all sociologists have agreed that it is appropriate to adopt the methodology of the natural sciences. These sociologists believed that the subject matter of the social and natural sciences is fundamentally different. While natural sciences deal with matter, social sciences deal with man and his behaviour. Since human beings are conscious beings, their action is meaningful. Hence, for these sociologists, methods of natural sciences alone would be inadequate. They instead emphasised on the interpretive methodology to understand the subjective meanings that underlie social action.

Thus, on the basis of the above discussion, two broad traditions within sociology could be identified.

1. Those who advocated the use of scientific and quantitative methods (positivists)
2. Those who supported the use of more humanistic and qualitative methods (anti-positivists)

However, in recent years, the new-generation sociologists have started questioning such rigid divisions between quantitative and qualitative methodologies. Most sociologists instead advocate a combination of both quantitative and qualitative methods in sociological research.

Quantitative Research Methods

Quantitative research in sociology is largely associated with the 'positivist tradition'. Early sociologists belonging to the positivist tradition, such as Comte, Spencer, Durkheim, etc., believed that the methods and procedures of natural sciences could be adopted in sociology as well. Quantitative research is associated with a number of techniques of data collection such as survey, questionnaire, structured interview and secondary sources of data, etc. Some of the features of quantitative research in sociology are discussed next.

1. **Social Facts**: Early sociologists like Comte and Durkheim, who were positivists, placed particular emphasis on behaviour that can be directly observed. It argues that those aspects of behaviour which are not directly observable, such as meanings, feelings and purposes, are not particularly important and can be misleading. Durkheim went to the extent of stating that social facts should be treated as 'things'. This means that the belief systems, customs and institutions of society – the facts of the social world –

should be considered as things in the same way as the objects and events of the natural world.

2. **Statistical Data**: The second aspect of quantitative approach as advocated by positivists is the use of statistical data. Positivists believed that the behaviour of man, just like the behaviour of matter, can be objectively measured and, thus, it was possible to classify the social world in an objective way. For example, Durkheim collected data on social facts such as the suicide rate and the membership of different religions.

3. **Correlation**: The third aspect of positivist methodology entails looking for correlations between different social facts. A correlation is a tendency for two or more things to be found together, and it may refer to the strength of the relationship between them. For example, in his study of suicide, Durkheim found an apparent correlation between a particular religion, Protestantism, and a high suicide rate.

4. **Causation**: The fourth aspect of positivist methodology involves a search for causal connections. Positivists believed that on the basis of the data collected through quantitative methods, patterns could be identified and a cause-and-effect relation between two or more variables or social phenomena could be established. For example, Durkheim in his study of suicide had explained that low solidarity among the Protestants was the causal factor for high suicide rate among them.

5. **Generalisation and Replicability**: The quantitative researcher is invariably concerned to establish that his result of a particular investigation can be generalised to the larger population. Positivists like Comte and Durkheim believed that just as natural sciences could arrive at universal laws with regard to matter, laws of human behaviour can also be discovered in social sciences. They believed that laws of human behaviour can be discovered by the collection of objective facts about the social world, by the careful analysis of these facts and by repeated checking of the findings in a series of contexts (replication).

Positivism is based upon an understanding of science that sees science as using a mainly inductive methodology. An inductive methodology starts by collecting the data. The data are then analysed, and out of this analysis theories are developed. Once the theory has been developed, it can then be tested against other sets of data to see if it is confirmed or not. If it is repeatedly confirmed (replicated), then positivists like Comte, Durkheim, etc. assume that they have discovered a law of human behaviour (Haralambos and Holborn, 2014).

Qualitative Research Methods

As mentioned earlier, qualitative research methods in sociology are largely advocated by sociologists belonging to social action approach who emphasise on the interpretive understanding of human social behaviour. These sociologists prefer sacrificing a certain precision of measurement and objectivity in order to get closer to their subjects, to examine the social world through the perspective of the people they are investigating. They sometimes refer to quantitative researchers as those who 'measure everything and understand nothing'. Qualitative research fundamentally refers to that approach to the study of the social world which seeks to describe and analyse the culture and behaviour of humans and their groups from the point of view of those being studied. As discussed earlier, quantitative data are data in a numerical form, for example, official statistics on crime, suicide and divorce rates. By comparison, qualitative data are usually presented in words, e.g. an ethnographic account of a group of people living in poverty, providing a full and in-depth account of their way of life, or a transcript of an interview in which people describe and explain their attitude towards and experience of religion. Compared to quantitative data, qualitative data are usually seen as richer, more vital, as having greater depth and as more likely to present a true picture of a way of life, of people's experiences, attitudes and beliefs. Participant observation, unstructured interview, focus group discussion, life history or case study method are some of the major methods or techniques of data collection in qualitative research. The main intellectual undercurrents which tend to be viewed as providing qualitative research with their distinct methodology are Weberianism, symbolic interactionism, phenomenology, ethnomethodology, etc. Some of the features of qualitative research in sociology are discussed next.

1. **Empathetic Description of Social Reality**: Since social action theorists believe that social action is meaningful, they focus on the interpretation of the meanings that social actors have probably given to their act. The most fundamental characteristic of qualitative research is its express commitment to viewing events, actions, norms, values, etc. from the perspective of the people who are being studied. This is explicitly stated by Weber in his *Verstehen* methodology.

2. **Contextualism**: Social action theorists believe that social action does not exist in isolation, rather it is expressed in a given socio-economic, political and historical context. Hence, qualitative research exhibits a preference for contextualism in its commitment to understanding events, behaviour, etc. in their respective context. It is almost inseparable from another theme in qualitative research, namely 'holism', which entails an undertaking to examine social entities – schools, tribes, firms, slums, delinquent groups, communities or whatever – as wholes to be explicated and understood in their entirety.

3. **Emphasis on Processual Dimension**: Qualitative research views social life in processual and dynamic terms, rather than static terms. The emphasis on process can be seen as a response to the qualitative researcher's concern to reflect the reality of everyday life which, they tend to argue, takes the form of streams of interconnecting events. The general image that qualitative research conveys about the social order is one of interconnection

and change. For example, symbolic interactionists explain social order as a 'negotiated order'.

4. **Flexibility**: Qualitative researchers tend to favour a research strategy which is relatively open and unstructured. Such strategy allows them access to unexpectedly important topics which may not have been visible to them had they foreclosed the domain of study by a structured, and hence, potentially rigid strategy.

However, some sociologists, in recent years, have questioned the need for such a rigid division between quantitative and qualitative methodology and have advocated combining the two approaches. Alan Bryman has suggested a number of ways in which a plurality of methods – a practice known as *triangulation* – can be useful.

1. Quantitative and qualitative data can be used to check on the accuracy of the conclusions reached on the basis of each.
2. Qualitative research can be used to produce hypotheses which can then be checked using quantitative methods.
3. The two approaches can be used together so that a more complete picture of the social group being studied is produced.
4. Qualitative research may be used to illuminate why certain variables are statistically correlated. For example, Durkheim concluded in his study on suicide that the rate of suicide varies from religion to religion because of their varying degree of solidarity.

Bryman believes that both quantitative and qualitative research have their own advantages. Neither can produce totally valid and completely reliable data, but both can provide useful insights into social life. He argues that each has its own place and they can be most usefully combined. Generally, quantitative data tend to produce rather static pictures, but they can allow researchers to examine and discover overall patterns and structures in society as a whole. Qualitative data are less useful for discovering overall patterns and structures, but they allow a richer and deeper understanding of the process of change in social life (ibid.).

Many of the debates about the merits of particular research methods focus on questions of 'reliability' and 'validity'. In the natural sciences, data are seen to be 'reliable' if other researchers using the same methods of investigation on the same material produce the same results. By replicating an experiment, it is possible to check for errors in observation and measurement. Once reliable data have been obtained, generalisations can then be made about the behaviour observed. No sociologist would claim that the social sciences can attain the standards of reliability employed in the natural sciences. Many would argue, however, that sociological data can attain a certain standard of reliability. Generally speaking, quantitative methods are seen to provide greater reliability. They usually produce standardised data in a statistical form: the research can be repeated and the results checked. Qualitative methods are often criticised for failing to meet the same standards of reliability. Such methods may be seen as unreliable because the procedures used to collect data can be unsystematic, the results are rarely quantified and there is no way of replicating a qualitative study and checking the reliability of its findings.

Further, data are considered 'valid' if they provide a true picture of what is being studied. A valid statement gives a true measurement or description of what it claims to measure or describe. It is an accurate reflection of social reality. Data can be reliable without being valid. Studies can be replicated and they produce the same results, but those results may not be a valid measure of what the researcher intends to measure. For instance, statistics on church attendance may be reliable but they do not necessarily give a true picture of religious commitment.

Supporters of qualitative methods often argue that quantitative methods lack validity. Statistical research methods may be easy to replicate, but they may not provide a true picture of social reality. They are seen to lack the depth to describe accurately the meanings and motives that form the basis of social action. They use categories imposed on the social world by sociologists, categories that may have little meaning or relevance to other members of society. To many inter-pretive sociologists, only qualitative methods can overcome these problems and provide a valid picture of social reality.

Researchers are sometimes attracted to quantitative methods because of their practicality. Quantitative methods are generally less time-consuming and require less personal commitment. It is usually possible to study larger and more repre-sentative samples which can provide an overall picture of society. Qualitative research often has to be confined to the study of small numbers because of prac-tical limitations. It is more suited to providing an in-depth insight into a smaller sample of people. Hence, most sociologists today tend to combine both quantita-tive and qualitative methods in their social research to enhance its reliability as well validity.

Concepts and Hypothesis

In our discussion on 'Scientific Method and Sociological Research' in Chapter 3, we have learned that a social scientist starts his research by defining precisely what it is that he wants to know. This he does by formulating a clear and verifi-able hypothesis. Let us now discuss hypothesis and its relevance in sociological enquiry in detail.

According to Theodorson and Theodorson, a hypothesis is a tentative state-ment asserting a relationship between certain facts. Bailey has also said that a hypothesis is a proposition stated in a testable form which predicts a particular relationship between two or more variables. Since statements in hypothesis have to be put to empirical investigation, the definition of hypothesis excludes all such statements which are merely opinions or value judgements, for example, *'All politicians are corrupt'*. In other words, a hypothesis carries clear implications for testing the stated relationship, that is, it contains variables that are measurable and also specifies how they are related. A statement that lacks variables or that does not explain how the variables are related to each other is no hypothesis in scientific sense. Variables are measurable phenomena whose values can change. In social sciences, variables may be understood as the social characteristics that can be converted into measurable forms and analysed. This point will become clearer in our subsequent discussion on operationalisation of concepts (Ahuja, 2008).

In social sciences, the social scientists tend to study and explore the various aspects of social reality and interrelationship among them. Since social reality is infinite, social scientists make sense of this infinite social reality through logical abstractions. These logical abstractions or mental constructs are nothing but the 'concepts'. Hence, when a social scientist is carrying out research to test his hypothesis, he is actually exploring the relationship between the two concepts. Thus, in general, variables in social sciences are nothing but the concepts which are the part of the research. However, in particular, variables are described as the specific characteristics or attributes of the more general concepts. You will soon learn that in order to carry out research, the variables or the concepts used in the hypothesis should be clearly defined and operationalised. This point will be discussed in detail with examples in our subsequent discussion on operationalisation of concepts. Further, the terms 'independent variable', 'dependent variable' and 'extraneous variable' used commonly in research have already been discussed in our earlier discussion on the 'scientific method'.

A few examples of hypothesis are cited below:

- suicide rates vary inversely with social integration
- urbanisation leads to proliferation of nuclear families
- literacy rate is directly related to average marital age
- children from broken homes more likely tend to be delinquents

Hypothesis formulation is of fundamental importance in any research. A hypothesis looks forward. It provides direction to research. Without it, research is unfocused and may be reduced to a random empirical wandering. Results of such unguided research would be of little use. The hypothesis is the necessary link between theory and the investigation that leads to the discovery of additions to knowledge. Goode and Hatt argue that theory and hypothesis are very closely interrelated. Hypotheses are the deduced propositions from the existing theory. These hypotheses, when tested, by means of empirical investigations, are either proved or disproved. Hence, in turn, hypothesis testing leads to either revalidation or reformulation of the theory (Goode and Hatt, 2006).

Let us now discuss a few essential characteristics of a good hypothesis. The most fundamental of them all is that a hypothesis must be conceptually clear. This means that the variables or the concepts used in the hypothesis should be clearly defined and operationalised. Operationalisation of concepts refers to the process of defining the concepts in terms of those attributes which could be empirically observed during research. In other words, operationalisation refers to the process of converting concepts in their empirical measurements. For example, the concept of anomie, in general terms, is defined as a 'state of normlessness' in society. Now, anomie could be observed in social, economic and political systems of a given society. For instance, the concept of anomie in social sphere may be operationalised by identifying the quantifiable attributes such as incidence of suicide, crime, honour killings, etc. on which empirical data can be collected. Similarly, in political sphere, the concept of anomie may be operationalised when it is explained in terms of the attributes like stability of the government, corruption in the government, people's perception about the government, etc. In the economic sphere, the concept of anomie may be operationalised when it is defined in terms of attributes like economic inequality, poverty, unemployment, etc.

Second, the variables or the concepts used in hypothesis should be commonly accepted and communicable. In simpler words, it implies that there should be uniformity in the definition and meaning of the concepts used in hypothesis. Once the concepts have been clearly defined and operationalised by means of their empirical referents, a hypothesis must also specify the relationship between the variables. A hypothesis that does not explain how the concepts are related to each other is no hypothesis in scientific sense. For example, suicide rates vary inversely with social integration.

Another important characteristic of a good hypothesis is that it should be related to the available techniques of data collection and interpretation. In other words, a hypothesis must be so formulated keeping in mind the availability as well as applicability of the techniques of data collection in the respective field (socio-geographical area identified to carry out the research). Further, a good hypothesis must be related to a body of theory. As stated earlier, one of the key features of any scientific discipline is its cumulative nature. Likewise, sociological theories are built upon one another, extending and refining the older ones and producing the new ones. This would be possible only if the hypotheses are related to a body of theory (Ahuja, 2008).

Dear Learner, so far we have discussed the meaning of hypothesis, its relevance in sociological enquiry and some characteristics of a good hypothesis. We have discussed that a hypothesis is a tentative statement asserting a relationship between two or more concepts or variables. What do you understand by concept? What is the relevance of concepts in sociology? What are the problems associated in defining the concepts in sociology? Let us now try to understand and answer these questions.

Concepts are the logical abstractions or mental constructs created from sense impressions, percepts or experiences. Concept formation is an essential step in the process of sociological reasoning. Concepts are the tools with which we think, criticise, argue, explain and analyse. We build up our knowledge of the social world not simply by looking at it but through developing and refining concepts which will help us make sense of it. Concepts, in that sense, are the building blocks of human knowledge. Concepts help in comprehending the reality that a science is engaged in studying. Concepts act as mediums of short-cut communication among those associated with the enquiry (social scientists).

Concepts and hypotheses are the core of social research. For any social research to be fruitful, it is important that the concepts or variables mentioned in the hypothesis are operationalised. As discussed earlier, operationalisation of concepts refers to the process of defining concepts in terms of those attributes which could be empirically observed during research. In other words, operationalisation refers to the process of converting concepts in their empirical measurements. For example, the concept of alienation is generally explained in terms of powerlessness, meaninglessness, normlessness, social isolation and self-estrangement. Now, in a given workplace, powerlessness could be empirically measured in terms of the indicators such as participation in the administration, degree of control over the decision-making process, grievance redressal mechanism, etc.

Let us now discuss the various problems in defining concepts in sociology. Social reality is dynamic in character, and so are the concepts in sociology. Sociology being a relatively young discipline relies more and more on empirical research for verification and validation of the existing theories and concepts. Hence, new findings lead to modification of the established concepts and theories. In other words, it leads to re-conceptualisation or re-specification of a concept. For example, earlier the personality differences between men and women were explained in biological terms. However, later-day research by anthropologists like Margaret Mead, who in her work *Sex and Temperament in Three Primitive Tribes* studied three tribes, namely Arapesh, Mundugumor and Tchambuli (in the western Pacific), concluded that personality patterns were culturally determined rather than biologically. In brief, her comparative study revealed a full range of contrasting gender roles. Among the Arapesh, both men and women were peaceful in temperament and neither men nor women engaged in fight. Among the Mundugumor, the opposite was true: both men and women were of violent temperament. Among the Tchambuli, gender role reversal was found. While the men 'primped' and spent their time decorating themselves, the women worked and were the practical ones. Similarly, you can also discuss here how the concepts of class, caste (*jati*), etc. have undergone changes with new findings put forward by later day researches.

Second, sociology as a discipline is rapidly attaining maturity with the contributions of several established and highly reputed schools like the British school, the American school, the French school and the German school. But the contributions from diverse schools of thought give rise to the problem of ensuring uniformity in the definition and meaning of the concepts. Concepts develop from a shared experience. Since each school of sociological thought puts forward its own set of concepts and defines the concept in the context of its unique social setting, it gives rise to the problem of communication. For example, the concepts of *Gemeinschaft* and *Gesellschaft*, which were coined by the German sociologist Ferdinand Tonnies, have no English equivalent. The terms *Community* and *Association*, which are English translations of these words, do not convey the particular sociological meaning of these two German words.

Third, due to the very subject matter of sociology, the terms used to denote scientific concepts may also have meanings in other frames of reference. For instance, the term 'bureaucracy', which implies a particular type of social structure, may either be seen as a rationally designed authority structure or as an administrative institution characterised by red-tapism, corruption and official disregard for the public interest.

Another problem associated with defining the concepts in social sciences is that the same term may refer to different phenomena. For example, the term 'function' in one sense may be used to denote the contributions which a given practice or belief makes towards the continued existence of society. However, the term function may also be used to denote the causal relationship between two variables; for example, in determining to what extent one variable (proliferation of nuclear families) is the function of another variable (industrialisation).

Further, in social sciences, different terms or concepts may be used to refer to the same or similar phenomena. For example, the terms like formal–informal, organic–mechanistic, primary–secondary, community–association, etc. overlap to a great degree in their meaning. Another problem with regard to concepts in social sciences is that a given concept may have no immediate empirical referent. For example, the concepts like social system, social structure, etc. have no immediate empirical referents or quantifiable attributes. At best they can be studied by observing the patterns of relations among the members of a given society (Goode and Hatt, 2006).

Thus, a social scientist must define the concepts as precisely as possible and operationalise the concepts in order to conduct a meaningful and result-oriented research.

Techniques of Data Collection

We have earlier discussed some of the fundamental characteristics of quantitative (positivist) and qualitative (anti-positivist) research methodologies. However, in practice, the distinctions between positivist and anti-positivist research methodologies are not as clear-cut as the previous sections have shown. They have been placed at opposite ends of the spectrum for purposes of emphasis and illustration. A large body of sociological research falls somewhere between the two extremes. In the same way, the methods of data collection discussed in the following sections cannot be neatly categorised as aspects of positivist or anti-positivist methodologies. However, certain methods are regarded as more appropriate by supporters of one or other of these perspectives.

Let us now discuss some of the important techniques employed by the social scientists for collecting data from the field. The need for adequate and reliable data is ever increasing for taking policy decisions in different fields of human activity. There are two ways in which the required information may be obtained:

1. complete enumeration survey (also known as the census method)
2. sample method

Under the complete enumeration survey method or census method, data are collected for each and every unit (person, household, field, shop, factory, etc., as the case may be) belonging to the population or universe, which is the complete set of items that are of interest in any particular situation. Since every unit is covered, this method ensures greater accuracy. However, it is a highly time- and money-consuming exercise, and that is why it is used very rarely and selectively for some specific purposes only, such as census. This is more true of underdeveloped countries where resources constitute a big constraint. Also, if the population is infinite, the method cannot be adopted. 'Population' here refers to 'all those people with the characteristics which the researcher wants to study within the context of a particular research problem'. A population could be all students in a school, all patients in a hospital, all prisoners in a prison, etc. Hence, in modern times, very little use is made of complete enumeration survey. How to collect the data then? It is through the adoption of sampling technique that a large mass of data pertaining to different aspects of human activity are collected these days (Gupta, 1990).

Sampling

As mentioned earlier, when the population is relatively large or widely dispersed, researchers survey only a sample. Sampling is simply the process of learning about the population on the basis of a sample drawn from it. In the sampling technique, instead of every unit of the universe, only a part of the universe is studied and the conclusions are drawn on that basis for the entire universe. A sample is not studied for its own sake. The basic objective of the sample study is to draw inference about the entire population which it claims to represent. In other words, sampling is only a tool which helps to know the characteristics of the universe or population by examining only a small part of it.

Features of a Good Sample

Since conclusions are drawn on the basis of the study of a small part of the entire universe or population, it is necessary that a sample possesses certain essential characteristics. First, a sample should be representative enough. In other words, a sample should be so selected that it truly represents the universe, otherwise the results obtained may be misleading. Second, the size of sample should be adequate in relation to the universe it tends to represent, otherwise it may not represent all the characteristics of the universe. Third, all items of the sample should be selected independent of one another, and all items of the universe should have equal chance of getting selected in the sample. Last but not the least, there should be homogeneity between the units of the sample and that of the universe.

Types of Sampling

There are basically two types of sampling: probability sampling and non-probability sampling. Probability sampling (also known as random sampling) is one in which every unit of the population has an equal probability of being selected for the sample. It offers a high degree of representativeness. This implies that the selection of sample items is independent of the person making the study – that is, the sampling operation is controlled so objectively that the items will be chosen strictly at random. Hence, it provides estimates which are essentially unbiased. However, this method is expensive, time-consuming and relatively complicated since it requires a large sample size and the units selected are usually widely scattered. Also, it requires a very high level of skill and experience for its use. Non-probability (or non-random) sampling makes no claim for representativeness, as every unit does not get the chance of being selected. It is the researcher who decides which sample units should be chosen.

Probability sampling today remains the primary method for selecting large, representative samples for social science and business researches. Some of the important sampling designs or methods under this category are simple random sampling, stratified random sampling, systematic (or interval) sampling, cluster sampling and multi-stage sampling.

Simple Random Sampling

Random sampling refers to the sampling technique in which each and every item of the population is given an equal chance of being included in the sample. The selection is, thus, free from personal bias because the investigator does not exercise his discretion or preference in the choice of items. Since selection of items in the sample depends entirely on chance, this method is also known as the method of chance selection. Some people believe that randomness of selection can be achieved by unsystematic and haphazard procedures. But this is quite wrong. However, the point to be emphasised is that unless precaution is taken to avoid bias and a conscious effort is made to ensure the operation of chance factors, the resulting sample shall not be a random sample. Random sampling is sometimes referred to as 'representative sampling'. If the sample is chosen at random and if the size of the sample is sufficiently large, it will represent all groups in the universe. A random sample is also known as a 'probability sample' because every item of the universe has an equal opportunity of being selected in the sample. To ensure randomness of selection, one may adopt any of the following methods.

1. *Lottery Method*: This is a very popular method of taking a random sample. Under this method, all items of the universe are numbered on separate slips of paper of identical size and shape. These slips are then folded and mixed up in a container or drum. A blindfold selection is then made of the number of slips required to constitute the desired sample size. The selection of items, thus, depends entirely on chance.

2. *Table of Random Numbers*: The lottery method discussed above becomes quite cumbersome to use as the size of population increases. An alternative method of random selection is that of using the table of random numbers. Three such tables are available: (i) Tippett's table of random numbers, (ii) Fisher and Yate's numbers and (iii) Kendall and Babington Smith's numbers.

The merits of random sampling lie in the fact that since the selection of items in the sample depends entirely on chance, there is no possibility of personal bias affecting the results. Further, as the size of the sample increases, it becomes increasingly representative of the population. However, the use of random sampling necessitates a completely catalogued universe from which to draw the sample. But it is often difficult for the investigator to have up-to-date lists of all the items of the population to be sampled. This restricts the use of random sampling method (Gupta, 1990).

Stratified Random Sampling

In this sampling method, the population is divided into various strata or classes, and a sample is drawn from each stratum at random. For example, if we are interested in studying the consumption pattern of the people of Delhi, the city of Delhi may be divided into various parts or zones, and from each part a sample may be taken at random. However, the selection of cases from each stratum must be done with great care and in accordance with a carefully designed plan as otherwise random selection from the various strata may not be accomplished.

Stratified sampling may be either proportional or disproportional. In proportional stratified sampling, the cases are drawn from each stratum in the same proportion as they occur in the universe. For example, if we divide the city of Delhi into four zones A, B, C and D with 40, 30, 20 and 10 per cent of the total population, respectively, and if the sample size is 1,000, then we should draw 400, 300, 200 and 100 cases, respectively, from zones A, B, C and D, i.e. sample is proportional to the size in the universe. In disproportional stratified sampling, an equal number of cases is taken from each stratum, regardless of how the stratum is represented in the universe. Thus, in the above example, an equal number of items from each zone may be drawn, that is, 250. This approach is obviously inferior to the proportional stratified sampling.

The most important merit of the stratified random sampling is that it is more representative. Since the population is first divided into various strata and then a sample is drawn from each stratum, there is little possibility of any essential group of the population being completely excluded. A more representative sample is thus secured. Stratified sampling is frequently regarded as the most efficient system of sampling. However, utmost care must be exercised in dividing the population into various strata. Each stratum must contain, as far as possible, homogenous items as otherwise the results may not be reliable. However, this is a very difficult task and may involve considerable time and expense.

Systematic or Interval Sampling

This method is popularly used in those cases where a complete list of the population from which a sample is to be drawn is available. It involves obtaining a sample of items by drawing every nth item from a predetermined list of items. In other words, it involves randomly selecting the first respondent and then every nth person after that; 'n' is the sampling interval. For example, if a complete list of 1,000 students of a college is available and if we want to draw a sample of 200, then this means we must take every fifth item (i.e. $n = 5$). The first item between one and five shall be selected at random. Suppose it comes out to be three. Now we shall go on adding five and obtain numbers of the desired sample. Thus, the second item would be the 8th student, and the third would be the 13th student and so on.

Systematic sampling differs from simple random sampling in that in the latter the selections are independent of each other; in the former, the selection of sample units is dependent on the selection of a previous one. The systematic sampling is more convenient to adopt than the random sampling or the stratified sampling method. The time and work involved in sampling by this method are relatively smaller. It is a rapid method and eliminates several steps otherwise taken in probability sampling. However, critics of this method argue that it ignores all persons between two nth numbers with the result that the possibility of overrepresentation and underrepresentation of several groups is greater.

Cluster Sampling

This sampling implies dividing the population into clusters and drawing random samples either from all clusters or from selected clusters. This method is used when (a) cluster criteria are significant for the study, and (b) economic considerations are significant. In cluster sampling, initial clusters are called primary sampling units; clusters within the primary clusters are called secondary sampling units; and clusters within the secondary clusters are called multi-stage clusters. When clusters are geographic units, it is called area sampling. For example, dividing one city into various wards, each ward into areas, each area into neighbourhoods and each neighbourhood into lanes. We can take an example of a hospital. The issue is to ascertain the problems faced by doctors, patients and visitors in different units and to introduce some reformative programmes. Administratively, it will not be viable to call all doctors from all units, nor a large number of patients admitted in different units like cardiology, neurology, orthopaedic, gynaecology and so on. Treating each unit as a cluster, randomly selected doctors and patients – say 2 doctors and 3 patients, or about 50 people all together – from all units may be invited for discussion. On the basis of such discussion, suggestions by the stakeholders may be submitted to higher authorities for necessary action.

The advantage of cluster sampling is that it is much easier to apply this sampling design when large populations are studied or when a large geographical area is studied. Further, the cost involved in this method is much less than in other methods of sampling. The disadvantages of this sampling method are that each cluster may not be of equal size, and hence the comparison so done would not be on an equal basis. The chances of sampling error are greater as there could be homogeneity in one cluster but heterogeneity in other.

Multi-stage Sampling

As the name implies this method refers to a sampling procedure which is carried out in several stages, but only the last sample of subjects is studied. Suppose it is decided to take a sample of 5,000 households from the state of Uttar Pradesh. At the first stage, the state may be divided into a number of districts and a few districts are selected at random. At the second stage, each district may be subdivided into a number of villages, and a sample of villages may be taken at random. At the third stage, a number of households may be selected from each of the villages selected at the second stage. In this way, at each stage the sample size becomes smaller and smaller. The merit of multi-stage sampling is that it introduces flexibility in the sampling method, which is lacking in the other methods. It enables existing divisions and subdivisions of the population to be used as units at various stages. It permits the fieldwork to be concentrated despite covering a large area. Another important advantage in this sampling design is that it is more representative. Further, in all cases, complete listing of population is not necessary. This saves cost. However, a multi-stage sample is in general less accurate than a sample containing the same number of final stage units which have been selected by some suitable single stages process.

Let us now discuss about the non-probability sampling. In many research situations, particularly those where there is no list of persons to be studied (e.g. widows, alcoholics, migrant workers), probability sampling is difficult and inappropriate to use. In such a research, non-probability sampling is the most appropriate one. Non-probability sampling procedures do not employ the rules of probability theory, do not claim representativeness and are usually used for qualitative exploratory analysis. Some of the important sampling designs under this category are convenience sampling, purposive or judgement sampling, quota sampling, snowball sampling and volunteer sampling.

Convenience Sampling

This sampling is also known as 'accidental' or 'haphazard' sampling. In this sampling, the researcher studies all those persons who are most conveniently available or who accidentally come in his contact during a certain period of time in the research. For example, the researcher engaged in the study of university students might visit the university canteen, library, some departments, playgrounds and *verandahs* and interview certain number of students. Another example is of election study. During election times, media personnel often present man-on-the-street interviews that are presumed to reflect public opinion. In such a sampling, representativeness is not significant. The most obvious advantage of convenience sample is that it is quick and economical. But it may be a very biased sample. The possible sources of bias could be: (i) the respondents may have a vested interest to serve in cooperating with the interviewer, and (ii) the respondents may be those who are vocal and/or want to brag. Convenience samples are best utilised for exploratory research when additional research will subsequently be conducted with a probability sample.

Purposive Sampling

Purposive sampling is also known as judgement sampling. In this sampling, the choice of sample items depends exclusively on the discretion of the investigator. In other words, the investigator exercises his judgement in the choice and includes those items in the sample which he thinks are most typical of the universe with regard to the characteristics under investigation. For example, if a sample of 10 students is to be selected from a class of 60 for analysing the spending habits of students, the investigator would select 10 students who, in his opinion, are representative of the class. This method, though simple, is not scientific because there is a big possibility of the results being affected by the personal prejudice or bias of the investigator. Thus, judgement sampling involves the risk that the investigator may establish foregone conclusions by including those items in the sample which conform to his preconceived notions. For example, if an investigator holds the view that the wages of workers in a certain establishment are very low, and if he adopts the judgement sampling method, he may include only those workers in the sample whose wages are low and thereby establish his point of view, which may be far from the truth. Since an element of subjectiveness is possible, this method cannot be recommended for general use. However, because of simplicity and easy adaptability, this method is quite often used by businessmen in the solution of everyday problems. Indeed, if applied with skill and care, the judgement method can be of great help to businessmen. At least, it helps deriving somewhat better solutions to the problems than could be obtained without it.

Quota Sampling

Quota sampling is a type of judgement sampling. In a quota sample, quotas are set up according to given criteria, but within the quotas the selection of sample items depends on personal judgement. For example, in a radio listening survey, the interviewers may be told to interview 500 people living in a certain area and that out of every 100 persons interviewed, 60 are to be housewives, 25 farmers and 15 children. Within these quotas, the interviewer is free to select the people to be interviewed. The cost per person interviewed may be relatively small for a quota sample, but there are numerous opportunities for bias which may invalidate results. Because of the risk of personal prejudice and bias entering the process of selection, the quota sampling is rarely used in practical work.

Snowball Sampling

In this technique, the researcher begins the research with the few respondents who are known and available to him. Subsequently, these respondents give other names who meet the criteria of research, who in turn give more new names. This process is continued until 'adequate' number of persons are interviewed or until no more respondents are discovered. For instance, in studying wife batter-ing, the researcher may first interview those cases whom he knows, who may later on give additional names and who in turn may give still new names. This method is employed when the target population is unknown or when it is dif-ficult to approach the respondents in any other way. Reduced sample sizes and costs are a clear advantage of snowball sampling. Bias enters because a person known to someone (also in the sample) has a higher probability of being similar to the first person. If there are major differences between those who are widely known by others and those who are not, there may be serious problems with snowball sampling.

Volunteer Sampling

In this sampling, the respondent himself volunteers to give information he holds. The success of the research is dependent on the 'rich' information given by the respondents. However, there is a possibility that the informants may not truly represent the population, i.e. they may not have the aggregate characteristics of the population. Further, the personal leanings of the researcher of being preju-diced against certain types of persons, say, untouchables or religious minorities, may also affect the validity of the findings (Ahuja, 2008).

On a review of the pros and cons of the various methods of sampling, it is clear that stratified sampling and systematic sampling methods based on ran-dom principle are more reliable, and hence, these methods are more widely used than others. Let us now briefly discuss the merits of the sampling procedure in general. The sampling technique has the following merits over the complete enumeration survey:

1. Sampling is essentially useful in cases where the universe if large and scattered.
2. It consumes less time. Since sampling is a study of a part of the population, considerable time and labour are saved when a sample survey is carried out. Time is saved not only in collecting data but also in processing it.
3. Less cost is incurred in sampling compared to other techniques of data collection in terms of the cost involved. This is a great advantage particularly in an underdeveloped economy where much of the information would be difficult to collect by the census method for lack of adequate resources.
4. Sampling yields more reliable results. This is because more effective precautions can be taken in a sample survey to ensure that the information is accurate and complete. Moreover, it is possible to avail of the services of experts and to impart thorough training to the investigators in a sample survey which further reduces the possibility of errors. Follow-up work can also be undertaken much more effectively in the sampling method.
5. Since the sampling technique saves time and money, it is possible to collect more detailed information in a sample survey. For example, if the population consists of 1,000 persons in a survey of the consumption pattern of the people, the two alternative techniques available are as follows:
    (a) We may collect the necessary data from each of the 1,000 people through a questionnaire containing, say, ten questions (census method), or
    (b) We may take a sample of 100 persons, i.e. 10 per cent of population, and prepare a questionnaire containing as many as 100 questions. The expense involved in the latter case may be almost the same as in the former, but it will enable nine times more information to be obtained (Gupta, 1990).

However, despite the various advantages of sampling, it is not altogether free from limitations. Some of the difficulties involved in sampling are stated next.

1. A sample survey must be carefully planned and executed, otherwise the results obtained may be inaccurate and misleading.
2. Sampling generally requires the services of experts for the proper planning and execution of the survey. In the absence of qualified and experienced persons, the information obtained from sample surveys cannot be relied upon.
3. If the information is required for each and every unit in the domain of study, sample method cannot be adopted.

To appreciate the need for sample surveys, it is necessary to understand clearly the role of sampling and non-sampling errors in complete enumeration and sample surveys. The errors arising due to drawing inferences about the population on the basis of few observations (sample) is termed as sampling errors. Clearly, the sampling error in this sense is non-existent in a complete enumeration survey, since the whole population is surveyed. However, the errors mainly arising at the stages of ascertainment and processing of data which are termed non-sampling errors are common both in complete enumeration and sample surveys.

Sampling Errors

Even if utmost care has been taken in selecting a sample, the results derived from the sample may not be representative of the population from which it is drawn, because samples are seldom, if ever, perfect miniatures of the population. This gives rise to sampling errors. Sampling errors are, thus, due to the fact that samples are used and to the particular method used in selecting the items from the population. Sampling errors are of two types: biased and unbiased. Biased errors are those which arise from any kind of bias in selection, estimation, etc. Bias may arise either due to a faulty process of selection or faulty method of analysis. Unbiased errors, on the other hand, arise due to chance differences between the members of the population included in the sample and those not included. The simplest and the only certain way of avoiding bias in the selection process is for the sample to be drawn either entirely at random or at random, subject to restrictions, which, while improving the accuracy, are of such a nature that they do not introduce bias in the results.

Non-sampling Errors

When a complete enumeration of units in the universe is made, one would expect that it would give rise to data free from errors. However, in practice it is not so. For example, it is difficult to completely avoid errors of observation or ascertainment. Similarly, in the processing of data tabulation errors may be committed affecting the final results. Errors arising in this manner are termed non-sampling errors, as they are due to factors other than the inductive process of inferring about the population from a sample. Thus, the data obtained in a census by complete enumeration, although free from sampling errors, would still be subject to non-sampling errors, whereas the results of a sample survey would be subject to sampling errors as well as non-sampling errors.

Non-sampling errors can occur at every stage of planning and execution of the census or survey. Such errors can arise due to a number of causes, such as defective methods of data collection and tabulation, faulty definitions, incomplete coverage of the population or sample, etc. More specifically, non-sampling errors may arise from one or more of the following factors.

1. Data specification being inadequate and inconsistent with respect to the objectives of the census or sample survey
2. Inappropriate statistical unit

3. Inaccurate or inappropriate methods of interviews, observation or measurement with inadequate or ambiguous schedules, definitions or instructions
4. Lack of trained and experienced investigators
5. Lack of adequate inspection and supervision of primary staff
6. Errors due to non-response, i.e. incomplete coverage in respect of units
7. Errors in data processing operations such as coding, punching, verification, tabulation, etc.
8. Errors committed during presentation and printing of tabulated results

These sources are not exhaustive but are given to indicate some of the possible sources of error. In some situations, the non-sampling errors may be large and deserve greater attention than the sampling error. While, in general, sampling error decreases with increase in sample size, non-sampling error tends to increase with the sample size. In the case of complete enumeration, non-sampling error and in the case of sample surveys both sampling and non-sampling errors require to be controlled and reduced to a level at which their presence does not vitiate the use of final results (Gupta, 1990).

Survey

The most common type of empirical, or quantitative, research in sociology is the survey, which consists of systematically questioning people about their opinions, attitudes or behaviours. A social survey involves the collection of standardised information from a sample selected as being representative of a particular group or population. The group from which the sample is drawn may be the population as a whole, a particular class, ethnic, gender or age group, etc., depending upon the objective of the researcher. In a survey, standardised information is obtained by asking the same set of questions to all members of the sample. Questionnaires and structured interviews are two important and popular techniques of data collection in a social survey.

Social surveys are broadly divided into two categories: descriptive and analytical. Descriptive surveys are used to describe the world as it is. In other words, descriptive surveys are concerned with description rather than explanation. It aims to provide an accurate measurement of the distribution of certain characteristics in a given population. For example, a survey may be conducted in a city or town to measure the extent of poverty in the given population. Here the researcher and his team would be interested in collecting the data on average per capita income of the working-class stratum or the population below poverty line, etc. In other words, they aim to measure the extent of poverty in a given population rather than to explain the causes of poverty. Analytical surveys, on the other hand, are concerned with explanation. They are designed to test hypotheses about the relationships between a number of factors or variables. For example, an analytical survey may seek to discover possible relationships between social class and educational attainment, gender and occupation, etc. Analytical surveys are not simply concerned with discovering relationships but also with explaining them (Haralambos and Heald, 2006).

Analytical surveys are usually designed to test the effects of a number of variables or factors on some other variable. For example, a researcher may suggest that social class differences in some way cause or determine variations in educational attainment. However, there may be other factors also affecting educational attainment, and they must also be considered if the influence of social class is to be accurately assessed. For example, variables such as caste, gender and ethnicity may account for some variation in educational attainment. As a result, researchers usually gather data on a range of factors which might influence the variable in question. The method used to analyse relationships between variables is known as 'multivariate' or 'variable analysis'. With the aid of various statistical techniques, the analyst attempts to measure the effects of a number of variables upon other variables. This method was pioneered in sociology by Emile Durkheim in his study of suicide.

Official statistics revealed significant variations in suicide rate between European societies. Durkheim's research indicated that predominantly Protestant societies had a higher rate of suicide in comparison to societies where Catholicism was the majority faith. But before a causal relationship could be claimed between religion and suicide rates, it was necessary to eliminate other possibilities. For example, could variations in suicide rates be the result of differences in national cultures? To test this possibility, Durkheim held the variable of national culture constant by examining differences in suicide rates between Catholics and Protestants within the same society. The relationship still held. Within the same society Protestants had higher suicide rates than Catholics. To ensure greater objectivity in his research, Durkheim then went a step further and examined the possibility that regional differences rather than religion might account for variations in suicide rates. He found, for example, that Bavaria had the lowest suicide rate of all the states in Germany and it also had the highest proportion of Catholics. Yet, might the suicide rate be due to the peculiarities of Bavaria as a region rather than its predominantly Catholic population? To test this possibility Durkheim compared the suicide rates and the religious composition of the various provinces within Bavaria. He found that the higher the proportion of Protestants in each province, the higher the suicide rate. Again, the relationship between religion and rates of suicide was confirmed. By eliminating variables such as national culture and region, Durkheim was able to strengthen the relationship between religion and suicide rates and provide increasing support for his claim that the relationship is a causal one (ibid.).

Let us briefly discuss some of the major steps normally involved in survey research. First, before a survey is begun, the issues to be explored must be clearly defined. At the same time, the target population to be interviewed is selected. The target population might be identified on the basis of the characteristics that the researcher is interested in examining. It could either be a particular gender or age group, or any specific socio-economic section of the society, etc. This first step is crucial, for if the population is not correctly specified, the results of the survey may be meaningless. For example, if the aim of the research is to predict the results of an election, it is very important that the population chosen consist only of those persons who will actually vote in that election.

Second, if the population is large, time and cost will almost always make it impractical to interview the entire population. So, the second step in surveying is to pick an appropriate sample of the population to interview. A sample is a limited number of selected cases drawn from a large group. Careful procedures have been established for selecting samples. The better the sampling procedure, the more closely the sample will resemble the entire population and the more accurate will be the generalisations or predictions. In other words, if generalisations are to be made from the findings of a social survey, it is essential that the sample is representative. This is often accomplished by means of a 'random sample'. We have already discussed the various types of sampling techniques and their merits and limitations. Once the researcher is satisfied that he has obtained a representative sample, he can begin the survey proper and feel some justification in generalising from its findings.

Once the sample is selected, the third step in survey research is to interview or administer the questionnaire to the selected people and to collect the data. At this point a major consideration is the precision of the questions. Do the questions really pinpoint the issues concerned? Are they phrased in such a way that they will be interpreted correctly and similarly by each person interviewed, i.e. the respondents. In addition to being precise and unambiguous in meaning, a survey question must also be neutrally stated.

For most accurate results, the entire sample must be interviewed, particularly if the sample is small. If some people refuse to answer or are unavailable for interviewing, the sample is no longer representative and, consequently, the accuracy of the data may be reduced. Non-response is frequently a serious problem when questionnaires are sent by mail, for refusals to respond to mailed questionnaires tend to be high. Replies often come only from those who have some interest in the particular issue, thus introducing a bias into the survey findings. To assure maximum response, most major attitude surveys and public opinion polls are conducted through personal interviews. These interviews range from the highly structured to be highly unstructured.

A structured interview consists of a set of questions and answers which are always stated in the same way and in the same sequence. The answers are, thus, easily compiled and generalised. Most public opinion polls use structured interviews. For other research purposes, where more extensive information about individual attitudes or behaviour is desired, the unstructured interview has many advantages. An unstructured interview may consist of open-ended questions (How do you feel about the inter-caste marriages or caste-based reservations?) or even just a list of topics to be discussed. It is possible for the interviewer to introduce bias into the survey. He may, for example, use expressions or make comments that encourage the respondent to answer in a certain way. In an unstructured interview he may influence the answers by the way he phrases the questions. It is important that interviewers be suited to their task and that they be well trained in the techniques of interviewing. The final step in survey research is the tabulation, analysis and interpretation of the data. In all but the smallest surveys, this step normally involves the use of computers.

There are several possible sources of error in survey results. Sampling error is the degree to which the selected sample misrepresents the population as a whole. Other major sources of error arise from problems in observation and measurement, processing the data and analysing the findings. A basic problem with all surveys is that what people say may not always agree with how they act. People sometimes conceal their attitude purposely. An individual prejudiced against lower castes in India, for example, may act in a discriminatory fashion towards them, but because he knows that this prejudice is socially disapproved of, he will not admit it to an interviewer. Research that is well designed and carried out can help to overcome these difficulties, but the sociologist must be constantly aware that attitudes expressed in interviews are not always perfect expressions of underlying values, and that actions do not always reflect stated attitudes. The success of any survey is, however, ultimately dependent on the quality of its data. At the end of the day a social survey stands or falls on the validity of its data.

Case Study

Case study method is an ideal methodology when a holistic, in-depth investigation is needed. Frederic Le Play is reputed to have introduced the *case study* method into social science. He used it as a handmaiden to statistics in his studies of family budgets. Herbert Spencer was one of the first sociologists to use case materials in his ethnographic studies.

Case study is an intensive study of a case which may be an individual, an institution, a system, a community, an organisation, an event or even the entire culture. Robert K. Yin has defined case study as 'an empirical inquiry that investigates a contemporary phenomenon within its real-life context, when the boundaries between phenomenon and context are not clearly evident, and in which multiple sources of evidence are used'. It is, thus, a kind of research design which usually involves the qualitative method of selecting the sources of the data. It presents the holistic account that offers insights into the case under study. It is worth noting that while a case study can be either quantitative or qualitative, or even both, most case studies lie within the realm of qualitative methodology. It is the preferred strategy when 'how, who, why and what' questions are being asked, or when the focus is on a contemporary phenomenon within a real-life context (Ahuja, 2008).

Case studies have been used in varied social investigations, particularly, in sociological studies, and are designed to bring out the details from the viewpoint of the participants by using multiple sources of data. It is, therefore, an approach to explore and analyse the life of social unit, be it a person, a family, an institution, a culture group or even an entire community. Its aim is to determine the factors that account for the complex behaviour patterns of the unit and the relationships of the unit to its surroundings. Case data may be gathered, exhaustively, on the entire life cycle or on a definite section of the cycle of a unit but always with a view to ascertain the natural history of social unit and its relationship to the social factors and forces involved in its environment. In other words, through case studies researchers attempt to see the variety of factors within a social unit as an integrated whole. When attention is focused on the development of the case, it is called 'case history'. For example, how a particular boy became a juvenile delinquent because of lack of parental control, impact of peers, lack of attention by teachers and money earned through cheap means, and then became an adolescent thief and a sex criminal and ultimately a professional pickpocket is tracing criminality through case history method.

Data, for case studies, can be collected by primary as well as secondary sources. Two main sources of primary data collection are interviews and observations. Interviews may be structured or unstructured. Most commonly, it is the unstructured interview which is used by the investigators. The observation method used could be either participant or non-participant, while the secondary data can be collected through a variety of sources like reports, records, newspapers, magazines, books, files, diaries, etc.

Sjoberg has identified some essential characteristics of case study method, which are as follows:

1. The case study 'strives towards a holistic understanding of cultural systems of action'. Cultural systems of action refer to sets of interrelated activities engaged in by the actors in a social situation.
2. Case study research is not sampling research. However, selection of the items or sources must be done so as to maximise what can be learned, in the limited period of time available for the study.
3. Because they are intensive in nature, case studies tend to be selective, focusing on one or two issues that are fundamental to understanding the system being examined.
4. 'Case studies are multi-perspectival analyses'. This means that the researcher considers not just the voice and perspective of the actors but also of the relevant groups of actors and the interaction between them.

According to Black and Champion, some of the advantages of case study design are:

1. Case study makes holistic and in-depth study of the phenomenon possible.
2. It offers flexibility with respect to using methods for collecting data, e.g. questionnaire, interview, observation.
3. It could be used for studying any specific dimension of the topic in detail.
4. It can be conducted in practically any kind of social setting.
5. Case studies are relatively inexpensive.

However, practically, the case study method is very time-consuming and demanding of the researcher. The possibility of becoming involved emotionally is much greater than in survey research, thus making detached and objective observation difficult and sometimes impossible. Another problem in the use of case study method is that since only one example of a social situation or group is being studied, the results may not be representative of all groups or situations in the category. In other words, the particular mental hospital ward, slum or suburb may not be typical of all mental hospital wards, slums or suburbs. Critics of the case study method believe that the study of a small number of cases can offer no grounds for establishing reliability or generality of findings. Some dismiss case study research as useful only as an exploratory tool. Yet, researchers continue to use the case study research method with success in carefully planned and crafted studies of real-life situations, issues and problems. In comparison to survey, the case study method is more intensive, while survey research is more extensive in nature. In other words, surveys are usually conducted on a fairly large scale in contrast to case studies that tend to be more intensive but on a smaller scale. Case study is done in terms of limited space and broader time, whereas survey is done in terms of limited time with broader space. Case study is inward looking, while survey method is outward looking.

Interviews

Interviews are one of the most widely used methods of gathering data in sociology. They consist of the researcher asking the interviewee or respondent a series of questions. Bingham and Moore have described interview as 'a conversation with a purpose' (Ahuja, 2008). According to Goode and Hatt (2006), 'Interviewing is fundamentally a process of social interaction'. Interviews can be classified as 'structured' or 'unstructured' though many fall somewhere between these two extremes.

In a structured interview, there is a set of predetermined questions which the interviewer is required to put before the interviewee (respondent) to collect the required information. In this type of interview, the wording of the questions and the order in which they are asked remains the same in every case. The result is a fairly formal question and answer session. However, unstructured interviews are more like an informal conversation. In an unstructured interview, there are no specifications in the wording of the questions or the order of the questions. The interviewer usually has particular topics in mind to cover but few, if any, preset questions. There are no specifications in the wording of the questions or the order of the questions. He has the freedom to phrase questions as he likes, ask the respondent to develop his answers and probe responses which might be unclear and ambiguous. This freedom is often extended to the respondent, who may be allowed to direct the interview into areas which interest him (Haralambos and Heald, 2006).

Data from structured interviews are generally regarded as more reliable. Since the order and wording of questions are the same for all respondents, it is more likely that they will be responding to the same stimuli. Thus, different answers to the same set of questions will indicate real differences between the respondents. Different answers will not, therefore, simply reflect differences in the way questions are phrased. Thus, the more structured or standardised an interview, the more easily its results can be tested by researchers investigating other groups. The structured interview reduces the interviewer's bias to the minimum. This form of interview is largely employed in quantitative research. By comparison, data from unstructured interviews are seen as less reliable. Questions are phrased in a variety of ways, and the relationship between the interviewer and the respondent is likely to be more intimate. It is unclear to what degree the answers are influenced by these factors. Differences between respondents may simply reflect differences in the nature of the interviews. It is therefore more difficult to replicate an unstructured interview but the greater flexibility of unstructured interviews may strengthen the validity of the data. They provide more opportunity to discover what the respondent 'really means'. Ambiguities in questions and answers can be clarified and the interviewers can probe for shades of meaning (ibid.).

Structured interviews are largely employed in quantitative research. Such interviews are regarded as appropriate for obtaining answers to questions of 'fact' such as the age, sex and income of the respondent. Unstructured interviews, on the other hand, are seen as more appropriate for eliciting attitudes, opinions and interests. Interview data are often taken as indications of respondents' attitudes and behaviour in everyday life, although what a person says in an interview may have little to do with his normal routines. Even if the respondent does his best to provide honest answers, he may be unaware of the taken-for-granted assumptions which he employs in everyday life.

Various studies have suggested, though, that interviews pose serious problems of reliability and validity. This is partly due to the fact that interviews are interaction situations. Thus, the results of an interview will depend in part on the way the participants define the situation, their perceptions of each other and so on. Most studies have been concerned about the effects of interviewers on the respondents. The significance of what has come to be known as 'interviewer bias' can be seen from the research conducted by Katz. The classic study of socio-economic status of interviewers was conducted by Katz in 1942 in a lower-class area in Pittsburgh. Katz compared the results obtained by a group of interviewers who were blue-collar industrial workers with the results obtained by middle-class interviewers. Katz found that low-income industrial workers consistently gave more radical answers on labour issues to the blue-collar lower-class interviewers than to the middle-class interviewers. Katz concluded that lack of rapport between lower-class respondents and middle-class interviewers led to bias in response (Bailey, 1994). In a similar study, J. Allan Williams Jr. concluded that the greater the status differences between interviewer and respondent, the less likely the respondent will be to express his true feelings. In a series of interviews organised in 1960s, Williams found drastic difference in the responses of the respondents when interviewed by black and white interviewers at different points of time. Williams found that on issues such as civil rights demonstrations and school desegregation, black respondents often tended to give the answers they felt that white interviewers wanted to hear. These findings suggest that when status differences are wide, as is often the case with middle-class sociologists interviewing members of the lower working class, interview data should be regarded with caution (Haralambos and Heald, 2006).

Interviewers, like everybody else, have values, attitudes and expectations. However, no matter how much the interviewer tries to disguise his views, they may well be communicated to the respondent. This is particularly likely in the more informal situation of the unstructured interview. As a result, the interviewer may 'lead' the respondent whose answer will then reflect something of the interviewer's attitudes and expectations. This can be seen from a study conducted by Stuart A. Rice in 1914: 2,000 destitute men were asked, among other things, to explain their situation. There was a strong tendency for those interviewed by a supporter of prohibition to blame their demise on alcohol, but those interviewed by a committed socialist were much more likely to explain their plight in terms of the industrial situation. To counter this problem, interviewers are often advised to be 'non-directive', to refrain from offering opinions, to avoid expressions of approval and disapproval. It is suggested they establish 'rapport' with their respondents, that is, a warm, friendly relationship which implies sympathy and understanding, while at the same time guarding against communicating their own attitudes and expectations (ibid.).

However, despite these limitations, interviews do have certain advantages. They are less costly and time-consuming and can cover much larger samples. Further, the response rate of the interview method is high, particularly when compared to mailed questionnaires. Most importantly, the validity of the information can be checked. Since the respondent's confidence can be sought through personal rapport, in-depth probing is possible. The interviewer can explain difficult terms and clear up any confusion and misunderstandings. He gets the opportunity to observe the non-verbal behaviour of the respondent, which thus enables him to record the responses in the right perspective.

Questionnaires

A questionnaire consists of a list of preset questions to which respondents are asked to supply answers. Questionnaire poses a structured and standardised set of questions, either to one person or to a small population, or most commonly to respondents in a sample survey. Structure here refers to questions appearing in a consistent, predetermined sequence and form. Researchers who use questionnaires regard them as a comparatively cheap, fast and efficient method for obtaining large amounts of quantifiable data on relatively large numbers of people.

Questionnaires may be administered in a number of ways. Questionnaires may either be distributed by mail or by hand, through arrangements such as the 'drop-off', where a fieldworker leaves the questionnaire for respondents to complete by themselves, with the provision either for mailing the complete form back to the research office or for a return call by the fieldworker to collect the questionnaire. A questionnaire administered in a face-to-face interview, or over the telephone (growing in popularity among researchers), is generally termed a 'schedule'. Often, they are given to individuals by interviewers, in which case they take the form of structured interviews. This method was used by Goldthorpe and Lockwood in the affluent worker study and by Young and Willmott in their survey of family life in London conducted in 1970. This method has the advantage of having a trained interviewer on hand to make sure that the questionnaire is completed according to instructions and to clarify any ambiguous questions. However, questionnaires administered by interviewers involve the problem of 'interviewer bias'. Further, this method is expensive in comparison to other alternatives available such as postal questionnaire. As its name suggests, a postal questionnaire is mailed to respondents with a stamped addressed envelope for return to the researcher. It is a cheaper method of data collection, especially if the respondents are dispersed over a large geographical area. However, the response rate of postal questionnaires is low. In deciding upon one of these methods, the researcher balances the cost, probable response rate and the nature of the questions to be posed.

It is important to note that the set of structured questions in which answers are recorded by the interviewer himself is called *interview schedule*, or simply the *schedule*. It is distinguished from the questionnaire in the sense that in the questionnaire the answers are filled in by the respondent himself. Though the questionnaire is used when the respondents are educated, schedule can be used for both the illiterate and the educated respondents. The questionnaire is especially useful when the respondents are scattered in a large geographical area but the schedule is used when the respondents are located in a small area so that they can be personally contacted. The wording of the questions in the questionnaire has to be simple, since the interviewer is not present to explain the meaning and importance of the question to the respondent. In the schedule, the investigator gets the opportunity to explain whatever the respondent needs to know.

Questionnaires could broadly be classified into three types: *standardised questionnaire, open-ended questionnaire* and *close-ended questionnaire*. Standardised questionnaires are those in which there are definite, concrete and pre-ordained questions with additional questions limited to those necessary to clarify inadequate answers or to elicit more detailed responses. The questions are presented with exactly the same wording and in the same order to all the respondents. The reason for standardised questions is to ensure that all the respondents are replying to the same set of questions. Here the respondents or the researcher mark certain categories of reply to the questions asked, for instance, 'yes/no/don't know' or 'very likely/likely/unlikely/very unlikely'. Standardised questionnaires have the advantage that responses are easy to compare and tabulate, since only a small number of categories are involved. On the other hand, because the standardised questions do not allow for subtleties of opinion or verbal expressions, the information they yield is likely to be restricted in scope.

Open-ended questions allow the respondent to compose his own answers rather than choosing between a number of given answers. For example, 'What's your view on the reservation policy in India?' Open-ended questionnaires are designed to permit a free response from the subject rather than one limited to certain alternatives. This may provide more valid data since he can say what he means in his own words. However, this kind of response may be difficult to classify and quantify. Answers must be carefully interpreted before the researcher is able to arrive at certain conclusion.

Close-ended or fixed-choice questions, on the other hand, require the respondent to make a choice between a number of given answers. For example, 'Do you agree with the reservation policy in India?' The answer choices given are, 'yes', 'no', and 'partly'. From the point of view of the interpretation of questionnaires, the closed question is preferable. The results are unambiguous and comparable. With an open question, the heterogeneous answers must first be ordered into classes (codified) before they can be interpreted. Constructing classes in this way is sometimes very laborious and a challenging task. From the point of view of the reliability of interview data also, the closed question is preferable. This is because that the response to an open-ended question is subjected to the perception and linguistic ability of the respondent and under certain circumstances this can produce serious distortions.

Although the content of questionnaires is governed by the purpose of the study, many problems of communication may still arise on all surveys regardless of the content. Much careful attention and experimentation are needed to produce effectively worded questions. The language should be concise and directed towards producing uniformity of understanding among the respondents. Great care is therefore needed in designing a questionnaire. Sometimes the main survey is preceded by a 'pilot study', which involves giving the questionnaire to a group similar to the population to be surveyed. This helps to clear up any ambiguity in the wording of questions and to ensure their relevance to future respondents. Ideally, the questions should mean the same thing to all respondents. As earlier discussed, this is extremely difficult to ensure, particularly if respondents are drawn from different social classes and ethnic groups. In addition, the researcher must be aware of the meaning respondents give to the question. He cannot simply assume that they will share his interpretation (Haralambos and Heald, 2006).

More importantly, questions must not only elicit stable or reliable answers but they must also provide the kind of information, which the researcher wants. More often, the problem of truth is a much more complex one. A good questionnaire will contain some 'check questions' on crucial issues, variously placed within the document, designed to parallel or confirm each other. Sometimes, these will explore other facets of the same behaviour. Usually, the cross-check question is a kind of *specification*. That is, a general question is checked by specific reference.

Questionnaires provide data which can be easily quantified. They are largely designed for this purpose. Those who adopt a positivist approach insist that this kind of measurement is essential if sociology is to progress. They argue that only when the social world is expressed in numerical terms can precise relationships be established between its parts. Only when data are quantified by means of reliable measuring instruments can the results of different studies be directly compared. Without quantification, sociology will remain on the level of impressionistic guesswork and unsupported insight. It will, therefore, be impossible to replicate studies, establish causal relationships and support generalisations. The questionnaire is one of the main tools of measurement in positivist sociology (ibid.).

Operationalisation of concepts is an important aspect in the construction of a questionnaire. This means concepts are defined in terms of their empirical referents and, thus, put into a form which can be measured. Sociologists classify the social world in terms of a variety of concepts. For example, social class, power, family, religion, alienation and anomie are concepts used to identify and categorise social relationships, beliefs, attitudes and experiences which are seen to have certain characteristics in common. In order to transpose these rather vague concepts into measuring instruments, a number of steps are taken. First, an operational definition is established. This involves breaking the concept down into various 'components' or 'dimensions' in order to specify exactly what is to be measured. Thus, when Robert Blauner attempted to operationalise the concept of alienation, he divided it into four components: powerlessness, meaninglessness, isolation and self-estrangement. Once the concept has been operationally defined in terms of a number of components, the next step involves the selection of 'indicators' for each component. Thus, an indicator of Blauner's component of powerlessness might be an absence of opportunities for workers to make decisions about the organisation of work tasks. Finally, indicators of each dimension are put into the form of a series of questions, which will provide quantifiable data for measuring each dimension (ibid.).

However, whether such procedures succeed in producing valid measurements of human behaviour is open to question. Scholars belonging to phenomenological tradition often reject the entire procedure of operational definitions, selecting indicators, constructing questionnaires and quantifying the results. They argue that rather than providing a valid picture of the social world, such operations merely serve to distort it. From the phenomenological perspective, the social world is constructed by its members. Hence, phenomenologists argue that the job of the sociologist should be to investigate how members construct or perceive their world. According to phenomenologists, positivist research procedures merely impose sociological constructs, categories and logic on that world. Thus, when Blauner seeks to measure alienation, he is employing a concept which may have no reality in the social world. Phenomenologists argue that instead of imposing sociological categories and measuring instruments on the social world, sociologists should discover whether workers even categorise jobs in terms of satisfaction or not, and if so, investigate the procedures they employ to arrive at such categorisation.

There is little doubt that questionnaires are rather inexpensive and for that reason quite attractive. This is not merely a question of saving money but also of saving administrative time and talent, e.g. by using the mail system instead of a costly *ad hoc* staff of interviewers. One special advantage lies in the simultaneity of access. If it is important to reach all respondents at the same time, this is probably easier by means of questionnaires than interviews.

Observation

Observation is a method that employs vision as its main means of data collection. It implies the use of eyes rather than of ears and the voice. It is accurate watching and noting of phenomena as they occur with regard to the cause-and-effect or mutual relations. It is watching other persons' behaviour as it actually happens without controlling it. For example, observing the life of street children or a religious ceremony in any community.

Lindzey Gardner has defined observation as 'selection, provocation, recording and encoding of that set of behaviours and settings concerning organisms *in situ* (naturalistic settings) which are consistent with empirical aims'. In this definition, *selection* means that there is a focus in observation and also editing before, during and after the observations are made. *Provocation* means that though observers do not destroy natural settings, they can make subtle changes in natural settings, which increase clarity. *Recording* means that observed incidents/events are recorded for subsequent analysis. *Encoding* involves simplification of records (Ahuja, 2008).

According to Black and Champion, the major purpose of observation is to capture human conduct as it actually happens. In other methods, we get a static comprehension of people's activity. In actual situation, they sometimes modify their views, sometimes contradict themselves and sometimes are so swayed by the situation that they react differently altogether. They further argue that observation can be used as a tool of collecting information in situations where methods other than observation cannot prove to be useful, e.g. voter's behaviour during election time or worker's behaviour during strike.

Participant observation is one of the most important qualitative methodologies in which the researcher participates in the daily life of the population under study, observing things that happen, listening to conversations, informally questioning people. This may be done covertly, as when a sociologist becomes a prison inmate in order to study the effectiveness of rehabilitation programmes. It may also be done openly, by joining a group in the formal role of the observer.

In other words, participant observation is a method in which the investigator becomes a part of the situation he is studying. He involves himself in the setting and group life of the research subjects. He shares the activities of the community, observing what is going on around him, supplementing this by conversations and interviews. One of the pioneering uses of participant observation by sociologists in a modern setting is recorded in William Foote Whyte's *Street Corner Society: The Social Structure of an Italian Slum*.

Street Corner Society is a study of an Italian American street-corner gang in a low-income district of south Boston. Whyte spent three and a half years living in the area as a participant observer. Whyte studied lower-class 'slum' street-corner groups by joining and talking informally with the members. He gained access to the first group through a social worker, became friendly with the group's leader, was introduced to other groups and finally was accepted as 'one of them' although he did not have to 'play their game all the way'. By 'hanging out' on the street corner for a period of time, Whyte gained much valuable information about the group's goals and structure and the motivations of its members.

Supporters of participant observations have argued that, compared to other research techniques, it is least likely to lead to the sociologist imposing his reality on the social world he seeks to understand. It, therefore, provides the best means of obtaining a valid picture of social reality. With a structured interview – a predetermined set of questions which the interviewee is requested to answer – or a questionnaire – a set of printed questions to which the respondent is asked to provide written answer – the sociologist has already decided what is important. With preset questions, he imposes his framework and priorities on those he wishes to study. By assuming the questions are relevant to his respondents, he has already made many assumptions about their social world. Although the participant observer begins his work with some preconceived ideas, for example, he will usually have studied the existing literature on the topic he is to investigate; he at least has the opportunity to directly observe the social world (Haralambos and Heald, 2006).

However, the success of participant observation depends initially upon the acceptance of the observer by the group he wishes to study. Once accepted, the participant observer must gain the trust of those he observes to be successful. Further, there are also the challenges of objectivity and value-neutrality. Since the observer participates in the events, sometimes he becomes so involved that he loses objectivity in observation. He may start interpreting events subjectively. Further, his presence may sensitise the subjects that they do not act in a natural way. In other words, his presence will to some degree influence the actions of those he observes. In this way he may modify or change the social world he wishes to investigate.

Positivists who argue that research methods in sociology should be drawn from the natural sciences are, however, highly critical of participant observation. They argue that the data obtained from participant observation lack 'reliability' since there is no way of replicating a study and checking the consistency of its results. Since the success of participant observation relies heavily on the rapport between the researcher and his respondents, his interpretive skills and personality, the exact replication of studies using this method are difficult, if not impossible. Hence, it is not possible to generalise from such studies. However, the value of participant observation studies seems to lie in providing useful insights which can then be tested on larger samples using more rigorous and systematic methods.

The above criticisms derive mainly from those who adopt a strongly positivist approach. Others would argue that what the findings of participant observation lack in reliability, they often more than make up for in validity. By coming face to face with social reality, the participant observer at least has the opportunity to make valid observations. Many would argue that the systematic questionnaire surveys favoured by many positivists have little or no chance of tapping the real social world (ibid.).

In non-participant observation, the observer remains detached and does not participate or intervene in the activities of those who are being observed. He merely observes their behaviour. Sometimes, this places the persons being observed in an awkward position and their conduct becomes unnatural. But some say that though initially the observer's behaviour may affect the behaviour of the observed, after a little while, less and less attention is paid to his presence. This type of observation is more useful as a tool of data collection because the observer can choose the situations to be observed and can record the data freely. This is because the observer is not required to participate actively in the social processes at work in the social field he is observing. Since he is not himself immediately affected by the demands of the situation, he can concentrate his whole attention more easily on systematic observation of the situation and what is happening in it.

Content Analysis

Bernard Berelson defined content analysis as 'a research technique for the objective, systematic, and quantitative description of manifest content of communications'. Content analysis is a research tool focused on the actual content and internal features of media. It is used to determine the presence of certain words, concepts, themes, phrases, characters or sentences within texts or sets of texts and to quantify this presence in an objective manner.

Content analysis or textual analysis is a methodology in the social sciences for studying the content of the communication. Earl Babbie defines it as 'the study of recorded human communications, such as books, websites, paintings, and laws'. Harold Lasswell formulated the core questions of content analysis: 'Who says what, to whom, why, to what extent and with what effect?' Ole Holsti offers a broad definition of content analysis as 'any technique for making inferences by objectively and systematically identifying specified characteristics of messages'.

In other words, content analysis is a research tool used to determine the presence of certain words or concepts within texts or sets of texts. Researchers quantify and analyse the presence, meanings and relationships of such words and concepts, and then make inferences about the messages within the texts, the writer(s), the audience and even the culture and time of which these are a part.

Texts can be defined broadly as books, book chapters, essays, interviews, discussions, newspaper headlines and articles, historical documents, speeches, conversations, advertising, theatre, informal conversation or really any occurrence of communicative language. To conduct a content analysis on any such text, the text is coded, or broken down, into manageable categories on a variety of levels – word, word sense, phrase, sentence or theme – and then examined using one of content analysis' basic methods: conceptual analysis or relational analysis. Conceptual analysis can be thought of as establishing the existence and frequency of concepts in a text. Relational analysis builds on conceptual analysis by examining the relationships among concepts in a text.

Content analysis is a product of the electronic age. Though content analysis was regularly performed in the 1940s, it became a more credible and frequently used research method since the mid-1950s, as researchers started to focus on concepts rather than simply words, and on semantic relationships rather than just presence. While both traditions still continue today, content analysis now is also utilised to explore mental models, and their linguistic, affective, cognitive, social, cultural and historical significance. Due to the fact that it can be applied to examine any piece of writing or occurrence of recorded communication, content analysis is used in large number of fields, ranging from marketing and media studies to literature and rhetoric, ethnography and cultural studies, gender and age issues, sociology and political science, psychology and cognitive science, as well as other fields of enquiry.

For example, in a research project on gender issues, the content of the text books (particularly the stories) was analysed and it was found how gender relations prevailing in our society manifested themselves, as well as got reinforced by the gender roles described in the various stories. The girl child often was depicted as an obedient child, helping the mother in the household chores. On the other hand, the boy was often portrayed as school going, naughty and aiming high in life. Similarly, the content analysis of the local newspapers in rural hinterland could throw light on the prevailing caste relations and the nature of the caste conflict.

Bernard Berelson has identified the various uses of content analysis. Some of them are listed below:

1. It reveals international differences in communication content.
2. It can detect the existence of propaganda.
3. It can identify the intentions, focus or communication trends of an individual, group or institution.
4. It helps in describing attitudinal and behavioural responses to communications.
5. It can determine psychological or emotional state of persons or groups.

Content analysis offers several advantages to researchers who consider using it. Some of them are as follows:

1. It is an unobtrusive means of analysing interactions. One of the significant advantages of content analysis is that it is an *unobtrusive* method, i.e. it has no effect on the subject being studied. In other methods (like interview, observation, experiment, etc.), the researcher is directly involved with

persons. Content analysis eliminates the source of 'response bias' that threatens research whenever the respondents are directly questioned or observed.

2. It looks directly at communication via texts or transcripts, and hence gets at the central aspect of social interaction.
3. It can allow for both quantitative and qualitative operations.
4. It can provide valuable historical/cultural insights over time through analysis of texts.
5. It makes possible a variety of cross-cultural studies that would likely be unfeasible using other methods.
6. It provides insight into complex models of human thought and language use.

Content analysis suffers from several disadvantages, both theoretical and procedural. Some of them are as follows:

1. Since content analysis is a heavily planned method, it lacks the spontaneity often required in the field research.
2. It can be extremely time-consuming.
3. Content analysis is subject to increased error, particularly when relational analysis is used to attain a higher level of interpretation.
4. It is often devoid of theoretical base, or attempts too liberally to draw meaningful inferences about the relationships and impacts implied in a study.
5. It often disregards the context that produced the text, as well as the state of things after the text is produced.
6. Some required documents may not be available to the researcher, which may affect the conclusions.
7. It is susceptible to coder's bias (Ahuja, 2008).

One of the leading debates among the users of content analysis is whether analysis should be quantitative or qualitative. Berelson, for example, suggests that content analysis is 'objective, systematic, and quantitative'. Similarly, Silverman dismisses content analysis from his discussion of qualitative data analysis 'because it is a quantitative method'. Selltiz et al., however, state that concerns over quantification in content analysis tend to emphasise 'the procedures of analysis', rather than the 'character of the data available'. Selltiz et al. suggest also that heavy quantitative content analysis results in a somewhat arbitrary limitation in the field by excluding all accounts of communication that are not in the form of numbers as well as those that may lose meaning if reduced to a numeric form (definitions, symbols, detailed explanations, photographs and so forth). Other proponents of the content analysis, notably Smith, suggest that some blend of both quantitative and qualitative analysis should be used. Smith explains that he has taken this position 'because qualitative analysis deals with the forms and antecedent-consequent patterns of form, while quantitative analysis deals with duration and frequency of form'. Abrahamson suggests that 'content analysis can be fruitfully employed to examine virtually any type of communication'. As a consequence, content analysis may focus on either quantitative or qualitative aspects of communication messages.

Another controversy concerning the use of content analysis is whether the analysis should be limited to *manifest content* (those elements that are physically present and countable) or extended to more *latent content*. In the latter case, the analysis is extended to an interpretive reading of the symbolism underlying the physical data. For example, an entire speech may be assessed for how radical it was, or a novel could be considered in terms of how violent the entire text was. In other words, manifest content is comparable to the *surface structure* present in the message, and latent content is the *deep structural* meaning conveyed by the message. Holsti has tried to resolve this debate:

> It is true that only the manifest attributes of text may be coded, but this limitation is already implied by the requirement of objectivity. Inferences about latent meanings of messages are therefore permitted but ... they require corroboration by independent evidence.

One reasonable interpretation of this passage, and a similar statement made by Berelson, suggests that although there are some dangers in directly inferring from latent symbolism, it is nonetheless possible to use it. To accomplish this sort of 'deciphering' of latent symbolic meaning, researchers must first incorporate independent corroborative techniques (for example, agreement between independent coders concerning latent content or some non-content analytic source). Finally, and especially when latent symbolism may be discussed, researchers should offer detailed excerpts from relevant statements (messages) that serve to document the researchers' interpretations.

Focus Group

Focus group is a qualitative research method of data collection in social sciences. Over the past decade, focus groups and group interviews have emerged as popular techniques for gathering qualitative data, both among sociologists and across a wide range of academic and applied research areas.

David L. Morgan has defined focus groups as 'a research technique that collects data through group interaction on a topic determined by the researcher'. This definition has three essential components. First, it clearly states that focus groups are a research method devoted to data collection. Second, it locates the interaction in a group discussion as the source of the data. Third, it acknowledges the researcher's active role in creating the group discussion for data collection purposes.

Thus, on the basis of this definition, focus groups should be distinguished from groups whose primary purpose is something other than research, for example, therapy, education, decision-making, etc. Further, it is useful to distinguish focus groups from procedures that utilise multiple participants but do not allow interactive discussions, such as nominal groups and Delphi groups. Finally, focus groups should be distinguished from methods that collect data from naturally occurring group discussions where no one acts as an interviewer. However, there is a difference of opinion among scholars on the issue whether focus groups should be distinguished from other types of group interviews. On the one hand are the scholars who use an inclusive approach and treat most forms of group interviews as variants of focus groups. On the other hand, there are scholars who use an exclusive approach and treat focus group as a distinct technique which should not be confused with other types of group interviews. In this regard, Frey and Fontana argue that group interviews can be distinguished from focus groups on the basis of three features:

- first, group interviews are conducted in informal settings
- second, group interviews use non-directive interviewing
- third, group interviews use unstructured question formats

Similarly, Stewart and Shamdasani associate focus groups with more or less directive interviewing styles and structured question formats. However, applied demographers such as John Knodel, who have held focus group interviews throughout the world, concluded that focus groups can be adapted to a wide variety of settings and culture practices. Hence, in actual practice, it would be quite difficult to apply the above-mentioned classification as the methodology of focus groups or group interviews is largely dependent on the purpose of a particular project as well as the sociocultural context.

Today, focus groups, like other qualitative methods, are being used across a wide variety of research areas including education, public health, marketing research, etc. In recent years, two specific areas where the applied use of focus groups has had a major and continuing link to sociology are family planning and HIV/AIDS. Studies conducted in these areas suggest that the use of focus groups facilitated better understanding of knowledge, attitudes and practices with regard to contraception in the Third World countries. Further, an important aspect of focus group method is that it facilitates participatory research. Various studies have suggested that use of focus group method in HIV/AIDS research has not only facilitated a better understanding of the problems being faced by at-risk groups, but it also serves to 'give a voice' to such marginalised groups (Morgan, 1996).

Uses of Focus Groups in Combination with Other Methods

Focus groups can be used either independently or in combination with other methods such as individual interviews, surveys, etc.

Focus Groups and Individual Interviews

Both focus groups and individual interviews are qualitative techniques of data collection. But while focus groups and group interviews provide greater breath to the research, individual interviews, on the other hand, provide greater depth. Various researchers have often used in-depth individual interviews as a follow-up to focus group studies in order to ascertain the degree of consistency or discrepancy in the responses of the participants.

Focus Groups and Surveys

Morgan has described four ways of combining quantitative and qualitative methods using survey and focus groups as example. The four ways of combining the methods are based on 'which method received the primary attention and whether the secondary method served as a preliminary or follow-up study'.

First combination: *Survey as the primary method and focus group for preliminary study*

The first combination contains studies in which surveys are the primary method and focus groups serve in a preliminary capacity. Survey researchers typically use this design to develop the context of their questionnaires. Because surveys are inherently limited by the questions they ask, it is increasingly common to use focus groups to provide data on how the respondents themselves talk about the topics of the survey.

For example, in order to carry out a survey on the factors that influence the voting behaviour of people in rural areas, a preliminary focus group study may be undertaken to list various important factors and issues that people take into account when voting such as caste, religion, socio-economic status of the contestants, etc. The data thus collected from this preliminary focus group study may be used to design the questionnaire for the survey study.

Second combination: *Focus groups as the primary method and survey for preliminary study*

In the second combination, focus groups are the primary method, while surveys provide preliminary inputs. Studies following this research design make use of the data obtained from survey in selecting samples for focus groups to carry out a detailed analysis.

For example, a preliminary survey study may be carried out to know about the opinion of students regarding implementation of semester system. After determining the general opinion of the students either for or against the semester system, a more intense and detailed focus group study may be carried out to find out the reasons that students give for their respective opinion.

Third combination: *Survey as the primary method and focus group as a follow-up*

The third combination uses survey as the primary method and focus group as a follow-up study. This type of research design is increasingly being used for interpreting the survey results and in determining the degree to which the results of both methods are in conformity or at variance with each other. For example, if a survey study finds out that people in rural areas give high priority to caste factor during voting, it may be cross-checked by a follow-up focus group study.

Fourth combination: *Focus group as the primary method and survey as a follow-up*

The fourth combination uses focus group as the primary method and survey as a follow-up. For example, if a focus group study suggests caste as the most important factor determining the voting behaviour of people in rural India, it can be cross-checked by a follow-up survey.

In comparison, survey offers more breadth to research both in terms of coverage of area and coverage of issues. Focus group offers more depth to research by means of in-depth and detailed investigation over a topic.

Strength and Weakness of Focus Groups

Morgan and Krueger argue that compared to other methods, the real strength of focus groups is not simply in exploring what people have to say, but in providing insights into the sources of complex behaviours and motivations. They view this advantage of focus groups as a direct outcome of the interaction in focus groups. What makes the discussion in focus groups more than the sum of separate individual interviews is the fact that the participants both query each other and introduce themselves to each other. Morgan and Krueger argue that such interaction offers valuable data on the extent of consensus and diversity among the participants. This ability to observe the extent and nature of interviewees' agreement and disagreement is a unique strength of focus groups.

The weaknesses of focus groups, like their strengths, are linked to the process of producing focused interactions, raising issues about both the role of the moderator in generating the data and the impact of the group itself on the data. Agar and MacDonald, and Saferstein from their respective studies have concluded that the behaviour of the moderator has consequences for the nature of group interviews.

Sussman et al. in their study administered questionnaires before and after focus group discussion to find out if the focus group discussion changed the participants' attitudes. They found that the attitudes became more extreme after the group discussion. In other words, after the focus group discussion, there was a polarisation effect on the attitudes of the participants. Thus, it could be concluded that 'group effect' also influences the response of participants in a focus group.

Further, critics argue that only a limited range of topics can be researched effectively in groups. It is argued that some sensitive issues may be unacceptable for discussion among some categories of research participants. However, this assumption is being questioned in the light of widespread use of group interviews to study various sensitive issues like sexual behaviour, etc. (Morgan, 1996).

Comparative Method

Comparative method refers to the study of different types of groups and societies in order to determine analytically the factors that lead to similarities and differences in specified patterns of behaviour.

Comparative method is an integral component of the positivist tradition in sociology. The founding fathers of sociology like Auguste Comte, Herbert Spencer and Emile Durkheim laid great emphasis on the use of 'comparative method' in any sociological enquiry. In the nineteenth century, when sociology as a discipline was still in its infancy stage, the principal attraction of the comparative method lay in the belief that it could be used for discovering scientific laws about human society and culture. The strong advocates of the comparative method believed in the possibility of a natural science of society that would establish regularities of coexistence and succession among the forms of social life by means of systematic comparisons. Unlike natural sciences, sociology cannot make proper use of experimental method in the study of any particular social phenomena in a laboratory due to certain moral and ethical reasons. But a sociologist can surely experiment in the laboratory of the world by employing the comparative method.

Not only was the early use of the comparative method tied to the idea of a natural science of society, it was, more specifically, tied to the theory of evolution. A large part of nineteenth-century anthropology was concerned with the origins of phenomena and the reconstruction of the stages through which they had evolved from simplest to their most complex forms. The classification and comparison of the forms of social life became an indispensable part of this process of reconstruction (Beteille, 2009).

The central place assigned to comparison was signalled by Durkheim when he wrote: 'Comparative sociology is not a special branch of sociology; it is sociology itself'. Durkheim regarded the comparative method as the counterpart in the social sciences of the experimental method pursued in natural sciences. He recognised that social fact could only be observed, not artificially produced, under experimental conditions. Therefore, Durkheim favoured a comparative-historical approach because sociologists could not carry out experiments and had to rely on the method of indirect experiment, that is, the comparison of similar cases in a systematic way. In this regard, it is important to note that Durkheim, following J.S. Mill's *System of Logic*, refers appreciatively to the 'method of concomitant variations' as the procedure of the comparative method. He calls it 'instrument par excellence of sociological research'. Please note that concomitant variation simply refers to the method of establishing statistical correlation between two variables. For example, Durkheim in his study of suicide found that Germany, a Protestant-dominated country, reported a high suicide rate, whereas Spain, a Catholic-dominated country, reported a low suicide rate. Hence, he arrived at the conclusion that the rate of suicide is correlated with the religious faith in a society.

However, in this regard, S.F. Nadel in his work *The Foundations of Social Anthropology* argues that the notion of concomitant variations does not mean the same thing in J.S. Mill's *System of Logic* and in Durkheim's sociological treatise. Nadel argues that while for Mill concomitant variations imply quantitative correlation, Durkheim makes and advocates the use of comparative method with concomitant variations to arrive at qualitative correlations. For instance, after having arrived at a statistical correlation between the suicide rate and a particular religion, he further explores what makes people of a particular religious faith more or less prone to suicide. The answer he arrived at was solidarity. The lower degree of solidarity or social integration among the Protestants made them prone to greater suicidal tendencies, while higher solidarity among the Catholics, affirmed by the age-old institution of Church, resulted in relatively fewer suicides. Hence, Durkheim concluded that 'the rate of suicide is inversely proportional to the degree of solidarity'.

A.R. Radcliffe-Brown (1881–1955), in Britain, was another strong advocate of the comparative method. Radcliffe-Brown borrowed a great deal from Durkheim, including the idea that societies were governed by laws that could be discovered by the application of the proper method. That method was the comparative method based on observation, description and comparison of societies as they actually existed. He often used the term 'comparative sociology' as a synonym for social anthropology. He argued that in comparative sociology or social anthropology, the purpose of comparison is to explore the varieties of forms of social life as a basis for the theoretical study of human social phenomena. In his essay 'The Comparative Method in Social Anthropology', Radcliffe-Brown further extended the argument of Durkheim to explain why a particular totem is chosen by a society or group as its totem. In a comparative analysis of various tribes of Australia and north-west America, he found various instances whereby a tribe was divided into two exogamous moieties and each moiety represented by particular natural specie as its totem. For example, in case of Australian aborigines in New South Wales, the two moieties were represented by eaglehawk and crow. On the basis of his comparative study, he concluded that the selection of a particular set of natural species as the totem by the two exogamous moieties of a tribe is also associated with their inter-group social relations. He found it common that natural species were placed in pairs of opposites, with certain degree of resemblances as well as differences. He interpreted the resemblances and differences of animal species in terms of social relationships of friendship and antagonism in human society.

Thus, on the basis of his comparative study he arrived at a higher order generalisation that relationships of mutual alliance and antagonism are universal to human society. However, the manner in which these relationships of alliance and opposition get reflected may vary from society to society. For example, in his comparative study of the institution of marriage, he found that the expression of relationships of alliance and opposition may take the form of joking and avoidance relationship. In joking relationship, members of opposite divisions are permitted or expected to indulge in teasing each other, in verbal abuse or in exchange of insults. Joking relationships serve to protect the delicate relationships between persons who are bound together in one set of ties and yet separated by other ties. For example, the members of different lineages are socially separated from each other, but, if they marry each other, they are also allied. Joking, thus, is one way of defusing the tensions of certain delicate relationships. Another response is avoidance or extreme respect. It prevents conflicts that might arise through divergence of interest. In many societies, a man is required to avoid any close social contact with the mother of his wife and others (Radcliffe-Brown, 1958).

However, André Béteille in his essay 'Some Observations on the Comparative Method' argues that the great wave of enthusiasm for the comparative method belongs to the past, and today there are probably more sceptics than enthusiasts. Among the sceptics, Franz Boas, Goldenweiser and Evans-Pritchard are some of the important names. For example, Franz Boas objected to the sweeping generalisations made through the use of comparative method, and recommended studies on a more limited geographical scale. He clearly stated his preference for 'historical method' over and above the comparative method. Similarly, Evans-Pritchard recommended intensive comparative investigation in a limited area rather than going for universal generalisations. Similarly, scholars belonging to the phenomenological tradition argue that the application of this method is not as simple as it may appear because social units have different meanings in different societies. For instance, the institution of marriage among Hindus is regarded as an indissoluble and sacred bond between husband and wife. Muslim marriage, on the other hand, is not a religious sacrament but a secular bond. It is a social or civil contract, which can be terminated (Beteille, 2009).

However, despite these criticisms and limitations of comparative method, its significance in sociology cannot be undermined. For example, Durkheim and Weber in their respective works have clearly highlighted the importance of comparative method as a scientific for sociological enquiry for a comprehensive understanding of social reality.

Historical Method

As discussed earlier, enquiries in social sciences could be classified in two categories: the nomothetic and the ideographic. According to this classification, the ideographic sciences are those which study unique and unrepeatable events, while the nomothetic sciences attempt to make generalisations. We can, thus, call sociology as a nomothetic science and history as an ideographic science. Historians try to increase our accurate knowledge of unique phenomena of the past, whereas sociologists try to seek information about certain uniformities in social behaviour under specific conditions. This, in principle, is the difference between the two modes of enquiry. However, the data of history are also widely used now by sociologists. On the other hand, historians have also started using data generated by sociologists for their own writings.

Historical method is one of the important methods to analyse the process of social change that occurred in the past. It involves the study of origins, development and transformation of social institutions over a period of time. The historical method in sociology has taken two principal forms. The first is that of early sociologists, initially influenced by the philosophy of history and later by biological theory of evolution. It concentrates upon the origin, development and transformation of social institutions, societies and civilisations. It is concerned with the whole span of human history with all the major institutions of society, as in the works of Comte, Spencer, Hobhouse, etc. It was also employed by Karl Marx in conjunction with dialectical materialism in understanding the human societies. Marx talked of dialectical materialism to explain change as a historical phenomenon. According to Marx, the history of all the hitherto societies is the history of class struggle. He classified the evolution of human society in terms of the following stages, viz. primitive communism, ancient society, feudal society, capitalist society and communism.

Yet another form of historical method is characteristic of the works of Max Weber. This is exemplified, especially, in his studies of the origins of capitalism, the development of modern bureaucracy and the economic influence of the world religions. The main methodological features of these studies are that particular historical changes of social structures and types of society are investigated and are compared in certain respects with changes in other societies. In this manner, both causal explanations and historical interpretations find a place in the social explanation. A very convincing illustration of this approach of Weber is to be found in his treatment of the growth of capitalism in Europe, as he brings out in his book *The Protestant Ethic and the Spirit of Capitalism*.

P.V. Young, in her book *Scientific Social Surveys and Research*, describes sources of historical data highlighting both the adequacy and the limitations of historical data. The social scientists generally confine themselves to three major sources of historical information: (i) documents and various historical sources to which historians themselves have access, (ii) materials of cultural history and of analytical history and (iii) personal sources of authentic observers and witnesses. When, how and under what circumstances these sources are to be used depends upon the discretion of the researcher's interest, the scope of the study and the availability of the sources. Historical data have some limitations, which arise mainly because historians cannot describe all the happenings in time and space available at the time of writing history. Personal biases and private interpretations, often, enter unconsciously, even when honest attempts are made to select and interpret pertinent facts.

LET'S THINK

Dear Learner, I am sure that by now you must have understood the technicalities and complexities of sociological research. You must have also understood the challenges that are associated with sociological research, especially with regard to maintaining reliability and validity, in other words, objectivity in research. Can you now think of a social problem that you may wish to investigate? Develop a hypothesis and prepare your research design. What techniques of data collection would you choose for the purpose of your research and why?

For Practice

Q1. Analyse the changing notion of the 'field' in sociological research with suitable examples.

Q2. Comparative sociology is not a special branch of sociology; it is sociology itself. Discuss.

Q3. Participant observation is the most effective tool for collecting facts. Comment.

Q4. Compare and contrast the quantitative research methodology with qualitative research methodology. Which of the two in your opinion is best suited for sociological research?

Q5. Formulate a hypothesis, research design and list the research techniques you would use to understand the influences on marriage choices among young people.

Model Answers

Q. Compare and contrast the quantitative research methodology with qualitative research methodology. Which of the two in your opinion is best suited for sociological research?

A. Methodology is an integral aspect of any scientific discipline. In sociology, two major methodological traditions could be identified, viz. quantitative and qualitative methods.

Quantitative research in sociology is largely associated with the 'positivist tradition'. Early sociologists belonging to the positivist tradition, such as Auguste Comte, Herbert Spencer, Emile Durkheim, etc., believed that social reality can be studied with the same methods and procedures as that of natural sciences. This assertion of positivist was largely based on the following assumptions. First, they viewed social reality as an objective reality and believed that the behaviour of man, like the behaviour of matter, can be objectively measured. Second, they placed particular emphasis on behaviour that can be directly observed, and ignored those aspects of behaviour which are not directly observable, such as subjective meanings, feelings and motives unique to an individual actor. Some of the key features of quantitative research in sociology are: (i) it focuses on the study of social facts and treats social facts as 'things', (ii) it relies on statistical data to establish correlation and cause-and-effect relationship between two or more variables and (iii) it assumes the cause-and-effect relationship so arrived can be universally generalised subject to empirical verification and replication. The study of suicide by Durkheim could be cited as one of the best demonstrations of the application of this methodology. Quantitative research is associated with a number of techniques of data collection such as survey, questionnaire, structured interview and secondary sources of data, etc. Quantitative methodology facilitates extensive research and, thus, adds more breadth to research. Though it offers high reliability, it scores low in validity.

On the other hand, some scholars argued that in order to have a complete understanding of man's social behaviour, it is not only important but also necessary to take into account the unique meanings, motives and values that underlie such behaviour. These scholars, such as Max Weber, G.H. Mead, etc., are largely associated with the anti-positivist tradition and emphasise on the interpretative understanding of social action. They advocate the use of qualitative research methods such as participant observation, unstructured interview, focus group, case study method, etc. to understand human social behaviour. Some of the key features of qualitative research in sociology are as follows:

(i)   it focuses on empathetic description of reality,
(ii) it exhibits a preference for contextualism and
(iii) views social life as dynamic and emphasises on its processual dimension.

Malinowski, W.F. Whyte, Srinivas, André Béteille, etc. used qualitative research methods, participant observation to be more specific, in their respective studies. Qualitative methodology facilitates intensive research and, thus, adds more depth to research. Though it offers high validity, it scores low in reliability.

However, most sociologists in contemporary times suggest a combination of both research methodologies in their social research to enhance its reliability as well validity. For example, Alan Bryman has suggested a number of ways in which a plurality of methods – a practice known as *triangulation* – can be useful.

Q. Formulate a hypothesis, research design and list the research techniques you would use to understand the influences on marriage choices among young people.

A. Sociology is a scientific study of society and all phenomena and processes that unfold within it. Sociological theories are arrived at on the basis of empirical research. Sociological research, thus, is not a random search for facts. It is a guided research that begins with defining precisely the objective of the research. A clearly defined and verifiable hypothesis is, thus, the first step in sociological research which guides and directs sociological research.

A hypothesis is a tentative statement asserting a relationship between two or more variables, though there could be several factors that may influence the marriage choices of young people, such as caste, religion, region, education, career orientation, etc. However, in the light of the research problem stated above, one of the possible hypotheses could be: 'Increase in literacy rate is directly proportional to the average marital age' or 'Increase in education tends to increase the incidence of inter-caste marriages in India'.

The next step is to develop a research design. A research design is a plan for the collection, analysis and evaluation of data. It involves:

Step 1: Identification of a suitable field. It could be a group of undergraduate students in a university or young people visiting a mall.

Step 2: Choice of a sampling method (for a representative sample).

Step 3: Selection of appropriate techniques of data collection as per field requirements. For example, if the sample size is large and dispersed, then considering the time and cost factor, a survey through questionnaire would be more suitable. However, if the sample is small, then data can be collected with the help of an interview schedule or structured interview. Some of the sample questions could be: 'What is your name?', 'What is your caste/religion?', 'What are your educational qualifications?', 'For marriage, which of the following factors is most important for you?' (caste, religion, education, income, etc.), 'At what age would you prefer to get married?' (15–20 years, 20–25 years, 25–30 years, etc.).

Step 4: Cross-checking of data. Let's say if the primary technique of data collection was a quantitative method, e.g. questionnaire, then these findings can be cross-checked with the help of a qualitative method, e.g. an interview. This process of cross-checking the reliability and validity of data by adopting a plurality of methods is called triangulation by Alan Bryman.

Step 5: Data analysis in the next step in order to identify certain patterns, if any, and establish a cause-and-effect relationship between variables as proposed in the hypothesis.

Step 6: Report writing. The findings of the research are finally submitted as a report for further verification.

Sociological findings thus arrived at could facilitate the understanding of the complex social reality and contribute significantly in the formulation of social policy and bringing about necessary social reforms.

References

Ahuja, Ram. *Research Methods*. Jaipur: Rawat Publications, 2008.

Bailey, K.D. *Methods of Social Research*. New York: The Free Press, 1994.

Béteille, André. *Sociology: Essays on Approach & Method*. 2nd Edition. New Delhi: Oxford University Press, 2009.

Goode, W.J. and Paul K. Hatt. *Methods in Social Research*. New Delhi: Surjeet Publications, 2006.

Gupta, Akhil and James Fergusson. *Anthropological Locations: Boundaries and Grounds of a Field Science*. Berkeley: University of California Press, 1997.

Gupta, S.P. *Elementary Statistical Methods*. New Delhi: Sultan Chand, 1990.

Haralambos, M. and R.M. Heald. *Sociology: Themes and Perspectives*. New Delhi: Oxford University Press, 2006.

Haralambos, Michael, Martin Holborn, Steve Chapman and Stephen Moore. *Sociology: Themes and Perspectives*. 8th Edition. London: Collins, 2014.

Morgan, David L. 'Focus Groups', *Annual Review of Sociology*, 22, pp. 29–52, 1996.

Srinivas, M.N., A.M. Shah and E.A. Ramaswamy, eds. *The Fieldworker and the Field: Problems and Challenges in Sociological Investigation*. New Delhi: Oxford University Press, 2002.

Radcliffe-Brown, A.R. *Method in Social Anthropology*. New Delhi: Asia Publishing Corporation, 1958.

PART II
Sociological Thought

5

FOUNDING FATHERS OF SOCIOLOGY

Auguste Comte

About Comte

Isidore Auguste Marie Francois-Xavier Comte (1798–1857) was an influential French social theorist and philosopher. Comte is known as the father of sociology, a term he first used in 1839 to describe the new 'positive science of society'. Sociology was the first academic discipline to look specifically at human society. In the nineteenth century, in a series of books, Comte developed a general approach to the study of society. He believed that the sciences follow one another in a definite and logical order and that all enquiry goes through certain stages, arriving finally at the last, scientific stage. He thought that it was time for enquiries into social problems and social phenomena to enter the last stage and so he recommended that the study of society should become the science of society (Ransome, 2011).

Comte was born in Montpellier, France, during an era of revolutionary upheaval. His parents were staunch monarchists and conservative Roman Catholics. Unlike many French citizens who applauded the decline of the old order and the new promise of liberty, equality and brotherhood for all, Comte's parents despised the revolution and decried the persecution of Catholicism. As a minor official working in a regional tax office, Comte's father earned enough to provide adequately for his wife and his children. At age 9, Comte was enrolled in a local residential military school, the Lycie de Montpellier. There he quickly gained attention for both his intellect and mischievousness. Comte also became a source of distress to his parents at an early age. By the age of 13, he openly rejected his parents' deepest beliefs and declared himself to be a republican and a freethinker.

DOI: 10.4324/9781003291053-7

Comte's life was characterised by conflict and contradictions. He had been a brilliant student in school. Having mastered all the courses taught at his school, Comte took the entrance exam for Ecole Polytechnique in Paris, which was considered as the most prestigious scientific institution in the world of the time. Although he passed the exam with the fourth highest score in all of France, Comte, at 15, was a year too young to be allowed to begin his studies there. So, before entering the school, he spent a year taking advanced courses in mathematics at a local university and teaching mathematics at the Lycie de Montpellier. In 1814, he entered Ecole Polytechnique which was a renowned centre for scientific research. Although he was respected by students and teachers alike for his superior academic performance, Comte repeatedly got in trouble for questioning authority and breaking curfew regulations. An ardent republican who kept a copy of the Constitution of the United States in his desk, Comte took a central role in the informal political discussions that occurred among students after classes. His wit and humour made him a natural leader. At one point in 1815, he was imprisoned by the school for two weeks for talking back to a school official. But in 1816, a much more serious incident occurred. Comte led a students' protest against the administration over policy issues and on account of his participation in this demonstration, Comte was dismissed from the school. That ended Comte's formal education along with his chance of pursuing a career in government (Abraham and Morgan, 2010).

Comte supported himself by offering private tuitions in mathematics and with some assistance from his family. However, despite his extremely limited income, Comte's parsimony enabled him to attend the theatre and also to enjoy the services of prostitutes. In 1817, Comte met Claude Henri de Saint-Simon (1760–1825). Saint-Simon, then director of the periodical *Industrie*, was a creative, fertile, disorderly and tumultuous man who was to have a major and lasting influence on Comte's life and works. Saint-Simon was attracted by the brilliant young man who possessed a trained and methodical capacity for work, which Saint-Simon so conspicuously lacked. Comte became his secretary and close collaborator. Almost 40 years Comte's senior, Saint-Simon had led an interesting life. Born to a French family of minor nobility, he had run away from the home of an authoritarian father at the age of 19, arrived in the United States during the American Revolution and ended up as an officer and aide to General George Washington. After fighting in the final battle at Yorktown, Saint-Simon returned to France, and made and lost a number of fortunes before he devoted the rest of his life to philosophical pursuits. His goal was to develop an applied reformist philosophy suited to the industrial nature of modern society. Disorganised and contradictory in parts, Saint-Simon's philosophy looked to scientists to fulfil the role of society's new 'spiritual leaders' who would help bring in an era of progress and social stability (Coser, 2008).

Though a member of the French aristocracy, Saint-Simon became one of the earliest and most prominent Utopian socialists. Utopian socialists, one of the social thinkers, perhaps social dreamers, believed that the problems of the society of their time could be best solved by reorganising economic production. According to these scholars, the economic reorganisation could be achieved by depriving the proprietary class of the means of production of economic freedom, a foremost value of the time (Timasheff, 1967). However, the most interesting aspect of Saint-Simon was his significance to the development of both conservative (like Comte's) and radical Marxian theory. On the conservative side, Saint-Simon was largely concerned with the social stability and order. But, for this, he did not seek a return to life as it had been in the Middle Ages, as did Bonald and Maistre. Instead, being a positivist, he emphasised on the scientific study of social phenomena with the help of similar methods, as employed in natural sciences, to arrive at social laws. On the radical side, Saint-Simon saw the need for socialist reforms, especially the centralised planning of the economic system. But Saint-Simon did not go nearly as far as Marx did later. Although he, like Marx, saw the capitalists superseding the feudal nobility, he felt it inconceivable that the working class would come to replace the capitalists. Many of the Saint-Simon's ideas are found in Comte's work, but Comte developed them in a more systematic fashion (Ritzer and Stepnisky, 2014).

From 1817 to 1824, Comte worked as Saint-Simon's secretary and general assistant, editing, rewriting and even producing first drafts of articles for him. In 1824, Comte and Saint-Simon had a fallout that led to a permanent rift between them. Among the explanations put forth are the young Comte's rejection of the religious elements that Saint-Simon began to incorporate into his work, his jealousy of the senior philosopher's fame and his anger at Saint-Simon for publishing under his own name essays that Comte had written. Along with these, apparently, there was also a divergence among the two with regard to the strategy for social reform. Saint-Simon emphasised the need for immediate reform. He wanted to inspire the liberal industrialists and bankers who were his supporters to take prompt steps for the reorganisation of French society. Comte, in contrast, emphasised that theoretical work had to take precedence over reform activities, and that establishing the foundations of the scientific doctrine was more important for the time being than effecting any practical influence.

With the termination of collaboration with Saint-Simon, Comte was once more thrust into a marginal existence, tutoring and attempting to arouse interest in his ideas in a series of public lectures. Comte married Caroline Massine, a bookseller, who had formerly been a prostitute, in 1825. The marriage was a miserable failure, suffering through a perpetual tempest of confusions, misunderstandings and incompatibilities. In 1826, Comte began working on a series of public lectures on his philosophy to be held at his apartment. These lectures were to provide the foundation for *The Positive Philosophy* (1830–1842). These lectures drew a distinguished audience but were halted after three lectures when Comte suffered a nervous breakdown. The stress of the lectures, combined with worry over his meagre income and marital difficulties, contributed to his collapse (Caroline had recently left Comte after he had flown into a rage at her suggestion that she could supplement their income by allowing private visits from a wealthy lawyer). Comte was treated for 'mania' and institutionalised for months. It should be noted that Caroline stood by him during this difficult time. Comte continued to suffer from a depression that left him unable to work. Comte twice attempted suicide. After the second suicide attempt, when he was saved from drowning in the River Seine by a passing guard, Comte recovered sufficiently to begin to write again. His rescue on the second attempt convinced him that he had been saved in order to complete his life's work – the elaboration of a positivist philosophy (Adams and Sydie, 2016). Comte resumed his wretched life in neglect and isolation. During 1830–1842, Comte wrote his masterwork, the *Cours de philosophie positive*, i.e. *The Course of Positive Philosophy*, also popularly known as *The Positive Philosophy*. Throughout this period, Comte faced serious financial difficulties and continued to live miserably on the margin of the academic world. He had a series of low-paid, marginal academic jobs, such as appointments as a teaching assistant at Ecole Polytechnique in 1832 and as an external examiner in 1837, and as a mathematics teacher at a private school. Comte's attempts to get a regular academic appointment were futile, and in 1844 his appointment as an external examiner at the Ecole was not renewed. In addition, his marriage deteriorated, and Caroline left him just after the completion of *The Positive Philosophy*.

Volumes of *The Positive Philosophy* were published in 1830, 1835, 1838, 1839, 1841 and 1843. Although Comte had previously used the term 'sociology' (*sociologie*) in private correspondence, it was in *The Positive Philosophy* that this name for his proposed science of society first appeared in print. While working on this project, Comte discovered the principle of 'cerebral hygiene'. This discovery, in application to his life, meant that he stopped reading other's works in order to keep his mind uncontaminated by the thought of others. Comte's life became more bearable in 1844 when he met the young Clotilde de Vaux, a 30-year-old minor novelist who descended from an aristocratic family. At the age of 20, she had married to escape a tyrannical father. Her husband, a minor government official, was found to have embezzled government funds and disappeared when Clotilde was 25. Thus, when Comte and de Vaux met, both were already married to other individuals. Clotilde suffered from consumption; and two years after meeting Comte, she died. Comte vowed to devote the rest of his life to the memory of Clotilde and credited her with providing, through her love, the inspiration for his last major work, the organisation of a Religion of Humanity. As a result of this experience of love and deep emotion, Comte became obsessed with the primacy of emotion over intellect, of feeling over mind, such that he began to write and speak openly of his conviction that 'universal love' was the only real solution for all social problems of the time. He began to devise a Religion of Humanity with which he thought of himself as the high priest. Comte died on 5 September 1857, at the age of 59 (Abraham and Morgan, 2010).

Auguste Comte's works can be divided into two distinct phases: (1) the early scientific stage, between 1820 and 1842 and (2) the moralistic and quasi-religious stage, which began in the later 1830s and culminated between 1851 and

1854. The scientific phase involved the publication of several important articles and then, between 1830 and 1842, the five volumes of *The Course of Positive Philosophy*, where the science of society was formally established. The second period in Comte's life is marked by personal tragedy and frustration; during this period, he wrote *System of Positive Polity*, which represented his moralistic view of how society should be reconstructed. Despite the excessive moral preaching of this work, its vision of science as the tool for reconstructing society was to be an important element in sociology's mission as seen by later generations of French sociologists.

It is sometimes difficult to separate Comte's early essays from those of Saint-Simon, because the ageing master often put his name on works written by the young Comte. Yet his essay, 'Plan of the Scientific Operations Necessary for Reorganizing Society', which was written in 1822, just before his break with Saint-Simon, is clearly Comte's and represents the culmination of his thinking, while working under Saint-Simon. This essay also anticipates, and in fact presents an outline of, the entire Comtean scheme as it was to unfold over the succeeding decades. In this essay, Comte argued that it was necessary to create a 'positive science' based on the model of other sciences. This science would ultimately rest on empirical observations and like all sciences, it would seek to formulate the laws governing the organisation and movement of society, an idea implicit in Montesquieu's *The Spirit of Laws*. This new science was to be termed *social physics*. Later, however, on finding that a Belgian statistician, Adolphe Quetelet, had used this term to describe simple statistics, Comte reluctantly changed it to *sociology*. His agenda for sociology was to discover the natural laws of social phenomena, through observation and historical and comparative analyses. With this knowledge, he believed the new science would be able to help society overcome problems of disorder and conflict. Once the laws of human organisation have been discovered and formulated, they can be used to direct society. Scientists of society are thus to be social prophets, indicating the course and direction of human organisation. Comte did not urge revolutionary change, because he felt the natural evolution of society would make things better. Comte believed that social reforms guided by rational social laws derived from scientific sociological research would address social problems of the society.

Comte, like most French intellectuals, and European intellectuals in general, framed his ideas in response to the crises and conflicts that marked the aftermath of the French Revolution. In essence, the current crisis was cultural. France, like all of Europe, was undergoing a great cultural change that would eventually shape the destiny of all societies. The change involved a shift from a religious and metaphysical to a scientific world view. The cultural collision between the religious, metaphysical and scientific world views had reached a climax in nineteenth-century France.

The core of sociological theory of Comte broadly consists of his *perspective*, i.e. his assumptions towards social reality, the *Law of Three Stages* and the *hierarchy of sciences* in which sociology occupies the summit. Let's discuss these keys aspects of Comte's theory in detail.

Perspective

Comte's perspective about social reality was largely shaped by intellectual influences on him. He was influenced by the ideas of both, the conservatives and the Enlightenment scholars. On the conservative side, the ideas of Bonald and Maistre appealed to Comte. Comte, like Saint-Simon, acknowledged that society is an organic whole and its various parts exist in a mutual interrelationship giving rise to social stability and harmony. Thus, the family, the Church, the State, etc. exist in a delicate and finely adjusted balance. In the backdrop of social chaos and disorder in European society, particularly in France in the post-French revolution period, Comte, like Bonald and Maistre, realised that for social stability and harmony it is essential that society is bound by the ties of moral community. This led Comte to emphasise the primacy of society or group over individuals.

Comte's sociology rests on the assumption of social realism – implying that society is a 'real being' and an objective reality – having its own independent existence over and above individuals comprising it. The key to Comte's new science was the idea that society has a 'real' existence with properties separate and also different from those of individuals. In fact, individual human beings are absent from Comte's sociology; he is almost entirely concerned with society (Adams and Sydie, 2016). The primacy that Comte accorded to society over the individual was also partly influenced by his perception of individuals. Rather than viewing individuals as rational beings, Comte saw them as beings whose emotional instincts tended to dominate their rational intellectual abilities. He argued that individuals were incapable of self-control and in order to live together harmoniously, they needed to be socially and morally regulated by society (Ashley and Orenstein, 2007).

Comte's sociology began with the premise that every science has its own separate subject matter. Departing from the conventional wisdom of many Enlightenment thinkers, Comte thought that it was a mistake to conceive of society as a collection of individuals. Instead, he believed that society consisted of social interaction, social rules and institutions that are independent of the psychology of individuals. He did not view the individual as a 'true social unit'; indeed, he relegated the study of the individual to biology – an unfortunate oversight because it denied the legitimacy of psychology as a distinct social science. The most basic social unit, he argued, is 'the family'. It is the most elementary unit from which all other social units ultimately evolved. Comte argued that it is family that produces individuals, and not individuals who produce families.

Comte's social realism was so extreme that he insisted that, whereas society is real, the individual exists only as an 'abstraction'. The denial of individual life as having an independent existence from social reality is clearly demonstrated in Comte's hierarchical classification of the sciences. Comte presented sociology as directly following biology in reference to the complexity of the 'reality' on which each science focuses. With his denial of an individual reality, Comte excluded psychology from an intermediate position between the science of living organisms (biology) and the science of society (sociology). What most theorists would view as individual psychological phenomena (thoughts, feelings, wishes, etc.), Comte ascribed to either biological or social reality.

However, despite being partly influenced by conservatives, Comte could not accept their retrograde vision. He did not seek a return to life as it had been in the Middle Ages, as did Bonald and Maistre. To him, the good society was not to be found in the medieval past but in a future yet to come. Comte shared the optimistic and futuristic vision of Enlightenment scholars. He clung to the idea of social progress, even though beholden to the vision of social order (Coser, 2008).

The Law of Three Stages
(also known as *'The Law of Human Progress'*)

Comte presents his views on society and social change in his Law of Three Stages. According to Comte, intellectual development (or the development of human mind or knowledge) is closely linked with the social development (or social change). Comte thought that he had discovered a law governing the progress of the human mind. According to the so-called Law of Three Stages, the human mind (or knowledge) passes through three stages of thought: the theological, the metaphysical and the positive.

In the *Theological Stage*, the human mind explains the origin and nature of any phenomena by reference to supernatural entities (e.g. spirits, divine beings, gods). A Christian world view would exemplify the theological stage.

In the *Metaphysical Stage*, explanations are not supernatural, but are based on intuition, guesswork and reason but are not supported by any conclusive empirical evidence. Comte used western European history from the Reformation to the end of the French Revolution to illustrate the metaphysical stage. The metaphysical stage corresponded roughly to the Middle Ages and the Renaissance.

In the *Positive Stage*, explanations are based on both observed facts and logical reasoning. Religious or philosophical speculation gives way to the discovery of natural and social laws. The positive stage represents the era of the modern sciences.

Comte argued that corresponding to the three stages of mental progress, there are three stages of society. For Comte, there was a direct correlation between the evolution of the human mind and the evolution of human society. As one develops, so does the other. Human history is fundamentally the history of the progress of mind and society (Abraham and Morgan, 2010). On the basis of his studies of history of science and other social institutions, Comte maintained that all societies develop at a gradual rate from what he termed a 'theological stage' to a 'positive stage' passing through an intermediate, transitional and chaotic 'metaphysical stage' (Figure 5.1). Comte drew on ethnographic and

Stage	Time Period	Everything Explained by	Dominated by	Primary Social Unit
Theological Stage	Early Humankind	Supernatural	Priests and Military	Family
Metaphysical Stage	Middle Ages	Abstract	Churches (Clergy) and Lawyers	State
Positive or Scientific Stage	Post-Renaissance	Scientific Observation	Industrial Administrators and Scientific Moral Guides	Entire Human Race

FIGURE 5.1 The Law of Human Progress

Western (particularly French) historical data to illustrate the predominant characteristics of the theological, metaphysical and positive stage of societal evolution. Societies were distinguished in terms of their contributions to order and progress.

- *Theological Stage*: Military men and priests dominate, and the major social unit is the family. This stage offers order but no progress.
- *Metaphysical Stage*: The priests' dominance is challenged by lawyers, and the major social unit is the state. This stage offers progress, usually of the revolutionary kind, but no order and often anarchy.
- *Positive Stage*: Order and progress are reconciled under the guidance of scientists and industrialists, who act on behalf of the major social unit – humanity (Adams and Sydie, 2016).

Comte believed that the new scientific-industrial society will become the society of all mankind. This is the ultimate stage in a series of successive transformations the human race goes through and each stage is decidedly superior to the previous one. Social change is viewed as a linear, directional progressive process. Humanity is moving towards the same goal or endpoint, even if at varying rates. Driving social development is the evolution of the human mind. Changes in social and political institutions are correlated with cultural evolution. Comte held that all humanity evolves through these three social stages; history culminates in the positive age.

Comte believed that 'intellectual evolution', i.e. the evolution of human thought, is the most important basis of his explanation of human progress. However, he did not rule out other causal factors. For example, he considered *growth in human population* a major factor which determines the rate of social progress. The more the population there, the more the *division of labour*. Comte believed that the division of labour was the fundamental cause of the growing complexity of society. The more the division of labour in a society, the more evolved it will become. Thus, he saw division of labour as a powerful force in the progress of social evolution. Solidarity and cooperation must, therefore, characterise the relationship of individuals to each other in society. Within this context, Comte coined the word 'altruism'.

Thus, as social systems develop, they become increasingly differentiated, and yet like all organisms, they maintain their integration. This view of social structure led Comte to the problem that Adam Smith had originally suggested with such force: how is integration among parts maintained in the face of increasing differentiation of functions? This question was to occupy French sociology in the nineteenth century, culminating in Durkheim's theoretical formulations.

Comte's proposed solution to this problem reveals much about how he viewed the maintenance of social structure. First, the potentially disintegrating impact of social differentiation is countered by the centralisation of power in government, which will then maintain fluid coordination among system parts. Second, the actions of government must be more than 'material'; they must also be 'intellectual and moral'. Hence, human social organisation is maintained by (1) mutual dependence of system parts on one another, (2) centralisation of authority to coordinate exchanges of parts and (3) development of a common morality or spirit among members of a population. To the extent that differentiating systems cannot meet these conditions, pathological states are likely to occur.

In presenting this analysis, Comte felt that he had uncovered several laws of social statics, because he believed that differentiation, centralisation of power and development of a common morality were fundamentally related to the maintenance of the social order. Although he did not carry his analysis far, he presented Durkheim with both the basic question and the broad contours of the answer.

Hierarchy of the Sciences

Comte's second-best known theory, that of hierarchy of the sciences, is intimately connected with the Law of Three Stages. Comte believed that like individuals and societies, sciences also pass through similar stages of development, viz. theological, metaphysical and positive stage. But different sciences progress at different rates. The differential rate of advancement to the positive stage formed the basis of what Comte presented as the 'hierarchy of the sciences'. According to Comte, this hierarchical arrangement of sciences coincided with:

1. the order of their historical emergence and development
2. the order of their dependence upon each other (i.e. each rests on the one that precedes it and prepares the way for the one that follows it)
3. the increasing degree of complexity of their subject matter
4. the decreasing degree of their generality

Comte further stated that the hierarchy moved from the study of the 'most general, simple, abstract and remote phenomena known to us, and those that affect all others without being affected by them', i.e. mathematics, to the 'most particular, compound, concrete phenomena, and those which are the most interesting to Man', i.e. sociology (ibid.).

> The abstract and theoretical sciences form a hierarchy in which the more concrete and complex sciences succeed the more general and abstract sciences. The hierarchy, determined by the natural law of mental progress, is based on the order in which positive method comes to be adopted in the disciplines. The base of the hierarchy is mathematics, followed by astronomy, because these are the sciences in which the positive method comes to be adopted first. In time, they are followed by physics, chemistry, much later biology, and finally sociology.
>
> *(Abraham and Morgan, 2010)*

Thus, thought about the physical universe (inorganic world) reaches the positive stage before conceptions of the organic world, because the inorganic world is simpler and organic phenomena are built from inorganic phenomena. In Comte's view, astronomy was the first science to reach the positivistic stage, then physics, next came chemistry, and after these three had reached the positivistic (scientific) stage, thought about organic phenomena could become more positivistic. The first organic science to move from the metaphysical to the positivistic stage was biology (physiology). And with biology now a positivistic doctrine, sociology could move away from the metaphysical speculations of the seventeenth and eighteenth centuries (and the residues of earlier theological thought) toward a positivistic mode of thought. Thus, the final arrangement of the sciences in terms of their emergence and complexity on this basis can be portrayed as shown in Figure 5.2.

Later, however, when Comte settled on 'love' as the basic principle of existence, he added 'Morals' as the last, most 'positive' of the sciences.

Sociology has been the last to emerge, Comte argued, because it is the most complex and because it has had to wait for the other basic sciences to reach the

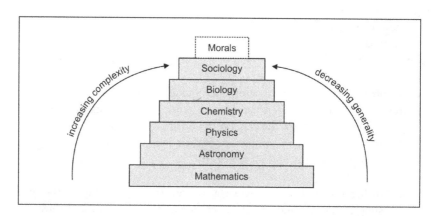

FIGURE 5.2 Hierarchy of the Sciences

positivistic stage. According to Comte, all sciences pass through the three stages, the theological, the metaphysical and, finally, the positive stage. But the individual sciences do not move through these three stages simultaneously. In fact, the higher a science stands in hierarchy, the later it shifts from one stage to another. He argued that all the sciences, except sociology, have reached the positive stage but with the development of sociology the process will be complete.

For the time, such a line of argument represented a brilliant advocacy for a separate science of society, while at the same time it justified the lack of scientific rigour in social thought when compared with the other sciences. Moreover, though dependent on, and derivative of, evolutionary advances in the other sciences, sociology will study phenomena that distinguish it from the lower inorganic phenomena as well as the higher organic science of biology.

Each science in Comte's hierarchy builds on the science that precedes it, so sociology is a distinct science but 'closely connected, from first to last, with biology'. Sociology and biology are closely connected because they are synthetic sciences – that is, they examine the parts of any phenomenon in relation to the whole. In contrast, the analytical sciences at the base of the hierarchy focus on isolated phenomena.

Thus, Comte considered mathematics to be the source of all sciences and he spoke of sociology as the 'crowning edifice', i.e. science of sciences, or, in other words, queen of all sciences. Unlike the other sciences, which analyse one narrow segment of life, sociology integrates all knowledge about humanity. Comte relied upon biology for his guiding social imagery and language. Society is visualised in organic terms, as a system whose 'needs' are met by the normal operation of its functionally interdependent parts. Like any organism, society grows in a slow, continuous and linear way, exhibiting a movement from simplicity to complexity and from potentiality to self-realisation. Sociology was to be the science of society; its aim was to discover the universal laws that govern the organisation and evolution of humanity.

Much as Saint-Simon had emphasised, Comte saw sociology as an extension of the study of 'organisms' in biology to 'social organs'. Hence, sociology was to be the study of social organisations. This emphasis forces the recognition that society is an 'organic whole' whose components stand in relation to one another. To study these parts in isolation is to violate the essence of social organisation and to compartmentalise inquiry artificially. For, as Comte emphasised, 'there can be no scientific study of society, either in its conditions or its movements, if it is separated into portions, and its divisions are studied apart'. Implicit in this emphasis is a mode of analysis that later came to be known as functionalism (Coser, 2008).

Comte advocated that sociology be concerned with the discovery of the most general, most fundamental social laws. Such laws would indicate the ways in which society could be changed. That is, sociology could determine what *is*, what *will be* and what *should be*, because it discovers what conforms to human nature (Adams and Sydie, 2016). Comte was so firmly convinced of the correctness of his views that he sent a copy of his *Positive Philosophy* to Emperor Nicholas I of Russia, writing him a letter in which he took it for granted that the autocratic ruler (who, interestingly, was well trained in mathematics) would initiate reforms elevating Russia to a positive society.

Methodology

As stated earlier, despite being a child of Enlightenment age, Comte was sceptical about the rationality of the human mind. Feelings rather than reason rule the mind. According to Comte, man is not and cannot be by instinct a positivist – his emotions are more likely to be governed by superstition and fear than by cool analysis and logical description. Man is not by nature a positivist; he is not naturally scientific. However, Comte argued that man becomes a positivist gradually through the evolution and progress of society and the human mind. With time, through systematic observation and experimentation, man develops such ability to carry out scientific analysis. This happens when the study of society and its problems enters positive stage with the emergence of a distinct science 'sociology'.

> Comte's aim was to create a naturalistic science of society, which would both explain the past development of mankind and predict its future course. … The society of man, Comte taught, must be studied in the same scientific manner as the world of nature. It is subject to basic laws just as is the rest of the cosmos, even though it presents added complexities. Natural science, Comte argued, had succeeded in establishing the lawfulness of natural phenomena. It discovered that these phenomena, from the falling of stones to the movement of planets, followed ordered sequences of development. In the world of nature, science had succeeded in progressively contracting the realm of the apparently nonordered, the fortuitous and the accidental. The stage was now set for a similar endeavor in the study of society.
>
> *(Coser, 2008)*

Here Comte is suggesting that social reality (society) is the ultimate level of reality and has an objective and independent existence over and above individuals who comprise it. Hence, Comte considers social reality, as an organic whole, the subject matter of sociology. Further, since Comte is sceptical about the rationality of the human mind, Comte believes that sociology, as a positive science, would discover the universal laws that govern the organisation and evolution of humanity. These laws, then, would serve as the basis of social reforms in order to restore social order and harmony in society.

Being a positivist, he emphasised on the scientific study of social phenomena with the help of similar methods, as employed in natural sciences, to arrive as social laws. In sum, then, Comte believed that sociology could be modelled after the natural sciences. It could seek and discover the fundamental properties and relations of the social universe, and like the other sciences, it could express these in a small number of abstract principles. Observations of empirical events could be used to generate, confirm and modify sociology's laws. And once well-developed laws had been formulated, they could be used as tools or instruments to modify the social world.

Auguste Comte defined sociology as a discipline dealing with scientific study of society. He argued that '*from science comes precision, and from precision comes action*'. He summed up the objective of sociology as a scientific discipline in his famous phrase '*to know, to predict, to control*'. Comte was the first social thinker to take seriously methodological questions – that is, how are facts about the social world to be gathered and used to develop, as well as to test, theoretical principles? Comte argued that as a science that rejects metaphysical concerns and concentrates on the discovery of invariable laws, sociology should rely on four methods for learning about social phenomena: (1) observation, (2) experimentation, (3) comparison and (4) historical analysis. Each of these is discussed below:

Observation: For Comte, positivism was based on use of the senses to observe 'social facts' – a term that the next great French theorist, Emile Durkheim, was to make the centre of his sociology. But most important, observation is 'first directed, and finally interpreted, by some theory'. Comte argued that any isolated, empirical observation is 'idle' unless it is connected 'at least hypothetically, with some law'. In a statement that would be echoed in Durkheim's work, Comte stated that 'No social fact can have any scientific meaning till it is connected with some other social fact'. Until the connections are made through theory, information is anecdotal, having no 'rational utility' (Adams and Sydie, 2016). Comte, thus, is rightly credited for firmly establishing sociology as a science of social facts, and thereby liberating thought from the debilitating realm of morals and metaphysical speculation.

Experimentation: Comte believed that experiments similar to natural science experiments were difficult, although not impossible, in sociology. He distinguished between two types of experiment: direct and indirect. Comte recognised that, as in biology, direct experiments are difficult on such a complex and dynamic organism as society. However, the indirect experiment is possible for both biology and sociology. The analysis of a pathology – biological or social – involves the investigation of cases in which the 'natural laws, either of harmony or succession, are disturbed by any causes, special or general, accidental or transient'. Thus, social disturbances are 'analogous to diseases in the individual organism'. The study of physical and social suffering discloses the 'the real laws of our nature, individual or social' – that is, they disclose what is normal and right (ibid.).

In particular, he thought that, much as is the case in biology, pathological events allowed 'the true equivalent of pure experimentation' in that they introduced an artificial condition and allowed investigators to see normal processes reasserting themselves in the face of the pathological condition. Much as the biologist can learn from the study of disease, so can social physicists learn about the normal processes of society from the study of pathological cases. This view of sociological experiments was to inspire later thinkers, such as Durkheim; in many ways, it still guides the modern rationale for the study of deviance.

Comparison: Comparative method is an integral component of the positivist tradition in sociology. Comte believed that three forms of comparison are possible in sociology: comparison of human and animal societies, comparison of all existing human societies and comparison of societies at different stages of development. Comparative method involved the study of different types of groups and societies in order to determine analytically the factors that lead to similarities and differences in specified patterns of behaviour. The strong advocates of the comparative method believed in the possibility of a natural science of society that would establish regularities of coexistence and succession among the forms of social life by means of systematic comparisons.

Historical Analysis: Comte originally classified historical analysis as a variation of the comparative method (that is, comparing the present with the past). But his 'law of the three stage' indicates the importance of a broad historical process. He thought that the laws of social dynamics could ultimately be developed only with careful observations of the historical movement of societies. In sum, then, Comte saw these four basic methods as appropriate to sociological analysis. His formulation of the methods is, of course, quite deficient by modern standards. We should recognise, however, that prior to Comte little attention had been paid to how social facts were to be collected. And thus, although the specifics of Comte's methodological proposals are not always useful, their spirit and intent are most important. Sociology was, in his vision, to be a theoretical science capable of formulating and testing the laws of social organisation and change. His formulation of sociology's methods added increased credibility to this claim.

Social Statics and Dynamics

According to Auguste Comte, all societies undergo changes. He stated that 'it would be a mistake, to expect a new social order any more than a new intellectual order to emerge smoothly from the death throes of an old'. He argued that 'the passage from one social system to another can never be continuous and direct'. Thus, social evolution is marked by alternative 'organic' and 'critical' periods. According to Comte, all societies undergo change and such transition from one stage to another is marked by periods of instability and disturbance. He uses the concept of organic period to denote that stage of society which is characterised by social stability, intellectual harmony and in which various parts of society are in equilibrium. However, he argues that when old traditions and institutions get disturbed, intellectual harmony is lost and there is disequilibrium, then it implies that the society is passing through the critical period. Comte believed that Europe in his own time was passing through such a critical phase that was preparatory to the emergence of the positivistic organic state. Since the contemporary European society was entering the positivistic stage, new forms of knowledge must be based on the positive science methods. Comte argued that such positive science of social life would hasten the process of transition to the new organic state. Sociology was to be such a positive science of society.

Thus, Comte conceived of sociology as consisting of two parts: statics and dynamics. *Social statics* analyses the structure and functioning of society; it describes the elementary parts of society, their functions and interconnections.

Social dynamics investigates the evolution of humanity; it reveals the source of change and its stages and direction. Comte's aim was nothing less than to sketch the universal laws of social statics and dynamics, a project that he began in *The Course of Positive Philosophy* (1830–1842) and completed in the *System of Positive Polity* (1851–1854). Statics reveals the diversity of a particular society out of which the principles of social order can be discovered. Dynamics reveals the successive and necessary laws of progress for human beings and societies. In other words, while social statics is primarily concerned with the aspects of social stability and equilibrium among various parts of society, social dynamics is concerned with the aspects of social change and transition. But the two are vitally connected: order is the basic condition for progress, and progress tends to consolidate social order. Thus, Comte theorised that social change is dialectical. That is, each stage prepares the ground for the transition to the next, higher stage (ibid.).

For Comte, while statics is a theory of order or harmony between the conditions of man's existence in society, dynamics is a theory of social progress, which amounts to the fundamental development or evolution of society. Order and progress are closely interlinked because there cannot be any social order if it is not compatible with progress, while no real progress can occur in society if it is not consolidated in order. Thus, although we distinguish between static and dynamic sociology for analytical purposes, the static and dynamic laws must be linked together throughout the system (Timasheff, 1967).

Critical Evaluation

Let's now evaluate the contributions of Comte. It is beyond any doubt that by delineating the subject matter of sociology and providing a broad description of procedural steps, Comte laid down the foundation of a positive science of society. However, the chief limitation of Comte's work was that he never himself tried to apply the methodology he advocated to carry out the scientific studies of social life. For all of his advocacy of a science of society and his insistence that as a theoretical science sociology was capable of formulating and testing the laws of social organisation and change, Comte himself did not develop any true sociological laws. Though Comte believed that his Law of Three Stages was the equivalent of Newton's law of gravitation for the understanding of social dynamics, critics argued that it was more of a historical description than a law. Further, Comte violated his own logic and straightway jumped to making prescriptions about social reconstruction. This was apparent in 1850s when he began to formulate his Religion of Humanity, with himself as high priest. In the four volumes of the *System of Positive Polity*, published between 1851 and 1854, Comte intended to reconstruct society on the basis of a new religious spirit. In much the same way that his early mentor, Saint-Simon, basked in the glory of a quasi-religious movement in his late years, so Comte proclaimed himself 'the Founder of Universal Religion' and as 'the Great Priest of Humanity'. However, many events converged to change the direction of Comte's thought in his later career. The frustration over not receiving an academic appointment and the death of his love, Clothilde de Vaux, were probably the most significant forces that took him away from the search for the laws of the social universe towards the Religion of Humanity. As a result, Comtean positivism became a term of disrepute. Former enthusiasts for his positivist sociology were dismayed by his reversion to religion, especially one modelled on the medieval Catholic Church. The majority of his former admirers eventually repudiated him.

Later scholars also raised doubts about Comte's advocacy for a positive science of society. Comte's vision for sociology was for it to become a 'positive science'. He wanted sociology to apply the same rigorous scientific methods to the study of society that were being used in natural sciences to study nature (or matter). Positivism holds that science should be concerned only with observable entities that are known directly to experience. On the basis of careful observations, one can infer laws that explain the relationship between the observed phenomena. By understanding the causal relationships between events, scientists can then predict how future events will occur. A positivist approach to sociology aims for the production of knowledge about society based on empirical evidence drawn from observation, comparison and experimentation. But, as we have learned in early chapters, social action theorists or anti-positivists tend to disagree with such propositions. For them, social action is meaningful, subjective and contextual. They deny any possibility of universal generalisations in social sciences.

Nevertheless, despite these criticisms, it is important to remember Comte's formative role in establishing the case for a science of society. Although humans had thought about their condition for centuries, he explicitly recognised the need for, and nature of, sociological theory. It is in this recognition that his great contribution resides. It is with Comte that sociological theory explicitly emerges. Comte's contribution resides not so much in his actual theoretical principles as in the vision of social science that his work represented. Later sociologists, such as Spencer in England and, later, Durkheim in France, were to build on the suggestive leads in Comte's analysis of statics and dynamics. And most important, Comte provided an image of what sociology could be; although his work was rejected in his later years, it resurfaced in the last decades of the nineteenth century and stimulated a burst of sociological activity. For whatever the flaws in his grand scheme, he had the right vision of what a science of society should be. And although it remained for others to execute this vision, he understood better than his contemporaries and better than many scholars today that a science of society must seek the fundamental principles by which patterns of social organisation are created, maintained and changed. For this reason, then, sociological theory first emerged with Auguste Comte. Along with Saint-Simon, Comte was also credited with making significant contributions to the development of modern socialism. Later, Marx had termed Comte's theory of positive philosophy as 'scientific socialism'.

Herbert Spencer

About Spencer

Sociology came into its own as an autonomous discipline with the appearance of the sociological works of the Englishman Herbert Spencer (1820–1903), who is considered one of the most brilliant intellects of modern times. Herbert Spencer was a contemporary of Auguste Comte and like Comte he too was trying to establish sociology as the science of society. Spencer is often categorised with Comte in terms of their influence on the development of sociological theory, and hence he is also called the 'second founding father of sociology'.

Along with some similarities, there are also some important differences between Comte and Spencer. Let's first look at similarities among them. First, Comte and Spencer both shared a commitment for a positive science of society. Second, both viewed society as an organism. In other words, both emphasised on the study of society as a whole and focused on the interrelationships between its various parts (or social institutions). Third, and most importantly, Spencer, like Comte, had an evolutionary conception of historical development. Both believed in progress and also had deep faith in the unity and irreversibility of historical development. Evolutionary doctrine was central to the ideas of both of them. However, Spencer was critical of Comte's evolutionary theory on several grounds. Specifically, he rejected Comte's Law of Three Stages. He argued that Comte was content to deal with evolution in the realm of ideas, in terms of intellectual development. Spencer, however, sought to develop an evolutionary theory in the real, material world (Ritzer and Stepnisky, 2014).

Among the differences, the most important was Spencer's acceptance and advocacy of a *laissez-faire* doctrine. Unlike Comte, Spencer was not interested in social reforms. He felt that state should not intervene in individual affairs except in the rather passive function of protecting people. He wanted social life to evolve free of external control. Thus, unlike Comte, Spencer had very different expectations from sociology. Whereas Comte wanted sociology to guide men in building a better society in which to live, Spencer countered that the new science should demonstrate to the modern state that mankind should not interfere or tamper with the natural processes occurring within society – a pure *laissez-faire* social policy serves society's interests best and sociology demonstrates how and why that is true (Abraham and Morgan, 2010). On account of these assumptions, Spencer was also called a *social Darwinist*. Further, Spencer was individualist in his outlook. He emphasised upon the individual, whereas Comte focused on larger units such as the family. Spencer stated that 'Every man has freedom to do all that he wills, provided he fringes not the equal freedom of any other man' (Adams and Sydie, 2016).

Let's now briefly look at the biography of Spencer. Spencer was born in a middle-class family in Derby, England. His father, George Spencer, was a schoolmaster. He and his whole family were staunch nonconformists and were individualists in outlook. Spencer was the eldest of nine children and the only one to survive into adulthood. It is said that he was too ill as a child to attend school, and hence he never went to a conventional school. He was taught at home by his father and uncle. In his autobiography, Spencer credited his father with having taught him to think freely and also shaping his personality in his father's image: eccentric, egoistical and solitary. According to his autobiography, his training in mathematics was the best. In spite of not receiving a systematic training in other subjects like natural sciences, literature, history, he wrote outstanding treatises on biology and psychology.

> He was a prolific and very influential scholar, but lived alone and suffered from a sketchily defined nervous disorder, opium addiction, chronic insomnia, depression, etc. Auguste Comte and other acquaintances urged him to marry, claiming that a sympathetic wife would cure his afflictions, but he rejected their advice, explaining that it was too hard to find a woman who was both smart and attractive; plus, he recognised that he was too difficult to please.
>
> *(Abrahamson, 2010)*

In 1837, Spencer started working as a civil engineer for a railway, an occupation he held until 1846. During this period, Spencer continued to study on his own and began to publish scientific and political works. In 1848, Spencer was appointed as an editor of *The Economist*, and his intellectual ideas began to solidify. By 1850, he had completed his first major work, *Social Statics*. In 1853, Spencer received an inheritance that allowed him to quit his job and live for the rest of life as a gentleman scholar. At one time, he became a close friend of the poet, George Eliot, but their relationship did not materialise into marriage, and Spencer never married anyone thereafter. Spencer never earned a university degree or held an academic position. As he grew more isolated, and physical and mental illness mounted, Spencer's productivity as a scholar increased. Eventually, Spencer began to achieve fame not only within England but also internationally. As one scholar had remarked: 'In the three decades after the Civil War it was impossible to be active in any field of intellectual work without mastering Spencer' (Ritzer and Stepnisky, 2014).

Dear Learner, it is important to note that Spencer belonged to the Victorian world which was far removed from the chaotic and conflict-ridden social universe of Comte and Marx. While riots and revolutions marred the society in which Comte and Marx grew to intellectual maturity, mid-Victorian England was as far removed from the dangers of revolution and violent upheavals as a modern society can be. The mid-Victorian age was a confident and pleasant age. Popular radicalism was checked with reformed capitalism and it seemed to most contemporaries that England was now safely settled on a course that would bring it ever-increasing affluence and prosperity. The basis for this optimism lay in the growing material prosperity, industrial production and foreign trade of Britain that had by now become a workshop of the world. The general standard of living of the British population was rapidly rising. Spencer was deeply influenced by these social conditions. On the intellectual plane, Spencer was influenced by the ideas of Adam Smith, Charles Darwin, etc. He was also exposed to the ideas of Auguste Comte and borrowed the term 'sociology' from Comte. However, he vehemently tried to deny any intellectual debt to Auguste Comte.

Spencer later wrote several books but his *First Principles* (1862) and *Principles of Sociology* (1876) are worth mentioning here. Spencer reached the peak of his popularity in 1882, when he visited the United States. In last years of his life, Spencer continued to write on issues of the day. But increasingly, his individualism and his assumptions about evolutionary necessity – which led him to conclude, for example, that any welfare provisions for the poor and deprived interfered with 'natural' social progress – reduced public interest in his work. He died a sad man because he believed that his life work had not achieved its goal as much as he expected. Spencer died on 8 December 1903.

Theory of Evolution

The evolutionary doctrine is the very foundation of Spencer's sociology. According to him, the social process is unique and so sociology as a science must explain the present state of society by explaining the initial stages of evolution and applying to them the laws of evolution. Spencer's entire scheme of knowledge rested upon the belief that 'evolution' was the key concept for the understanding of the world as a whole and of man's place within it.

Spencer was deeply influenced by the ideas of his contemporary Charles Darwin and his books like *The Origin of Species* and *Descent of Man*. Darwin's ideas had brought a revolutionary change in the understanding of how life evolved on earth from a simple unicellular organism to multicellular complex organisms, like human beings themselves. Spencer, like Darwin, believed in the notion of 'the survival of the fittest'. Interestingly, Spencer claimed that it was he who coined the phrase 'survival of the fittest' several years before Darwin's work on natural selection (Ritzer and Stepnisky, 2014).

For Spencer, reality was governed by the Cosmic Law of Evolution. The law of evolution, according to Spencer, was the supreme law of every becoming. Spencer outlined his ideas about evolution in *First Principles* (1862) where he stated that 'evolution is an integration of matter and concomitant dissipation of motion during which matter passes from an indefinite incoherent homogeneity to a definite coherent heterogeneity'. Thus, on the basis of cosmic law, he argued that the inorganic phase of evolution is followed by the organic evolution, which in turn is followed by evolution of the super-organic.

Inorganic Evolution → Organic Evolution → Super-organic Evolution

While at inorganic stage 'matter' developed, at organic stage 'life' developed and at super-organic stage 'society' came into being. According to him, sociology was the science of super-organic phenomena, more exactly of super-organic evolution. Super-organic was the term he used for social life.

Spencer believed that throughout all times there actually has been social evolution from a simple, homogeneous structure to a complex, heterogeneous one. Spencer described societies as evolving from simple, undifferentiated systems, dominated by religion, to complex, differentiated systems, dominated by science and industry. He concluded that societies were in balance at both extremes, but went through a period of disequilibrium during the transition (Abrahamson, 2010).

Spencer, like Darwin, believed that nature had the power to get rid of the weak and unfit. The fittest people are those who are healthy and more intelligent. For him, the state was a 'joint-stock company for the mutual protection of individuals'. According to him, nature is more intelligent than human beings and therefore, the government should stop interfering in the process of this evolution. He asked the government to prohibit such activities as education and healthcare schemes, other social welfare measures, etc. Thus, for Spencer, the Victorian *laissez-faire*, i.e. free market type society (where there was no government intervention and individuals were free to compete with each other), was the apex of all societies.

However, having said that, Spencer acknowledged that evolution did not imply a 'latent tendency to improve, everywhere in operation' or that evolution was 'inevitable in each particular society, or even probable'. Social change occurred in response to specific physical and social conditions. Evolution was not a series of inevitable stages but a process of adaptation, and disintegration was as likely as integration. In sum, the evolution of societies is accompanied by a growth in size and complexity that results in specialisation, differentiation and a corresponding need for integration of the parts (Adams and Sydie, 2016). Thus, according to Spencer, evolution is a twin process of differentiation and integration whereby a simple or less differentiated form transforms itself into a more complex and differentiated form. He also stated that the degree of differentiation is directly proportional to the need for integration.

Organic Analogy

Spencer's conception of the nature of social reality was largely influenced by biology. Adopting organic analogy, he argued that society, like an individual organism, is an integrated whole. He argued that like a biological organism, society is also made up of various parts and subparts which are interconnected. In case of society, these parts are social institutions and that more or less a persisting network of these interdependent parts constitutes the social structure.

In comparing human society with an organism, which is essentially what organic analogy means, Herbert Spencer, however, noted the differences between the biological organism and society. He maintained that 'a society', as an entity, is something more, and other, than an 'organism', even though human 'organisms' (individuals) are members of it. It is a total system of elements of social organisation and their interdependent functions. It is a super-organic entity: an organisational entity over and above the level of the organism. Following this, Spencer accepted the ideas that a society was more than a collective name for a number of individuals. That is, it is not just a collection of several individuals but a distinct entity. The whole is more than its parts. Thus, a house is more than a mere collection of bricks, wood and stone. It involves a certain ordering of parts. However, being an individualist, Spencer believed that unlike biological organisms, where the parts exist for the benefit of the whole, in society it is the whole which exists for the benefit of the parts, i.e. the individuals in society.

Spencer further argued that social structure persists due to the contribution of these parts towards the fulfilment of the needs of the society. This contribution of the parts is termed 'function'. He was one of the first sociologists to use the concept of 'social function'. He argued that in a society these parts have to perform primarily three social functions, viz. regulatory, operative and distributive. While regulatory function is performed by political institutions, operative function is performed by social institutions like family, marriage, kinship, etc. and the distributive function is performed by economic institutions which involves distribution of goods and services.

Further, like organisms, societies are also characterised by increase in size and complexity. He argued that an increase in size of a society is followed by an increase in complexity resulting due to the increase in division of labour or differentiation of parts. This societal growth or evolution may be caused either due to the internal growth of population or due to the change in social environment. Sociology is the study of this process of social evolution. It is important to note that Spencer's theory of social evolution included the notion of progress and development. He further argued that since this interrelationship between parts and subparts is subject to continuity, patterns could be identified and generalisations be made. In other words, a scientific study of society is possible.

Types of Societies

According to Spencer, the study of society like all positive sciences should be based on comparative method. The basic source of sociological knowledge should be the empirical data relating to the nature of social institutions in different societies. This data must be analysed from the evolutionary perspective so as to trace the course of societal evolution. For Spencer, in order to study the society from the evolutionary perspective, one has to identify the societies' earlier state of evolution and then trace the path taken by the society in the course of its evolution to the present state. Such a study of evolution, including the passage through definite states, must be based on empirical data. Here, Spencer encountered a methodological problem regarding the collection of authentic data related to earlier stages of social evolution. The difficulty arises because societies unlike organisms do not leave behind any fossils. However, Spencer tried to resolve this problem by assuming that the simple societies of Africa and Asia can be treated as contemporary fossils. Thus, the ethnological data from these societies can give an idea about the past stages of evolution of the complex societies like those of Europe.

Hence, Spencer collected a wealth of information regarding the nature of social institutions in the tribal and agrarian societies of Asia and Africa. However, the data that he collected was only second-hand data acquired through correspondence with the colonial officers and travellers who visited these societies. Spencer himself never went out to visit any of these societies to acquire first-hand data. Spencer built two classificatory systems of society based on his theory of social evolution.

Spencer's first classificatory system is based on the 'degree of composition'. In order to systematise this data in the form of an evolutionary sequence, Spencer arranged this data into social types on the basis of increasing complexity of the political institutions. Spencer argued that since evolution is a twin process involving differentiation and integration, the degree of differentiation is directly proportional to the need for integration. Since political institutions are the primary societal arrangements to bring about integration, the more differentiated a society, the more specialised and complex will be the political institutions. Thus, the nature of the political institution is an indicator of the degree of evolution. Based on the above reasoning, Spencer built a classificatory typology in which he arranged the social types in an ascending order on the basis of the degree of complexity of social organisation indicated by the nature of the political institutions. For Spencer, this typology represented the universal model of societal evolution. He stated that in the process of social evolution, societies move from simple to various levels of compound on the basis of their degree of composition. He proposed the following classificatory scheme: Simple society, Compound society, Doubly compounded society and Trebly compounded society.

Spencer's second classificatory system is based on 'construction of types', where he presented another parallel explanatory typology with the extreme polarities of a militant and an industrial type of society. Here, Spencer explained the evolution of societies in terms of transition from military to industrial societies. The militant society is characterised by the predominance of offensive and defensive military actions. Human relationships in such societies are marked by compulsory cooperation. Such societies have a highly centralised pattern of authority and social control, and a set of myths and beliefs which reaffirm the hierarchical nature of society. Further, the social life is marked by rigorous discipline and a close identity between public and private life. On the other hand, in the case of an industrial society, military activity and organisation are only peripheral in nature. The greater part of society concentrates on human production and welfare. Such societies are characterised by voluntary cooperation and recognition of people's personal rights. There is also a separation of the economic realm from political control of the government. Such societies also witness increasing growth of free associations and institutions. Although Spencer sees a general evolution in the direction of industrial societies, he recognises that it is possible that there will be periodic regressions to warfare and more militant societies (Ritzer and Stepnisky, 2014).

However, in Spencer's view, the final stage of evolution was not yet achieved.

He argued that the industrial society would give way to the 'ethical society', which will be totally free from external regulation and would be characterised by voluntary commitment on the part of the members to societal norms. Spencer was aware that societies need not fit into either of the classificatory systems totally. They still, however, served the purpose of models to aid classification.

Critical Evaluation

Unlike Comte, Spencer enjoyed enormous acceptance and universal recognition for his ideas during his lifetime. Spencer's contributions particularly in terms of providing a fresh perspective to view the social phenomena laid the foundation of the science of society. Spencer not only defined the subject matter of sociology but also suggested a methodology for a comparative study of societal evolution. The problem of the relationship between man and society was solved by Spencer along the line of extreme individualism: the individual was paramount; the society should not interfere with men; the individual has to act and, acting, will do the best for himself and society (Timasheff, 1967).

Timasheff observes that though Spencer wrote several treatises on sociology, he never presented a formal definition of the discipline. For Spencer, sociology was the science of super-organic phenomena, more exactly, of super-organic evolution. Further, critics argue that Spencer himself did not follow the methodology that he advocated for sociological enquiry. Spencer had stated:

> We must learn, by inspection, the relations of coexistence and sequence in which social phenomena stand to one another. By comparing societies of different kinds and societies in different stages, we must ascertain what traits of size, structure, function, are associated with one another.

Spencer, in fact, selected materials from the most diversified cultures, widely separated in time and space. He picked up facts from here and there and combined them together in an arbitrary manner to support his evolutionary hypothesis. Such a procedure, of course, is entirely out of keeping with the rules of logic and principles of scientific method (ibid.).

Further, his advocacy of a *laissez-faire* doctrine also came under scrutiny in early twentieth century given the turmoil in Europe and America caused by war, inflation, unemployment, etc. There was a growing feeling that society and politics need some rational control. Critics also argue that his explanation regarding the social evolution of societies from simple to compound, and so on, was also faulty. His law of evolution is a cosmic law and, therefore, his theory is, strictly speaking, a philosophical theory rather than sociological theory. For example, Spencer should have realised that societies at the same stage of evolution, according to the principle of the differentiation of social structure, do not necessarily possess similarities in politics, religion, morals, etc. and contrarily, similar types of government and forms of religion are found among different structural types of societies (Abraham and Morgan, 2010).

By the end of nineteenth century, the tide of criticism started emerging against the ideas and approach laid down by Spencer, so much so that Spencer himself died a sad man finding the new developments in the world going against his expectations. Many of Spencer's theories had to be greatly modified or even abandoned in the course of the development of sociology, but the contributions of this pioneer can hardly be exaggerated. Spencer's most important legacy was his functional perspective, which became the dominant theoretical perspective in the mid-twentieth-century sociology, as well as an important perspective in anthropology.

LET'S THINK

Dear Learner, I hope that after reading this chapter you would appreciate the intellectual efforts of the founding fathers of sociology. Just imagine, how difficult a task is to convince others about your own ideas, particularly when your ideas stand in sharp contrast with the existing dominant ideas. The founding fathers of sociology surmounted this challenge with great enthusiasm and perseverance. Now, can you relate to some of the ideas of these scholars in contemporary context. Let's say Comte's Law of Three Stages, also popularly known as the Law of Human Progress. Do you really think that science has replaced religion in developed societies, particularly in the West? If yes, then, how would you explain religious revivalism, and more importantly, religious fundamentalism world over? Similarly, can you relate Spencer's theory of evolution to explain the developments in contemporary societies?

For Practice

Q1. Human history is fundamentally the history of the progress of mind and society. Comment.

Q2. Write a short note on *Social Statics* and *Social Dynamics*.

Q3. Write a short note on *Organic Analogy*.

Q4. Evolution is a twin process of differentiation and integration. Discuss this statement in light of Spencer's contributions.

Model Answers

Q. Human history is fundamentally the history of the progress of mind and society. Comment.

A. Auguste Comte, the founding father of sociology, believed that the development of human mind (or knowledge) is closely linked with the social development (or social change). Comte thought that he had discovered a law governing the progress of the human mind. Comte presented his views on society and social change in his Law of Three Stages. According to the so-called Law of Three Stages, the human mind passes through three stages of thought: the theological, the metaphysical and the positive.

According to Comte, in the theological stage, the human mind explains the origin and nature of any phenomena by reference to supernatural entities (e.g. spirits, divine beings, gods). A Christian world view would exemplify the theological stage. In the metaphysical stage, explanations are not supernatural, but are based on intuition, guesswork and reason; however, they are not supported by any conclusive empirical evidence. The metaphysical stage corresponded roughly to the Middle Ages and the Renaissance. In the positive stage, explanations are based on both observed facts and logical reasoning. Religious or philosophical speculation gives way to the discovery of natural and social laws. The positive stage represents the era of the modern sciences.

Comte argued that corresponding to the three stages of mental progress, there are three stages of society. Comte drew on ethnographic and Western (particularly French) historical data to illustrate the predominant characteristics of the theological, metaphysical and positive stage of societal evolution. The theological stage, in terms of political dominance, was dominated by the priests and ruled by military men, and the major social unit is the family. In the metaphysical stage, the priests' dominance is challenged by lawyers, and the major social unit is the state. The positive stage, which was just dawning, will be dominated by industrial administrators and scientific moral guides, and will have the entire human race as the operative social unit.

Comte believed that the new scientific-industrial society will become the society of all mankind. This is the ultimate stage in a series of successive transformations the human race goes through and each stage is decidedly superior to the previous one. Social change is viewed as a linear, directional progressive process. Humanity is moving towards the same goal or endpoint, even if at varying rates. Driving social development is the evolution of the human mind. Changes in social and political institutions are correlated with cultural evolution. Comte held that all humanity evolves through these three social stages; history culminates in the positive age.

Thus, for Comte, there was a direct correlation between the evolution of the human mind and the evolution of human society. As one develops, so does the other. Human history, thus, is fundamentally the history of the progress of mind and society

Q. Evolution is a twin process of differentiation and integration. Discuss this statement in light of Spencer's contributions.

A. Spencer is often categorised with Comte in terms of their influence on the development of sociological theory; hence, he is also called the 'second founding father of sociology'. Spencer was deeply influenced by the ideas of his contemporary Charles Darwin on evolution. Spencer too believed that reality was governed by the Cosmic Law of Evolution. According to Spencer, sociology as a science must explain the present state of society by explaining the initial stages of evolution and applying to them the laws of evolution.

Spencer took an extreme position on social evolution by advocating *laissez-faire* doctrine, i.e. free market type society (where there was no government intervention and individuals were free to compete with each other). He asked the government to prohibit such activities as education and healthcare schemes, other social welfare measures, etc. For Spencer, the Victorian *laissez-faire* was the apex of all societies. On account of these assumptions, Spencer was also called a *social Darwinist*.

According to Spencer, evolution is a twin process of differentiation and integration whereby a simple or less differentiated form transforms itself into a more complex and differentiated form. He also stated that the degree of differentiation is directly proportional to the need for integration. Spencer built two classificatory systems of society based on his theory of social evolution. Spencer's first classificatory system is based on the degree of composition. Since political institutions are the primary societal arrangements to bring about integration, the more differentiated a society, the more specialised and complex will be the political institutions. Thus, keeping the nature of the political institution as an indicator of the degree of evolution, Spencer proposed the following classificatory scheme: Simple society → Compound society → Doubly compounded society → Trebly compounded society. Spencer's second classificatory system is based on the construction of types, where he presented another parallel explanatory typology with the extreme polarities of a militant and an industrial type of society.

Spencer's ideas on social evolution and *laissez-faire* economy came under severe criticism in later years. Critics even argued that Spencer himself did not follow the methodology that he advocated for sociological enquiry. However, despite these criticisms, Spencer's ideas are still partly relevant in understanding some of the contemporary developments. For example, it can be seen that as societies are becoming increasingly more complex and heterogeneous, a greater need is being felt for a secular basis for integration.

Unlike small-scale, simple and homogeneous societies where religion served as a source of integration, large-scale, modern and plural societies need a secular ideology for integration.

References

Abraham, Francis and John Henry Morgan. *Sociological Thought*. New Delhi: Macmillan, 2010.

Abrahamson, Mark. *Classical Theory and Modern Studies: Introduction to Sociological Theory*. New Delhi: PHI Learning, 2010.

Adams, Bert N. and R.A. Sydie. *Sociological Theory*. New Delhi: SAGE Publications, 2016.

Ashley, David and David Michael Orenstein. *Sociological Theory: Classical Statements*. 6th Edition. New Delhi: Dorling Kindersley, 2007.

Coser, Lewis A. *Masters of Sociological Thought*. 2nd Edition. Jaipur: Rawat Publications, 2008.

Ransome, Paul. *Social Theory*. Jaipur: Rawat Publications, 2011.

Ritzer, George and Jeffrey Stepnisky. *Sociological Theory*. 9th Edition. New York: McGraw-Hill Education, 2014.

Timasheff, Nicholas S. *Sociological Theory: Its Nature and Growth*. 3rd Edition. New York: Random House, 1967.

6

KARL MARX

About Marx

Karl Marx was born in 1818 in the city of Trier in Prussia (now Germany). He grew up in a prosperous middle-class Jewish family. Marx's father was a lawyer who had converted to Protestantism to escape the social difficulty suffered by Jews in German society. Born in a bourgeois household and brought up by a highly educated lawyer, Marx naturally thought of pursuing an advanced university education upon completing his early studies at the Trier gymnasium. At the age of 17, in 1835, Karl Marx entered the University of Bonn to study law. The following year, unlike most German students who attend several universities before sitting for the university degree examinations, he journeyed to Berlin to study on the university faculty. It was in Berlin that Marx first read the works of the famous German idealist philosopher Georg Wilhelm Friedrich Hegel (1770–1831) whose theoretical writings influenced him throughout his life. Law was abandoned and Marx took up the study of philosophy.

In 1841, at the age of 23, Marx received his doctorate degree from the University of Jena for his thesis on Greek natural philosophy. Having destroyed his chances of taking up a university teaching career due to his radical and outspoken views, shortly after completing his studies, he began writing for a radical left-wing paper in Cologne, *Rheinische Zeitung*, and became its editor in 1842. Following the forced closure of the paper by the government because of a series of radically controversial articles by Marx on social conditions, Marx and his fiancée, Jenny, married and moved to Paris in 1843 (Abraham and Morgan, 2010). The move to Paris was crucial for Marx for two reasons. First, still aged only 26, Marx wrote his most important philosophical work known as the 1844 *Paris Manuscripts*. Although these were not published until 1930 (and were not widely read until the 1950s), it is here that he introduced the concept of alienation

DOI: 10.4324/9781003291053-8

and laid the philosophical foundations for much of his later work. The second important event was meeting his lifelong friend Friedrich Engels (1820–1895). Despite being heir to flourishing textiles business with factories in Germany and a mill in Manchester, Engels had developed a reputation as a forthright critic of capitalist industry in his book, published in 1845, *The Condition of the Working Class in England*. Engels had been managing one of his father's factories until he felt overwhelmed by the miserable living conditions of the working class. Marx and Engels shared a socialist political outlook and their collaboration lasted until Marx's death in 1883 (Ransome, 2011).

During this period, Europe was facing the consequences of industrialisation in terms of increasing poverty and social distress among working classes. Low wages, long hours and poor working conditions led to growing social unrest and worker protest, and eventually in 1848 to social revolution in France and throughout Europe. In Paris, Marx took up the study of political economy by reading the works of Adam Smith and David Ricardo. As social and political questions began to become more pressing, Marx became involved in the socialist movement. With this began an open criticism of society and eventually a more intense focus on economic problems. But, as it happened in Germany two years before, the governmental authorities, this time of Guizot in Paris, expelled Marx and many of his associates. In 1845, Marx and his family were forced to leave Paris by the authorities there and they spent the next three years in Brussels. Moving to Brussels, he re-established contact with like-minded German refugees there, especially a socialist organisation called the German Workers' Educational Association. This organisation interestingly had headquarters in London and was federated with the Communist League of Europe. It was against this background that in 1848, the Communist League asked Marx and Engels to draw up a worker's charter. This led to *The Communist Manifesto* of 1848, which had an enormous impact on the worker's movement throughout Europe (Morrison, 2012). Just prior to that, he had published *The Holy Family* (1845) and *The Poverty of Philosophy* (1847). Another book, *The German Ideology*, was written in 1845–1846, but was not published until 1932.

Marx and Engels returned to Paris in 1848 following the outbreak of revolution in Germany, assuming the editorship of the radical paper, *Neue Rheinische Zeitung*. But the circumstances which initially appeared to be favourable soon turned unfavourable. As a result, failing to work out a working-class–bourgeoisie alliance against the feudal government, Marx was given an ultimatum by the government in August 1849 to either retire to the French hinterlands or leave the country. Marx opted for the latter and moved to London with his wife and children, where he established permanent residence. Arriving in London in 1849 at the age of 31, Marx's life was just half over – a refugee thrice, twice exiled as an editor of a radical political paper, and once as the author of *The Communist Manifesto*. Given his firm belief in his ideas, fierce struggle that he waged against the most power authorities and supreme sacrifices that he made, it seemed that he had much to live and hope for (Abraham and Morgan, 2010).

However, the early London years were difficult for Marx's family. Except for the one-pound sterling he received for each article he wrote on European affairs for the American radical newspaper *The New York Daily Tribune*, he had nothing. After securing an admission card to the British Museum's reading room, Marx spent most of his time in the social, economic and political analyses of the industrial capitalism of the day. For years, the family lived in abject poverty, a condition relieved periodically by financial support from Engels. Three children died in the Marx household owing to malnutrition and impoverishment during the time he was completing the first volume of *Capital* (or *Das Kapital*). This took a heavy psychological toll on Marx and his wife, but nonetheless he persisted in his relentless intellectual endeavours rather than attempting to find employment that would alleviate the family's economic distress.

It was here, in London, that Marx saw first-hand the collapse of rural economy, the development of industrial capitalism and the migration of the agricultural worker to the cities of industry. Workers often lived in conditions of extreme poverty and unhygienic conditions. Working hours fluctuated between 16 and 18 hours per day on an average and wages were extremely low – at times, even below the rate of subsistence. The condition of women and child labourers was even worse. In the absence of any legal limit on the working hours per day, many employers often extended it beyond the point to which it could be humanly tolerated. It was at this point that Marx formed his lifelong interest in the social and economic conditions of industrial workers (Morrison, 2012). The initial few years in London proved productive, intellectually and literally, producing such works as *The Class Struggles in France* (1850) and *The 18th Brumaire of Louis Bonaparte* (1852). By 1859, he had sketched an outline of his work *A Contribution to the Critique of Political Economy*. During these years, Marx also spent a great deal of time researching for his major work, the three-volume *Capital*. The first volume was published in 1867 and volumes two and three, edited by Engels after Marx's death, in 1885 and 1894. Also important from the period is a collection of 'fragments' or 'notes', which he wrote as a 'preliminary work' to *Capital* and was eventually published in 1953 as *Grundrisse*.

Despite his early involvement in London with a secret society known as the Communist League, Marx primarily lived the life of a scholar and not that of a revolutionary political organiser. He wrote about economic and political matters but remained aloof from activists for well over a decade. However, this changed in 1864 when he undertook an instrumental role in the foundation of the working-class movement known as the First International. From 1864 to 1872, Marx worked with the First International, which was filled with strife and in which various anarchists, in particular, were opposed to Marx. Marx quit the organisation after writing *The Paris Commune*, following the fall of the Paris Commune in 1871. Marx, now wrecked by illness and broken health due to early poverty and by unfulfilled dreams, produced little during his last remaining years. Though a little comfortable towards the end of his life financially, and a distinct celebrity, for socialist leaders from all over the world came to visit him in London, he sustained two blows – the deaths of his eldest daughter and wife – from which he never recovered. Marx died on 14 March 1883. Appropriately, he died not on the barricades but in his favourite armchair. Before turning to some of his major ideas, however, it is important to make a distinction between two of Marx's roles: one, the advocate of communist revolution, and two, the theoretician and analyst. One need not to be in favour of a communist revolution to find much of value in Marx's insights.

Response to Hegel's Dialectical Idealism

Georg Wilhelm Friedrich Hegel (1770–1831) was a German philosopher who dominated the entire intellectual horizon of his day. In his key works, *The Phenomenology of Mind* (1807) and *The Philosophy of Right* (1821), Hegel developed a very ambitious philosophical system based on the premise that God (sometimes referred to as the 'Geist', 'Absolute Spirit' or the 'Absolute Idea') works through men to give shape to the material world (i.e. to create an ideal world order). For Hegel, the Absolute Spirit is the precondition of all nature. However, among all its creations, Man is something special, for he was created in God's image. He was endowed by the Creator with the potential for self-consciousness that could, when rationally cultivated, lead to the realisation of the essence of the Absolute Spirit (Larson, 1973). In other words, for Hegel, the essence of reality is Reason, but that the spirit of Reason (Geist or Absolute Spirit) manifests itself only gradually, revealing more and more facets of itself during the course of time (ibid.).

Hegel's philosophy aimed to give an account of history as a whole. Here, Hegel tends to take it for granted that his history is a collective one, i.e. it is a history of humanity as a whole, or of large groups of people, not of particular individuals. The history of all humanity can, he argued, be understood as a single, unified, organised and rational progress. However, progress is not smooth, continuous and cumulative. Rather, the progress of all humanity is marked by struggle, conflict and discontinuity, which nonetheless is of an essentially logical kind. Just as the seed is destined to turn into a plant of a specific kind, human beings – Hegel argues – are destined to develop towards complete freedom. For example, the ultimate objective of a seed is to realise its true potential, i.e. to grow into a plant. But it can realise its true potential only when it gets favourable conditions in terms of fertile soil, moisture, sunlight, etc. In the absence of such favourable conditions, true potential of a seed would never be realised. Similarly, human history can be compared with the life of a seed. According to Hegel, humanity must itself develop into what it has the potential to become. That is, to realise and express the essence of the Absolute Spirit. Human history, according to Hegel, is merely the unfolding of the potential which was present at the earliest stage of its being. Further, what human beings essentially are will never be fully expressed if their capacity for development is restricted or inhibited by circumstances (i.e. imperfect social institutions that may restrict human freedom). The true potential of humanity will only be fully realised when human beings enjoy complete freedom. Achievement of complete freedom, facilitated by the evolved social and political institutions, would mark the end of human history. Since history is a process of change through which humanity develops its true and full potential, when that has been realised there can be no further development and therefore no further history (Cuff et al., 2009).

In simpler words, according to Hegel, the ultimate purpose of human existence was the realisation of the essence of the Absolute Spirit and expression of the highest form of what he called the Absolute Spirit (or *Geist*). *Geist* is a German term, meaning literally 'spirit' or 'mind'. Hegel uses it to describe the role of an all-pervasive moral and ethical force which unites all of humanity in its quest for enlightenment and civilisation. The Geist or Absolute Spirit was not a physical or material entity but an abstract expression of the moral and ethical qualities and capacities, the highest cultural ideals, which, he argued, were the ultimate expression of what it is to be a human being. For Hegel, material life was the practical means through which this quest for the ultimate realisation of human consciousness, the search for a really truthful awareness of reality, could be expressed. Material life, which included such things as the economy, the political institutions of the state and other social organisations in civil society, is a means to this higher end and not an end in itself (Ransome, 2011). In other words, with the emergence of evolved social and political institutions that facilitate complete human freedom, the true potential of humanity and the ultimate purpose of human existence would be realised.

So, in what sense does humanity develop? For Hegel, the primary manifestation of development was the development of the intellectual life, of the *mind* or *spirit*. In other words, Hegel offered a kind of evolutionary theory of the world in idealistic terms, i.e. in terms of ideas or consciousness. Those who assert the primacy of mind over matter are called *idealists*. Hegel is termed as an idealist because he thought that the true nature of history and human existence was to be understood in terms of the development of ideas, thought or consciousness. Self-awareness, the rational ability to realise the meaning of the creative spirit, had to be developed – it was not an inherent certainty. As a process, self-awareness or consciousness follows a dialectical pattern in which thought leads to action, reaction and their eventual unity. The idea of the dialectic comes from ancient Greek philosophy and describes a situation in which truth is arrived at through a process of debate or conversation. In the beginning, a particular point of view (or idea) is stated. This is challenged by an alternative view (or counter-idea), and eventually a third view emerges, which is superior to both of them. The first phase, the *thesis*, describes a state of affirmation and unity; the second, the *antithesis*, is a process of negation; and the third phase, the *synthesis*, is the process by which the antagonism or contradiction between thesis and anti-thesis is resolved. But this is not the end of the dialectical process. The newly arrived synthesis now becomes a new thesis and so on.

Thus, according to Hegel, the process by which human quest for the ultimate truth is carried on involves a *dialectical* process in which one state of awareness about the nature of reality (thesis) is shown to be false by a further and higher state of awareness (anti-thesis) and is finally resolved in a final and true state of awareness (synthesis). For example, during early stages, human beings were endowed only with the most basic level of consciousness, that is, ability to acquire a sensory understanding of the world around them. They could understand things like the sight, smell and feel of the social and physical world. Overtime, humans developed the ability to be conscious of, to understand, themselves. With self-knowledge and self-understanding, people began to understand that they could become more than what they were. Hence, in terms of Hegel's dialectical approach, a contradiction developed between what humans were and what they felt they could be. The resolution of this contradiction lay in the development of an individual's awareness of his or her place in the larger spirit of society. Individuals come to realise that their ultimate fulfilment lies in the development and expansion of the spirit of society as a whole. Thus, in Hegel's scheme, individuals evolve from an understanding of things to an understanding of self to an understanding of their place in the larger scheme of things (Ritzer and Stepnisky, 2014).

Thus, according to Hegel, the entire process of human history was the progress of the human *Geist* towards self-realisation. However, the true potential of humanity, that is, to understand and express the essence of the Absolute Spirit, will only be fully realised when human beings enjoy complete freedom. Achievement of complete freedom, facilitated by the evolved social and political institutions, would mark the end of human history. For Hegel, material life was the practical means through which this quest for the ultimate realisation of human consciousness, the search for a really truthful awareness of reality, could be expressed. Hegel uses the same dialectical approach in suggesting that the contradictions or imperfections of the family and of civil society (corresponding with thesis and anti-thesis) are finally resolved by the institutions of the state, which correspond with the new ethical synthesis.

Modern society, according to Hegel, is divided into three separate domains: family, civil society and state. These three spheres of social existence are different spheres of ethical development in which individual self-determination is realised in larger ethical communities. The three institutions are organised on three different principles or value systems. The family is based on the value system of '*particular altruism*', encouraging individuals to sacrifice their own personal interests for the good of their family members and relatives. In Hegel's formulation, family is the domain of private life based on love and trust, where there is no space for individual egos.

Civil society, on the other hand, is characterised by the value system of '*universal egoism*' where individuals place their own interests before those of others, and behave selfishly and instrumentally towards others. Hegel begins his treatment of civil society by baldly stating its two leading principles. The first is the pursuit of self-interest. In civil society, everyone seeks their own good, regarding others simply as a means for their own ends. The second principle is that everyone satisfies his self-interest only if he also works to satisfy the self-interest of others. Hence, people relate to one another strictly on the basis of self-interest. Since they see public life only as a means to satisfy their own ends, Hegel describes civil society as the stage of 'the alienation of ethical life'.

It is worth noting here that Hegel, like eighteenth-century Enlightenment thinkers, conceptualised civil society as a sphere consisting of people involved in market. Thus, civil society in Hegel's system comprised an economic system where formally free and equal individuals could engage in work and trade. Civil society for Hegel was a 'system of needs' where individuals pursued their freely chosen economic goals. It was also a system of mutual interdependence of individuals where exchange was the main medium of need fulfilment. Hegel placed great value on civil society chiefly because it was a necessary stage in the development of freedom. He saw civil society as another manifestation of the fundamental principle of the modern world: the right of subjectivity or individual freedom. Hence, he praised its many liberties: equality of opportunity, the right to pursue one's self-interest and the freedom to buy and sell goods in the marketplace. This freedom, according to Hegel, was absent in the ancient societies. Still, the freedom of civil society is not freedom in the full and positive sense; it is only a form of negative liberty, i.e. the right to pursue self-interests independent of the interference of others. Hegel sometimes describes the freedom of civil society as purely formal and abstract, because the content of our ends is still given to us by our desires and inclinations. It is therefore unlike the positive freedom of the state, where the content of our ends – the laws and ways of life of the state – is determined by reason (Beiser, 2006).

In civil society, according to Hegel, each individual was concerned with his own interests and no one cared about the whole. Civil society is the sphere of competition characterised by pursuit of private or sectional interests in an open market. It is based on the principle of unrestrained individual egoism. The freedom available to individuals here is only partial. Complete freedom, according to Hegel, also demands unity. But, in civil society, there is disunity. This disunity is brought about by the emergence of sectional and partial interests because of social and economic inequalities. In other words, a society organised on the principles of gain and profit left to its own rules would produce grave evils. Hence, Hegel argues that the institutions of civil society only provide partial space for self-determination of individuals and the freedom they offer is somehow formal and empty. Civil society, thus, cannot provide people with a self-determined ethical life because of its inability to produce freedom and integration. Modern society, therefore, needs another form of sociability to overcome the problems arising from civil society. According to Hegel, this function is performed by the state (Bhargava and Acharya, 2008).

Thus, an ethical sphere higher than both the family and civil society must be found for the realisation of human freedom. The state, according to Hegel, is the ethical sphere of universality, freedom and integration. The state is based on the value system of *'universal altruism'*. The state is founded on freedom instead of coercion and so it is the final realisation of the 'Absolute Spirit' in history. In his *Philosophy of Right* (1821), he portrayed the state as an ethical ideal and the highest expression of human freedom, which was realised as human beings acted in accordance with their reason. The state reconciles individual freedom with the values of the community; in the realisation of the community, each individual would find his or her own fulfilment while simultaneously contributing to the well-being of the whole. The state thus provides the practical means of expressing the universal Spirit. With his grand philosophical system, Hegel had attempted to show that human history had a goal, the most salient features of which were the creation of a reasonable state and the realisation of the concept of freedom. Hegel argued persuasively that 'History is the growth of Reason to consciousness of itself, and the constitutional, legalistic state is the culmination of history' (Abraham and Morgan, 2010). Since Hegel believed that the Prussian state of his time had made the greatest advances towards realising freedom and reason, as a professor in Berlin he became somewhat of a 'state philosopher' for Prussia.

Hegel's *dialectical idealism* can be understood with the help of Figure 6.1 which attempts to explain the evolution of human *Geist* and realisation of the essence of the Absolute Spirit. Note that for Hegel, material life (i.e. socio-economic and political institutions that facilitate complete freedom to individuals for self-determination) was the practical means for the realisation of the essence of the Absolute Spirit (i.e. the truthful awareness of reality).

To summarise, it may be argued that Hegel applied the idea of dialectical change to the history of human society, in particular to the realm of ideas. Hegel saw historical change as a dialectical movement of men's ideas, thoughts or consciousness. He believed that society is essentially an expression of these thoughts. Thus, in terms of dialectic, conflict between incompatible ideas produces new concepts which provide the basis for social change. Given these assumptions,

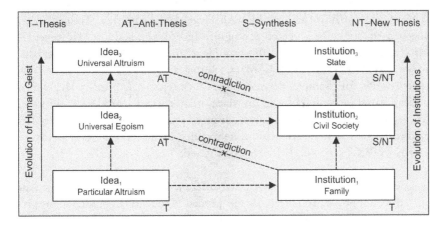

FIGURE 6.1 Hegel's Conception of Family, Civil Society and State

Hegel's philosophical system is also known as 'dialectical idealism'. It is a subjective theory in which change is originally held to occur at the level of consciousness, which later manifests itself in material life, i.e. social, economic and political institutions, etc. To Hegel, this process of evolutionary change in consciousness (Geist) occurs largely beyond the control of individuals. Individual actors are reduced to little more vessels swept along by the inevitable evolution of consciousness. In any case, where people seemed to be moving towards greater consciousness of the world, as it could be, there seemed no need for any revolutionary change; the process was already moving in the 'desired' direction. Whatever problems did exist lay in consciousness, and the answer therefore seemed to lie in changing thinking (Ritzer and Stepnisky, 2014). These assumptions of Hegel, however, were later criticised as to be metaphysical and Eurocentric.

Marx's education at the University of Berlin was shaped by Hegel's ideas as well as by the split that developed among Hegel's followers after his death. The 'Old Hegelians' continued to subscribe to the master's ideas, while the 'Young Hegelians', although still working in the Hegelian tradition, were critical of many facets of his philosophical system. Marx soon became interested in the ideas of Young Hegelians, particularly that of Ludwig Feuerbach. Law was abandoned, and joining these Young Hegelians, Marx took up the study of philosophy. Feuerbach was critical of Hegel's excessive emphasis on consciousness and the spirit of society. Instead, Feuerbach advocated materialist philosophy which emphasised on the material reality of real human beings. In his critique of Hegel, Feuerbach focussed on religion. To Feuerbach, God is simply a projection by people of their human essence onto an impersonal force. People, on the one hand, project a series of positive characteristics onto God, for example, he is almighty, supreme, holy, kind, loving, etc. On the other hand, people reduce themselves to being imperfect, powerless and sinful. Feuerbach argued that this kind of religion must be overcome and hence he emphasised on materialist philosophy which focussed on real people and their materialistic conditions.

Marx was partly influenced by both Hegel and Feuerbach. Trained in the Hegelian tradition, he accepted the significance of the dialectic. However, he was critical of some aspects of the way Hegel used it. While Hegel tended to apply the dialectic only to ideas, Marx felt that it should be applied to material aspects of life, for example, the economy. Marx rejects the priority Hegel gives to ideas, mind or consciousness. To Marx, matter is not a product of mind; on the contrary, mind is simply the most advanced product of matter. Though Marx rejected Hegel's content orientation, he retained his dialectical structure. In his famous work *Capital* (Vol. I, 1867), Marx stated:

> My dialectic method is not only different from the Hegelian, but is its direct opposite. To Hegel, the life-process of the human brain, i.e. the process of thinking, which, under the name of 'the Idea', he even transforms into an independent subject, is the demiurgos of the real world, and the

real world is only the external, phenomenal form of 'the Idea'. With me, on the contrary, the ideal is nothing else than the material world reflected by the human mind, and translated into forms of thought.

(Larson, 1973)

For Marx, it is quite inadequate to regard human history, the development of society itself, as merely a by-product of the quest for ultimate knowledge in the abstract realm of human consciousness. So, Marx reverses Hegel's approach by arguing that the quest for knowledge should not begin with abstract conceptions in the realm of ideas, but with a positive analysis of actually existing material things in the real physical world. While Hegel, in common with all idealist thinkers, argues that the most truthful version of the world is the one that we hold in our consciousness, Marx proposed the opposite or materialist view – that the most real version must be the one we can actually touch and feel. Unlike Hegel, Marx would not ascribe an independent, determinate role to ideas or philosophical conception, for they, he believed, reflected, rather than caused, changes in social and material life (Figure 6.2). For materialist thinkers, the really real world is not the one we create in our minds but the untidy, crowded, noisy physical matter that surrounds us. Thus, if we want to know about the real reality, and provide a truthful account of it, social theory must begin with an analysis of real things and not become preoccupied with their 'ideal' representation in our thoughts. Even the most perfectly polished mirror needs something to reflect or it has no purpose at all. Worse still, it might be used to project a completely false image or ideology. The intention of Marx becomes clear with his famous statement: '*the philosophers have interpreted the world, the point however is to change it*' (Ransome, 2011).

Marx argues that the source of change lies in contradictions in the economic system in particular and in society in general. As a result of the priority he gives

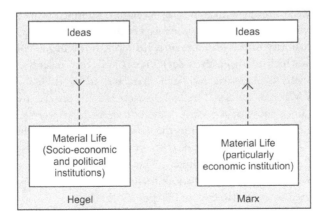

FIGURE 6.2   Hegel and Marx: A Comparison

to economic factors, to 'material life', Marx's view of history is often referred to as 'dialectical materialism' or 'historical materialism'. Since man's ideas are primarily a reflection of the social relationships of economic production, they do not provide the main source of change. It is in contradictions and conflict in the economic system that the major dynamic for social change lies. Since all parts of society are interconnected, however, it is only through a process of interplay between these parts that change occurs.

Historical Materialism as a Perspective

Before we discuss Marx's ideas in detail, it is worth noting that Marx was not a sociologist and did not consider himself one. Although his work is too broad to be encompassed by the term *sociology*, there is a sociological theory to be found in Marx's work. Marx is well known as a philosopher, economist and social activist. As stated earlier, he received his doctorate in philosophy at the age of 23. However, because of his radical views, he never became a professor and spent most of his adult life in exile and poverty.

Marx was repulsed by the poverty and inequality that characterised the nineteenth century. Unlike many of his contemporaries, he refused to consider poverty as a natural or a God-given condition. Instead, he viewed poverty and inequality as human-made conditions fostered by a system that was built around private property and that protected only the interests of the wealthy. As a result, he devoted his intellectual efforts to understanding – and eliminating – that system. Many of Marx's ideas are of more interest to political scientists and economists than to sociologists, but he did play a major role in alerting sociologists towards the importance of economic systems, social conflict and social change (Brinkerhoff et al., 2017).

At the time, when most scholars believed that society generally functioned smoothly and that social change, when it happened, evolved slowly and peacefully, Marx, on the other hand, argued that social change resulted from harsh conflict between groups with opposing economic interests. Marx's radical and revolutionary ideas influenced many scholars of that time, particularly in Europe. But for the majority of early sociologists, his work was a negative force, something against which to shape their sociology. Until very recently, sociological theory, especially in America, has been characterised by either hostility to or ignorance of Marxian theory. The basic reason for this rejection of Marx was ideological. Since most of the early sociological theorists were greatly influenced by the conservative reaction to the disruptions of the Enlightenment and the French Revolution, Marxian ideas about revolutionary social change were clearly feared and hated by such thinkers. They were ready and eager to buy conservative ideology wrapped in a cloak of sociological theory, but not the radical ideology offered by Marx (Ritzer and Stepnisky, 2014).

Historical materialism as a perspective implies the basic assumptions of Marx about the individual and his capabilities, his relationship with other social actors and the social structure of society. In Marx's view, man is essentially a social being. Man is both the producer and the product of society. History is therefore the process of man's self-creation. According to Marx, the motivating factor underlying human history was not ideas about religion and society but the struggle for survival. Human history began with the struggle of man with nature in order to produce their means of subsistence, i.e. the production of food and shelter.

Marx argues that 'The first historical act is, therefore, the production of material life'. Production is a social enterprise since it requires cooperation. Men must work together to produce the goods and services necessary for life. From the social relationships involved in production develops a 'mode of life' which can be seen as an expression of these relationships. This mode of life shapes man's nature. In Marx's words, 'As individuals express their life so they are. What they are, therefore, coincides with their production, with *what* they produce and *how* they produce it'. Thus, the nature of man and the nature of society as a whole derive primarily from the production of material life (Haralambos and Heald, 2006).

In simpler terms, Marx argues that in order to survive, man must produce food and other material objects that are necessary for his survival. Since production is a social enterprise, man enters into social relationships with other men in order to produce goods and services necessary for life. Production also involves a technical component known as the *forces of production* (or means of production) which may include land, labour, raw material, technology (tools and machinery) and technical and scientific knowledge employed in the process of production. Forces of production are dynamic in nature, i.e. they continuously evolve with time. Further, each major stage in the development of forces of production gives rise to corresponding *relations of production* (social relations that men enter into in order to carry out production). The relations of production involve the relationship of social groups to the forces of production as well as with each other. Thus, the forces of production in a hunting and food gathering economy, agrarian economy or industrial economy will correspond to a particular set of social relationships.

Since man is also a product of society, he is shaped by the social relationships. An understanding of human history, therefore, involves an examination of these relationships, the most important of which are the relations of production. At the dawn of human history, when man supposedly lived in a state of primitive communism, the forces of production and the products of labour were communally owned. During the era of primitive communism, i.e. the earliest form of human society, each member of society produced both for himself and for society as a whole. Hence, there were no conflicts of interest between individuals and groups. Primitive societies, like hunting and gathering band, were largely subsistence economies which means that production could only meet basic survival needs. Since forces of production were communally owned, the relations of production too were egalitarian in nature.

However, as the mode of production changed to agriculture, it led to surplus production of goods, that is goods above the basic subsistence needs of the community. This led to an exchange of goods and development of trade and commerce. This was accompanied by the development of a system of private property. Marx argues that with the emergence of private property, and in particular, private ownership of the forces of production, the fundamental contradiction of human society was created. Private property and the accumulation of surplus wealth form the basis for the development of class societies. In particular, they provide the preconditions for the emergence of a class of producers and a class of non-producers. Some are able to acquire the forces of production and others are therefore obliged to work for them. The result is a class of non-producers which owns the forces of production and a class of producers which owns only its labour power. Through its ownership of the forces of production, a minority is able to control, command and enjoy the fruits of the labour of the majority. Since one group gains at the expense of the other, a conflict of interest exists between the minority who own the forces of production and the majority who perform productive labour. Marx uses the concept of '*class*' to highlight the mutually conflicting economic interests of these groups.

Marx used the term class to refer to the main strata in all stratification systems, though most modern sociologists would reserve the term for strata in capitalist society. From a Marxian view, a class is a social group whose members share the same relationship to the forces of production and as a result share common economic interest. According to Marx, Western society had developed through four main epochs: primitive communism, ancient society, feudal society and capitalist society. Primitive communism provides the only example of a classless society. Except primitive communism, all societies are divided into two major classes: a *ruling class* and a *subject class*. For example, masters and slaves in ancient society, lords and serfs in feudal society and capitalists and wage labourers in capitalist society. The power of the ruling class derives from its ownership and control of the forces of production. Thus, the ruling class is the ownership class and the subject class is the non-ownership class. Marx maintained that in all class societies, the ruling class exploits and oppresses the subject class. As a result, there is a basic conflict of interest between the two classes. Through its ownership of the forces of production, a minority is able to control, command and enjoy the fruits of the labour of the majority.

From a Marxian perspective, the relationship between the major social classes is one of mutual dependence and conflict. For example, in the feudal society, feudal lords and serfs were mutually dependent on each other for agricultural production. Though feudal lords owned the forces of production (also known as means of production) such as land, tools and technology, they could not carry out the production without the labour of serfs. Serfs too in turn depended on the feudal lords for their survival and security. Similarly, in capitalist society, the bourgeoisie (capitalists) and proletariat (wage labourers) are dependent upon each other. The wage labourer must sell his labour power in order to survive since he does not own a part of the forces of production and lacks the means to produce goods independently. He is therefore dependent for his livelihood on the capitalists and the wages they offer. The capitalists, as non-producers, are dependent on the labour power of the wage labourers, since without it, there would be no production. However, this mutual dependency of the two classes is not a relationship of equal or symmetrical reciprocity. Instead, it is a relationship marked by exploitation and oppression. In particular, the ruling class gains at the expense of the subject class and there is therefore a conflict of interest between them.

Further, with regard to the social structure of a society, Marx argues that a society forms a totality and can only be understood as such. The various parts of society are interconnected and influence each other. Thus, economic, political, legal and religious institutions can only be understood in terms of their mutual effect. Economic factors, however, exert the primary influence and largely shape other aspects of society. The following passage which appears in the preface to *A Contribution to the Critique of Political Economy* (1859) contains all the essential ideas of Marx's economic interpretation of history and social change:

> In the social production of their life, men enter into definite relations that are indispensable and independent of their will, relations of production which correspond to a definite stage of development of their material productive forces. The sum total of these relations of production constitutes the economic structure of society, the real foundation, on which rises a legal and political superstructure and to which correspond definite forms of social consciousness. The mode of production of material life conditions the social, political and intellectual life process in general. It is not the consciousness of men that determines their being, but, on the contrary, their social being that determines their consciousness.
>
> *(Larson, 1973)*

Taken together, the forces of production and the relations of production constitute the *mode of production* of any given society. Mode of production, in simplest terms, implies the way production of goods and services is organised in a given society. Marx also referred to it as the *economic infrastructure* or *base* of society. Marx argued:

> Social relations are closely bound up with productive forces. In acquiring new productive forces men change their mode of production; and in changing their mode of production, in changing the way of earning their living, they change all their social relations. The hand-mill gives you society with the feudal lord; the steam-mill, society with the industrial capitalist.
>
> *(Ransome, 2011)*

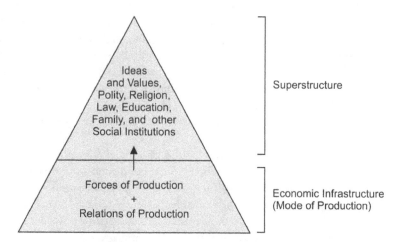

FIGURE 6.3 Historical Materialism as a Perspective

As per Marx, the other aspects of society, known as the *superstructure*, are largely shaped by the economic infrastructure (Figure 6.3). Thus, the political, legal and educational institutions and the belief and value system are primarily determined by economic factors.

In his work *Socialism: Utopian and Scientific* (1892), Engels systematically presented Marx's ideas on historical materialism. According to Engels, historical materialism

> designates that view of the course of history which seeks the ultimate cause and the great moving power of all important historic events in the economic development of society, in the changes in the modes of production and exchange, in the consequent division of society into distinct classes, and in the struggle of these classes against one another.

Taking cue from this explanation of Engels, we can look at historical materialism both as a perspective and as a methodology. The first part of Engel's statement which states that historical materialism 'designates that view of the course of history which seeks the ultimate cause and the great moving power of all important historic events in the economic development of society' explains historical materialism as a perspective. The second part of the statement which states that 'in the changes in the modes of production and exchange, in the consequent division of society into distinct classes, and in the struggles of these classes against one another' can be seen as an explanation of historical materialism as a methodology.

In the background of the above explanation of historical materialism as a perspective, we can better understand the statement of Marx, 'It is not the consciousness of men that determines their being, but, on the contrary, their social being that determines their consciousness'. Consciousness is defined as 'the totality of mental states and processes (perception, feelings, thoughts), mind at its widest sense, awareness'. In simpler words, consciousness here implies ideas, values and beliefs, or ideologies that people hold in a given society at a particular stage of its development and by which they make sense of their world. Social being, on the other hand, here refers to the material (economic) position of social actors and their relationship with each other, particularly their social relations of production. To be specific, social being here implies the position that an individual occupies in relation to production, i.e. relations between the ruling (ownership) class and the subject (non-ownership) class.

According to Marx, the power of the ruling class stems from its ownership and control of the forces of production. And since the superstructure of society – the major institutions, values and belief systems – is seen to be largely shaped by the economic infrastructure, the relations of production will be reproduced in the superstructure. As a result, the dominance of the ruling class in relation to production will be reflected in the superstructure. Hence, be it political or legal system, religious or educational system, or any other social system of society, all would largely reflect ruling class interests. For example, Marx recognised Western democracy as yet another form of bourgeois oppression. To Marx, politics mirrors the inequalities of capitalist society, and democracy simply creates the illusion of political representation. From a Marxian perspective, political power derives from economic power.

Marx believed that economic power was the most important facet of power in any society and that as long as there was economic inequality, there could be no political equality. In this sense, he did not believe there could be a real democracy until a level economic playing field was established. Parliamentary representation, in Marx's view, was one of the many ways in which the bourgeoisie attempted to control the proletariat. While conceding formal democracy, their grip on economic power ensured that the bourgeoisie could manipulate politics and society to suit their interests. For example, economic power ensured that the mass media were under the control of the agents of the bourgeoisie and could present a view of the world that coincided with their interests. This was achieved largely by removing controversial economic ideas from the public arena. Nor did the existence of competing political parties convince him of the value of democracy. Rather they were organised elites (oligarchies) who inevitably betrayed the interests of the people they were supposed to be representing. This led the mass of the population towards political apathy, as they were frustrated by their leaders' inability to change things for the better. Marx, therefore, looked not to the widening of parliamentary structures in a communist society but to a withering away of the state itself as a direct democracy was established (Churton and Brown, 2017).

Likewise, the various ownership rights of the capitalist class will be enshrined in and protected by the laws of the land. For example, under capitalism, the legal system protects capitalist's wealth, and the family allows capitalists to pass their property from one generation to the next. Similarly, religious institutions sanction the ruling class domination by attributing it as the will of the God, and educational system socialises the young into dominant concepts and ideas of the age. Hence, the various parts of the superstructure can be seen as instruments of ruling class domination and as mechanisms for the oppression of the subject class. In the same way, the position of the dominant class is supported by beliefs and values which are systematically generated by the infrastructure. Marx refers to the dominant concepts of class societies as *ruling class ideology* since they justify and legitimate ruling class domination and project a distorted picture of reality. The term 'ideology' may be defined as a system of ideas that tend to explain and legitimise the existing beliefs and practices of a given social group or society. The term is also used to refer to any comprehensive and mutually consistent set of ideas by which a social group makes sense of the world. Lefebvre defines an ideology as an integrated system of ideas that is external and coercive of people. For example, in capitalist society, the emphasis on freedom, illustrated by phrases such as 'the free market', 'free democratic societies' and 'the free world', is an illusion which disguises the wage slavery of the proletariat.

According to Marx, ruling class ideology produces *false class consciousness*, i.e. a false picture of the nature of the relationship between social classes. Members of both classes tend to accept the status quo as normal and natural and are largely unaware of the true nature of exploitation and oppression. In other words, members of both social classes are largely unaware of the true nature of their situation, of the reality of the relationship between ruling and subject classes. The members of the ruling class assume that their particular interests are those of society as a whole, and the members of the subject class accept this view of reality and regard their situation as a part of the natural order of things. This false consciousness is due to the fact that the relationships of dominance and subordination in the economic infrastructure are largely reproduced in the superstructure of society. Thus, in all class-based societies, the consciousness of all members of society is infused with ruling class ideology which proclaims the essential rightness, normality and inevitability of the status quo. In this way, the conflict of interest between the classes is disguised and a degree of social stability produced, but the basic contradictions and conflicts of class societies remain unresolved.

Marx was well aware that most people living in an industrial capitalist system do not recognise how capitalism shapes the operation of their entire society. Most people, in fact, regard the right to own private property or pass it on to their children as 'natural'. In the same way, many of us tend to see rich people as having 'earned' their money through long years of schooling and hard work; we see the poor, on the other hand, as lacking skills and the personal drive to make more of themselves. Marx rejected this type of thinking, calling it false consciousness, *explaining social problems as the shortcomings of individuals rather than as the flaws of society*. Marx was saying, in effect, that it is not 'people' who make society so unequal but rather the system of capitalist production. False consciousness, he believed, hurts people by hiding the real cause of their problems (Macionis, 2015).

According to Marx, for long periods of history, men are largely unaware of the contradictions which beset their societies. This is because man's consciousness, his view of reality, is largely shaped by the social relationships involved in the process of production, or, in other words, relations of production. Marx maintains that, 'it is not the consciousness of men that determines their being, but, on the contrary, their social being that determines their consciousness'. The primary aspect of man's social being is the social relationships he enters into for the production of material life. Since these relationships are largely reproduced in terms of ideas, concepts, laws and religious beliefs, they are seen as normal, natural and just. Thus, when the law legitimises the rights of private property, when religious beliefs justify economic arrangements and the dominant concepts of the age define them as natural and inevitable, men will be largely unaware of the contradictions they contain. As a result, the contradictions within the economic infrastructure are compounded by the contradiction between man's consciousness and objective reality. This consciousness is false. It presents a distorted picture of reality since it fails to reveal the basic conflicts of interest which exist in the world which man has created. For long periods of time, man is at most vaguely aware of these contradictions, yet even a vague awareness produces tension. This tension will ultimately find full expression and be resolved in the process of dialectical change.

Applied to human society, Marxian dialectical materialism has been popularly interpreted as meaning *economic determinism*. The label is not without justification. Marx and his close collaborator, Friedrich Engels, purposely, but not naively, emphasised the dominating influence of the economic facts of life. Engels presented Marx's 'materialist conception of history' in a systematic and simplified manner, and referred to it as '*historical materialism*'. Subsequently, it was Georgi Plekhanov (1856–1918), the father of Russian Marxism, who later introduced the term *dialectical materialism* to Marxist literature.

Let us briefly examine at this point what many see as the central issue of Marxism, the question of 'economic determinism'. Critics have often rejected Marxism on this basis, though they admit that the charge of economic determination is more applicable to certain of Marx's followers than to Marx himself. Although Marx did not consistently argue for a crude economic determinism, he left no doubt that he considered the economy to be the foundation of the whole sociocultural system. The forces (means) and relations of production, in the Marxian sense, constitute the basic structure of society on which are built all other social institutions, particularly the state and legal system. Viewed in these terms, history can be presented as a mechanical process directed by economic forces which follow 'iron laws'. From Marxian perspective, man is portrayed as being compelled to act in terms of the constraints imposed by the economy and who passively responds to impersonal forces rather than actively constructing his own history. The economic infrastructure determines the superstructure, and man's consciousness is shaped by economic forces independent of his will and beyond his control. Further, it is argued that the contradictions in the capitalist infrastructure will inevitably result in its destruction. Thus, in this way, Marx can be presented as a crude positivist who sees causation solely in terms of economic forces.

However, on closer examination, Marx's writings prove more subtle and less dogmatic than many of his critics have suggested. Although he gives priority to economic factors, they form only one aspect of the dialectic of history. Thus, from this perspective, the economy is the primary but not the sole determinant of social change. Thus, Marx rejects a simplistic, one-directional view of causation. Instead, Marx admits that the idea of the dialectic involves an interplay between the various parts of society such as the economic, political, legal, religious, educational and social systems, etc. Marx rejects the view of unidirectional causation proceeding solely from economic factors and argues that the various parts of society are interrelated in terms of their mutual effect. Marx described the economic infrastructure as the 'ultimately determinant element in history'. Yet he added:

> if somebody twists this into saying that the economic element is the *only* determining one, he transforms that proposition into a meaningless, abstract and senseless phrase. The economic situation is the basis, but the various elements of the superstructure ... also exert their influence upon the course of the historical struggle and in many cases preponderate in determining their *form*.

Thus, the various aspects of the superstructure have a certain degree of autonomy and a part to play in influencing the course of history. They are not automatically and mechanically determined by the infrastructure (Haralambos and Heald, 2006).

Further, Marx consistently argued that 'man makes his own history'. In other words, the history of human society is not the product of impersonal forces, rather it is the result of man's purposive activity. In Marx's view, 'It is not *history* which uses men as a means of achieving – as if it were an individual person – *its* own ends. History is *nothing* but the activity of men in pursuit of their ends'. Marx argued that since men make society, only men can change society. Radical change results from a combination of true consciousness of reality and direct action. Thus, in a capitalist society, members of the proletariat must be fully aware of their situation and take active steps in order to change it. Although a successful revolution depends ultimately on the economic situation, it requires human initiative. Men must make their own utopia.

Hence, Marx offers not only a structural theory of social change which locates the source of change in the economic infrastructure, but also introduces agency or creative action of the actors involved. Marx argued that social change requires meaningful action by people who gain consciousness through struggle. Thus, Marxian theory is a halfway between structural and social action approaches.

The replacement of false consciousness by (true) class consciousness, then, can only come about because of changes taking place within the system at the structural level; but once this happens, creative action to overthrow the system is taken by subjects working collectively. As Marx and Engels put it, '*Men make their own history, but not under circumstances of their own choosing*' (Bilton et al., 2016).

Yet the label of *economic determinism* that was frequently applied to Marx's theory by his critics as well as misinterpretation of his ideas could also be accounted to some extent for his widely scattered writings. Most of his contemporaries learned about his ideas through the political speeches, manifestos and pamphlets. Given the antagonism of governments of several countries against his radical views, bans on his publications and his frequent exiles, such misinterpretation of Marx's ideas could be well understood.

Historical Materialism as a Methodology

Till now we have discussed historical materialism as a perspective of Karl Marx whereby he places greater emphasis on the role of economic factors in shaping the overall social structure of society and triggering social change. But, how does social change actually occur? To understand it, we will now look at historical materialism as a methodology used by Marx to account for social changes in human society. As discussed earlier, in the second part of Engels' definition of historical materialism 'in the changes in the modes of production and exchange, in the consequent division of society into distinct classes, and in the struggles of these classes against one another', we can trace an explanation of historical materialism as a methodology.

In simpler words, as a methodology, historical materialism seeks to explain social change in terms of the dialectical movement of forces of production and relations of production in the mode of production (economic infrastructure) of a given society. According to Marx and Engels, the source of social change lies in the mode of production of any given society. So, at first, the change occurs in the way production of goods and services is organised in a society, forces of production in particular. This leads to the division of society into distinct classes with mutually conflicting economic interest. As a result, the conflict between these classes becomes inevitable. So, the class that benefits from the existing economicarrangement or mode of production tends to preserve it and fights hard to maintain the status quo, while the class that feels deprived or marginalised in the existing arrangement tries to change it. Hence, a struggle ensues between these classes for protecting and promoting their respective class interests against one another. This struggle is ultimately resolved by the subsequent changes in the relations of production and in the mode of production. It is worth mentioning here that while the forces of production change in an evolutionary manner, the relations of production (often) change in a revolutionary manner. This is because the ruling class which benefits from the existing economic arrangement tries to preserve the status quo with its full might, even resorting to violent means.

This is how Marx explains that changes in a given mode of production or economic infrastructure subsequently lead to change in society in dialectical manner. Hence, historical or dialectical materialism can be seen as a methodology put forward by Marx to explain social change.

In methodological terms, a comparative analysis of Hegel's dialectical idealism and Marx's historical materialism (dialectical materialism) can be understood with the help of the diagrammatic presentation shown in Figures 6.4 and 6.5.

As discussed earlier, Hegel applied the idea of dialectical change to the history of human society, in particular to the realm of ideas. Hegel saw historical change as a dialectical movement of men's ideas, thoughts or consciousness. He believed that society and its various socio-economic and political institutions are essentially an expression of these thoughts. Thus, in terms of the dialectic, conflict between incompatible ideas produces new concepts which provide the basis for social change (Figure 6.4). For example, during traditional times, people in India might have thought about the idea of caste endogamy as one of the ways to regulate sexual relations. Overtime, the practice of caste endogamy got institutionalised and it acquired the form of an institution. This may be considered as *thesis* in dialectical terms. However, during India's freedom struggle, its national leaders stressed on the value of secularism partly due to the contact with the West and partly due to the plural character of Indian society. Thus, the value of secularism emerged as the anti-thesis of the primordial, particularistic and collective identity of caste. As a result, Special Marriage Act was enacted in 1954 by the Parliament of India to provide for a special form of marriage for the people of India and all Indian nationals in foreign countries, irrespective of the religion

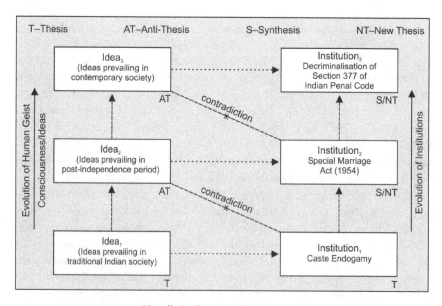

FIGURE 6.4 Hegel's Dialectical Idealism as a Methodology

or faith followed by either party. This can be viewed as the *synthesis* which subsequently became the new thesis. However, overtime certain sections of society demanded for a broader interpretation of values of equality and freedom, and asserted for the legal recognition of the same sex relationships. Thus, giving rise to a new anti-thesis. Recently, adopting a more liberal stance towards consensual sexual relationships between adults, Supreme Court of India partly decriminalised Section 377 of the Indian Penal Code, which deemed homosexual intercourse as a criminal offence earlier. This again can be seen as a new synthesis.

Marx rejects the priority Hegel gives to ideas, mind or consciousness in explaining social change, but he retained his dialectical approach. Marx argues that the source of change lies in contradictions in society in general, and in the economic system in particular. According to Marx, each major stage in the development of forces of production gives rise to corresponding relations of production (social relations that men enter into in order to carry out production). The relations of production involve the relationship of social groups to the forces of production as well as with each other. Thus, the forces of production in a hunting and food gathering economy, agrarian economy, or industrial economy will correspond with a particular set of social relationships. In other words, a given mode of production may be considered as *thesis* in dialectical terms. For example, prior to scientific and commercial revolution, and industrial revolution, the major forces of production in European society primarily comprised land, raw material, simple tools and technology, etc. Marx argued that each major stage in the development of forces of production gives rise to corresponding relations of production. Hence, at this stage of development, these forces of production gave rise to feudal relations of production which was characterised by the asymmetrical and exploitative relationship between feudal lords and serfs. The relationship between feudal lords and serfs was also hereditary and paternalistic in nature.

As stated earlier, according to Marx, the source of social change lies in the mode of production of any given society. So, at first, the change occurs in the way production of goods and services is organised in a society, forces of production in particular. But why do forces of production evolve and how does one mode of production displace the previous one? According to Marx, conflict is the engine that drives social change. Sometimes societies change at a slow, *evolutionary* rate. But they may erupt in rapid, *revolutionary* change. In the opening lines of *The Communist Manifesto* (1848), Marx states, 'The history of all societies up to the present is the history of the class struggle'. This statement embodies three important but separate propositions. The first is that people who share similar economic position constitute a class and also tend to act together as a group. The second is that economic classes are the most important groups to be found in society; their history is the history of human society. The third is that the economic interest of these classes is mutually antagonistic, and the outcome of their class struggle and conflicts defines how society develops. Thus, Marx's theory of class is not simply a theory of social structure; it is also a theory of social change (Wallace and Wolf, 2012).

A new historical epoch is created by the development of superior forces of production by new social group. These developments take place within the framework of the previous era. As discussed earlier, production also involves a technical component known as the *forces of production* (or means of production) which may include land, labour, raw material, technology (tools and machinery) and technical and scientific knowledge employed in the process of production. Marx argued that forces of production are dynamic in nature, that is, they continuously evolve with time. Over time, people become better and better at organising their ways of working. The development in the tools and techniques of production could also be partly accounted for the sheer inventiveness of human beings and their natural capacity for creative imagination. These assumptions of Marx are indicative of the influence of political economist Adam Smith on him.

According to Marx, at a particular stage of development of a society, newly emerging forces of production come into conflict with the existing relations of production. How? Marx argued that forces of production develop faster than relations of production and they may also conflict with each other.

At a certain stage of their development, the material forces of production in society come into conflict with the existing relations of production, or – what is but a legal expression for the same thing – with the property relations within which they had been at work. From the forms of development of the forces of production, these relations turn into their fetters. Then comes the period of social revolution. With the change of the economic foundation, the entire immense superstructure is more or less rapidly transformed (Abraham, 2010).

New forces of production develop within the womb of the then existing mode of production and overtime give rise to a new ownership class, i.e. the owners of new forces of production. Soon, the economic interests of this newly emerging ownership class come into conflict with the existing relations of production, which are largely in favour of the traditional ruling class of that time. In other words, the economic interests of the newly emerging ownership class, which is usually in minority, comes into direct conflict with the economic interests of the then existing dominant ruling class, which also happens to be a minority, thus leading to the emergence of contradiction (anti-thesis) within a given mode of production.

Marx argued that since ownership of the forces of production brings wealth, status and power, the class that at any particular historical juncture has this power is going to be very unwilling to let it go. It is important to understand that developments in the forces of production become inseparable from the class that stands to gain the most from their introduction. As long as there is no significant change in the principal forces of production in a particular society, the status quo will be maintained. For example, the agricultural mode of production in feudal society confers great power on the landowning class. However, when an alternative way of making living, in terms of new forces of production, begins to emerge, this generates a great deal of conflict between the old agricultural way of life and the landowning class, and the emerging industrial forces of production and the capitalists who own and control them. Thus, an established property or ownership class comes into conflict with an emerging one (Ransome, 2011).

For example, the early merchants and industrialists who spearheaded the rise of capitalist mode of production emerged during the feudal mode of production. As mentioned in Chapter 1, in the European feudal system, land belonged to the king, and feudal lords (*vassals*) held land in the name of the king. Private ownership in land did not exist and, thus, land was not a saleable commodity. The survival and stability of the feudal aristocracy was largely dependent on the exploitation of the labour of serfs, who were tied to land and feudal lord by hereditary and paternalistic ties. These conditions and relations of production were not conducive for the growth of the newly emerging class of early merchants and industrialists, also known as *bourgeoisie* or capitalists.

After scientific and commercial revolution, Europe witnessed growth of trade and commerce and as a result new forces of production emerged such as surplus capital and advanced technology. Growth of trade in Europe was accompanied by the increasing use of money. Money had little use in feudal societies. In traditional feudal society, a feudal manor was more or less self-sufficient for its needs. There was very little of buying and selling and whatever there was, was done through barter. The use of money indicated far-reaching changes in economy. Land was the indicator of a man's wealth. Some people had wealth, particularly the Church and sometimes the nobles, in the form of gold and silver, but it was idle wealth. It could not be used to make more wealth. With the growth of trade and manufactures, this changed, marking the beginning of the transition from feudal economy to capitalist economy in which wealth is used to make a profit. This is done by investing money in business, in trade and industry. The profits made are reinvested to make further profits. Such wealth or money is called 'capital'. Money, not the landed property, increasingly became the measure of man's wealth. Early merchants and capitalists emerged as owners of new forces of production, thus constituting a new ownership class (bourgeoisie), though in minority.

The bourgeoisie or capitalist class had accumulated vast amount of capital on account of expansion of trade and commerce. As a result, it sought private property rights in land for the investment of their capital and to make more profit. Furthermore, for the growth of urbanisation and industrialisation, it was necessary that there was a free flow of labour which could work in cities and factories. Instead of the historical paternalistic ties between feudal lords and serfs, contractual wage-labour relationships between capitalists and workers suited the interests of this newly emerging (ownership) class. Thus, the economic interests of the new ownership class, which was in minority, came into direct conflict with the economic interests of the existing ruling class of feudal society, i.e. feudal aristocracy, which was also in minority. Hence, contradiction (anti-thesis) emerged within feudal mode of production. Marx argued that the class struggles (until the emergence of capitalism) of history have been between minorities.

However, a mere division of society into two classes with mutually opposed economic interest, in itself, is not sufficient enough for its revolutionary transformation. For class conflict to unfold and revolution to occur, Marx argues that members of the exploited and oppressed subject class must develop a *subjective* awareness of the *objective* reality in order to transform itself into a revolutionary force, i.e. a class for itself. Objective reality implies the existing exploitative relations of production in a class-based society whereby the minority ruling class by virtue of its ownership and control of forces of production exploits and oppresses the majority subject class. Subjective awareness, on the other hand, implies a realisation by the subject class of this objective reality which is the real cause of their exploitation, and subsequently leading to their mobilisation and collective action. It is important to note that in case of feudal society, the non-ownership class, i.e. serfs did not develop such awareness. Given the hereditary and paternalistic relations with their feudal lords, serfs could not realise that the real cause of their exploitation and oppression was the private ownership and control of the forces of production by the feudal aristocracy. As a result, instead of protesting and revolting against the system, serfs continued to work and sacrifice their lives for their feudal lords for centuries in the name of loyalty. Hence, the conflict between the ownership (minority feudal aristocracy) and non-ownership class (majority serfs) did not take place. Instead, it was the conflict between the economic interests of the newly emerging ownership class (minority bourgeoisie) and the existing ruling class (minority feudal aristocracy) that led to the French revolution and transformation of feudal society to capitalist one.

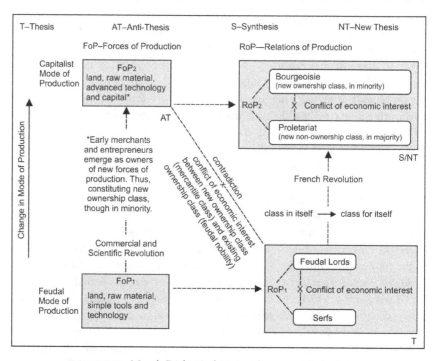

FIGURE 6.5 Marx's Dialectical Materialism as a Methodology

While talking about the revolutionary transformation of a given mode of production, Marx distinguished between a 'class in itself' and a 'class for itself'. For Marx, a class in itself is simply a social group whose members share the same relationship with the forces of production and as a result share common economic interest. Marx argues that a social group fully becomes a class only when it becomes a class for itself. At this stage, its members have developed true class consciousness and class solidarity. In other words, it means that the false class consciousness has been replaced by a full awareness of the true situation, by a realisation of the nature of exploitation. Members of a class develop a common identity, recognise their shared interests and unite, thereby producing class solidarity. The final stage of class consciousness and class solidarity is reached when members realise that only by collective action can they overthrow the ruling class and when they take positive steps to do so. Marx argued that the struggle between the two classes, viz. existing feudal aristocracy and the emerging capitalist class, with mutually conflicting economic interests, was ultimately resolved by the subsequent changes in the feudal mode of production and its replacement with the capitalist mode of production after French Revolution. However, such change in the relations or mode of production often tend to be violent and revolutionary in nature.

A class becomes a class for itself when the forces of production have developed to the point where they cannot be contained within the exiting relations of production. In Marx's words, 'For an oppressed class to be able to emancipate itself, it is essential that the existing forces of production and the existing social relations should be incapable of standing side by side'. Revolutionary change requires that the forces of production on which the new order will be based have developed in the old society. Therefore, the 'new higher relations of production never appear before the material conditions of their existence have matured in the womb of the old society'. This process may be illustrated by the transition from feudal to capitalist society. Industrial capitalism gradually developed within the framework of feudal society. In order to develop fully, it required, 'the free wage labourer who sells his labour-power to capital'. This provides a mobile labour force which can be hired and fired at will and so efficiently utilised as a commodity in the service of capital. However, the feudal relations of production, which involved 'landed property with serf labour chained to it', tended to prevent the development of wage labourers. Eventually, the forces of production of capitalism gained sufficient strength and impetus to lead to the destruction of the feudal system. At this point, the rising class, the bourgeoisie, became a class for itself and its members united to overthrow the feudal relations of production. When they succeeded, the contradiction between the new forces of production and the old relations of production was resolved. Thus, the establishment of capitalist mode of production can be seen as *synthesis* that emerged out of the contradiction present in the feudal mode of production. Marx further argued that once a new economic order is established, the superstructure of the previous era is rapidly transformed. The contradiction between the new infrastructure and the old superstructure has now ended. Thus, the political dominance of the feudal aristocracy was replaced by the power to the newly enfranchised bourgeoisie. The dominant concepts of feudalism such as loyalty and honour were replaced by the new concepts of freedom and equality. In terms of the new ideology, the wage labourer of capitalist society is free to sell his labour power to the highest bidder. The relationship between employer and employee is defined as a relationship between equals, the exchange of labour for wages as an exchange of equivalents. But the resolution of old contradictions does not necessarily mean an end to contradictions in society. As in previous eras, the transition from feudalism to capitalism merely results in the replacement of an old set of contradictions by a new.

Marx argued that the class struggles of history have been between minorities. For example, capitalism developed from the struggle between the feudal aristocracy and the emerging capitalist class, both groups in numerical terms forming a minority of the population. Major changes in history have involved the replacement of one form of private property by another and of one type of production technique by another. For example, capitalism involved the replacement of privately owned land and an agricultural economy by privately owned capital and an industrial economy (Haralambos and Heald, 2006).

Marx saw history as divided into a number of time periods, each being characterised by a particular mode of production. Marx believed that Western society had developed through four main epochs: primitive communism, ancient society, feudal society and capitalist society. To Marx, early hunting and food gathering societies formed primitive communist societies. Communism is a system in which people commonly own and equally share food and other things they produce. Since such societies are basically subsistence type, there is little or no surplus. Everyone does the same kind of work, there are no class differences, and thus there is little chance of social conflict.

With the advancement of technology, surplus production and emergence of institution of private property, social inequality made its appearance in human society. Among horticultural, pastoral and early agrarian societies – which Marx lumped together as the 'ancient world' – warfare was frequent, and victors turned their captives into slaves. This marked the beginning of the development of class-based societies. Thus, the ancient mode of production was characterised by the emergence of two class: masters and slaves. Further, the development of agriculture brings still more wealth to a society's elite but does little for most other people, who labour as serfs and are barely better off than slaves. Marx argued that in feudal society while the elite or nobility enjoyed all the privileges, the class of serfs largely remained deprived. As Marx saw it, the state supported the feudal system, assisted by the church, which claimed that this arrangement reflected the will of God. This is why Marx thought that feudalism was simply 'exploitation, veiled by religious and political illusions'. Hence, the feudal mode of production was marked by the presence of two classes: feudal lords (nobility) and serfs.

Gradually, with the commercial and scientific revolution, as trade steadily increased, cities grew, and merchants and skilled craftsmen formed the new capitalist class or *bourgeoisie*. Bourgeoisie is a French word meaning 'people of the town'. In the late eighteenth and early nineteenth centuries, the bourgeoisie also controlled factories, became richer and richer and so they soon rivalled the feudal landowning nobility. For their part, the nobles looked down their noses at this upstart 'commercial' class, but in time, these capitalists took control of European societies. Thus, these new productive forces started to break down the feudal order. Industrialisation also led to the formation of the proletariat or the working class. As discussed in Chapter 1, during enclosure movement, a large number of landowners converted fields once ploughed by serfs into grazing land for sheep to produce wool for the textile mills. Forced from the land, millions of people migrated to cities and had little choice but to work in factories. Marx envisioned these workers one day joining together to form a revolutionary class that would overthrow the capitalist system. Thus, capitalist mode of production too was beset with two antagonistic classes: bourgeoisie and proletariat (Macionis, 2015).

Capitalism and Its Critique

Industrial capitalism, according to Marx and Engels, emerges at the point in history when agriculture ceases to be the main source of livelihood and is replaced by manufacturing, first in rural workshops but eventually in large factories in the towns. Capital may be defined as money or other forms of wealth, which may not be needed for immediate consumption, but can be used to finance further production of goods and services for private gain (profit), thus, in turn, producing further more capital. In a capitalist economy, various forces of production like land, labour, raw materials and machinery used to produce them are given a monetary value. The capitalist invests his capital in the production of goods and earns profit by selling those goods at a value greater than their cost of production. Capitalism therefore involves the investment of capital in the production of commodities with the aim of maximising profit. Capital is privately owned by a minority, the capitalist class. In Marx's view, such capital that is accumulated in terms of profits by capitalists is gained from the exploitation of the mass of the population, the working class. Marx argued that capital, as such, produces nothing. Only labour produces wealth. Yet the wages paid to the workers for their labour are well below the value of the goods they produce (Figure 6.6). The difference between the value of wages and commodities is known as 'surplus value'. This surplus value is appropriated in the form of profit by the capitalists (Haralambos and Heald, 2006). The whole point of capitalism is to produce commodities as cheaply as possible, sell them for the highest price and thus make large profit. Marx believed that although other factors such as changes in the price of raw materials or equipment, or variations in the supply and demand for any particular commodity, will affect the selling price of the commodity, this

FIGURE 6.6 A Marxist View of the Class System under Capitalism. *Source:* Industrial Worker, 1911, Wikimedia Commons

does little to alter the fact that the fundamental source of surplus value was the labour power of the worker, a value that cannot be quantified until after the commodity has been sold and thus its surplus value realised. For Marx, therefore, profit is the most accurate way of measuring the value that the worker has added to the product, but for which he has not been paid (Ransome, 2011).

According to Marx, the Western society had developed through four main epochs: primitive communism, ancient society, feudal society and capitalist society. Each stage of development being characterised by a particular mode of production. While explaining social change, Marx stated: 'The history of all societies up to the present is the history of the class struggle'. However, here, Marx made a significant observation. Marx argued that the class struggles of history (till the emergence of capitalism) have been between minorities. As mentioned earlier, according to Marx, forces of production are dynamic and develop faster than relations of production. Marx argued that at a particular stage of development of a society, newly emerging forces of production come into conflict with the existing relations of production. Overtime, the economic interests of the owners of new forces of production, i.e. new ownership class, come into conflict with the existing relations of production, which are largely in favour of the traditional ruling class of that time. In other words, the economic interests of the newly emerging ownership class, which is usually in minority, come into direct conflict with the economic interests of the then existing dominant ruling class, which also happens to be a minority. Thus, this leads to the emergence of contradiction within a given mode of production.

Marx believed that the class struggle which would transform capitalist society to socialist or communist society would involve none of these processes. Marx argued that the class struggle that would transform capitalism would be between the bourgeoisie and the proletariat, a minority versus a majority. The proletariat, the non-ownership class in capitalist society, need not wait for the emergence of new forces of production and new classes for initiating change in the existing relations of production. Marx argued that as capitalism advances, certain conditions and developments would transform the proletariat into class for itself. Subsequently, the proletariat would overthrow the bourgeoisie and seize the forces of production, the source of power. Property would be communally owned and, since all members of society would now share the same relationship with the forces of production, a classless society would result. Since history is the history of the class struggle, history would now end. The communist society which replaces capitalism will contain no contradictions, no conflicts of interest and therefore be unchanging. Industrial manufacture would remain as the basic technique of production in the socialist or communist society which would replace capitalism.

However, the final epoch of history, the socialist or communist society which Marx believe would eventually supplant capitalism, will not result from a new force of production. Instead, it will develop from a resolution of the contradictions contained within the capitalist system. Marx believed that the basic contradictions contained in a capitalist economic system would lead to its eventual destruction. Let us now discuss the two fundamental contradictions that are inherent in the capitalist system. First, there is a contradiction between the forces of production, in particular the labour power of the workers which produce wealth, and the relations of production which involve the appropriation of much of that wealth by the capitalists. Marx maintained that only labour produces wealth. Thus, wealth in capitalist society is produced by the labour power of the workers. However, much of this wealth is appropriated in the form of profits by the capitalists, the owners of the forces of production. The wages of the workers are well below the value of the wealth they produce. Second, there exists a related contradiction between the technical organisation of labour and the nature of ownership. As capitalism developed, the workforce was increasingly concentrated in large factories where production was a social enterprise. Yet the forces of production are privately owned, the profits are appropriated by individuals. Thus, the contradiction between the forces and relations of production lies in the social and collective nature of production and the private and individual nature of ownership. Marx, however, argued that the social and collective production would make it easier for workers to organise themselves against the capitalists as it would facilitate better communication and encourage a recognition of common circumstances and interests.

Thus, Marx argued that the capitalist society by its very nature is unstable. Marx believed that these and other contradictions would eventually lead to the downfall of the capitalist system. He believed that the conflict of interest between capital and labour, which involves one group gaining at the expense of the other, could not be resolved within the framework of a capitalist economy. Marx was convinced that these contradictions and antagonisms can only be resolved by the transformation of capitalist society. He argued that apart from the basic contradictions of capitalist society, certain factors in the natural development of a capitalist economy will hasten its downfall. These factors will result in the polarisation of the two main classes in capitalist society, viz. a minority bourgeoisie and a majority proletariat. First, with the advancement of capitalism, the increasing use of machinery will result in a homogeneous working class. Since 'machinery obliterates the differences in labour' members of the proletariat will become increasingly similar in terms of their skills. The differences between skilled, semi-skilled and unskilled workers will tend to disappear as machines remove the skill required in the production of commodities. This process is also called the process of *homogenisation* of working class.

Second, the difference in wealth between the bourgeoisie and the proletariat will increase. For example, with increasing competition, in order to maintain the same margin of profit, a capitalist tends to cut down his variable cost (for example, wages of workers) since constant or fixed capital (for example, in plant and machinery) remains unchanged. According to Marx, even though the real wages and living standards of the proletariat may rise, its members will become poorer in relation to the bourgeoisie. This may happen in a situation where by modestly increasing the wages, a capitalist may force the workers to produce more, thus generating even higher surplus or profit for him. This process is known as *pauperisation*. The term pauperisation means an increasing impoverishment of the proletariat. Further, for Marx, capitalist economies would always be subject to periods of boom and recession. The periods of economic boom would be characterised by high rates of employment, business confidence, profitability and rising standards of living. The periods of economic recession would be characterised by crises in profitability, poor business confidence, high rates of unemployment, business bankruptcy and declining standards of living.

As a result, this leads to *immiserisation* of the proletariat. Immiserisation literally implies the growing misery of the workers in capitalism, for example, due to frequent unemployment.

Third, though early capitalism operated on the principle of free market economy, with the advances of capitalism, it tends to develop monopolistic tendencies. The competitive nature of capitalism means only the largest and most wealthy companies will survive and prosper. Marx argued that competition will depress the intermediate strata, those groups lying between the two main classes, into the proletariat. According to Marx, the 'petty bourgeoisie', the owners of small businesses, would not be able to compete with large businesses. Thus, the petty bourgeoisie, having been driven out of business, will eventually 'sink into the proletariat'. Hence, the processes of homogenisation, pauperisation, immiserisation and the depression of the intermediate strata into the proletariat will result in the *polarisation* of society into two major antagonistic classes in capitalist society, viz. a minority of monopoly capitalists and a majority of impoverished proletariat. As mentioned earlier, a mere division of society into two classes with mutually opposed economic interest, in itself, is not sufficient enough for its revolutionary transformation. For class conflict to unfold and revolution to occur, Marx argues that members of the exploited and oppressed subject class must develop a *subjective* awareness of the *objective* reality in order to transform itself into a revolutionary force, i.e. a class for itself (Figure 6.7).

Marx believed that the contradictions of capitalism were sufficient to transform the proletariat into a class for itself and bring about the downfall of the bourgeoisie. The proletariat will become subjectively aware of the objective reality or, in other words, a class for itself for two reasons. First, by herding

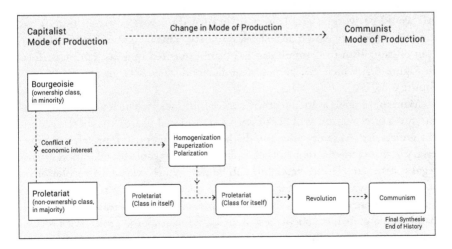

FIGURE 6.7 Marx: Capitalism to Communism

them together into factories, the bourgeoisie weld them together, as they discuss and recognise their common interests. In factories, wrote Marx and Engels, the bourgeoisie oversees the production of products, but 'produces, above all, its own grave-diggers' (Adams and Sydie, 2016). Second, Marx highlighted the role of intelligentsia in conscientisation of the workers, that is, creating awareness among the proletariat and subsequently leading to the development of the true class consciousness among them. Marx and Engels believed that a few members of the bourgeoisie who understand history will break away and join the proletariat. According to Marx and Engels,

> Just as, therefore, at an earlier period, a section of the nobility went over to the bourgeoisie, so now a portion of the bourgeoisie goes over to the proletariat, and in particular, a portion of the bourgeoisie ideologists, who have raised themselves to the level of comprehending theoretically the historical movement as a whole.
>
> *(ibid.)*

Thus, once the proletariat transforms into a class for itself, the class antagonism would be articulated. That is, the class conflict would become open and manifest. Marx believed that this conflict cannot be resolved within the framework of capitalist society. This conflict, according to Marx, can only be resolved by a radical transformation of the capitalist mode of production into a communist one. In order to achieve this, the proletariat would resort to political action and capture state power. For Marx, the state is an executive organ of the ruling class and hence preserves the existing relations of production. Thus, in order to change the existing capitalist relations of production and abolish the institution of private property, the proletariat must first capture state power. With the abolishing of the institution of private property, class divisions would cease to exist in communist society. There would be no owner and no non-owner. All would be workers and communally own the forces of production. Thus, communist society would be a classless society. This revolutionary transformation of capitalism to communism has been presented in a diagrammatic form in Figure 6.7, which can be better understood when seen in continuation to Figure 6.5.

Marx and Engels argued that the communist society which would arise from the ruins of capitalism will begin with a transitional phase, 'the dictatorship of the proletariat'. Absolute power in the hands of self-conscious proletariat is necessary to dismantle the remnants of capitalism such as capitalist education system, legal system, etc. This dictatorship will be essential to every post-revolutionary society for a while, as the rest of the world goes through the revolution. Marx and Engels noted that because bourgeoisie ownership of the means of production had become global, producing a worldwide proletariat, the proletariat's revolution would also have to be global in focus. If private ownership remained anywhere in the world, a bourgeoisie would continue to exploit its workforce, and the proletariat's revolution could not succeed. Thus, *The Communist Manifesto* concludes:

> Let the ruling classes tremble …. The proletarians have nothing to lose but their chains. They have a world to win. Working men of all countries, unite!
>
> *(Abrahamson, 2010)*

Once the communist system has been fully established, the cause of dictatorship and therefore its existence will end. Since the state had always been the instrument of class oppression in the hands of the ruling class, Marx and Engels believed it would eventually shrivel or wither away for lack of a purpose. The communist society of the new era is without classes, without contradictions. The dialectical principle now ceases to operate. The contradictions of human history have now been negated in a final harmonious synthesis. In light of the Marxian assertion about withering away of the state, critics questioned that 'Why, then, has the state not withered away in avowedly communist societies of the twentieth century?' In response to this, later Marxists argue that it cannot wither away anywhere until the worldwide revolution is complete, because the force at the disposal of capitalist nations is always a threat. The final revolution, then, is still one historical stage away, but it will end class-based history as we know it. In this communist world, machines will serve workers, not dominate them. Distribution of products will be equal and complete, with each worker also an owner (Adams and Sydie, 2016).

Marx's presumptions about the division of labour in communist society are interesting. However, before that, let's discuss Marxian views about division of labour in general. Marx's views differed from that of the classical functionalist sociologist Emile Durkheim on several grounds. First, Durkheim regarded division of labour as a social fact and increase in division of labour as a societal necessity to fulfil the increasing demand of goods and services. Marx, on the other hand, looked at human labour in a creative sense. In fact, to Marx, productive labour is what separates human beings from animals. Through productive labour, man objectifies himself, expresses and externalises his creative being. Marx, thus, looks at productive labour in terms self-fulfilment, an end in itself. Second, Durkheim primarily focuses on the functional consequences of division of labour for the society as whole. For example, in his work *The Division of Labour* (1893), Durkheim explains how the nature of division of labour in a society is closely linked with the nature of social solidarity. On the contrary, Marx highlighted the inevitability of class conflict in the contemporary capitalist society, given the existing nature of division of labour. Further, Marx asserts the exploitative and alienating aspects of the division of labour in all class-based societies. Third, Durkheim foresaw an ever-increasing division of labour in modern society resulting in individuals engaged in different and often highly specialised occupations. Marx instead believed that the increasing mechanisation and automation would have an 'homogenisation effect' on the working class. It would obliterate the differences among the working class. The members of the proletariat will become increasingly similar in terms of their skills.

Marx, while commenting on division of labour, stated:

> in a capitalist society, the individual becomes a hunter, a fisherman, a shepherd, or a critical critic, and must remain so if he does not want to lose his means of livelihood; while in communist society … society regulates the general production and thus makes it possible for me to do one thing today and another tomorrow, to hunt in the morning, fish in the afternoon, rear cattle in the evening, criticize after dinner, just as I have in mind, without ever becoming hunter, fisherman, shepherd, or critic.
>
> *(ibid.)*

In communist society, according to Marx, production would not be geared to generation of profits. Instead, production would be carried out for the sake of satisfaction of human needs. Thus, the consumption of goods and services would be based on the principle of 'from each according to his ability, to each according to his needs'. In Marx's view, man would lead a wholesome life in communist society.

Asiatic Mode of Production

According to Marx, Western society had developed through four main epochs: primitive communism, ancient society, feudal society and capitalist society. Primitive communism provides the only example of a classless society. While explaining social change in terms of modes of production, Marx identified four modes of production: the *Asiatic, Ancient, Feudal* and *Capitalist*. The history of the West, according to Marx, could be understood in terms of the dialectical transformation of the primitive communist society to ancient, feudal and, finally, capitalist modes of production. Asiatic mode of production, which does not constitute a stage in Western history, is distinguished by the subordination of all people to the state. In his reference to Asian countries, particularly India, Marx used the term Asiatic mode of production. The theory of the Asiatic mode of production was devised by Karl Marx around the early 1850s. It is argued that Marx at first regarded Asian society as a special society which was stagnant and devoid of history. Later, however, he overcame this view and argued that the Asiatic mode of production was begotten out of the dissolution of primitive society and was the earliest form of class society.

The essence of the theory has been described as

> [The] suggestion … that Asiatic societies were held in thrall by a despotic ruling clique, residing in central cities and directly expropriating surplus from largely autarkic and generally undifferentiated village communities. (https://en.wikipedia.org/wiki/Asiatic_mode_of_production)

The Asiatic mode of production is characteristic of primitive communities in which ownership of land is communal. These communities are still partly organised on the basis of kinship relations. State controls the use of essential economic resources, and directly appropriates part of the labour and production of the community. Sometimes, Marx and Engels stressed the dominant role the state played in Asiatic societies because of its monopoly of land ownership, its control over irrigation systems, or its sheer political and military power. At other times, they suggested that it was the communal nature of landholding and self-sufficiency of villages that isolated the inhabitants of different villages from one another and so made them prey to state domination (Marshall, 1998).

The Asiatic mode of production does not seem to be distinguished by the subordination of slaves or serfs, but by the subordination of all workers to the state. Marx tended to chronologically overlap the Asiatic mode of production with the ancient and feudal mode of production of the West. The Asiatic mode of production constitutes one of the possible forms of transition from classless to class societies; it is also perhaps the most ancient form of this transition. It contains the contradiction of this transition, i.e. the combination of communal relations of production with emerging forms of the exploiting classes and of the state. Marx did not leave behind any systematic presentation of the history of India. He set down his observations on certain current Indian questions which attracted public attention, or drew materials from India's past and contemporary conditions of his times to illustrate parts of his more general arguments. The concept of Asiatic mode of production is therefore inadequate for an understanding of Indian history and society.

The Asiatic mode of production is a notion that has been the subject of much deliberation on the part of Marxist and non-Marxist commentators alike. The Asiatic mode of production has endured much controversy and contest from many scholars and is the most disputed mode of production outlined in the works of Marx and Engels. Questions regarding the validity of the concept of the Asiatic mode of production were raised in terms of whether or not it corresponds to the reality of certain given societies. Some have rejected the whole concept on the grounds that the socio-economic formations of pre-capitalist Asia did not differ enough from those of feudal Europe to warrant special designation. Some argue that the Asiatic mode of production is not compatible with archaeological evidence.

Alienation

The term alienation has had long and varied use in many fields besides sociology: philosophy, theology, law and psychiatry. Alienation is a socio-psychological condition which denotes a state of 'estrangement' of individuals from themselves or from others, or from a specific situation or process. This concept gained currency in the writings of Hegel and was later developed by Feuerbach before Marx adopted it in his early writings.

According to Hegel, the noted German idealist philosopher, the ultimate purpose of human existence was to express the highest form of what he called the human Geist or 'Spirit'. This Spirit was not a physical or material entity but an abstract expression of the moral and ethical qualities and capacities, the highest cultural ideals which, he argued, were the ultimate expression of what it is to be a human being. For Hegel, material life was the practical means through which this quest for the ultimate realisation of human consciousness, the search for a really truthful awareness of reality, could be expressed. Material life, which included the economy, the political institutions of the state and other social organisations in civil society, is a means to this higher end and not an end in themselves.

Hegel uses the concepts of *lack of sublation* and *estrangement* to describe the sense of insecurity or unease that people might experience at moments when they recognise the shortcomings of their mental understanding of reality. Hegel uses the term sublation to describe the need social actors have to feel at ease with their understanding of reality and how they fit into it. Lack of sublation shows itself as a feeling of estrangement, of not fitting in, of being at odds with the world and being confused about the nature of reality. For Hegel, estrangement was a cognitive or psychological state of being whose resolution depends on acquiring a more thorough understanding of what reality is and how individual consciousness comes to terms with its place within it. For Hegel, as Marx puts it, 'all estrangement of human nature is therefore nothing but estrangement of self-consciousness' (Ransome, 2011). In simpler words, alienation occurs, for Hegel, when people are not able to recognise themselves in the culture (the existing socio-economic and political institutions), finding it foreign to their self-conceptions. While Hegel contended that alienation was widespread, he did not consider it necessarily inevitable. With the emergence of the state, alienation among humans would end. The state, according to Hegel, is the ethical sphere of universality, freedom and integration. The state is based on the value system of *'universal altruism'*. Hegel portrayed the state as an ethical ideal and the highest expression of human freedom, which was realised as human beings acted in accordance with their reason. The state reconciles individual freedom with the values of the community, and in the realisation of the community each individual would find his or her own fulfilment while simultaneously contributing to the well-being of the whole. The state thus provides the practical means of expressing the universal Spirit.

In response to Hegel, Marx argues that alienation is less to do with how social actors meet their philosophical needs and more with meeting their physical needs. Human contentment requires a settled material life at least as much a settled consciousness (ibid.). According to Marx, Hegel placed too much emphasis upon alienation as a state of mind, and too little attention to alienation in relation to material social conditions arising out of a system of private property. In addition, Marx claimed that Hegel exaggerated the degree to which political institutions acted autonomously, and thereby failed to recognise the degree to which they actually served the interests of economically dominant sections of society (Abrahamson, 2010).

Several years before Marx wrote about alienated labour, Ludwig Feuerbach published *The Essence of Christianity* (1841). In this book, Feuerbach not only criticised religion (as did most of the Young Hegelians, including Marx and Engels), but he also went a step further and tried to explain why it exists. Feuerbach bases religion in man's worldly existence and believes that, in religion, man expresses his dream of a different and better world. It is not God who has created man, as religion teaches, but it is man who has created (the concept of) God. Man has objictified his own being in God and then provided his creation with a creative force of his own. In this way, the object, the concept of God which is created by man, has become the subject and the true subject, man, has made himself an object. In this way, man has become estranged – alienated – from himself and, according to Feuerbach, religion expresses this alienation of man from himself.

Though Marx applauded Feuerbach's emphasis on materialism, he was far from fully satisfied with Feuerbach's position. While Feuerbach focussed on the religious world, Marx believed that it was the entire social world, and the economy in particular, that had to be analysed. Further, Feuerbach failed to include the most important of Hegel's contributions, the dialectic, in his materialist orientation, particularly the relationship between people and the material world. Finally, Marx argued that Feuerbach, like most philosophers, failed to emphasise *praxis* – practical activity – in particular, revolutionary activity. As Marx put it, 'The philosophers have only *interpreted* the world, in various ways; the point, however, is to *change* it' (Ritzer and Stepnisky, 2014).

For Hegel and Feuerbach, thus, alienation was a metaphysical concept. Marx transformed it into a sociological one in his work *The Economic and Philosophic Manuscripts* (1844). Marx believed that humanity has an essential nature which is realised through creative work. Marx, thus, looked at human labour in a creative sense. From a historical materialist perspective, Marx looks at the course of human history in terms of a progressive development of the forces of production, a steady increase in man's control over nature. This is paralleled by a corresponding increase in man's alienation, an increase which reaches its height in capitalist society. To Marx, alienation is a situation in which the creations of man appear to him as alien objects. They are seen as independent from their creator and invested with the power to control him. As per Marx, man creates his own society, but he will remain alienated until he recognises himself within his creation. Until that time, he will assign an independent existence to objects, ideas and institutions and be controlled by them. In the process, he loses himself, he becomes a stranger in the world he has created, he becomes alienated.

Marx explains that how religion provides an example of men's alienation. Borrowing the ideas from Feuerbach, Marx argues that 'Man makes religion, religion does not make man'. However, members of society fail to recognise this fact and they assign to the gods an independent power, a power to direct their actions and shape their destiny. The more man invests in religion, the more he loses himself. In Marx's words, 'The more man puts into God, the less he retains of himself'. In assigning his own powers to supernatural beings, man becomes alienated from himself. Religion appears as an external force controlling man's destiny, whereas, in reality, it is man-made (Haralambos and Heald, 2006). Religion is nothing but a reflection of society. It was society that created God, in its image, not vice versa. From a historical materialist perspective, the economic infrastructure to a large extent influences and shapes the superstructure. Hence, in all class-based societies, the institutions in the superstructure largely reflect the interests of the economically dominant ruling class. Religion too, being a part of the superstructure of society, tends to protect, legitimise and promote the ruling class interests. Marx looks at religion as one of the agencies to promote the ruling class ideology and thereby promote the false class consciousness among the members of the subject class. In Marx's view, religion 'perverted' consciousness because it was the product of a 'perverted' world.

Marx, on the one hand, contended that religion provided a genuine outlet for the suffering of the masses. In the mid-nineteenth-century cities that Marx was analysing, most working-class families barely survived because of dreadful working conditions, meagre wages and unsanitary living conditions that led to epidemics. Their distress was real and it found expression in religion. In Marx's words, 'Religion is the sigh of the oppressed creature'. It was in that sense that he called religion as the opium or opiate of the masses; that is, religion acted like a sedative to numb people's pain. On the other hand, religion also acted like a sedative, it did nothing to alleviate the underlying problem. It merely covered up the pain temporarily. Worse yet, Marx condemned religion for leading people to seek solutions to their problems in the wrong place. Marx believed it was necessary to confront religion precisely because it reflected the society that needed to be changed (Abrahamson, 2010). If man is to find himself and abolish the illusions of religion, he must 'abandon a condition which requires illusions'. He must therefore eradicate the source of alienation in the economic infrastructure.

In Marx's view, productive labour is the primary, most vital human activity. Marx looks at productive labour in terms of self-fulfilment, an end in itself. In fact, to Marx, productive labour is what separates human beings from animals. In the days of the medieval guilds and before, people were absorbed in their work. They took raw materials, made them into products and consumed them. According to Marx,

> Owner-producer-merchant-consumer were all the same person, and creative labour gave meaning to human life. Next came the separation of the merchant class. The merchant mediates between producer and consumer, and eventually goods are no longer traded for goods, but for money. Then came the separation of owner and worker in production, especially under capitalist industrialisation. This is the completion of self-estrangement or alienation.
>
> *(Adams and Sydie, 2016)*

For Marx, thus, alienation results from the breaking apart of the owner-worker-product-consumer syndrome. He further argues that alienation is not peculiar to industrial capitalism; neither the slave nor the serf owns his means of production or its product. However, in capitalist industrial society, alienation has become the common condition of life. Marx stated:

> The alienation of the worker in his product means not only that his labour becomes an object, an external existence, but that it exists outside him, independently, as something alien to him, and that it becomes a power on its own confronting him. It means that life which he has conferred on the object confronts him as something hostile and alien.
>
> *(ibid.)*

According to Marx, man is essentially a creative being who realises his essence and affirms himself in labour or production, a creative activity carried out in cooperation with others and by which the external world is transformed. The process of production involves transformation of human power into material objects or 'objectification' of human creative power. In other words, in the production of objects, man 'objectifies' himself, he expresses and externalises his being. However, if the objects of man's creation come to control his being, then man loses himself in the object. The act of production then results in man's alienation. This occurs when man regards the products of his labour as commodities, as articles for sale in the marketplace. The objects of his creation are then seen to control his existence. They are seen to be subject to impersonal forces, such as the law of supply and demand, over which man has little or no control. In Marx's words, 'the object that labour produces, its product, confronts it as an alien being, as a power independent of the producer'. In this way, man is estranged from the object he produces, he becomes alienated from the most vital human activity, that is, productive labour.

Marx looked into important characteristics of industrial society – the mechanisation of production and a further specialisation of the division of labour – as contributing to the alienation of the workforce. However, he stressed that the capitalist economic system, rather than industrialisation as such, is the primary source of alienation. In the capitalist society, division of labour and the institution of private property develop to their highest level and relations become contractual; consequently, alienation also reaches the highest level. According to Marx, alienation reaches its height in capitalist society where labour is dominated by the requirements of capital, the most important of which is the demand for profit. These requirements determine levels of employment and wages, the nature and quantity of goods produced and their method of manufacture. The worker sees himself as a prisoner of market forces over which he has no control. He is subject to the impersonal mechanisms of the law of supply and demand. He is at the mercy of the periodic booms and slumps which characterise capitalist economies. The worker therefore loses control over the objects he produces and becomes alienated from his product and the act of production. His work becomes a means to an end, a means of obtaining money to buy the goods and services necessary for his existence. Unable to fulfil his being in the products of his labour, the worker becomes alienated from himself in the act of production. Therefore, the more the worker produces, the more he loses himself. In Marx's words, 'the greater this product the less he is himself' (Haralambos and Heald, 2006).

According to Marx, alienation in capitalism manifests itself in four ways. First, the worker is alienated from the product of his labour, since what he produces is appropriated by the capitalist and the worker has no control over it.

Second, the worker is alienated from the act of production itself because all decisions as to how production is to be organised are taken by the capitalist.

Third, in addition to the fact that wage labour alienates man from his product and his productive activity, which distinguishes him from animals, he also becomes alienated from his species. After all, according to Marx (and Hegel), his 'species-being' is determined by his conscious productive activity, which is also a goal in itself. Under conditions of wage labour, however, labour is not a goal in itself, but only a means of maintaining life. For the worker, labour ceases to offer an intrinsic satisfaction and instead becomes only a means for survival. The labour, therefore, is no longer voluntary, rather it acquires a form of forced labour. This too means that what distinguishes man from animals, the free, conscious activity of life, disappears. In other words, according to Marx, man is distinguished from an animal by his creative ability to do labour, but due to the above-mentioned aspects of alienation, man loses his distinctly human quality and gets alienated from his real human nature or his 'species-being'. The capitalist system stratifies man, destroys the human qualities and renders man to a state worse than animal. No animal has to work for its survival at other's bidding, while man has to do that in a capitalist system.

Marx argued that in human functions, i.e. work, people are like animals. It is to be noted that Marx regarded work as a central human activity. The work of humans in capitalism is entirely forced. They feel no joy. They are like oxen hitched to a wagon. Meanwhile, it is only in the functions they share with animals (i.e. eating, drinking, procreating) that people feel human because they have an opportunity to behave freely, to make choices. In capitalistic systems, Marx observed, the irony is: 'The animalistic becomes the human and the human the animalistic' (Abrahamson, 2010). Marx also stated that 'The worker only feels himself outside his work, and in his work feels outside himself. He is at home when he is not working, and when he is working, he is not at home' (Adams and Sydie, 2016). In short, a common fear among thinkers in the early industrial era was that people, now slaves to the new machines, would be stripped of their humanity. No one captured this idea better than the comic actor Charlie Chaplin, who wrote and starred in the 1936 film *Modern Times*. According to Marx, thus, industrial capitalism alienates workers from their human potential.

Fourth, the form of wage labour prevalent in the capitalist society also leads to social alienation. Consequently, man ultimately becomes alienated from that which is a product of his actions: society. In other words, the worker in a capitalist system is also socially alienated, because social relations became market relations, in which each man is judged by his position in the market, rather than his human qualities. Through work, Marx claimed, people build bonds of community. Industrial capitalism, however, makes work competitive rather than cooperative, setting each person apart from everyone else and offering little chance for companionship (Macionis, 2015).

According to Marx, in capitalism, both the capitalists and the workers are alienated. Capitalists are alienated since they regard the goods and services produced by the workers merely as things to sell and sources of profit. They do not care who makes or buys these items, or how the worker who make them feel about the products of their labour, or how buyers use them. Their only concern is with making profit. In addition, capitalists are alienated by knowing that they do no productive labour. And as consumers, the only difference is that the capitalists can buy and own more things than the workers can. Commodities, such as television set, cars, etc., become fetish for the consumer – an item that in a hollow way pretends to give meaning to life. Fetishes are commodities that may have no actual use value or utility, but they are still desired by the consumers just for the sake of it. In contemporary society, much conspicuous consumption – such as fancy car, branded clothing, prestigious home, etc. is, Marx would say, a matter of fetishism.

According to Marx, the market forces which are seen to control production are not impersonal mechanisms beyond the control of man, they are man-made. Alienation, therefore, is the result of human activity rather than external forces with an existence independent of man. If the products of labour are alien to the worker, they must therefore belong to somebody. This somebody, according to Marx, is no other than the capitalist himself who owns and controls the forces of production and the products of labour, and who appropriates for himself the wealth that labour produces. Alienation, therefore, springs not from impersonal market forces but from the relations of production between classes. Marx argues that an end to alienation, thus, involves a radical change in the pattern of these relationships. This will come when the contradiction between man's consciousness and objective reality is resolved. Then man will realise that the situation in which he finds himself is man-made and therefore subject to change by human action (Haralambos and Heald, 2006).

Hence, given the priority Marx assigns to economic factors, an end to alienation involves a radical change in the economic infrastructure. To Marx, the solution would be the abolition of private property and of the division of labour (specialised tasks) which also serves to alienate the worker. The replacement of private property with communal ownership of the forces of production under communism will restore the owner-worker-consumer syndrome (Adams and Sydie, 2016).

Please note that the theory of alienation was unknown until the 1930s, but since the 1960s, it has become extremely important and much discussed and used in so-called humanistic Marxism. Since Marx, the term *alienation* has undergone a lot of change of meaning. It has become one of the important concepts in mainstream sociology, especially in the writings of the American sociologists of the 1950s and 1960s. Let us now discuss the views of some other scholars on alienation.

Max Weber (1864–1920), a German sociologist, disagreed with Marx regarding the factors leading to alienation and believed that alienation was an inevitable feature of modern industrial society irrespective of whether the means of production are owned privately or collectively. For Weber, the cause of alienation lies in the rationalisation of social life and predominance of bureaucratic organisations in modern industrial societies. The compulsive conformity to impersonal rules in bureaucratic organisations renders people into mere cogs in giant machines and destroys their human qualities.

The American sociologist C. Wright Mills, in a study of the American middle classes entitled *White Collar*, applies Marx's concept of alienation to non-manual (white-collar) workers. While Marx highlighted alienation largely in manufacturing sector, Mills turned attention towards alienation in the tertiary sector of the economy in advanced capitalist societies. To Mills, advanced capitalism has led to a 'shift from skills with things to skills with persons'. Just as in manufacturing sector manual workers (blue-collar workers) become like commodities by selling their 'skills with things', a similar process occurs in tertiary or service industry when non-manual workers (white-collar workers) sell their 'skills with persons' on the open market. Mills refers to this sector of the economy as the 'personality market'. According to Mills, a market value is attached to personality characteristics and as a result people sell pieces of their personality. Therefore, managers and marketing executives are hired not simply because of their academic qualifications and experience, but for their ability to get on with people. For example, the salesman is given a job for his apparent warmth, friendliness and sincerity. Since the aspects of personality are bought and sold like any other commodity on the market, capitalism not only exploits the worker of his physical labour but also his emotional labour. Thus, individuals feel alienated from their true selves. Their expression of personality at work is false and insincere. Mills gives the example of a girl working in a department store, smiling, concerned and attentive to the whims of the customer. He states:

> in the course of her work, because her personality becomes, the instrument of an alien purpose, the salesgirl becomes self-alienated. At work she is not herself. In the salesroom, in the boardroom, in the staffroom, in the conference room, men and women are prostituting their personalities in pursuit of personal gain.
>
> *(Haralambos and Heald, 2006)*

Similarly, the French sociologist and journalist Andre Gorz argues that in capitalist society, man is alienated from both work and leisure. The two spheres of life reinforce each other. According to Gorz, alienation at work leads the worker to seek fulfilment in leisure. However, just as the capitalist system shapes his working day, it also shapes his leisure activities. It creates the passive consumer who finds satisfaction in the consumption of the product of the manufacturing and entertainment industries. Leisure simply provides a 'means of escape and oblivion', a means of living with the problem rather than an active solution to it.

Like Gorz, Herbert Marcuse also presents a pessimistic view of work and leisure in industrial capitalist society. Herbert Marcuse was a German-American philosopher and sociologist associated with the Frankfurt School of Critical Theory. In his work *One Dimensional Man*, Marcuse argues that the potential for personal development is crushed in advanced industrial society. Marcuse argues that work is 'exhausting, stupefying, inhuman slavery'. Leisure simply involves 'modes of relaxation which soothe and prolong this stupefaction'. It is based on and directed by 'false needs' which are largely imposed by a mass media controlled by the establishment. Needs are false if they do not result in true self-fulfilment and real satisfaction. Marcuse claims that 'Most of the prevailing needs to relax, to have fun, to behave and consume in accordance with the advertisements, to love and hate what others love and hate belong to this category of false needs'. Members of society no longer seek fulfilment in themselves and in their relationships with others. Instead, 'The people recognise themselves in their commodities; they find their soul in their automobile, hi-fi set, split-level home, kitchen equipment'. The circle is now complete: industrial man is alienated from every sphere of his life (ibid.).

Marxian perspectives on the nature of work and leisure, however, are open to a number of criticisms. First, critics argue that these views are based partly on a rather vague picture of what man could and ought to be. It can be argued that these views say more about the values of particular sociologists than it does about man's essential being. Second, Marxist scholars tend to ignore the subjective meanings held by members of society. If people tend to claim fulfilment in work and/or leisure, there is a tendency to dismiss their views as a product of false class consciousness. Third, Marxian perspectives are very general. In other words, they tend to lump together diverse occupations and leisure activities and create a simple model of 'man in industrial society', thus presenting an overly simplified explanation of man and his existence in capitalist society.

Where Marx was pessimistic about the division of labour in society, Emile Durkheim (a functionalist) was cautiously optimistic. Marx saw the specialised division of labour trapping the worker in his occupational role and dividing society into antagonistic social classes. Durkheim saw a number of problems arising from the specialisation of industrial society but believed the promise of the division of labour outweighed the problems. Whereas Marx's solution to the problem of alienation was radical – the abolition of capitalism and its replacement by socialism – Durkheim believed that the solution to anomie can be provided within the existing framework of industrial society. He outlined his views in his work *The Division of Labour in Society*, first published in 1893. Durkheim saw alienation as a consequence of the condition of *anomie*, which refers to the break-down of norms in society leading to experienced normlessness. You will learn more on this in the chapter on Emile Durkheim.

Another sociologist Melvin Seeman used the insights of Marx, Emile Durkheim and others to construct what is often considered a model to recog-nise the five prominent features of alienation: powerlessness, meaninglessness, normlessness, isolation and self-estrangement. However, Seeman simply treats them as subjective dispositions which can be measured with the help of atti-tude scales. Seeman was part of a surge in alienation research during the mid-twentieth century when he published his paper 'On the Meaning of Alienation' in 1959.

Robert Blauner, an American sociologist, offers an altogether new perspective on alienation. In his famous study entitled *Alienation and Freedom*, Blauner examines the behaviour and attitudes of manual workers in the printing, textile, automobile and chemical industries. He sees production technology as the major factor influ-encing the degree of alienation that workers experience. For Blauner, alienation is made up of both objective and subjective conditions. Objective conditions mainly referred to the technology employed in particular industries. Blauner argues that technology largely determines the amount of judgement and initiative required from workers and the degree of control they have over their work. From an analysis of various forms of technology, he assesses the degree of alienation they produce. Subjective conditions or feelings, on the other hand, refer to the attitudes and feel-ings that workers have towards their work. This information can be obtained from the workers employed in different industries through questionnaires.

Blauner considers workers' attitudes as a valid measure of their level of alienation. So, if workers express satisfaction with their work, they are not alienated. Blauner, thus, rejects Marxian views which argue that workers in capitalist society are automatically alienated because of their objective posi-tion in relation to production. From a Marxian perspective, if workers express satisfaction with their jobs, this is an indication of false consciousness. Blauner identifies four dimensions of alienation: the degree of control workers have over their work; the degree of meaning and sense of purpose they find in work; the degree to which they are socially integrated into their work; and the degree to which they are involved in their work. In terms of these four dimensions, the alienated worker has a sense of powerlessness, meaninglessness, isolation and self-estrangement.

Robert Blauner, on the basis of his findings, presented the relationship between technology and alienation in the form of an inverted U-curve. According to him, the level of alienation is low in craft industries like printing but it increases in the machine-based textile industry. Blauner saw alienation reaching its height with mass production industry based on mechanised assembly line technology like automobile industry, but in the process industries with high degree of automation, alienation tends to decline because workers feel more involved and responsible.

Unlike Marx, Blauner believes that automation reverses the 'historic trend' towards increasing alienation in manufacturing industry. It restores control, meaning, integration and involvement to the worker. Blauner examines work in the chemical industry which involves the most recent development in production technology. For example, in the case of oil and chemical industries, although the product is manufactured automatically, the worker has considerable control over and responsibility for production. Workers in chemical plants are involved in continuous monitoring and checking of control dials which measure factors such as temperature and pressure. Blauner states that these decisions require 'considerable discretion and initiative'. In direct contrast to assembly line workers, none of the process workers felt they were controlled or dominated by their technology. Further, Blauner argues that in continuous process technology, the dominant job requirement is responsibility. This emphasis on responsibility restores meaning and purpose to work. It is an important source of satisfaction and accomplishment. According to Blauner, process technology halts the increasingly specialised division of labour (Figure 6.8). It integrates the entire production process and since workers are responsible for the overall process, they can see and appreciate their contribution to the finished product. Their sense of purpose is increased by the fact that process workers operate in teams with collective responsibility for the smooth running of the machinery. Again, this encourages the individual worker to feel a part of the overall production process.

Thus, as can be seen from the discussion above, the meaning of alienation has undergone change in contemporary times. It is no longer based upon objective conditions alone, rather it has come to be identified with subjective dispositions as well.

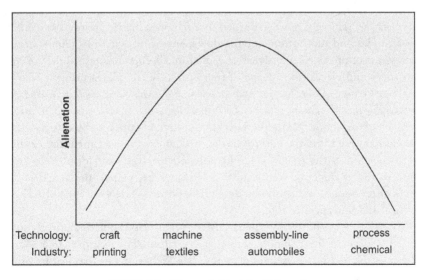

FIGURE 6.8   Blauner's Model of Alienation

Marx: An Assessment

We conclude our discussion by making some observations about the impact of Marx's ideas on social theory and on the social theorists who came after him. As we know that Karl Marx never saw himself in the role of a sociologist, his prime concern was to bring about a revolutionary transformation in the then contemporary European society. Nevertheless, the ideas of Karl Marx have greatly contributed to the development of modern sociology. In fact, he is the founder of the 'conflict tradition' in modern sociology and his ideas have stimulated a lively debate which has further enriched the discipline.

Marx contributed a new perspective and a new methodology to the study of social phenomena. He highlighted the role of economic factors in shaping the various institutions of society. This has been accepted as an academic methodology in social sciences. The long-lasting significance of Marx's theory of historical materialism is that he goes far beyond the point of just adopting a materialist orientation in philosophical terms; he puts this approach to work in developing a detailed theory about the emergence of modern capitalist society. To the extent that Marx's theory accounts successfully for the emergence of capitalist society during the nineteenth century, this reinforces the general reliability, not only of his own theory of historical change, but also of the materialist and realist approaches in social theory as a whole.

However, Marxian ideas have also been criticised on various accounts. Many of his critics have argued that history has failed to substantiate Marx's views on the direction of social change. Let's look at some of the important criticisms of Marxian theory in detail one by one.

First, and most importantly, particular criticism has been directed towards the priority that Marx assigns to economic factors in his explanation of social structure and social change. For instance, Max Weber in his study *The Protestant Ethic and the Spirit of Capitalism* argued that religious beliefs provided the ethics the attitudes and motivations for the development of capitalism. Since ascetic Protestantism preceded the advent of capitalism, Weber maintained that at certain times and places, the aspects of superstructure can play a primary role in directing change. Thus, *one potential weakness of the Marxist approach is its tendency to underplay the role of ideas, values and beliefs as a motivator of social action.* The priority given to economic factors by Marx has also invited criticisms by elite theorists who have argued that the control of the machinery of government rather than the ownership of the forces of production provides the basis for power. They point to the example of communist societies where, despite the fact that the forces of production are communally owned, power is largely monopolised by a political and bureaucratic elite.

Second, scholars have also criticised Marx's two-class model as an overly simplified version of the complex reality of capitalism. For example, like Marx, Weber also sees class in economic terms. But Weber argues that factors other than the ownership or non-ownership of property are also significant in the formation of classes. He argues that classes develop only in market economies in which individuals compete for economic gain. He defines a class as '*a group of individuals who share a similar position in a market economy and by virtue of that fact receive similar economic rewards*'. Thus, in Weber's terminology, a person's 'class situation' is basically his 'market situation'. This implies that those who share a similar class situation also share similar life chances. Their economic position will directly affect their chances of obtaining those things defined as desirable in their society, for example, access to higher education and good quality housing. Thus, according to Weber, the classes are a feature of modern capitalist societies. All pre-capitalist societies, thus, were status-based societies. While class refers to the unequal distribution of economic rewards, status refers to the unequal distribution of 'social honour'. Status, in traditional societies, was largely based on ascriptive criteria such as age, gender, caste, ethnicity, etc.

Thus, while Marx recognises class as the only possible basis for group formation and collective action, Weber identifies status (honour) and parties (power) as the other bases along with class. Weber defines 'parties' as groups which are specifically concerned with influencing policies and making decisions in the interests of their membership. In Weber's words, parties are concerned with the acquisition of social 'power'. According to Weber, political parties may represent the interests of classes or status groups, or both.

Third, Weber also rejects Marx's thesis of polarisation of classes. Like Marx, Weber argues that the major class division is between those who own the forces of production and those who do not. However, Weber sees important differences in the market situation of the propertyless groups in society. According to Weber, different occupations enjoy differing market values, depending upon the various skills and services offered by them. For example, in capitalist society, white-collar workers like managers, administrators and professionals receive relatively high salaries in comparison to blue-collar workers because of the demand for their services. Weber identified four distinct classes in capitalist society:

1. the propertied upper class
2. the propertyless white-collar workers
3. the petty bourgeoisie
4. the manual working class

Instead of polarisation of classes, Weber sees a diversification of classes and an expansion of the white-collar middle class. Though Weber sees some decline in the numbers of the petty bourgeoisie, the small property owners, due to competition from large companies, he argues that they enter white-collar or skilled manual trades rather than being depressed into the ranks of unskilled manual workers. More importantly, Weber argues that the white-collar 'middle class' expands rather than contracts as capitalism develops. He argues that capitalist enterprises and the modern nation state require a 'rational' bureaucratic administration which involves large numbers of administrators and clerical staff (Haralambos and Heald, 2006).

Fourth, Weber also rejects Marx's view of the inevitability of the proletariat revolution. Given the heterogeneity of class structure in capitalism, Weber sees no reason why those sharing a similar class situation should necessarily develop a common identity, recognise shared interests and take collective action to further those interests. Weber argued that dissatisfied workers may respond in a variety of ways. They may grumble, work to rule, sabotage industrial machinery, take strike action or attempt to organise other members of his class in an effort to overthrow capitalism. However, Weber admits that a common market situation may provide a basis for collective class action but he sees this only as a possibility.

In this regard, it may also be noted that, according to Marx, the inherent contradictions present within the capitalist system and the subsequent class conflict would lead to its eventual destruction. Critics, however, claim that class conflict, far from growing in intensity, has become institutionalised in advanced capitalist society. For example, Ralf Dahrendorf, a German sociologist, examined the nature of conflict in industry with particular reference to the role of trade unions. He argues that by the latter half of twentieth century, trade unions were generally accepted as legitimate by employers and the state. Dahrendorf regards this as the major step towards industrial democracy and the institutionalisation of industrial conflict.

At this point, it would be useful to learn about some of the important observations of Ralf Dahrendorf. Dahrendorf claims that the social structure of advanced societies has undergone some very significant changes since Marx's time. These changes have resulted in a 'transformed' capitalism, and the modern industrial societies are organised in terms of 'imperatively coordinated associations', i.e. associations of people controlled by a hierarchy of authority and power. Dahrendorf highlights three significant changes that have occurred in advanced industrial societies. First, modern industrial societies have witnessed a *decomposition of capital*. This implies the separation of ownership and control over large corporations such as joint stock companies where the ownership (in the form of equity) lies with the public at large while the control is exercised by the management, professionals, technocrats and other experts. Second, in contrast with the Marxian assumption of homogenisation of the proletariat, diverse occupational groups with different skills and statuses have emerged in advanced industrial societies. Dahrendorf calls this as *decomposition of labour*, a disintegration of the manual working class. Third, Dahrendorf argues that the tension between labour and capital is recognised as a principle of the structure of the labour market and has become a legal institution of society. As workers have become increasingly skilled, educated and better paid, they have become more integrated into the middle layers of society. The traditional sources of discontent and labour militancy have been dissolved. The basis for class struggle is gone. Conflicts now develop within imperatively coordinated associations (institutional structures such as business organisations, unions and so forth) and are resolved rationally and fairly through mediation, arbitration or adjudication. Dahrendorf calls it as *institutionalisation of class conflict* in modern industrial societies.

A number of sociologists have argued that largely through trade unionism, the working class has been integrated into capitalist society. Trade unions form the major groups representing the interests of employees in general and the manual working class in particular. Conflict between employers and employees has been institutionalised in terms of an agreed-upon set of rules and procedures. The net result is increasing stability in industrial society. No longer is the working class seen as a threat to social order as Marx believed; there is less and less chance of the kind of class conflict which Marx predicted.

The American sociologist, Seymour M. Lipset has also argued that trade unions 'serve to integrate their members in the larger body politic and give them a basis for loyalty to the system'. Through trade unions, the interests of the working class are represented at the highest level and in this way the working class as a whole is integrated into 'the larger body politic'. The picture which emerges from this discussion is one of fully-fledged interest groups – trade unions – effectively representing workers' interests. Industrial conflict has been institutionalised and the working class has been integrated into both the capitalist enterprise and society as a whole.

Having explained social change from a dialectical materialist perspective in terms of developments in the forces of production combined with changes in the nature of property relations, the simple message that Marx and Engels want to get across in *The Communist Manifesto* is that, as surely as night follows day, the capitalist mode of production is about to be replaced by a socialist or communist mode of production. The only remaining question was exactly *when* this might happen and whether some kind of intervention might be required to make sure it did. Marx and Engels certainly felt that by forming the Communist Party, and by spelling out the principles of historical change according to their own theory in the *Manifesto*, they could, as it were, give history a bit of a push in the right direction.

The working class, it seemed, could not be relied upon to make history happen as it should, but would need the help of 'fresh elements of enlightenment and progress' supplied even by the bourgeoisie to show them the way. There are strong hints, at least in sections of the *Manifesto* drafted by Engels, that the overthrow of capitalism was unlikely to be a peaceful affair:

> the Communists openly declare that their ends can be attained only by the forcible overthrow of all existing social conditions. Let the ruling classes tremble at a Communist revolution. The proletarians have nothing to lose but their chains. They have a world to win.
>
> *(Ransome, 2011)*

The validity of Marx and Engel's theory would have been considerably strengthened if a revolution had occurred in the modern society during the latter part of the nineteenth century. The fact that this has not yet happened rather suggests that either the theory was not complete or they had a poor sense of timing. Critics argue that Marx's predictions about the downfall of capitalism have not come true. Contrary to his belief, socialism has triumphed in predominantly peasant societies, whereas capitalist societies show no signs of destructive class war.

> It is clear that there are serious problems with Marx's account. When socialist revolution has occurred, it has mainly been in societies on the threshold of entering capitalism, such as Russia in 1917, or via a nationalist populism, such as China in 1949, rather than in mature capitalist states ripe for change. Second, in Western states, the working class has enjoyed an increase in wages in real terms, while the development of the welfare state has ameliorated some of the worse effects of unemployment. Third, state socialism in Europe collapsed like a house of cards between 1989 and 1992, and the ensuing charge towards capitalism in former communist states in Central and Eastern Europe took place.
>
> *(Bilton et al., 2016)*

Fifth, turning to his idea of communist society, critics argue that Marx's classless and stateless society is a utopia. There can be no society without an authority structure or a regulatory mechanism which inevitably leads to a crystallisation of social relations between the rulers and the ruled, with inherent possibilities of internal contradiction and conflict. Critics have argued that history has not borne out the promise of communism contained in Marx's writings. Socialist or communist societies are societies in which the forces of production are communally owned. Marx believed that public ownership of the forces of production is the first and fundamental step towards the creation of an egalitarian society. This would abolish at a stroke the antagonistic classes of capitalist society. Classes, defined in terms of the relationship of social groups to the forces of production, would now share the same relationship – that of ownership – to the forces of production. Social inequality would not, however, disappear overnight. There would be a period of transition during which the structures of inequality produced by capitalism would be dismantled.

Marx was rather vague about the exact nature of the communist utopia which should eventually emerge from the abolition of private property. He believed that the state would eventually 'wither away' and that the consumption of goods and services would be based on the principle of 'to each according to his needs'. Whether he envisaged a disappearance of all forms of social inequality, such as prestige and power differentials, is not entirely clear. One thing that is clear, though, is that the reality of contemporary communism is a long way from Marx's dreams. Significant social inequalities are present in communist regimes and there are few, if any, signs of a movement towards equality. The dictatorship of the proletariat clings stubbornly to power and there is little indication of its eventual disappearance.

Frank Parkin, in his study of Eastern European societies, observed that East European communism has not resulted in the abolition of social stratification.

Identifiable strata, which can be distinguished in terms of differential economic rewards, occupational prestige and power, are present in all socialist states. He identified the following strata in East European communist societies: white-collar intelligentsia (professional, managerial and administrative positions), skilled manual positions, lower or unqualified white-collar positions and unskilled manual positions. He concluded that although income inequalities are not as great as in capitalist societies, they are still significant.

Milovan Djilas, a Yugoslavian writer, also argues that those in positions of authority in communist societies use power to further their own interests. He claims that the bourgeoisie of the West have been replaced by a new ruling class in the East. This 'new class' is made up of 'political bureaucrats' occupying high ranks in the Communist Party. Djilas argues that though in legal terms the forces of production are communally owned, in practice they are controlled by the new class for its own benefit. Political bureaucrats direct and control the economy and monopolise decisions about the distribution of income and wealth. According to Djilas, this new class is even more exploitive than the bourgeoisie because its power is unchecked by political parties. Djilas argues that in a single party state, political bureaucrats monopolise power. In explaining the source of their power, Djilas maintains the Marxian emphasis on the forces of production. He argues that the new class owes its power to the fact that it controls the forces of production. Others have reversed this argument claiming that in communist societies economic power derives from political power. Thus, T.B. Bottomore argues that the new class 'controls the means of production because it has political power' (Haralambos and Heald, 2006).

These arguments also find support from Weber who rejects the Marxian view that political power necessarily derives from economic power. In other words, political inequality may also lead to economic inequality as stated above. Further, Weber argues that the class forms only one possible basis for power and that the distribution of power in society is not necessarily linked to the distribution of class inequalities. In other words, power distribution may also occur along status lines.

Sixth, critics argue that Marx misjudged the extent of alienation in the average worker. The extent and intensity of alienation and frustration which Marx 'witnessed' among the workers of his day is not 'typical' of today's capitalism or its worker who tends to identify increasingly with a number of 'meaningful' groups – religious, ethnic, occupational and local. This is not to deny the existence of alienation, but to point out that alienation results more from the structure of bureaucracy and mass society than from the economic exploitation. Further, Robert Blauner argues that alienation needs to be understood in terms of both objective and subjective conditions. He further argues that automation reverses the 'historic trend' towards increasing alienation in manufacturing industry and produced non-alienated worker (Abraham and Morgan, 2010).

In recent times, some scholars have argued that in certain respects, the overall picture of stratification in communist societies is similar to that of the West. According to some American sociologists, the stratification systems in all industrial societies, whether capitalist or communist, are becoming increasingly similar. This view is popularly known as 'convergence theory'. Clark Kerr, one of the main proponents of convergence theory, argues that modern industrial economies will necessarily produce similar systems of social stratification. According to Kerr, the same technology calls for the same occupational structure around the world – in steel, in textiles, in air transport. Kerr assumes that technical skills and educational qualifications will be rewarded in proportion to their value to industry. Since the demands of industry are essentially the same in both East and West, the range of occupations and occupational rewards will become increasingly similar. As a result, the stratification systems of capitalist and communist societies will converge (Haralambos and Heald, 2006).

Convergence theory, however, has been subject to strong criticism and its propositions are still a matter of debate. It is to be noted that convergence theory does not argue that the stratification systems of East and West are the same, only that they will become increasingly similar. On this particular point, only time will provide the final answer.

Francis Fukuyama, an acclaimed American political philosopher, has also prophesied the 'end of history'. Fukuyama's conception of the end of history is based on the worldwide triumph of capitalism and liberal democracy.

> In the wake of the 1989 revolutions in Eastern Europe, the dissolution of the Soviet Union and a movement towards pro-capitalism and multi-party democracy in other regions, Fukuyama argued, the ideological battles of earlier eras are over. The end of history is the end of alternatives … Capitalism has won in its long struggle with socialism, contrary to Marx's prediction, and liberal democracy now stands unchallenged. We have reached, Fukuyama asserts, 'the end point of mankind's ideological evolution and the universalization of Western democracy as the final form of human government.
>
> *(Giddens, 2008)*

Critics argue that although this currently seems to be the case, it is very doubtful that history has come to a stop in the sense that we have exhausted all alternatives open to us. Who can say what new forms of economic, political or cultural order may emerge in the future? For example, just as the thinkers of medieval times had no inkling of the industrial society that was to emerge with the decline of feudalism, so can we not at the moment anticipate how the world will change over the coming century.

Although Marx's predictions regarding the future of capitalist societies have been largely disproved by the developments of history in the twentieth century, Marx's concepts of historical materialism, class and class conflict and his theory of social change (if shorn of the prophetic elements) yet remain a valuable contribution to social sciences in understanding the social structure and change in the society. Marxian ideas have stimulated further debate and research which enriched sociology as a discipline. Judging from the constant reinterpretations, impassioned defences and vehement criticisms of Marx's work, his ideas are as alive and relevant today as they ever were.

LET'S THINK

- Dear Learner, in this chapter we have learned about Marx's ideas on social structure and social change. Try to think about the social structure of your society in terms of base and superstructure. Do you agree with Marx's view that the superstructure and its various institutions in a given society are largely shaped by the interests of the ruling class? Try analysing the social, political and legal institutions from this perspective.
- Reflect upon the idea of communism as stated by Marx. How would you explain the developments taking place in various socialist or communist countries? Contemporary China is a particularly interesting nation to examine in relation to base and superstructure because of the way elements of capitalism have been emerging within an otherwise controlled communist system.

For Practice

Q1. Write short notes on:
   (a) historical materialism
   (b) class in itself and class for itself
Q2. Analyse Marxian conception of historical materialism as a critique of Hegelian dialectics.
Q3. 'It is not the consciousness of men that determines their being, but on the contrary it is their social being that determines their consciousness'. Examine Karl Marx's notion of mode of production in the light of this statement.
Q4. Do you accept that Marxism offers a prefabricated theory of social change? Discuss critically.
Q5. Analyse Marxian theory of social change. Is it useful to comprehend the changes in the developing societies?

Model Answers

Q. Write a short note on historical materialism.

A. In his theory of historical materialism, Karl Marx argues that the conflict of economic interest between antagonistic classes is the primary cause for social change. This was in contrast to Hegel's historical or dialectical idealism. Hegel, the great German philosopher, had explained social change largely in terms of evolution of the human consciousness or ideas. Unlike Hegel, who gave primacy to ideas or mind, Marx gave primacy to matter in explaining social change. As a result of the priority he gives to economic factors, to 'material life', Marx's view of history is often referred to as 'historical materialism' or 'dialectical materialism'. Though Marx rejected Hegel's content orientation, he retained his dialectical structure. In other words, while Hegel tended to apply the dialectic only to ideas, Marx felt that it should be applied to material aspects of life, for example, the economy.

Historical materialism can be understood both as a perspective and as a methodology. As a perspective, it highlights Marx's emphasis on the role of economic infrastructure (base) in shaping the superstructure of society. The economic infrastructure is comprised of both forces of production and relations of production. Further, as a methodology, it describes the significance of the concept of class and class conflict in explaining social change in a dialectical manner. According to Marx, social change unfolds in a dialectical manner when at a certain stage of development of a society, newly emerging forces of production come into conflict with the existing relations of production. This gives rise to antagonistic classes who have mutually opposed economic interest. For example, the class struggle between the traditionally dominant feudal aristocracy and the newly emerging bourgeoisie subsequently led to the French Revolution and transformation of feudal mode of production to the capitalist one. Marx stated that '*The history of all hitherto existing society is the history of class struggles*'.

Weber, however, criticised Marxian theory for its mono-causal economic determinism and instead argued that the superstructure can also influence the base (economic structure). For instance, Max Weber in his study *The Protestant Ethic and the Spirit of Capitalism* argued that religious beliefs provided the ethics, attitudes and motivations for the development of capitalism. Dahrendorf also questioned the inevitability of proletarian revolution and talked about decomposition of labour and capital, and institutionalisation of conflict in modern industrial society. Despite its limitations, Marxian concept of historical materialism has contemporary relevance both as a perspective and as a methodology. However, Marxian theory of revolutionary change has only limited applicability to the extent that it can help us in understanding the cause of discontent as well as revolutionary tendencies in various Third World societies such as India (e.g. naxalism) which are marked by gross economic inequalities. In the Indian context, A.R. Desai has used Marxian approach to explain the rise of nationalism in India in his famous work *Social Background of Indian Nationalism*.

Q. Write a short note on 'class in itself' and 'class for itself'.

A. In his theory of social change, Marx argues that for a successful (revolutionary) transition of society from one stage to another, class in itself must transform into class for itself. For Marx, a class in itself is simply a social group whose members share the same relationship to the forces of production and as a result share common economic interest. But a class in itself transforms into a 'class for itself' when its members have developed true class consciousness and class solidarity. In other words, its members realise the real cause of their exploitation as well as the fact that only by collective action they can over throw the ruling class.

This process may be illustrated by the transition from feudal to capitalist mode of production. According to Marx, industrial capitalism gradually developed within the framework of feudal society. However, feudal relations of production were not conducive for the growth of the newly emerging class of early merchants and industrialists, also known as *bourgeoisie* or capitalists. Instead of the historical paternalistic ties between feudal lords and serfs, contractual wage-labour relationships between capitalists and workers suited the interests of this newly emerging (ownership) class. When the bourgeoisie developed this true class consciousness and its members united to overthrow the feudal relations of production, at this point, the bourgeoisie, became a class for itself. Further, with regard to transition of capitalist mode of production to communism, Marx argued that the contradictions of capitalism were sufficient to transform the proletariat into a class for itself and bring about the downfall of the bourgeoisie.

However, Marx's argument that in the capitalist society the processes of homogenisation, pauperisation, immiserisation and polarisation would inevitably transform the proletariat into a class for itself was later challenged and modified by Max Weber and Ralf Dahrendorf. Weber, for example, questions the polarisation thesis of Marx and instead finds evidence for the diversification of classes and an expansion of the white-collar middle class. Similarly, Dahrendorf too sees bleak chances for the proletarian revolution and instead asserts that the conflict between labour and capital has got institutionalised in modern industrial societies.

Yet, despite its limitations and if shorn of the prophetic elements, Marx's concept of class and class conflict remains a valuable contribution to social sciences in understanding the social structure and social change, particularly in developing societies like India which are marked by gross economic disparities. Recent marches of thousands of Indian farmers in Delhi and Maharashtra to highlight the deepening agrarian crisis are one of the several instances which keep Marx's concept of class and class conflict alive and relevant in contemporary times.

References

Abraham, Francis and John Henry Morgan. *Sociological Thought*. New Delhi: Macmillan Publishers, 2010.

Abrahamson, Mark. *Classical Theory and Modern Studies: Introduction to Sociological Theory*. New Delhi: PHI Learning, 2010.

Adams, Bert N. and R.A. Sydie. *Sociological Theory*. New Delhi: SAGE Publications, 2016.

Beiser, Frederick. *Hegel*. New York: Routledge, 2006.

Bhargava, Rajeev and Ashok Acharya, eds. *Political Theory: An Introduction*. New Delhi: Dorling Kindersley, 2008.

Bilton, Tony, Kevin Bonnet, Pip Jones, Tony Lawson, David Skinner, Michelle Stanworth and Andrew Webster. *Introductory Sociology*. 4th Edition. Hampshire: Palgrave Macmillan, 2016.

Brinkerhoff, David B., Rose Weitz and Suzanne T. Ortega. *Essentials of Sociology*. 9th Edition. New Delhi: Cengage Learning, 2017.

Churton, Mel and Anne Brown. *Theory & Method*. 2nd Edition. Hampshire: Palgrave Macmillan, 2017.

Cuff, E.C., W.W. Sharrock and D.W. Francis. *Perspectives in Sociology*. 5th Edition. India: Sirohi Brothers, 2009.

Giddens, Anthony. *Sociology*. 5th Edition. New Delhi: Wiley India, 2008.

Haralambos, M. and R.M. Heald. *Sociology: Themes and Perspectives*. New Delhi: Oxford University Press, 2006.

Larson, Calvin J. *Major Themes in Sociological Theory*. New York: David Mckay Company, 1973.

Macionis, John J. *Sociology*. 15th Edition. England: Pearson Education, 2015.

Marshall, Gordon. *Oxford Dictionary of Sociology*. New York: Oxford University Press, 1998.

Morrison, Ken. *Marx, Durkheim, Weber: Formations of Modern Social Thought*. 2nd Edition. New Delhi: SAGE Publications, 2012.

Ransome, Paul. *Social Theory*. Jaipur: Rawat Publications, 2011.

Ritzer, George and Jeffrey Stepnisky. *Sociological Theory*. 9th Edition. New York: McGraw-Hill Education, 2014.

Wallace, Ruth A. and Alison Wolf. *Contemporary Sociological Theory: Expanding the Classical Tradition*. 6th Edition. New Delhi: PHI Learning Private, 2012.

7

EMILE DURKHEIM

About Durkheim

Emile Durkheim was born in 1858, in Epinal, France. He grew up in a traditional, orthodox Jewish family. His father was a rabbi (as had been his grandfather and great-grandfather). The family was quite poor. Like his father before him, young Durkheim expected to become a rabbi. His training began early in Hebrew and the Old Testament and the Talmud. His Jewish parents nurtured their son's ambition in the strongly homogeneous and cohesive community of Jews. The Jewish minority status and his early contact with the disastrous Franco-Prussian War made a strong impression upon Durkheim, which is reflected in his constant fascination with the study of group solidarity. However, Durkheim changed his mind and later on even rejected the Jewish faith. He remained a non-believer for the rest of his life (Abraham and Morgan, 2010).

After two unsuccessful attempts, Durkheim finally secured admission in 1879 in the most prestigious postgraduate school of higher education, the École normale supérieure in Paris. Because he was so astute in the application of his fledgling scientific skills of political and social analysis and partly because of his rebellious demeanour vis-à-vis the more traditional ways of doing things at the École, Durkheim was not always in favour with the university establishment. Though his primary training was in philosophy, his strong personal interest was in politics and sociology. However, since sociology was not a subject of instruction either at the secondary schools or at the university, Durkheim embarked upon a career as a teacher in philosophy. Upon graduation in 1882, he taught philosophy in several provincial Lycees in the neighbourhood of Paris, from 1882 to 1887 (Coser, 2008).

In 1885, Durkheim was offered a scholarship to study in Germany for a year. One reason for the scholarship was Durkheim's views supporting the French Republic

DOI: 10.4324/9781003291053-9

and his advocacy of a 'secular morality based on science'. The other reason, in a sense, was France's defeat in Franco-Prussian War of 1870. Many French policy-makers attributed the defeat to France's outdated educational system and insisted on reforming the educational system, focusing on secularisation (Adams and Sydie, 2016). In Germany, at the famous Psychological Laboratory of the renowned psychologist Wilhelm Wundt in Leipzig, Durkheim was especially impressed with the scientific precision and objectivity in research. On his return from Germany in 1887, Durkheim began to publish articles, first on the German academic life and then critical articles on various kinds of scholarship, thereby gaining considerable recognition from the French academy. In 1887, Durkheim obtained a position at the University of Bordeaux. This first position was with the Department of Philosophy. It was not until 1896 that he was appointed a full professor of social science, the first such position in any French university. Durkheim introduced the first sociology course at the University of Bordeaux (ibid.). Shortly after his appointment as a faculty at the University of Bordeaux, he married Louise Dreyfus, a Jewish girl from a strong traditional family. They had two children, Marie and Andre. Little is known about family life except that Louise seems to have been a strong and supportive wife and encouraging mother (Abraham and Morgan, 2010).

Durkheim spent 15 years in Bordeaux (1887–1902), and they were the most productive of his career. During this period, he published numerous articles and completed three of his major books. His first book, *The Division of Labour in Society*, submitted as his French doctoral thesis at the Sorbonne, was published in 1893. Two years later, he published his second major study *The Rules of Sociological Method* (1895). Durkheim completed his Bordeaux trilogy in 1897 with his incomparable *Suicide*. In 1898, Durkheim founded *L'Annee Sociologique*, which became one of the most influential sociology journals in the world. His students and friends described him as very disciplined, serious and stern. Durkheim along with Max Weber must be credited with laying the cornerstone of the modern phase of sociological theory.

Four years later and as everyone was anticipating, Durkheim was called to the Sorbonne, Paris's great university and headquarters of the French intelligentsia. In 1902, he was appointed professor of the science of education; it was only in 1913 that the title changed to Science of Education and Sociology. After more than three quarters of a century, Comte's brainchild had finally gained entry at the University of Paris (Sorbonne). His final, and in many respects provocative, book came 15 years after his previous study and 10 years after going to the Sorbonne, entitled *The Elementary Forms of the Religious Life* (1912).

When the First World War struck Europe, it was a great blow to France. It was even more painful for Durkheim, a man so much committed to the understanding of social solidarity. It is said that half of his class from his Sorbonne student days were killed in combat. And, just before Christmas, 1915, Durkheim was notified that his only son, Andre, had died in a Bulgarian hospital from his war wounds. The loss was too great to bear; his health failed and in less than two years at the age of 59, Durkheim died on 15 November 1917 (ibid.).

Although Durkheim was aware of Marx's work, and was a contemporary of Max Weber (Durkheim died in 1917, Weber in 1920), his training and intellectual orientation were quite different. Marx built his social theory on the basis of the German idealist philosophy of Georg Wilhelm Friedrich Hegel, the British political economy of Adam Smith and David Ricardo, and the French socialist tradition. Weber's social theory developed out of the philosophical debates that dominated German intellectual circles in the 1880s. In contrast, Durkheim stood as the successor to a quite different current of thought in the French positivist tradition (Ransome, 2011).

Social Realism

It is important for us to remember that all great ideas or theories are basically the product of the given social and intellectual conditions. Thus, in order to appreciate the contributions of Durkheim, let's try to understand that how social and intellectual conditions of his time influenced his ideas. Durkheim lived through a very turbulent period in French history – the disastrous war with the Prussians, the chaos and sociopolitical turmoil which inevitably followed and the instability and internal conflicts of the Third Republic. Durkheim was also involved in the greatest political conflicts of his time known as the Dreyfus affair. In 1894, a French officer named Dreyfus was found guilty of treason for supposedly writing to the German embassy about secret French documents. What made the conviction especially controversial was that Dreyfus was a Jew and the French military had a notorious reputation for anti-Semitism. However, a few years later, Dreyfus was proclaimed innocent and Durkheim was among the first to sign a public appeal in Dreyfus behalf. Durkheim was deeply influenced by the vulnerability of political stability of the French society against the personal ambitions of certain aspiring individuals. Further, various instances of high-level corruption such as Panama Scandal (1892), etc. exposed the weakness and vulnerability of national institutions. These developments led Durkheim to conclude that unrestricted or unbridled individualism is mainly responsible for the chaos and conflict in French society. Hence, the primary concern of Durkheim was how to strengthen French society. In other words, how to restore social cohesion and unity in society.

Although Durkheim was considerably affected by both German and British social thoughts, his ideas were rooted overwhelmingly in French intellectual history. Durkheim was deeply influenced by both Enlightenment and conservative scholars. The ideas of Enlightenment scholars such as Montesquieu, Rousseau, Saint-Simon, Auguste Comte and Herbert Spencer find reflection in Durkheim's works. Durkheim had read Montesquieu in detail during his Latin doctoral thesis on the well-known French philosopher. From Montesquieu, Durkheim borrowed the idea of the connectedness of all social and cultural phenomena. Durkheim stated:

> Montesquieu saw quite clearly that all these elements form a whole and that if taken separately, without reference to others, they cannot be understood.

> He does not separate law from morality, trade, religion, etc. and above all he does not consider it apart from the form of society, which affects all other social phenomena.
>
> *(Coser, 2008)*

If Durkheim owes his holistic view of society to Montesquieu, his notion of social solidarity and the concept of *conscience collective* grew out of his reading of Rousseau's *The Social Contract* and his concept of *general will.*

Like Saint-Simon and Auguste Comte, Durkheim also felt the need for a positive science of society. Durkheim argued that laws should be discovered based on empirical observation of the social phenomena and these laws then can be used for social reconstruction. Thus, sociology, for Durkheim, was a means to create a systematic and scientific body of knowledge which could serve as the basis for social construction. However, unlike Saint-Simon and Comte, Durkheim cautioned the social scientists against moral preaching. Saint-Simon and Comte, in their later years, had started advocating sweeping social reforms which were not based on any empirical research, and as a result both fell into disrepute. Durkheim insisted that sociologist himself should not directly indulge in social reconstruction. The responsibility of the sociologist, according to Durkheim, is to discover social laws on the basis of empirical research. These laws, then, could be used by administrators or political leaders for social reconstruction, that is, to create a stronger, stable and cohesive society.

Durkheim was also influenced by ideas of Spencer. For Spencer, reality was governed by the Cosmic Law of Evolution. According to Spencer, evolution is a twin process of differentiation and integration whereby a simple or less differentiated form transforms itself into a more complex and differentiated form. Durkheim used Spencer's idea of differentiation (i.e. increase in the division of labour in society) in his very first work *The Division of Labour in Society,* published in 1893. But, in place of Spencer's radical individualism, Durkheim supported an equally radical sociological realism in which the only ultimate social reality is found in the group, not in the individual. In shaping Durkheim's perspective towards social reality as well as his methodology, an imprint of two of his teachers at the *Ecole Normale* is quite apparent. From the great historian Fustel de Coulanges', Durkheim learned much of the careful historical method of research that is especially evident in the historical sections of *The Division of Labour in Society.* In other words, from Coulanges', Durkheim learned how to conduct historical research, how to collect and process historical data and how to establish cause and effect relationship between two or more social phenomena with the help of historical data. Coulanges' left a deep impact on Durkheim's research methodology. From his other major teacher, the philosopher Emile Boutroux, Durkheim learned the distinction between different levels of reality and the notion of emergence as a crucial aspect of the philosophy of science. Boutroux shaped the basic assumptions or perspective of Durkheim towards social reality (Coser, 2008).

Another French figure who had a demonstrably important effect on Durkheim's thought is the neo-Kantian philosopher Charles Renouvier. His emphasis on the need for a science of ethics found an echo in Durkheim's work. From Renouvier, Durkheim got the idea of the need for a civil morality to strengthen the French society of his times. Morality is basically concerned with what is considered as morally right and what is not. In other words, it prescribes what one ought to do and what one ought not to do. It is important for us to understand that moral principles are not static or fixed. They change from one society to another and within a given society from time to time. Given the turbulent socio-economic and political conditions in France, it was only natural for Durkheim to emphasise on the moral regulation of social life.

However, Durkheim faced a dilemma in harmonising his idea of moral regulation of social life with the value of individualism that had become the dominant and the most cherished value in modern times. Though Durkheim acknowledged that individualism is an integral value of the modern society, he also believed that unregulated or unbridled individualism could lead to chaos and social disorder as had happened in France. It is worth mentioning here that Enlightenment scholars had emphasised individual freedom. They gave primacy to the individual over society and argued that society exists for the sake of individual. However, conservative scholars held an altogether different view. For example, conservative German scholars Schmoller and Schaffle argued that individual can't exist without society. They believed that individual can only exist as a part and product of society. Hence, they gave primacy to society over the individual.

Ideas of Schmoller and Schaffle appealed to Durkheim and he was convinced that if society is to be strengthened, the individual must be subordinated to society. Thus, the social and intellectual conditions prevailing in French society at that time predisposed Durkheim to search for an alternative basis of morality other than religion. Durkheim stressed the need for civic morality (secular morality) and advocated the idea of moral individualism. Durkheim knew that modern societies could not be based on a strictly collectivist ethos. Durkheim redefined the notion of individualism. For Durkheim, individualism was not necessarily the same as egoism. Durkheim believed that the autonomy of the individual is fundamental, but this autonomy also involves the capacity for moral reflection and moral obligations. Given the correct form of socialisation and the development of social relations, modern individuals would be able to strike a balance between individual independence and social bonding. This new form of individualism he termed as *moral individualism*. By moral individualism, Durkheim emphasised the need for moral regulation of social life. He believed that moral and ethical values should serve as a guide to social action. Moral individualism also implied the voluntary compliance of individuals to the new morality which Durkheim called *civic morality*.

All these problems of the French society, along with his own background of belongingness to a highly well-knit Jewish community, predisposed him towards a search for the basis of moral order in society. It made him assert the primacy of 'group' over the individuals and preoccupied him with exploring the sources of social order and disorder, the forces that make for regulation or deregulation in the body social. His overriding concern as a moral man and scientist was with the social order. Durkheim believed that the traditional sources of morality upon which the social order was built, especially religion, were no longer viable or valid without serious and rational alterations. The new source of moral integration, so necessary for the establishment and stability of society, would be found in the discipline designed to scientifically analyse social order, stability and continuity, viz. that of sociology (Abraham and Morgan, 2010).

Durkheim argued that when individuals come together and start living in a group, a new level of reality emerges, that is, social reality or society. In a given society, individuals interact and enter into relations with each other giving rise to a way of life (social currents, for Durkheim). For example, members of a given society may develop certain norms to regulate sexual behaviour of its members or to regulate the production, distribution and exchange of goods and services. Over a period of time, these norms or social currents crystallise and take the form of social institutions such as marriage, kinship, market, etc. Thus emerge social facts.

Durkheim argues that although society (and its various institutions) develops out of the continuous process of interaction of its individual members, it comes to acquire a unique and independent existence of its own. It cannot be simply explained by reducing it to a mere aggregation of individuals. Society is not a mere sum of individuals. In other words, it is more than the sum of its parts. Despite the fact that society is made up only of human beings, it can be understood only through studying the interactions rather than the individuals. The interactions have their own levels of reality. For Durkheim, society is a *reality sui generis*. Society has an objective existence; it is independent of the consciousness of the individual members who comprise it. It is external and enduring. Individuals may die and new members take their place, but society lives forever. This view of Durkheim (his perspective) is sometimes also described as 'sociological realism' because he ascribes the ultimate sociological reality to the group and not to the individual.

Durkheim further argues that since each science is concerned with its own chosen aspect of reality, a new level of reality, *social reality*, must therefore be studied by a new science, namely sociology. In keeping with the tradition of nineteenth-century thinkers like Comte, Spencer, etc., Durkheim believed that this new science of society must be built on the lines of positive sciences. This he thought would be possible because social reality has its own objective existence, independent of the consciousness of the individual members who comprise it. It is worth mentioning here that, like Spencer, Durkheim also viewed society as an integrated whole made up of interconnected and interdependent parts. These parts fulfil the needs of the society. This contribution of parts towards fulfilment of the needs of the whole is called 'function'. Thus, these contributions of the parts enable the society to persist. An attempt to explain the persistence of society should therefore take into account the consequences of the parts for the society as a whole.

Social Fact

Though sociology as an idea was born in France in the nineteenth century, there was no field of sociology per se in late nineteenth-century universities. There were no schools, departments or even professors of sociology. Durkheim wanted to turn this idea into a discipline, a well-defined field of study. There were scholars commenting upon social phenomena in sociological terms in one sense or the other, but there was as yet no disciplinary 'home' for sociology. Indeed, there was strong opposition from existing disciplines to the founding of such a field. The most significant opposition came from psychology and philosophy, two fields that claimed already to cover the domain sought by sociology. The dilemma for Durkheim, given his aspirations for sociology, was how to create for it a separate and identifiable niche (Ritzer and Stepnisky, 2014).

In order to separate it from philosophy, Durkheim argued that sociology should be oriented towards empirical research. Durkheim believed that scholars like Saint-Simon, Comte and Spencer, who thought of themselves as sociologists, ended up only in philosophising. In other words, they were more interested in abstract theorising rather than in studying the social world empirically. If the field continued in the direction set by Comte and Spencer, Durkheim felt, it would become nothing more than a branch of philosophy. Durkheim criticised both for relying on preconceived ideas of social phenomena instead of actually studying the real world. Comte was held guilty of assuming theoretically that the social world was evolving in the direction of an increasingly perfect society, rather than engaging in the hard, rigorous and basic work of actually studying the changing nature of various societies. Similarly, Spencer was accused of assuming harmony in society rather than studying whether harmony actually existed (ibid.).

Durkheim sets out his own view of these tasks in his influential book *The Rules of Sociological Method*, which was published in France in 1895. The key advance he makes on Comte's approach is to emphasise that it is possible to identify a category of social phenomena, or *social facts* as he calls them, which is objectively identifiable, and which can be studied quite independently of any grand system of analysis that might be applied to them:

> Here, then, is a category of facts with very distinctive characteristics: it consists of ways of acting, thinking, and feeling, external to the individual, and endowed with a power of coercion, by reason of which they control him. ... They constitute, thus, a new variety of phenomena; and it is to them exclusively that the term 'social' ought to be applied. And this term fits them quite well, for it is clear that, since their source is not in the individual, their substratum can be no other than society.
>
> *(Durkheim,* The Rules of Sociological Method, *1895)*

Thus, in order to help sociology move away from philosophy and to give it a clear and separate identity, Durkheim proposed that the distinctive subject matter of sociology should be the study of social facts. Briefly, social facts are the social structure and cultural norms and values that are external to, and coercive of, actors. Students, for example, are constrained by such social structures as the university norms and the value that a given society places on education. Similar social facts constrain people in all areas of social life. Crucial in separating sociology from philosophy is the idea that social facts are to be treated as 'things' and studied empirically. This means that social facts must be studied by acquiring data from outside of our own minds through observation and experimentation. This empirical study of social fact as things sets Durkheimian sociology apart from more philosophical approaches.

> A social fact is every way of acting, *fixed or not*, capable of exercising on the individual an *external constraint*: or again, every way of acting which is *general* throughout a given society, while at the same time existing in its own right *independent* of its individual manifestations.
>
> (Durkheim, The Rules of Sociological Method, *1895*)

Ritzer, in his book *Sociological Theory* (2014), states that Durkheim gave two ways of defining a social fact so that sociology is distinguished from psychology. First, it is experienced as an *external* constraint rather than an internal drive; second, it is *general* throughout the society and is not attached to any particular individual.

Durkheim argued that social facts cannot be reduced to individual, but must be studied as their own reality. Durkheim referred to social facts with the Latin term *sui generis*, meaning 'unique'. Durkheim claimed that social facts have their own unique character that is not reducible to individual consciousness. To assume that social facts could be explained by reference to individuals would be to reduce sociology to psychology. Instead, he argued that social facts can be explained only by other social facts. To summarise, social facts can be empirically studied, are external to the individual, are coercive of the individual and are explained by other social facts.

Thus, the subject matter of sociology, Durkheim proposed, should be the study of social facts. In simper terms, social facts are nothing but those aspects of social life which have an independent existence of their own, over and above their individual manifestations. According to Durkheim, social facts are those ways of acting, thinking and feeling which are capable of exerting an external constraint on individual members, which are generally diffused throughout a given society and which can exist in their own life independent of their individual manifestations. Examples of such social facts are religion, law, language, any form of socio-economic and political institutions, etc.

On the basis of the discussion above, let us summarise the major characteristics of social facts:

First, social facts have distinctive *social* characteristics and determinants which are not amenable to explanation on either the biological or the psychological level.

Second, they are *external* to the individual; it means that social facts are external to and independent of the individual members of the society.

Third, social facts are diffused throughout the collectivity and are commonly shared by most of the members. In other words, they are *general* throughout a given society. They are not the exclusive property of any single individual, rather they belong to the group as a whole. They represent the socially patterned ways of thinking, feeling and acting and exclude the individual idiosyncrasies.

Fourth, they *endure* through time outlasting any set or group of individuals.

Fifth, they are, in Durkheim's own words, 'endowed with *coercive* power, by virtue of which they impose themselves upon him, independent of his individual will'. In other words, social facts constrain the individual to abide by the social norms and code of conduct. People living in groups are not free to behave according to their volition. Instead, their behaviour follows the guidance laid down by the group and the group exercises a moral pressure on the individual members, compelling them to conform to group norms. According to Durkheim, true human freedom lies in being properly regulated by the social norms.

Sixth, social facts are not static but *dynamic* in nature. For example, as society evolves over a period of time, there is also a corresponding change in its socio-economic and political institutions (this point is important and we will come back to it in our discussion on 'Anomie').

Finally, Durkheim argued that social facts can be explained only by other social facts. It implies that in order to understand social consequences, one must look for social causes.

For Durkheim, sociology is a science of such social facts. Society or *Conscience Collective* is the ultimate social fact. Further the constituent social facts of the conscience collective exist in a state of interrelationship or interdependence. Therefore, these social facts have to be studied in terms of their interrelationship and interdependence with each other. According to Durkheim, what holds the society together as an ongoing concern is the cohesiveness between these interdependent parts. This 'cohesiveness' has been termed by him 'solidarity'.

Before proceeding further, I would like to briefly mention about the distinction that Durkheim made between two broad types of social facts – material and non-material. *Material social facts,* such as social structures, morphological facts such as population size and density, forms of technology, styles of architecture, legal codes, etc. are easier to understand of the two because they are directly observable. Clearly, such things as laws are external to individuals and coercive over them. More importantly, these social facts often express a far larger and more powerful realm of *moral forces* that are at least equally external to individuals and coercive over them. These are *non-material social facts.* The bulk of Durkheim's studies, and heart of his sociology, lies in the study of non-material social facts. He argued that a sociologist usually begins a study by focusing on material social facts, which are empirically accessible, in order to understand non-material social facts, which are the real focus of his work. Some of the examples of non-material social facts are morality, collective conscience, collective representations and social currents (Ritzer and Stepnisky, 2014).

Conscience Collective

As mentioned earlier, Durkheim defined sociology as the 'science of institutions, of their genesis and of their functioning'. Durkheim also noted that institutions comprise 'all the beliefs and all the modes of conduct instituted by the collectivity'. In other words, institutions contain all the social facts that sociology studies (Adams and Sydie, 2016). If sociology is defined as the study of institutions, and institutions are constituted of social facts, then sociology is fundamentally the study of social facts. Durkheim stated that society or *conscience collective* is the ultimate social fact. To deal with his interest in common morality, Durkheim developed the idea of the conscience collective. Conscience collective, a French term, when translated into English is collective conscience. In French, the word *conscience* means both 'consciousness' and 'moral conscience'. Durkheim characterised the collective conscience in the following way:

> The totality of beliefs and sentiments common to average citizens of the same society forms a determinate system which has its own life; one may call it the collective or common conscience. ... It is, thus, an entirely different thing from particular consciences, although it can be realized only through them.
>
> *(Durkheim,* The Division of Labour in Society, *1893)*

Ritzer (2014) highlights some of the important points in this definition. First, by 'totality of people's beliefs and sentiments', Durkheim appears to think of the collective conscience as occurring throughout a given society. In other words, Durkheim is suggesting that in every society there are certain beliefs and sentiments, and certain norms and values that are commonly shared by the members of a society. Second, Durkheim clearly conceived of the collective conscience as being independent and capable of determining other social facts. That is, conscience collective is an all-inclusive phenomenon which determines other aspects of social life. It is not just a reflection of a material base as Marx sometimes suggested. Finally, although he held such views of the collective conscience, Durkheim also wrote of its being 'realised' through individual consciousness.

In simpler words, we can describe collective conscience as 'the totality of beliefs and sentiments common to the average member of the society, which forms a determinate system with a life of its own'. Thus, collective conscience refers to the general structure of shared understandings, norms and beliefs. It links successive generations to one another. Individuals come in and go out of society, however collective conscience remains. Although collective conscience can only be realised through individuals, it has a form beyond a particular person, and operates at a level higher than him. It is therefore an all-embracing and amorphous concept. As we will see later, Durkheim employed this concept to argue that 'primitive' societies had a stronger collective conscience – that is, more shared understandings, norms and beliefs – than modern societies (Figure 7.1).

Durkheim, however, in his later works preferred a much more specific concept of *collective representations* over *collective conscience*. He believed that the concept of collective conscience was a very broad and amorphous idea, and hence could not be studied directly. At best it can be approached through related material social facts. Durkheim used the concept of collective representations in order to highlight the richness and diversity of the commonly shared beliefs and sentiments, for example, commonly shared cognitive beliefs (concepts), moral beliefs, religious beliefs, etc. Collective representations also cannot be reduced to individuals because they emerge out of social interactions, but they can be studied more directly than collective conscience because they are more likely to be connected to material symbols such as flags, icons and pictures, or connected to

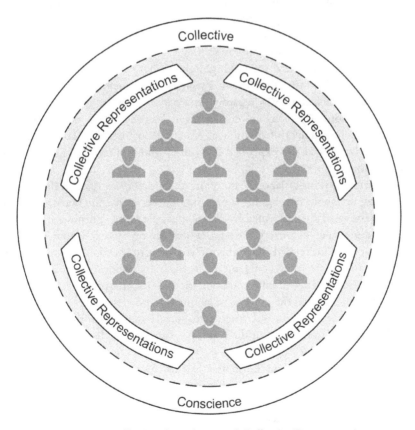

FIGURE 7.1   Collective Conscience and Collective Representations

practices such as rituals. Collective representations are socially generated and they refer to, and are, in some sense, about society. Collective representations are states of the collective conscience which are different in nature from the states of the individual conscience. Collective representations express collective sentiments and ideas which give the group its unity and unique character. Thus, they are an important factor contributing to the solidarity of a society.

Let us now look at some of the important ideas of Durkheim discussed in his major works.

The Division of Labour in Society (1893)

The Division of Labour in Society (1893) has been called sociology's first classic. It was Durkheim's first major theoretical work. It was written during the 1880s as part of his doctoral requirement and later published as a complete study in 1893 while Durkheim was at the University of Bordeaux. In this work, Durkheim traced the development of the relationship between individuals and society. Please note that since it was the first of his major works and his methodology for sociological research was still in its formative stage, it was to some extent a speculative exercise. Durkheim presented his methodological framework with clarity and precision in his second major work *The Rules of Sociological Method* (1895).

In his study on division of labour in society, Durkheim was primarily responding to the rise of industrial society highlighting both its positive and negative sides. The rise of industrial society was seen as a consequence of technological advancement which itself was regarded as a natural concomitant of increasing division of labour or specialisation. However, Durkheim was not the first to discuss the consequences of division of labour. Prior to him, classical economist Adam Smith had also explained division of labour in terms of its economic consequences.

The term 'division of labour' is used in social theory to refer to the process of dividing up labour among individuals in a group so that the main economic and domestic tasks are performed by different people for the purposes of the collective maintenance of society. The process of the division of labour therefore begins as soon as individuals form themselves into groups where, instead of living isolated or alone, they cooperate collectively by dividing their labour and by coordinating their economic and domestic activities for purposes of survival. Durkheim believed that the division of labour was therefore the result of a social process taking place within the structure of society rather than the result of the private choices of individuals or the result of organic traits that emerged during evolution (Morrison, 2012).

Classical economist Adam Smith was the first to introduce the term 'division of labour' into social thought and to discuss the role it played in the manufacturing process. However, Durkheim, in looking at the division of labour in different societies, made a distinction between what he called the 'social division of labour' and what Adam Smith had called the 'economic division of labour'. In the eighteenth century, Smith offered a purely economic interpretation of division of labour. He used the term 'economic division of labour' to describe what happens in the production process when labour is divided during manufacturing. Smith argued that when production tasks are divided between workers during the manufacturing process, it tends to increase the productivity. Smith noted that as soon as people divide their labour to perform various tasks and operations, the quantity of what they produce increases dramatically and that the process of dividing labour tends to accelerate the rate of production.

Durkheim rejected such a narrow and purely economic interpretation of division of labour. Durkheim argued that a purely economic interpretation of division of labour as given by Smith is sociologically inadequate. Since 'division of labour' is a social fact, it must be explained in terms of its overall social consequences and not simply in its economic consequences. The term 'social division of labour' was thus used by Durkheim to describe the *social links and bonds* which develop during the process that takes place in societies when many individuals enter into cooperation for purposes of carrying out joint economic and domestic tasks. Under these circumstances, Durkheim thought that the social division of labour was distinct from the economic division of labour.

> When used by Smith, the division of labour referred only to the process of dividing up labour for purposes of increasing the rate of production; whereas when used by Durkheim, it referred to the *principle of social cohesion* that develops in societies whose social links and bonds result from the way individuals relate to one another when their labour is divided along economic and domestic tasks.
>
> (Morrison, 2012)

In other words, in this study Durkheim explores the consequences of division of labour for the society as a whole. Beyond focusing explicitly on the social division of labour, Durkheim looked at the question of the overall unity of society. Generally speaking, he referred to this unity as social solidarity. He argued that what holds a society together is the cohesiveness or solidarity among its parts. Hence, in this study of social division of labour, Durkheim probes the relationship between division of labour and the manner in which solidarity comes about in a given society. Remember that his preoccupation with the idea of social order and solidarity was largely a by-product of his own background of belongings to a highly well-knit Jewish community and a very turbulent period in French history. This predisposed him towards a search for the basis of moral order in society.

Before proceeding further, let me just mention three important concerns which Durkheim was trying to address in his study of division of labour.

First, Durkheim wanted to study the social dimension of division of labour. He made a clear distinction between the economic and social consequences of division of labour.

Second, since Durkheim and many other before him had explained the rise of industrial society in terms of increase in division of labour, he wanted to study that how division of labour affects social solidarity. In other words, how the change in the division of labour affects the structure of the society and, consequently, the nature of social solidarity.

Third, in the post-Enlightenment period, when individualism was on rise, how does individual, while becoming more autonomous, also becomes more solidary. As Durkheim puts it:

> This work had its origins in the question of the relations of the individual to social solidarity. Why does the individual, while becoming more autonomous, depend more upon society? How can he be at once more individual and more solidary? Certainly, these two movements, contradictory as they appear, develop in parallel fashion. This is the problem we are raising. It appeared to us that what resolves this apparent antinomy is a transformation of social solidarity due to the steadily growing development of the division of labour. That is how we have been led to make this the object of our study.
>
> (Durkheim, The Division of Labour in Society, 1893)

Durkheim believed that the change in the division of labour has enormous implications for the structure of society. Durkheim was most interested in the changed way in which social solidarity is produced, in other words, the changed way in which society is held together and how its members see themselves as part of a whole. To capture this difference, Durkheim referred to two types of solidarity – mechanical and organic. Mechanical solidarity, according to Durkheim, is the characteristic feature of primitive societies where division of labour is minimal and individuality is zero. In simpler societies, people do basically the same thing, such as farming, and they share common experiences and consequently have common values. A society characterised by mechanical society is unified because all people are generalists. The bond among people is that they are all engaged in similar activities and have similar responsibilities. Individuals have little or no autonomy within the group. However, in this form of society, the division of labour is not in fact able on its own to provide enough in the way of social solidarity. The remainder comes from what Durkheim calls the *collective conscience*, 'the totality of beliefs and sentiments common to average citizens of the same society', which binds individuals together not so much in terms of their daily activity but in terms of the religious and cultural beliefs, the social and political ideology, they share. Such societies are characterised by collectivism.

It is important to note here that Durkheim takes both material and non-material aspects into account – shared ideas are as important as equality in material living conditions in primitive societies. A comprehensive, strong conscience collective is an essential characteristic of any primitive society. The conscience collective is basically religious in primitive societies. By religious, Durkheim means possessing a strong sense of right and wrong, of what is sacred, and this is manifest in the form of all the various rules, rituals and ceremonies that must be observed to show respect for the sacred. As a result of equality in material living conditions and customs, the intimacy of social life and the continuous reciprocal 'surveillance' of behaviour and the intense conscience collective which demands respect for rules and all that is held sacred, there will be a strong reaction to any form of deviancy in primitive societies. Deviancy is often regarded as a religious offence.

On the other hand, there is a comprehensive division of labour in modern societies. Individuals engage in different, often highly specialised occupations. When different people are assigned various specialised tasks, they no longer share common experiences. This diversity undermines the shared moral beliefs that are necessary for a society. Given the increasing diversity and differences in various occupations and professions, many theorists in Durkheim's day thought that high levels of conflict were inevitable in modern societies. Solidarity or a sense of collectivity would be weakened as a result of the numerous conflicts of interest resulting from all the differences. Durkheim, on the other hand, believed that as the division of labour increases and each individual becomes more specialised, each individual must rely more on others. It is important to note here that this specialisation includes not only that of individuals but also of groups, structures and institutions. The division of labour itself thus produces social solidarity. The function of division of labour in modern society is therefore social cohesion and harmony. Durkheim calls such solidarity resulting from high division of labour as organic solidarity (Adams and Sydie, 2016).

> The most remarkable effect of the division of labour is not that it increases the output of functions divided, but that it renders them solidary. Its role in all these cases is not simply to embellish or ameliorate existing societies, but to render societies possible which, without it, would not exist.
>
> *(Durkheim,* The Division of Labour in Society, *1893)*

Thus, in simpler words, it may be said that while mechanical solidarity arose from similarities or likeness of individuals in primitive society, organic solidarity, develops out of differences between individuals in modern societies. A society having organic solidarity is characterised by the weakening of collective conscience and restitutive law. Organic solidarity, according to Durkheim, is the product of increasing division of labour.

Anthony Giddens points out that the collective conscience in the two types of society can be differentiated on four dimensions – volume, intensity, rigidity and content (Table 7.1). Volume refers to the number of people enveloped by the collective conscience; intensity, to how deeply the individuals feel about it; rigidity, to how clearly it is defined; and content, to the form that the collective conscience takes in the two types of society (Ritzer and Stepnisky, 2014).

TABLE 7.1 The Four Dimensions of the Conscience Collective

Solidarity	Volume	Intensity	Rigidity	Content
Mechanical	Entire society	High	High	Religious
Organic	Particular groups	Low	Low	Moral individualism

Source: Ritzer, George and Jeffrey Stepnisky. *Sociological Theory.* 9th Edition. New York: McGraw-Hill Education, 2014.

For Durkheim, the division of labour was a material fact because it is a pattern of interactions in the social world. As mentioned earlier, Durkheim had stated that social facts must be explained by other social facts. Durkheim believed that a society's transition from mechanical to organic solidarity is a consequence of population growth. Increase in population, according to Durkheim, led to two consequences: increased physical density (i.e. the number of people per acre, or mile or the like) and increased moral or social density (i.e. the rate of social interactions among people in society). As per Durkheim, an increase in both physical and social density necessitates an increase in the division of labour in society. More people means an increase in the competition for scarce resources, and more interaction means a more intense struggle for survival among the basically similar components of society. Durkheim however argued that problems associated with increase in physical and social density usually are resolved through differentiation and, ultimately, the emergence of new forms of social organisation. The rise of the division of labour allows people to complement, rather than conflict with, one another. With the increase in the division of labour and corresponding specialisation, economic efficiency increases resulting in the increase of resources: thus, making the competition over resources more peaceful. Durkheim argues that in societies with high division of labour, greater differentiation allows people to cooperate more and to all be supported by the same resource base. Therefore, difference allows for even closer bonds between people than does similarity because it fosters greater interdependence. Thus, in a society characterised by organic solidarity, there are both more solidarity and more individuality than there are in a society characterised by mechanical solidarity. Individuality, then, is not the opposite of close social bonds but a requirement for them (Ritzer and Stepnisky, 2014).

For Durkheim, both division of labour and dynamic density are material social facts (Figure 7.2). However, as stated earlier, Durkheim's primary interest was in the study of non-material social facts. Since non-material social facts such as conscience collective or social solidarity could not be studied directly, sociologists should examine those material social facts that reflect the nature of, and changes in, non-material social facts. For example, in his work *The Division of Labour in Society*, Durkheim chose to study the difference between law in societies with mechanical solidarity and law in societies with organic solidarity.

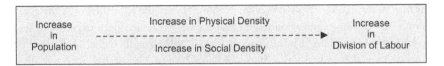

FIGURE 7.2   Division of Labour

Durkheim extensively analysed the institution of law in relation to the two types of societies because he believed that the nature of law in a society was the most 'visible symbol' of that society's type of social solidarity (Abrahamson, 2010). According to Durkheim, legal sanctions that enforced moral codes provided evidence of the nature of social solidarity. Legal sanctions represent society's reaction to the 'outrage to morality' resulting from a criminal act. Durkheim further goes on to say that a criminal act does not shock 'the common consciousness because it is criminal', but 'it is criminal because it offends that consciousness' (Adams and Sydie, 2016).

Durkheim argued that a society with mechanical solidarity is characterised by *repressive law*. This is because such society is based on likeness or similarities among people and as a result they tend to believe very strongly in a common morality. Any offence against their shared value system is taken very seriously, for example, theft might lead to the cutting off of the offender's hands, blaspheming might result in the removal of one's tongue, etc. Even minor offences against the moral system are likely to be met with severe punishment. Inflicting pain and suffering on the criminal serves to reaffirm the common consciousness and restore social solidarity. In contrast, a society with organic solidarity is characterised by *restitutive law*, where offenders must make restitution for their crimes. In such societies, offences are more likely to be seen as committed against a particular individual or segment of society than against the moral system itself. Because there is a weak common morality, most people do not react emotionally to a breach of the law. Instead of being severely punished for every offence against the collective morality, offenders in an organic society are likely to be asked to make restitution to those who have been harmed by their actions. Restitutive sanctions do not necessarily produce suffering for the criminal but consist in 'restoring the previous state of affairs'. Although some repressive law continues to exist in a society with organic solidarity (for example, the death penalty), restitutive law predominates, especially for minor offences (Ritzer and Stepnisky, 2014).

However, if Durkheim's theory of division of labour was correct, modern society would normally have evolved relatively free of conflict. But Durkheim himself was aware of that antagonism and powerful conflicts were commonplace in the nineteenth century. He put this down to the fact that development had not occurred along 'normal' lines and attempted to explain this anomaly. He thought this was partly due to the persistence into modern society some old disparities of power and wealth – from feudalism, for instance – which were incompatible with the new order. He also argued that very rapid changes and adjustments in any given period do not allow the various elements of society time to adjust to one another.

In order to explain this anomaly between 'what ought to be' and 'what is', Durkheim makes a distinction between '*normal*' and '*pathological*' forms of division of labour. He called the above description as normal division of labour. On the other hand, he explained the prevailing chaos and conflict of nineteenth century *laissez-faire* society, its wholly unregulated markets, extreme inequalities, etc. as the manifestations of the pathological or abnormal division of labour. He identified three abnormal forms, viz. anomic division of labour, forced division of labour and poorly coordinated division of labour.

Anomie, in literal sense, implies 'normlessness'. Durkheim used the concept of *anomie* to refer to the 'breakdown of the normative regulation' in a given society. 'Overspecialisation' of the institutions resulting from an increase in division of labour and insufficient regulation, according to Durkheim, was mainly responsible for the anomic situation in which various parts or organs of society were not properly integrated to each other. In sum, anomie involves a lack of integration among the components of a social system. However, Durkheim believed it was probably a temporary condition, due largely to the transition from mechanical to organic solidarity not being complete. Some institutions had changed or evolved more than others and there had not been enough time for each of the institutions to adjust with each other. For example, the economic institution had attained increased importance and evolved to an extent that the institution of family was no longer able to regulate its activities, and no other alternative means had yet emerged. Though Durkheim expected that over time the institutions would readjust to each other, but in the interim, there was anomie. Durkheim stated:

> If the division of labour does not produce solidarity it is because the rela- tion- ships between the organs are not regulated; it is because they are in a state of *anomie*. … We may say … that a state of *anomie* is impossible wher- ever organs linked to one another are in sufficient contact.
>
> (Abrahamson, 2010)

Durkheim argued that modern society is always prone to anomie, but it comes to the fore in times of social and economic crises. During the transitional phase of a society and in the absence of a strong common morality of mechanical solidarity, people might not have a clear concept of what is and what is not proper and acceptable behaviour. Even though the division of labour is a source of cohesion in modern society, it cannot entirely make up for the weakening of the common morality. Durkheim acknowledged the possibility of individuals becoming isolated and cut adrift in their highly specialised activities. They can more easily cease to feel a common bond with those who work and live around them. This, according to Durkheim, gives rise to anomie. It is important to note that, in principle, anomie could occur in a society characterised by either mechanical or organic solidarity. However, it is the specialised parts that especially require greater coordination. Organic solidarity is more prone to this particular pathology, but it is important to remember that Durkheim saw this as an abnormal situation. Durkheim believed that the modern division of labour has the capacity to promote increased moral interactions rather than reducing people to isolated and meaningless tasks and positions (Ritzer and Stepnisky, 2014).

Though Durkheim believed that people needed rules and regulation to tell them what to do, his second abnormal form of division of labour pointed to a kind of rule that could lead to conflict and isolation and therefore increase anomie. He called this the *forced division of labour*. By forced division of labour, Durkheim implied that outdated and traditional norms may force individuals, groups and classes into positions for which they are ill suited. In other words, traditional customs, economic power or status can determine who performs what jobs regardless of talent and qualification. The best example to understand this is the traditional caste system where allocation of social position and occupation was largely based on birth rather than merit. It is here that Durkheim comes closest to a Marxist position. Durkheim stated:

> If one class in society is obliged, in order to live, to take any price for its services, while another class can pass over this situation, because of the resources already at its disposal, resources that, however, are not necessarily the result of some social superiority, the latter group has an unjust advantage over the former with respect to the law.
>
> *(Ritzer and Stepnisky, 2014)*

However, Durkheim did not elaborate in detail on the fundamental causes of the extreme economic inequalities prevailing in the modern industrial societies of Europe in those times, as Marx did in terms of the ownership and non-ownership of the forces of production. Moreover, Durkheim saw this only as an aberration of the industrial society, occurring only in an abnormal situation. Under the heading of the forced division of labour, Durkheim discusses those socially structured inequalities which undermine solidarity. Durkheim argues that such socially structured inequalities restrict the opportunities of the lower classes and prevent the realisation of their abilities. As a result, resentment accumulates and men are led to revolutionary thoughts. The problem here is not lack of rules but rather the excess of them in that rules themselves are the cause of evil. The rules have in fact arisen in order to enforce the division of labour coercively. Individual specialism and occupations are not freely chosen but forced upon each person by custom, law and even sheer chance. Individuals find themselves estranged, resentful and aspiring to social positions which have been arbitrarily closed off to them.

The forced division of labour then brings about a situation which one modern author (Royce, 2015) has called the *anomie of injustice*. It is this which has produced class conflict and not, as Marx would have it, the inherently exploitative nature of capitalism. Nor did Durkheim consider that all inequality could be abolished. But whereas some inequalities are 'natural' and occur spontaneously, others are external inequality and can be mitigated. What in effect he is urging is the creation of what today is called 'equality of opportunity' or a meritocracy. For this to be possible, all forms of hereditary privilege should be abolished. 'There cannot be rich and poor at birth', he wrote, 'without there being unjust contracts.' (Lee, 2000)

The third form of abnormal division of labour, according to Durkheim, is the one where the specialised functions performed by different people are *poorly coordinated*. Durkheim stated that organic solidarity flows from the interdependence of the people, but if people's specialisations do not result in increased interdependence but simply in isolation, the division of labour will not result in social solidarity. Durkheim argued that for the division of labour to function as a moral and socially solidifying force in modern society, anomie, the forced division of labour and the improper coordination of specialisation must be addressed. Durkheim suggested a few broad guidelines to address the problems arising out of the abnormal or pathological division of labour. Remember that this was partly a speculative exercise since his conclusions were not based on any empirical research.

Durkheim argued that the conscience collective and religion would become less and less significant in a functionally differentiated society, due to the differences between people. With increasing differentiation in working and social life, as well as the weakening of the conscience collective as a binding force, modern society would be characterised by individualism. When individualism gains too much strength, it has the effect of destroying solidarity. To avoid total disruption, individualism must be counteracted through the development of new institutional bonds between people. Durkheim also modified the notion of individualism in his later writings. He reached the perception that individualism was not necessarily the same as egoism and the radical destruction of social bonds. It became clear to him that modern societies could not be based on strictly collectivist ethos. The problems associated with the division of functions and specialisation in modern societies could be solved only by assuming values and relations that took a high level of individualism for granted. He thought a more positive and more valuable type of individualism, one distinct from egoism, was in the process of emerging. This, he termed, *moral individualism*.

Durkheim believed that the autonomy of the individual is fundamental, but this autonomy also involves the capacity for moral reflection and moral obligations. Given the correct form of socialisation and the development of social relations, *modern* individualists would be able to strike a balance between individual independence and social bonding. In other words, rather than driving a wedge between individuals and society, the advanced division of labour gives rise to new kinds of individuals and endorses the strong notion of individuality. Modern society, just like modern industry, needs 'modern' individuals, just as individuals who want to behave in modern ways and to express modern attitudes and beliefs need an advanced division of labour where they can be expressed. The division of labour serves to reconcile the individual with society. In several works after 1893, he suggested certain measures to address abnormal division of labour. For instance, he advocated establishing new types of organisation in the economic sector – so-called corporations, which had certain similarities with the medieval guild system. The point was that those involved in a certain kind of occupation, employers and employees alike, should unite in a national organisation. He thought this would lead to the development of solidarity between actors, and thus counteract the tendencies towards ruthless competition and individualism. He cites the example of professional organisations, such as lawyers' organisations, which create professional ethics governing their work. According to him, this would go a long way in controlling the anomic state of professional, industrial and commercial life. He also thought school reforms, in the shape of new syllabuses and modes of cooperation, might restrain individualism. If children were educated in the spirit of solidarity at school, they would develop social habits that would also be important in adulthood. He also suggested restrictions on the right to divorce.

Many commentators have pointed to a tendency in the development of Durkheim's theories: early in his career, he expressed a strong belief in society's ability to develop solidarity and unity spontaneously. Later, he came to accentuate more and more the need for active political and moral regulation of social life, especially in the economic sphere. Eventually, he concluded that the basic principles of the modern market economy largely nurtured competition and egoism, and that the economy therefore had to be actively regulated in order to ensure widespread solidarity. We could not just wait for solidarity to evolve 'naturally'.

Let us now assess Durkheim's study of division of labour in terms of both its contribution to social theory and the criticisms it invited.

The key theme in Durkheim's sociological theory, the major theoretical issue he is concerned with throughout his work, is that of *the relationship of the individual to society.* In this book-length investigation, Durkheim analyses the individual versus society issue in terms of the different kinds of social solidarity that hold society and individuals together. One of the advantages of linking the individual versus society debate explicitly with the question of social solidarity is that it allows Durkheim to argue that developments in the demands of individuals and of modern notions of individuality are actually complimented by changes in the nature of society rather than being in opposition to them. Durkheim sees the emergence of modern individuals, and of modern notions of individuality, as an inevitable corollary of the advanced division of labour in society.

Durkheim's study of division of labour, though to an extent speculative, proved to be a landmark study as it was for the first time that the social significance of division of labour was explored in such a comprehensive manner. As stated earlier, prior to him division of labour was studied only in terms of its economic consequences. Durkheim was one of the first sociologists to explore the social dimension of division of labour. In this study, he explained that how with increase in the division of labour new forms of solidarity emerge in society to provide for its cohesiveness and stability. This finding opened new vistas of research in social sciences. It initiated a number of studies which attempted to explore that how and to what extent the experience at work can also have social implications. So much so that it gave rise to an altogether new branch of knowledge called *Sociology of Occupations and Professions*.

For example, Elton Mayo, a professor at the Harvard Business School, in his investigation (1927–1932) at the Hawthorne plant of the Western Electric Company in Chicago, found out that the 'sense of belongingness' to a social group is as important for a worker as the economic rewards. Mayo began with the assumptions of scientific management believing that the physical conditions of the work environment, the aptitude of the worker and financial incentives were the main determinants of productivity. The theory of scientific management was first spelt out in detail by Frederick W. Taylor whose book, *The Principles of Scientific Management* was published in America in 1911. Taylor assumed that man's primary motivation for work was financial. He argued that by increasing the monetary incentives paid to the worker, the productivity too can be maximised. In practice, this usually involved a wage incentive scheme based on piecework – payment according to the amount of work done. Taylor believed that the scientific planning of work tasks, the selection and systematic training of suitable workers for the performance of those tasks plus a carrot and stick system of financial incentives would maximise productivity. On the contrary, Mayo in his study found that the behaviour of the worker was largely a response to group norms rather than simply being directed by economic incentives. Most of the workers belonged to one or the other informal group. The researchers discovered that the workers had established a norm which defined a fair day's work, and that this norm, rather than standards set by management, determined their output. From the Hawthorne studies, and research which they largely stimulated, developed the human relations school. It stated that scientific management provided too narrow a view of man and that financial incentives alone were insufficient to motivate workers and ensure their cooperation.

However, though a remarkable study, Durkheim's study of division of labour also came under criticism on several accounts.

First, the concept of *conscience collective* as a common and determinate system of shared beliefs and sentiments was criticised on various accounts by other scholars. For Durkheim, the reality of society preceded the individual life. Durkheim frequently, especially in discussions on the collective conscience, reached a degree of sociological realism that seemed to deny altogether the social significance of individual volition or decision. Society is real, to be true, but so is the individual. And the two, it should be remembered, are always in interaction. Giving priority to one over the other is misleading in the long run.

Further, conflict theorists also argued, on Marxian lines, that modern industrial society is characterised by class divisions and extreme economic inequalities. Given the pluralistic character of modern society, it is difficult to conceive of an all-encompassing and shared value system which is based on consensus of all its members. Rather they argue that such collective conscience is nothing but a reflection of the values of the dominant classes in society. The values of the dominant classes are imposed on masses either by indoctrination through education and religion, or by coercion. In other words, it implies that the ideas and aspirations of the subaltern groups may find no representation in such body of belief systems.

Second, anti-positivist scholars also question the concepts of collective conscience and social facts. They argue that human behaviour is a meaningful behaviour, guided by meanings, motives and values. By defining collective conscience in terms of an all-embracing and determinate system and according primacy to groups over the individual has somehow subordinated the individual conscience to that of collectivity. Further, by focusing on the exteriority dimension and empirical study of the social facts, Durkheim leaves no room for the interpretative understanding of human behaviour.

Third, conflict theorists also question the suggestion offered by Durkheim, of state intervention in regulating the economy in order to address the problem of abnormal division of labour. Durkheim believed that the state, being an executive organ of the conscience collective, would work for the welfare of all sections of the society. However, conflict theorists argue that state is nothing but an executive organ of only the dominant classes and would only further their interests.

Fourth, conflict theorists also criticise Durkheim's theory for its conservative outlook. They argue that there is a built-in conservative bias in Durkheim's theory. By repeatedly emphasising on the normative regulation and collective morality, Durkheim's focus was primarily on explaining maintenance and sustenance of the stability and social order in society. Conflict theorists argue that Durkheim failed to account for conflict and conflict led change as Marx did.

Fifth, some scholars also argue that the solutions offered by Durkheim to address the problems of abnormal division of labour are overly simplified. For example, Durkheim explained the anomic division of labour in terms of the breakdown of the normative regulation in the society. As if by restoring the normative regulation alone, all problems associated with the increase in division of labour could be addressed. These scholars argue that there are certain inherent problems associated with the increase in division of labour such as de-skilling, fragmentation of work, alienation, etc. which Durkheim did not elaborate.

Further, there are also some problems with the Durkheim's view of the individual. Despite having made a number of crucial assumptions about human nature, Durkheim denied that he had done so. He argued that he did not begin by postulating a certain conception of human nature in order to deduce sociology from it. Instead, he said that it was from sociology that he sought an increasing understanding of human nature. However, Durkheim may have been less than honest with his readers, and perhaps even with himself.

One of Durkheim's assumptions about human nature is that people are impelled by their passions into a mad search for gratification that always leads to a need for more. If these passions are unrestrained, they multiply to the point where the individual is enslaved by them and they become a threat to the individual as well as to society. It can be argued that Durkheim's entire theoretical edifice, especially his emphasis on collective morality, was erected on this basic assumption about people's passions. However, Durkheim provides no evidence for this assumption, and indeed, his own theories would suggest that such an insatiable subject may be a creation of social structures rather than the other way around.

The Rules of Sociological Method (1895)

The Rules of Sociological Method was Durkheim's second major work. It was published in 1895, while he was at the University of Bordeaux. Largely a methodological study, the primary aim of this study was to outline the nature of sociological subject matter and to set out the steps of sociological investigation. As discussed earlier, Durkheim described 'social facts' in term of their exteriority, generality and constraint. He further argued that social facts are amenable to be studied by methods of positive sciences. Some of the important suggestions of Durkheim with regard to the scientific procedure to be adopted while studying social facts have been listed below:

Rules for the Observation of Social Facts

Durkheim said that social facts must be treated as '*things*'. As 'things' they have to be studied by the empirical method and not by intuition. While studying social facts as 'things', all preconceptions must be eradicated. Sociologists must emancipate themselves from the common place ideas that dominate the mind of the layperson and adopt an emotionally neutral attitude towards what they set out to investigate. Observation of social facts should be confined to their external attributes only which can be tested and verified.

In other words, when sociologists undertake the investigation of some order of social facts, they must consider them from an aspect that is independent of their individual manifestations. The objectivity of social facts depends on their being separated from individual facts, which express them. Social facts provide a common standard for members of the society. Social facts exist in the form of legal rules, moral regulations, proverbs, social conventions, etc. It is these that sociologists must study to gain an understanding of social life. The observation and study of social facts should be as definite as possible. Here, Durkheim insisted upon the clear definition of the range or area of observation. This would ensure that knowledge about social facts can be progressively ever more exact.

Rules for Distinguishing between the Normal and the Pathological Social Facts

Having stated rules for the observation of social facts, Durkheim makes a distinction between 'normal' and 'pathological' social facts. Durkheim argues that a social fact, which is 'general' to a given type of society, is 'normal' when it has utility for that societal type. In other words, this means that a normal social fact shall also be functional in the society in which it exists, while an abnormal or a pathological social fact shall have harmful consequences for the society. For example, let's take the example of crime. In general, we consider crime as pathological. However, Durkheim argues that from a scientific viewpoint it would be incorrect to call it pathological or abnormal.

First, because crime is a universal phenomenon occurring in almost every society in different degrees. What we call crime is actually a form of deviance from the established norms and expectations of a particular social group. According to Durkheim, deviance is relative in nature. This means that there is no absolute way of defining a deviant act. Deviance can only be defined in relation to a particular standard and no standards are fixed or absolute. As such deviance varies from time to time and place to place. In a particular society, an act which is considered deviant today may be defined as normal in the future. An act defined as deviant in one society may be seen as perfectly normal in another. For example, homosexuality was formerly considered a crime in various societies. But, in contemporary times, homosexual acts conducted between consenting adults in private are no longer illegal.

Durkheim further argued that acts of deviance could either be positively sanctioned (rewarded), negatively sanctioned (punished) or simply accepted without reward or punishment. In terms of the above definition of deviance, a soldier who risks his life above and beyond the normal call of duty in a battlefield may be termed deviant. Similarly, a scientist who breaks the rules of his discipline and through experimentation either discovers something new or invents something unique may also be termed as deviant. Their deviance is positively sanctioned: the soldier might be rewarded with a medal, the physicist with a Nobel Prize. Durkheim argued that if there were not occasional deviances or flouting of norms, there would be no change in human behaviour and, equally important, no opportunities through which a society can either reaffirm the existing norms or else reassess such behaviour and modify the norm itself.

To show that crime is useful to the normal evolution of morality and law, Durkheim cites the case of Socrates, who according to Athenian law was a criminal, his crime being the independence of his thought. But his crime rendered a service to his country because it served to prepare a new morality and faith, which the Athenians needed. It also rendered a service to humanity in the sense that freedom of thought enjoyed by people in many countries today was made possible by people like him. Thus, for Durkheim, crime is not only inevitable, it can also be functional. Durkheim argues that it only becomes dysfunctional when 'its rate is unusually high'. He believed that all social change begins with some form of deviance. Durkheim regarded some crime as 'an anticipation of the morality of the future' (Haralambos and Heald, 2006).

Rules for the Classification of Social Types

The founding fathers of sociology like Auguste Comte, Herbert Spencer and Emile Durkheim laid great emphasis on the use of 'comparative method' in sociological enquiry. They believed in the possibility of a natural science of society that would establish regularities of coexistence and succession among the forms of social life by means of systematic comparisons. The central place assigned to comparison was signalled by Durkheim when he wrote: 'Comparative sociology is not a special branch of sociology; it is sociology itself'. On the basis of systematic comparisons, Durkheim classified social phenomena into various types. For example, in his study of division of labour, Durkheim classified societies on the basis of mechanical and organic solidarity. Similarly, he used classificatory typologies in his studies of suicide and religion.

Durkheim also developed classification typology of social phenomena in terms of normal and pathological. For example, in his study of division of labour, he explained the prevailing chaos and conflict of nineteenth-century *laissez-faire* society, its wholly unregulated markets, extreme inequalities, etc. as the manifestations of the pathological or abnormal division of labour. He identified three abnormal forms, viz. anomic division of labour, forced division of labour and poorly coordinated division of labour. Durkheim argued that a social fact is normal or abnormal only in relation to a given social type. Thus, Durkheim attempts to outline a system for classifying societies according to their structure and complexity, a process Durkheim referred to as 'social morphology'.

Rules for the Explanation of Social Facts

For Durkheim, society is a *reality sui generis*. In other words, society has an objective existence. It is independent of the consciousness of the individual members who comprise it. Hence, a social phenomenon must be explained in terms of social causes and social consequences only. Thus, there are two approaches, which may be used in the explanation of social facts – the causal and the functional. The causal explanation of social fact is concerned with explaining 'why' the social phenomenon in question exists. The functional explanation, on the other hand, involves explaining the functions that the given social phenomenon performs for the existence and stability of the society as a whole. In other words, functional explanation involves explaining the social phenomenon in terms of the needs it fulfils of the given social type.

Durkheim further argues that since the subject matter of sociology has a social character – it is collective in nature – the explanation should also have a social character. Durkheim draws a sharp line between a psychological explanation and a sociological one. Since society has its own independent existence over and above individuals who comprise it, a sociological explanation thus must be social in character. Any attempt to explain social facts in terms of individual characteristics would make the explanation sociologically inadequate and false. Therefore, in the case of causal explanation 'the determining cause of a social fact should be sought among the social facts preceding it and not among the states of the individual consciousness'. Similarly, in the case of functional explanation, 'the function of a social fact always ought to be sought in its relation to some social end'.

Another very important point about Durkheim's logic of explanation is his stress upon the comparative nature of social science. To show that a given fact is the cause of another, 'we have to compare cases in which they are simultaneously present or absent, to see if the variations they present in these different combinations of circumstances indicate that one depends on the other'. According to Durkheim, experimentation is the crucial method for testing theories in science. However, experimentation is not possible in sociology. Therefore, the comparative method is the closest alternative to experimentation, for testing sociological explanations. Since sociologists normally do not conduct laboratory-controlled experiments but study reported facts or go to the field and observe social facts, which have been spontaneously produced, they use the method of indirect experiment or the comparative method. The comparative method is the very framework of the science of society for Durkheim. According to Durkheim, 'comparative sociology is not a particular branch of sociology; it is sociology itself, in-so-far as it ceases to be purely descriptive and aspires to account for fact'.

As can be seen from the above discussion, Durkheim, in order to establish sociology as a distinct scientific discipline, takes an extreme stance. This is reflected in his advocacy of positive science methodology to study social facts, and the definition of social facts in itself reflects his extreme sociological realism position. However, the positivists' emphasis on explaining a social phenomenon exclusively on the basis of its outwardly observable characteristics ignores the human side of social behaviour. This view fails to take into account the subjective dimension of human behaviour manifested in the unique meanings, choices and motives of an individual.

Suicide (1897)

Suicide was Durkheim's third book which was published in 1897. It is also regarded by many as the first empirical study in sociology. In this landmark study, Durkheim brings together conceptual theory and empirical research, and used considerable statistical ingenuity considered remarkable for his times. In general, there are several reasons why Durkheim took up the theme of suicide when he did. First, in nineteenth-century Europe, suicide was emerging as a major social problem and many felt that it was associated with the development of industrial society. Industrialisation had advanced individualism, accelerated social fragmentation and weakened the social bonds tying individuals to society. Second, growing dominance of economic institutions over other social institutions in industrial society which placed individual self-interest and economic gain over and above collective interest of society. Third, Dreyfus affair in 1894 also played a key role in highlighting the fragility of French national unity and drew attention to how much social fragmentation and egoistic forces had replaced the collective authority of society.

Further, factual evidence made available by comparative mortality data from different societies linked suicide to social factors such as industrial change, occupation, family life and religion, and this served to focus attention on society and social institutions rather than on complex psychological factors. Durkheim classified the statistical data contained in the records of suicidal deaths for the period according to age, religion, sex, occupation, military service and marital status, and this led directly to a search for the role played by social factors in the cause of suicide. Overall, Durkheim studied the records of 26,000 suicides, and his colleague, Marcel Mauss, aided in compiling the statistical tables on suicidal deaths relating to age and marital status. Durkheim defined suicide as 'all such cases of death resulting directly or indirectly from a positive or negative act, carried out by the victim himself, knowing that it will produce this result' (Morrison, 2012).

One of the primary aims Durkheim had in pursuing a social theory of suicide was to look for the social causes of suicide within the existing framework of society rather than looking at the psychological states of individuals who take their own lives. Examining what was popularly assumed to be the most individual and private act, and therefore more amenable to psychological than sociological explanation, was an audacious move on Durkheim's part. His emphasis on statistical analysis was primarily for two reasons. First, to refute theories based on biological, psychological, genetics, climatic and geographical factors. And second, to support with empirical evidence his own sociological explanation of suicide. At the time Durkheim began his study, suicide was largely treated as a nervous disorder and its causes were believed to derive from the psychological states of individuals. Many believed that suicide was the result of mental illness, depression, sudden tragedy, reversal of fortune and even personal setbacks and bankruptcy. In this light, suicide was seen by many as the result of a weak disposition and a psychological response to the burdens of life. Durkheim, however, pointed out that looking at suicide as an individual phenomenon must involve a psychological explanation, but that *suicide rates* were also a collective phenomenon. And hence, they must be explained sociologically (Adams and Sydie, 2016).

Durkheim displayed an extreme form of sociological realism in his study of suicide. He speaks of *suicidal currents* as collective tendencies that dominate some very susceptible individuals and catch them up in their sweep. The act of suicide at times, Durkheim believed, is interpreted as a product of these currents. Durkheim thus rejected the various extra-social factors such as heredity, racial characteristics, psychological and climatic factors as the cause of suicide. Durkheim also examined and rejected the imitation theory associated with one of his contemporaries, the French social psychologist Gabriel Tarde. According to the theory of imitation, people commit suicide (and engage in a wide range of other actions) because they tend to imitate the actions of others in society. However, upon examination of the data, Durkheim didn't find a significant correlation between imitation and suicide rate. Though Durkheim admitted that some individual suicides may be the result of imitation, it is such a minor factor that it has no significant effect on the overall suicide rate (Ritzer and Stepnisky, 2014).

Instead, Durkheim argued that suicide is a social fact and hence it must be explained in terms of social causes. For Durkheim, the critical factors in differences in suicide rates were to be found in differences at the level of social facts. Different groups have different collective sentiments, which produce different social currents. It is these social currents that affect individual decisions about suicide. In other words, changes in the collective sentiments lead to changes in social currents, which, in turn, lead to changes in suicide rates. Durkheim's central thesis is that suicide rate is a factual order, unified and definite, for each society has a collective inclination towards suicide, a rate of self-homicide which is fairly constant for each society so long as the basic conditions of its existence remain the same. The social character of suicide rates is demonstrated, Durkheim pointed out, by their variation in relation to the degree of solidarity in society (Abraham and Morgan, 2010).

No complete understanding of Durkheim's assertion that suicide had social causes is possible without looking at the concept of the '*social suicide rate*'. Durkheim arrived at the concept of the social suicide rate after a careful examination of the mortality data which had been obtained from public records of societies such as France, Germany, England, Denmark and Austria. These records contained information about cause of death, age, marital background, religion and the total number of deaths by suicide of the country from which they were gathered. As mentioned earlier, Durkheim was not interested in explaining the causes of individual cases of suicide, rather he looked at suicide as a social fact and intended to explain it in terms of social causes. In other words, Durkheim was interested in a sociological explanation of suicide, not a psychological one. The 'social suicide rate', therefore, was a term used by Durkheim to refer to the number of suicidal deaths in a given society and the extent to which the 'suicide rates' themselves could be looked upon as establishing a pattern of suicide for a given society. Thus, rather than looking at individual motives or psychological states, he began by looking at the 'social suicide rate' that existed in different countries.

After studying the rates, Durkheim made several key observations. First, he noticed that the rates varied from society to society. For example, they were higher in Germany in comparison to Italy, lower in Denmark in comparison to England and so on. Second, he observed that between 1841 and 1872, the number of suicidal deaths in each of the countries did not change dramatically and were considered to be stable. For example, between 1841 and 1842, the number of suicidal deaths in France were 2,814 and 2,866, respectively; whereas in Germany for the same years they were 1,630 and 1,598. As far as Durkheim was concerned, the stability of the rates within a given society was crucial since it meant that each society not only produced a 'quota of suicidal deaths' but that certain social forces were operating to produce what Durkheim saw as the 'yearly precision of rates' (Morrison, 2012).

The stability of suicide rates turned out to be decisive because when considered collectively, the rates pointed in the direction of underlying social causes. This led Durkheim to reason that the predisposing cause of suicide lay not within the psychological motives of the individual but within the social framework of society. Durkheim concluded that the observed stability of the rates meant that each society was a distinct social environment with different social characteristics, different religions, different patterns of family life, different military obligations and thus different suicide characteristics. Under these circumstances, each produced rate of suicidal deaths distinct from the other. Durkheim also noticed that when compared to the mortality rate, the suicide rate demonstrated a far greater consistency than did the general mortality rate, which fluctuated randomly.

Based on his observation of statistical data, Durkheim thus established the stability of the suicide rates. To support his conclusions, Durkheim argued that the stability of the rates showed that, while individual motives for suicide vary from case to case, the regularity exhibited by the social suicide rate was consistently stable. Further, though the suicide rates varied between societies, the stability of the rates within a particular society meant that each society produces a 'quota of suicidal deaths'. Thus, Durkheim took the position that the social suicide rate must represent a 'factual order' that is separate from individual disposition and, therefore, he thought it had a regularity which could be studied in its own right. In that the 'social suicide rate' is independent of individual suicide and has a stability of its own, it should therefore be the subject of a special study whose purpose would be to discover the social causes leading to a definite number of people that take their own lives in a given society.

For Durkheim, the social suicide rate was the clearest evidence for a social theory of suicide. Because, on the one hand, it established that different societies had different suicide rates, and, on the other hand, these rates changed very little over time within any given society. For example, between 1841 and 1842, France had 2,866 suicides, while Germany had 1,598 suicides. Durkheim argued that if suicide were entirely the result of individual causes and individual psychology, it would be difficult to explain why the French would be almost twice as likely to commit suicide in comparison with the Germans. Durkheim then reasoned that once we shift the focus from the study of individual suicides to the study of the 'collective suicide rate' – France's suicide rate in relation to Germany's suicide rate – it became apparent that the collective rates pointed in the direction of underlying social causes, which in turn indicated fundamental differences in the social framework that caused France to have 2,866 suicides each year, while Germany had only 1,598 (Morrison, 2012).

Based on the analysis of a mass of data gathered on many societies and cultures, Durkheim develops a classificatory typology of suicide based on two underlying social facts – integration and regulation (Figure 7.3). Integration refers to the strength of the social bonds existing between the individual and society. Regulation, on the other hand, refers to the degree of external constraint on people. Durkheim's typology of suicide is based on the degree of integration and regulation in society. For example, when integration is high, Durkheim calls that type of society altruistic. Low integration results in an increase in egoistic suicides. Fatalistic suicide is associated with high regulation, and anomic suicide

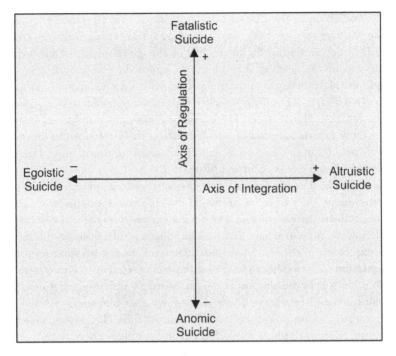

FIGURE 7.3 Durkheim's Theory of Suicide

with low integration (Ritzer and Stepnisky, 2014). Let us now discuss about these four types of suicide in detail.

Egoistic Suicide: Egoistic suicide results from the lack of integration of the individual into his social group. Durkheim believed that an individual acquires morality, values and sense of purpose from society. A well-integrated society, thus, provides a general feeling of moral support to get us through the uncertainties and disappointments of our daily life. Without this, individuals are liable to commit suicide at the smallest frustration. In a society marked by low degree of integration, an individual is isolated and potentially suicidal because the ties uniting him with others are broken because of the weakening of the social fabric. Durkheim believed that the cause of egoistic suicide is, therefore, the excessive individualism, which modern, industrial society tended to encourage. Durkheim further argued that less integrate groups within a society, such as, Protestants, unmarried men, urban dwellers, industrial workers, etc. are more prone to egoistic suicide (Adams and Sydie, 2016).

Altruistic Suicide: Altruistic suicide is the opposite of egoistic suicide. It is the result of the excessive integration of the individual into the group. The suicidal individual who is completely absorbed by the group feels it is his or her duty to commit suicide in order to benefit the group or collectivity. For example, the case of women in India, throwing themselves at the funeral pyre of their husbands (known as *sati* in India). Similarly, the case of Danish warriors killing themselves in old age or suicide of followers and servants on the death of their chiefs. As opposed to these obligatory altruistic suicides, there are optional varieties which do not require suicide but praise self-sacrifice or ultimate self-renunciation as a noble and praiseworthy act. Japanese Harakiri, self-immolation by Buddhist monks, self-homicide by army suicide squads and self-destruction in Nirvana under Brahminic influence (as in the case of ancient Hindu sages) illustrate other variants of altruistic suicide (Abraham and Morgan, 2010).

Anomic Suicide: Just as egoistic and altruistic suicide constitute two polar extremes on the axis of social integration, according to Durkheim, anomic and fatalistic suicide constitute two polar extremes on the axis of social regulation. Durkheim argues that anomic suicide results from normlessness or deregulation in society. Durkheim attributed anomic suicide to unlimited aspirations of individuals and the breakdown of regulatory norms in society. Durkheim believed that unlike animals, man's aspirations and desires are unlimited and insatiable. These desires, whether biological, psychological or social, can only be regulated by a moral force. Durkheim views collective order as the only moral force that can effectively restrain the social and moral needs. However, occasionally this mechanism breaks down and normlessness ensues (ibid.). Anomic suicide, according to Durkheim, was particularly prevalent in modern society, especially in the economic world where it has most victims.

> Rates of anomic suicide are likely to rise whether the nature of the disruption is positive (for example, an economic boom) or negative (an economic depression). Either type of disruption renders the collectivity temporarily incapable of exercising its authority over individuals. Such changes put people in new situations in which the old norms no longer apply but new norms have yet to develop. Periods of disruption unleash currents of anomie – moods of rootlessness and normlessness – and these currents lead to an increase in rates of anomic suicide.
>
> *(Ritzer and Stepnisky, 2014)*

However, just as in economic sphere, anomie in social, cultural and political sphere as well may predispose people to take the extreme step of committing suicide.

Fatalistic Suicide: Durkheim also discussed a fourth type of suicide which he called as fatalistic suicide. However, his discussion of fatalistic suicide was very brief and he mentioned it only in a footnote in *Suicide*. Fatalistic suicide was the opposite of anomic suicide. It was the result of excessive regulation. While Durkheim had little to say about the characteristics of fatalistic suicide, he cited as an example, the suicide of slaves who, seeing no alternative to life except enslavement under a master, take their own life. Durkheim described those who are more likely to commit fatalistic suicide as 'persons with futures pitilessly blocked and passions violently chocked by oppressive discipline'. In modern society, fatalistic suicide occurred among very young husbands and childless married women, but Durkheim insisted that in general it had 'little contemporary importance and examples are hard to find' (Adams and Sydie, 2016).

Durkheim concludes his study of suicide with an examination of what reforms could be undertaken to prevent it. He argues that most attempts to prevent suicide have failed because it has been seen as an individual problem. For Durkheim, attempts to directly convince individuals not to commit suicide are futile, since its real causes are in society. Of course, the first question to be asked is whether suicide should be prevented or whether it counts among those social phenomena that Durkheim would call normal because of its widespread prevalence. This is an especially an important question for Durkheim because his theory says that suicide results from social currents that, in a less exaggerated form, are good for society. We would not want to stop all economic booms because they lead to anomic suicides nor would we stop valuing individuality because it leads to egoistic suicide. Similarly, altruistic suicide results from our virtuous tendency to sacrifice ourselves for the community. The pursuit of progress, the belief in the individual and the spirit of sacrifice all have their place in society, and cannot exist without generating some suicides.

Durkheim admits that some suicide is normal, but he argues that the modern society has seen a pathological increase in both egoistic and anomic suicide. Here his position can be traced back to *The Division of Labour in Society*, where he argued that the anomie of modern culture is due to the abnormal way in which labour is divided so that it leads to isolation rather than interdependence. What is needed, then, is a way to preserve the benefits of modernity without unduly increasing suicides – a way of balancing these social currents. In our society, Durkheim believes, these currents are out of balance. In particular, social regulation and integration are too low, leading to an abnormal rate of anomic and egoistic suicides.

Many of the existing institutions for connecting the individual and society have failed, and Durkheim sees little hope of their success. The modern state is too distant from the individual to influence his or her life with enough force and continuity. The church cannot exert its integrating effect without at the same time repressing freedom of thought. Even the family, possibly the most integrative institution in modern society, will fail in this task since it is subject to the same corrosive conditions that are increasing suicide. Thus, Durkheim suggests two important measures to address the problem of abnormal rate of suicide in society, viz. emphasis on school reforms and formation of 'occupational associations'.

According to Durkheim, schools provided an excellent milieu for children for learning and internalising new cultural norms. For adults, Durkheim proposed another institution: the occupational associations. Durkheim advocated that all the workers, managers and owners involved in a particular industry should join together in an association that would be both professional and social. Unlike

Marx, Durkheim did not believe that there was a basic conflict of interest among the owners, managers and workers within an industry. For Marx, modern capitalist society was characterised by an inherent contradiction and fundamental conflict of economic interest between the bourgeoisie (the capitalist class) and the proletariat (the working class). Durkheim believed that any such conflict occurred only because the various people involved lacked a common morality which was traceable to the lack of an integrative structure. He suggested that the structure that was needed to provide this integrative morality was the occupational association, which would encompass 'all the agents of the same industry united and organised into a single group'. Such an organisation was deemed to be superior to such organisations as labour unions and employer association, which in Durkheim's view served only to intensify the differences between owners, managers and workers. Involved in a common organisation, people in these categories would recognise their common interests as well as their common need for an integrative moral system. That moral system, with its derived rules and laws, would serve to counteract the tendency towards atomisation in modern society as well as to help stop the decline in the significance of collective morality.

Mel Churton and Anne Brown state:

> Durkheim's analysis of society was primarily optimistic. He regarded social stability as of paramount importance and was confident that problems in society could be solved through social reform rather than radical action. He referred to the problems of society as pathologies, implying that they could be overcome or 'cured'. He construed the sociologist as a social physician whose job was to alleviate difficulties through structural reform. He even proposed that the difficulties in the workplace (which so concerned Marx) could be overcome if workers were encouraged to develop a common morality. He felt this could be achieved through the establishment of 'occupational associations', which could encompass 'all the agents of the same industry united and organized into a single group'. These would be superior to worker unions, which Durkheim felt only served to intensify the differences between owners and workers.
>
> (Churton and Brown, 2017)

Durkheim's analysis has had an enormous influence on all subsequent research into suicide, and many aspects of his theory have been confirmed by a number of studies, although many of these have also served to modify the original theory. Bearing in mind that many of the statistical techniques commonly used today had not been developed at the time, his statistical approach was very advanced. Still, he has been criticised both for his social realism perspective and for his positivist methodology. In his study *Suicide*, Durkheim displayed an extreme form of social realism and explained suicide as a product of suicidal currents. However, later-day scholars criticised this extreme sociological realism approach of Durkheim, and rather advocated a more comprehensive 'causal pluralism' approach to explain the phenomenon of suicide. They argued that apart from social factors, biological and psychological factors must also be explored while explaining suicide. Further, British sociologist J. Maxwell Atkinson has criticised Durkheim on his positivist methodology. Atkinson has raised doubts over the reliability and validity of the very data used by Durkheim in study *Suicide*. He maintains that the social world is a construction of actors' perceptions and subjective interpretations. As such it has no reality beyond the meanings given to it by social actors. Thus, an act of suicide is simply that which is defined as suicide by social actors. Certain deaths come to be defined as suicide by coroners (investigating officers), medical practitioners, newspaper reporters, family and friends of the deceased and so on. Definitions of suicide depend on their interpretation of the event. For Atkinson, suicide is not an objective fact, rather it is a subjective interpretation of the coroner. Thus, while some cases of unnatural death get classified as suicide and others are not, owing to the subjective interpretation by the coroner (Haralambos and Heald, 2006).

The Elementary Forms of Religious Life (1912)

Durkheim wrote *The Elementary Forms of Religious Life* between 1902 and 1911, and first published it as a complete study in 1912. By the time it was published, Durkheim had become one of the leading thinkers in French social thought. Durkheim's perspective of social realism and his concern for social regulation once again gets manifested in his study of religion. Religion, for Durkheim, is one of the forces that creates within individuals a sense of moral obligation to adhere to societal norms. Thus, Durkheim was primarily interested in identifying the principal elements of religion, the very core of the institution. Towards this end, he focused upon some small, isolated, preliterate Australian tribes and a few similar tribes that were native to North America. Studies such as Spencer and Gillen's *The Native Tribes of Central Australia* (published in 1899) and Benjamin Howitt's *Native Tribes of South Eastern Australia* were among the first to carry out ethnographic studies of the religious practices of tribal societies that had not been studied previously.

Following anthropological custom at the time, he referred to these small, isolated and preliterate societies as primitive. Their less complex social organisation, in Durkheim's view, would offer him an unfettered view of religion and its place within societies, both primitive and modern. Durkheim stated:

> At the foundation of all systems of belief ... [are] ... a certain number of fundamental representations or conceptions and of ritual attitudes which, in spite of the diversity of forms which they have taken ... fulfill the same functions everywhere. These ... elements ... constitute that which is permanent and human in religion.
>
> *(Abrahamson, 2010)*

Durkheim was primarily interested in the study of the original and most authentic essence of religion. For this, he focused on the study of the structure of primitive religions in order to provide an explanation of their elementary organisation. Most contemporary religions in modern society, he believed, had borrowed so much from each other that disentangling that which was original and authentic to them from that which had been taken over from other societies seemed hopeless. Thus, he wanted to move far back, to before the borrowing began, to the origins of religion where he could identify its most essential features. Hence, the title of his book, *The Elementary Forms of Religious Life* (ibid.).

In looking for the essence of religion, Durkheim's primary empirical referent was the society of the Arunta aborigines of Australia. This society, and other primitive societies, he believed, offered 'privileged cases ... because they are simple cases' in which 'life is reduced to its essential traits'; they are therefore 'less easily misunderstood'. Durkheim's study *The Elementary Forms of Religious Life* contains a description and a detailed analysis of the clan system and of totemism in the Arunta tribe of Australian aborigines. Durkheim began with a scrutiny of the two main theories of religion dominant at that time, viz. *animism* and *naturism*.

Animism means the belief in spirits. Animism refers to the belief that all objects, both animate and inanimate, are permanently or temporarily inhabited by spirits or souls. The spirits are conceived of as beings with an existence distinct from and therefore capable of surviving the death or destruction of, the persons, animals, plants or objects they inhabit (Scott, 1999). Edward B. Tylor, the distinguished English ethnologist, as well as Spencer himself supported the notion of 'animism', i.e. spirit worship as the most basic form of religious expression. Tylor believed this to be the earliest form of religion. According to Tylor,

> Animism derives from man's attempts to answer two questions, 'What is it that makes the difference between a living body and a dead one?' and, 'What are those human shapes which appear in dreams and visions?' To make sense of these events, early philosophers invented the idea of soul. The soul is a spirit being which leaves the body temporarily during dreams and visions, and permanently at death. Once invented, the idea of spirits was applied not simply to man, but also to many aspects of the natural and social environment. Thus, animals were invested with spirit, as were man-made objects. Tylor argues that religion, in the form of animism, originated to satisfy man's intellectual nature, to meet his need to make sense of death, dreams and visions.
>
> *(Haralambos and Heald, 2006)*

Naturism, on the other hand, means the belief that the forces of nature have supernatural power. F. Max Mueller, the noted German linguist, believes this to be the earliest form of religion. According to Mueller,

> Naturism arose from man's experience of nature, in particular the effect of nature upon man's emotions. Nature contains surprise, terror, marvels and miracles, such as volcanoes, thunder and lightning. Awed by the power and wonder of nature, early man transformed abstract forces into personal

agents. Man personified nature. The force of the wind became the spirit of the wind, the power of the sun became the spirit of the sun. Where animism seeks the origin of religion in man's intellectual needs, naturism seeks it in his emotional needs. Naturism is man's response to the effect of the power and wonder of nature upon his emotions.

(ibid.)

Durkheim rejected both of these explanations of religion because he felt that they failed to explain the universal key distinction between the sacred and the profane, and because they tended to explain religion in terms of either an illusion or a hallucination. For Durkheim, religion was neither an illusion nor a hallucination. Nor is religion defined by the notion of mystery or of the supernatural. Nor is the belief in a transcendental god the essence of religion, for there are several religions, such as Buddhism and Confucianism, without gods.

For Durkheim, religion was an eternal truth. He argued that it is inadmissible that systems of ideas like religion which have had such considerable place in history, to which people have turned in all ages for the energy they needed to live, and for which they were willing to sacrifice their lives, should be mere tissues of illusion. Rather, they should be viewed as so profound and so permanent as to correspond to a true reality. This true reality, according to Durkheim, is not a transcendent god but society itself. The central thesis of Durkheim's theory of religion is that throughout history, men have never worshipped any other reality, whether in the form of the totem or in the form of God, than the collective social reality transfigured by faith. Thus, religion, according to Durkheim, expressed the 'eternal truth that outside of us there exists something greater than us, with which we enter into communion'. Religion is the means by which individuals 'represent to themselves the society of which they are members' (Durkheim, 1912).

Accordingly, Durkheim defines religion as a 'unified system of beliefs and practices relating to sacred things, that is to say, things set apart and forbidden—beliefs and practices which unite into one single moral community called a Church, all those who adhere to them' (Durkheim, 1912). Beliefs and practices unite people in a social community by relating them to sacred things. Durkheim argues that this collective sharing of beliefs, rituals, etc. is essential for the development of religion. The sacred symbols of religious belief and practice refer not to the external environment nor to individual human nature but only to the moral reality of society (Abraham and Morgan, 2010). Thus, for Durkheim, the essence of religion is a division of the world into two kinds of phenomena, the sacred and the profane. In other words, all societies divide the world into two categories, 'the sacred' and 'the profane', or more simply, the sacred and the non-sacred. The sacred refers to things human beings set apart, including religious beliefs, rites, deities, or anything socially defined as requiring special religious treatment. Participation in the sacred order, such as in rituals or ceremonies, gives a special prestige, illustrating one of the social functions of religion. 'The sacred thing', wrote Durkheim, 'is *par excellence* that which the profane should not touch and cannot touch with impunity'. The profane is the reverse of the sacred. 'The circle of sacred objects', continued Durkheim, 'cannot be determined once for all. Its existence varies infinitely, according to the different religions' (Durkheim, 1912).

The dichotomy of the sacred and the profane arises out of the dualistic nature of life experience itself. Sacredness is essentially a matter of attitude on the part of the people towards various animate and inanimate objects. But it is not an intrinsic characteristic of the objects themselves. It is the society which designates certain objects as sacred and expects its members to show an attitude of awe and reverence towards these objects. For example, the holy water from Ganges is regarded as sacred by the Hindus despite the fact that Ganges these days is highly polluted. Thus, sacredness is a quality superimposed by society only. Further, according to Durkheim, the sacred is radically opposed to profane. Unlike the profane, the sacred is non-utilitarian and non-empirical, is strength giving and sustaining, elicits intense respect and makes an ethical demand on the believer.

Instead of animism and naturism, Durkheim took the religious practice of *totemism* among the Australian tribes as the key concept to explain the origins of religion. He sees their religion, which he calls totemism, as the simplest and most basic form of religion. As mentioned earlier, the sacred is not an intrinsic property of the object or thing; it is something that is added. Once the sacred attribution has been conferred, the object or thing becomes a symbol or totem of the group's identity. Ordinary objects, whether pieces of wood, polished stones, plants or animals, are transfigured into sacred objects once they bear the emblem of the totem. Durkheim writes:

> Totemism is the religion, not of certain animals or of certain men or of certain images, but of a kind of anonymous and impersonal force which is found in each of these beings, without however being identified with any one of them. None possesses it entirely, and all participate in it. So independent is it of the particular subjects in which it is embodied that it precedes them just as it is adequate to them. Individuals die, generations pass away and are replaced by others. But this force remains ever present, living, and true to itself. It quickens today's generation just as it quickened yesterday's and as it will quicken tomorrow's. Taking the word in a very broad sense, one might say that it is the god worshipped by each totemic cult; but it is an impersonal god, without a name, without a history, abiding in the world, diffused in a countless multitude of things.
>
> *(Abraham and Morgan, 2010)*

Australian aborigine society is divided into several clans. A clan is like a large extended family with its members sharing certain duties and obligations. Each clan has a totem, usually an animal or a plant. The totem is symbol. It is the emblem of the clan, 'It is its flag; it is the sign by which each clan distinguishes itself from all others'. However, the totem is more than this, it is a sacred symbol. The totem is 'The outward and visible form of the totemic principle or god'. Durkheim argues that if the totem, 'Is at once the symbol of god and of the society, is that not because the god and the society are only one?' Thus, he suggests that in worshipping God, men are in fact worshipping society. Society is the real object of religious veneration (Durkheim, 1912).

> Totem, Durkheim explained, refers to an implicit belief in a mysterious or sacred force or principle that provides sanctions for violations of taboos, inculcates moral responsibilities in the group, and animates the totem itself. The emphasis, in keeping with his overall emphasis upon social analysis of social phenomena, was upon the collective activities as the birthplace of religious sentiments and ideas. According to Durkheim, the essence of Totemism is the worship of an impersonal, anonymous force, at once immanent and transcendent. This anonymous, diffuse force which is superior to men and very close to them is in reality society itself.
>
> *(Abraham and Morgan, 2010)*

The totem, therefore, is the source of the moral life of the group or clan. The totem is a collective moral force that acts upon and is incorporated into the individual consciousness of each clan member. Worship of totem is therefore worship of clan. Durkheim further argues that the moral force of the clan is impressed upon the individual consciousness through collective rituals and ceremonies. Since man is a social animal, all individuals in society want to belong to the collectivity. They want social solidarity. They want to be moral beings. Durkheim argues that it is through participation in religion and ritual that their belonging and their moral solidarity are confirmed. Religion is therefore 'true', because it symbolises group or social solidarity, and the sacred is simply 'society transfigured and personified' (Adams and Sydie, 2016).

Durkheim further explains that how does man come to worship society? According to him, sacred things are 'considered superior in dignity and power to profane things and particularly to man'. In relation to the sacred, man's position is inferior and dependent. This relationship between man and sacred things is exactly the relationship between man and society. Society is more important and powerful than the individual. Once again, Durkheim's social realism is at display here. Durkheim argues that 'Primitive man comes to view society as something sacred because he is utterly dependent on it'. However, now the question arises that 'Why does man not simply worship society itself?' Why does he invent a sacred symbol like a totem? Durkheim answers this by saying that 'it is easier for him to visualise and direct his feelings of awe toward a symbol than towards so complex a thing as a clan' (Haralambos and Heald, 2006).

Durkheim's study of religion, thus, is one of the best demonstrations of the functional explanation of a social fact. He is trying to highlight the consequences of religion, which is a part of the society, for the society as a whole. The attitudes of reverence and respect which are expressed, through religious beliefs and rituals, towards the sacred objects are in fact an indirect expression of reverence for the society. Participation in religious worship builds respect for society's values and norms, hence, acting as an agency of social control. Further, collective participation in common rituals and holding common beliefs creates a sense of 'We-ness' among the members of the society and thus strengthens solidarity in the society.

In line with the basic premise of classical functionalism, Durkheim argues that social life is impossible without the shared values and moral beliefs which form the 'collective conscience'. Without shared values or value consensus, there would be no social order, social control, social solidarity or cooperation. In short, there would be no society. According to Durkheim, religion reinforces the collective conscience.

The social group comes together in religious rituals infused with drama and reverence. Together, its members express their faith in common values and beliefs. In this highly charged atmosphere of collective worship, the integration of society is strengthened. The members of society express, communicate and comprehend the moral bonds which unite them (ibid.).

Durkheim further argues that by defining the common values and beliefs as sacred, religion provides them with greater power to direct human action. The attitude of respect towards the sacred is the same attitude applied to social duties and obligations. Thus, in worshipping society, men are, in effect, recognising the importance of the social group and their dependence upon it. In this way, religion strengthens the unity of the group and promotes social solidarity.

Durkheim believed he had solved the religious–moral dilemma of modern society. It was presumed that religion, which had so far served as the basis of social solidarity and integration, would lose its appeal in modern society with the emergence of science. This might lead to disintegration of modern society. But Durkheim argued that if religion is nothing but the indirect worship of society, modern people need to only express their religious feelings directly towards the sacred symbolisation of society.

The source and object of religion, Durkheim pointed out, are the collective life – the sacred is at bottom 'society personified'. Therefore, a secular sociological explanation of religion could sound something like this – the individual who feels dependent on some external moral power is not a victim of hallucination but a responsive member of society. The substantial function of religion, said Durkheim, is the creation, reinforcement and maintenance of social solidarity. He argued that religious phenomenon emerges in any society when a separation is made between the sphere of the profane – the realm of everyday utilitarian activities – and the sphere of the sacred – the area that pertains to the numerous, the transcendental, the extraordinary (Figure 7.4) (Abraham and Morgan, 2010).

For Durkheim, religion is not only a social creation, but is in fact society divinised. Durkheim stated that the deities which men worship together are only projections of the power of society. Durkheim argued that if religion is essentially a transcendental representation of the powers of society, then the disappearance of traditional religion need not herald the dissolution of society. Furthermore, Durkheim reasoned that all that is required for modern men now was to realise directly that dependence on society, which before they had

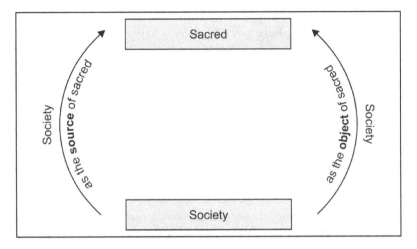

FIGURE 7.4   Society and the 'Sacred'

recognised only through the medium of religious representation. 'We must', he explained, 'discover the rational substitute for these religious notions that for a long time have served as the vehicle for the most essential moral ideas'. In modern society, Durkheim saw a need for some secular re-creation of the format and elements of religion. According to Durkheim, the critical institution for the re-creation of solidarity and moral equilibrium, replacing religion, was education. Thus, he advocated a new secular and humanistic religion for the modern society which is based on the ethos of rationality, secularism and humanism.

With this study of religion, Durkheim successfully demonstrated the application of functionalist methodology in sociology and social anthropology which subsequently influenced the works of B. Malinowski and A.R. Radcliffe-Brown. Durkheim's ideas remain influential, though they are not without criticism. Some social anthropologists and sociologists accept the fact that religion is important for promoting social solidarity and reinforcing social values, but they do not support the view that religion is the worship of society. For example, Malinowski, a social anthropologist, too used data from small-scale non-literate societies to develop his thesis on religion. In his study of Trobriand Islanders (New Guinea, southwest Pacific Ocean), Malinowski arrived at similar conclusions as that of Durkheim. Like Durkheim, Malinowski sees religion as reinforcing social norms and values and promoting social solidarity. Unlike Durkheim, however, he does not see religion reflecting society as a whole, nor does he see religious ritual as the worship of society itself. Instead, Malinowski argues that religion is concerned with specific situations of emotional stress which threaten social solidarity (Haralambos and Heald, 2006).

Malinowski argued that anxiety and tension tend to disrupt social life. Situations which produce these emotions include 'crises of life' such as birth, puberty, marriage and death. He argued that in all societies these life crises are surrounded with religious ritual. He saw death as the most disruptive of these events. Religion deals with the problem of death in the following manner.

A funeral ceremony expresses the belief in immortality, which denies the fact of death, and so comforts the bereaved. Other mourners support the bereaved by their presence at the ceremony. This comfort and support checks the emotions which death produces, and controls the stress and anxiety which might disrupt society. Death is 'socially destructive' since it removes a member from society. At a funeral ceremony, the social group unites to support the bereaved. This expression of social solidarity reintegrates society (ibid.).

Malinowski also discusses another category of events which cannot be fully controlled or predicted by practical means and which also produces tension and anxiety. Among the Trobrianders, Malinowski noted that such events were surrounded by ritual. He cites the example of fishing which is an important subsistence practice among the Trobrianders. Malinowski observed that Trobrianders went for fishing in both the lagoon and the open ocean. However, he noticed that in the lagoon, where there was no risk or uncertainty of any kind, there were no rituals associated with fishing. While fishing in the open sea is preceded by rituals to ensure a good catch and protect the fishermen. In the open sea, there is danger and uncertainty. For example, a storm may result in loss of life. Although Malinowski refers to these rituals as magic, others argue it is reasonable to regard them as religious practices. Again, here we can see rituals addressed to specific situations which produce anxiety. Rituals reduce anxiety by providing confidence and a feeling of control. As with funeral ceremonies, fishing rituals are social events. The group unites to deal with situations of stress, and so the unity of the group is strengthened (ibid.).

Here, we can see that while Durkheim analysed the functional aspect of religion for the society as a whole, Malinowski also talks of the functional consequences at the individual level, thus offering a critique to Durkheim's extreme social realism. Malinowski's distinctive contribution to the sociology of religion is his argument that religion promotes social solidarity by dealing with situations of emotional stress which threaten the stability of society.

In his essay, 'The Comparative Method in Social Anthropology', Radcliffe-Brown further extended the argument of Durkheim to explain why a particular totem is chosen by a society or a group as its totem. In a comparative analysis of various tribes of Australia and north-west America, he found various instances whereby a tribe was divided into two exogamous moieties and each moiety represented by particular natural species as its totem. For example, in case of Australian aborigines in New South Wales, the two moieties were represented by eaglehawk and crow. On the basis of his comparative study, he concluded that the selection of a particular set of natural species as the totem by the two exogamous moieties of a tribe is also associated with their intergroup social relations. He found it common that natural species were placed in pairs of opposites, with certain degree of resemblances as well as differences. He interpreted the resemblances and differences of animal species in terms of social relationships of friendship and antagonism in human society.

Further, Robert K. Merton argues that Durkheim's views on religion are more relevant to small, non-literate societies, where there is a close integration of culture and social institutions, where work, leisure, education and family life tend to merge and where members share a common belief and value system. They are less relevant to modern societies which have many subcultures, social and ethnic groups, specialised organisations and a range of religious beliefs, practices and institutions. Merton asserts that Durkheim's view that religion acts as an agency of social control and provided solidarity is true only for simple small-scale societies which practice a single common religion. In the case of modern industrial societies, religion has lost both these functions. Given the highly differentiated and diversified nature of modern societies, religion can no longer act as an agency of social control. Further, the existence of a plurality of religions quite often lead to inter-religious conflicts and therefore endanger solidarity rather than enhancing it. This could be seen in terms of the increasing communal violence at local level and deepening religious divide at international level.

Further, contrary to Durkheim's view that religion is in fact 'society divinised' and promotes solidarity in the society, Marx argues that religion is a part of the superstructure and thus it not only reflects but also reinforces the ruling class ideology. Marx further argues that religion acts as an opiate to dull the pain produced by oppression. In Marx's words, 'Religion is the sigh of the oppressed creature, the sentiment of a heartless world and the soul of soulless conditions. It is the opium of the people'. It does nothing to solve the problem, it is simply a misguided attempt to make life more bearable. As such, religion merely stupefies its adherents rather than bringing them true happiness and fulfilment. To Marx, religion is an illusion which eases the pain produced by exploitation and oppression. It is a series of myths which justify and legitimate the subordination of the subject class and the domination and privilege of the ruling class. It is a distortion of reality which provides many of the deceptions which form the basis of ruling class ideology and false class consciousness.

Durkheim, in his study of religion, pointed to two major functions of religion: social solidarity and social control. However, as evident from Max Weber's study of *The Protestant Ethic and the Spirit of Capitalism*, religion may also serve as an agent of social change. Weber's study of ascetic Protestantism argued that religious beliefs provided the ethics, attitudes and motivations for the development of capitalism, thus leading to the transformation of a predominantly feudal European society into a capitalistic one.

More recently, some scholars have highlighted an altogether new role that religion is playing in the contemporary world politics, as an ideology of protest. They argue that with welfare state failing to deliver on the basic amenities of life and communism still a utopia, religion has emerged as a potent ideology of protest by the disenchanted masses. This phenomenon is far more explicit and rampant mainly in the Third World developing countries. Rapidly spreading and powerful currents of Islamic fundamentalism could be cited as an example here. In the Indian context, we can also cite the example of Dalit movement led by Dr B.R. Ambedkar. In its later stage, Dalit movement also made use of Buddhist ideology of egalitarianism to protest against the social inequalities and injustice perpetrated by the traditional caste system.

Durkheim: An Assessment

Durkheim has exerted a great influence on the social sciences, especially the functionalist and structuralist schools of anthropology and sociology. His was the dominant theory of social science in France from the beginning of the twentieth century. After his death in 1917, many of his students refined his core ideas. In anthropology, central theorists like Radcliff-Brown and Levi-Strauss have built on the Durkheim an inheritance. In sociology, the structural functionalist Talcott Parsons refined many of Durkheim's ideas. Parsons's central role in sociology from World War II until the 1970s contributed to maintaining an interest in Durkheim, and Parsons's heirs still consider Durkheim an important forerunner.

Durkheim's theories have also been subjected to harsh criticism by later social scientists. Most of his most important ideas (for example, those on social facts and holism) have been rejected by many supporters of individualist positions, such as rational choice theory, exchange theory, symbolic interactionism and ethnomethodology. And his belief in integration and consensus, and his lack of concern with problems of power, have been criticised by supporters of more conflict-oriented theory, for example, Marxists.

Durkheim carved out a special field of study for sociology, established a sound empirical methodology and laid the foundation of structural functionalism, the dominant school of sociological theory today. It is a fact that despite some criticism to his concepts such as collective conscience and social facts, very few have surpassed his sociological realism or matched his substantive contribution to the many concerns of theoretical sociology.

One of the important contributions of Durkheim is that he delineated the subject matter of sociology with great precision and clarity. He was successful in distinguishing the phenomena studied by psychology and sociology. According to him, sociology must study social facts, those which are external to individual minds and which exercise coercive action on them. Durkheim showed convincingly that social facts are facts *sui generis*. In his *The Rules of Sociological Method*, he elaborated in detail the positivist methodology that a social scientist should adopt while studying a social phenomenon. Thus, to the main problems in socio logical theory of his times, Durkheim gave clear answers, both for theory and method. Durkheim faced up to complex methodological problems and demonstrated by implementing in his works the necessity of empirical research for a science of society.

Further, Durkheim was one of the first scholars to highlight the social consequences of division of labour. Prior to him, division of labour was explained in a narrow sense, limited only to its economic consequences. It was Durkheim who brought out vividly the social and cultural importance of division of labour. He analysed the nature and consequences of division of labour in terms of changing forms of social solidarity. In his book *The Division of Labour in Society*, Durkheim analyses the individual versus society issue in terms of the different kinds of social solidarity that hold society and individuals together.

Durkheim's study *Suicide* is also considered as a landmark study and the best demonstration of his application of social realism perspective and positivist methodology. It was for the first time that theoretical generalisations were arrived at on the basis of careful analysis of empirical data. This study gave sociology a firm footing among other social sciences and justified its claim of being a scientific discipline.

Durkheim also had emphasised that while studying any social phenomenon, a sociologist should seek for both causal as well as functional explanations. Durkheim's study of suicide is considered as the best demonstration of the causal explanation, while his study of religion is cited as an example of functional explanation in the sociological world. He argued that it is the business of the sociologists to establish causal connections and causal laws. Although many are sceptical about this approach, a great number of causal connections and functional correlations have been established by sociology with a reasonable degree of probability. While pleading for causal explanations, Durkheim argued that since experimentation is impossible in sociology, we should go in for indirect experimentation, by using the *comparative method*. This particular method continues to be used by sociologists.

Durkheim is also considered the pioneer of functional approach in sociology. Functional approach was later pursued by Malinowski and Radcliffe-Brown in studying various small-scale and pre-industrial societies. But it was Talcott Parsons and Robert K. Merton who revived functional approach and suitably modified classical functional approach to account for the dynamics unfolding in the modern industrial societies. Closely following Durkheim, Merton distinguished between 'manifest' and 'latent' functions. Also the idea of 'dysfunction' goes back to Durkheim's idea of pathological functions.

Without doubt, Durkheim shaped French sociology. His influence before World War II was insignificant, but following Talcott Parsons's *The Structure of Social Action* (1937) in which Durkheim was fully and admirably introduced to American sociology, his influence flourished. By the 1950s, he had become along with Weber the major influence in America and all Europe (Abraham and Morgan, 2010).

LET'S THINK

Dear Learner, in this chapter, we have learned about the ideas of Emile Durkheim regarding the perspective, subject matter and methodology to be adopted in sociology. However, we must remember that these ideas were advocated by

Durkheim at a time when sociology as an academic discipline was yet to born. Hence, the primary concern of Durkheim at that time was to convince the academic fraternity of the need for a distinct and scientific discipline to study society and to clearly demarcate the subject matter and methodology of the discipline. This explains that why we observe an extreme stance in the arguments of Durkheim, especially with regard to his perspective (social realism), subject matter (social fact) and methodology (positivist).

Though the contemporary sociology had abandoned some of his ideas on subject matter and methodology, especially in the post-Weberian era, but many of his ideas and insights still resonate in and guide sociological research. For example, do you think that Durkheim's theory of suicide can help us understand and explain the increasing suicide rate among students and farmers in India? Similarly, does his idea of sacred still hold relevance to understand the newly emerging symbols of collectivity in modern society such as national flag, national emblem or national anthem?

For Practice

Q1. Write a short note on social fact as 'thing'.
Q2. Write a short note on suicide as a social fact.
Q3. What is the focus of sociological analysis in the contributions of Emile Durkheim? Give your answer with the help of any one of his contributions.
Q4. Identify the similarities and differences between Marx's theory of 'alienation' and Durkheim's theory of 'anomie'.
Q5. Is the Durkheimian concept of religion entirely different from that of his predecessors? Why and how?

Model Answers

Q. Write a short note on social fact as 'thing'.

A. Emile Durkheim, in line with his social realism perspective, identified social facts as the subject matter of sociology. Social facts, according to Durkheim, are those ways of acting, thinking and feeling which are capable of exerting an external constraint on individual members, which are generally diffused throughout a given society and which can exist in their own life independent of their individual manifestations. Religion, law, language, any form of socio–economic and political institutions, etc. may be cited as some of the examples of social facts.

Arguing from a functional and positivist perspective, Durkheim asserted that society is a *reality sui generis*. In other words, society has an objective existence and it is independent of the consciousness of the individual members who comprise it. Likewise, the various facets of social reality, called social facts, too are general, external and coercive in nature. Having established the independent and objective character of social facts, Durkheim further argued that in the course of sociological enquiry, social facts must be treated as things. In other words, Durkheim is suggesting that social facts must be studied by empirical method and not by intuition. That is, while studying social facts as 'things', all preconceptions about such social facts must be abandoned by the researcher. Further, the observation of social facts should be confined to their external attributes only which can be tested and verified. Durkheim, in his study *Suicide*, demonstrated the application of positivist methodology in the study of social phenomena withconsiderable statistical ingenuity.

Later, however, Durkheim's ideas were criticised by scholars belonging to non-positivist or anti-positivist tradition in sociology, particularly by Max Weber. Weber argued that social action is a meaningful response of a social actor. Hence, unlike Durkheim, who gave primacy to society over the individual, Weber emphasised the mutual reciprocity between society and its institutions, and the voluntaristic action of the individual. Further, Weber argued that positivist methodology alone is inadequate to understand the subjective dimension of human behaviour and in its place he advocated *Verstehen*, an interpretative understanding of social action.

Despite these limitations, the significance of Durkheim's contributions in establishing sociology as a science cannot be undermined. However, it is also equally true that for a comprehensive understanding of social reality, subjective dimension of human behaviour must also be taken into account as highlighted by Weber.

Q. Identify the similarities and differences between Marx's theory of 'alienation' and Durkheim's theory of 'anomie'.

A. Alienation, in terms of Karl Marx, refers to a socio-psychological condition which denotes a state of 'estrangement' of individuals from themselves or from others, or from a specific situation or process. Anomie, on the other hand, implies 'normlessness' in literal sense of the term. Emile Durkheim used the concept of anomie to refer to the 'breakdown of the normative regulation' in a given society.

Both these concepts emerged in a common context and with a shared concern. Marx and Durkheim both were witness to profound socio-economic and political changes that were taking place in nineteenth- and twentieth-century Europe. Both tried to comprehend and explain the far-reaching effects of the newly emerging capitalistic society in terms of their respective concepts and theories. Both scholars were concerned with restoring peace and harmony in society, and believed that with the resolution of the problems of alienation and anomie, the social order will be restored in modern society. Further, both believed that the problems of alienation and anomie are rooted in the social structure of society. In other words, both scholars explained alienation and anomie primarily in terms of structural approach.

However, there are also some fundamental differences between the two concepts, particularly in terms of their cause, character and solution as offered by respective scholars. While for Marx institution of private property is the primary source of alienation in modern capitalist society, Durkheim held pathological division of labour responsible for anomic condition. Further, for Marx, alienation is a permanent feature of all class-based societies but reaches its peak in capitalist society, but for Durkheim, anomie is an aberration, temporary and transitory, and manifests only in times of social and economic crises. Last but not least, there is also a difference in terms of solution offered by Marx and Durkheim to address alienation and anomie. Arguing from conflict perspective, Marx believed that alienation can't be resolved with capitalistic framework. He asserted that the institution of private property must be abolished and communal ownership of forces of production must be established to end alienation. Durkheim, on the other hand, arguing from a functionalist perspective, proposed 'occupational associations' to harmonise the interests of both owners and workers. He also advocated work ethics and educational reforms to address anomie.

Despite the historical context that is associated with the emergence of these concepts, they are still partly relevant in contemporary times. Alienation continues to exist in multiple forms and economic inequality is only one of the major factors responsible for it. Recent studies by Robert Blauner even suggest a decline in alienation due to automation. Further, the solution offered by Marx to address alienation has been discredited by history. Anomie too is a useful concept for analysing social change, particularly in the contemporary Third World societies. However, Durkheim's assertion about its temporary nature can be questioned in the light of perpetual conflict in West Asia and Africa.

References

Abraham, Francis and John Henry Morgan. *Sociological Thought*. New Delhi: Macmillan Publishers India, 2010.

Abrahamson, Mark. *Classical Theory and Modern Studies: Introduction to Sociological Theory*. New Delhi: PHI Learning Private, 2010.

Adams, Bert N. and R.A. Sydie. *Sociological Theory*. New Delhi: SAGE Publications, 2016.

Churton, Mel and Anne Brown. *Theory & Method*. 2nd Edition. Hampshire: Palgrave Macmillan, 2017.

Coser, Lewis A. *Masters of Sociological Thought*. 2nd Edition. Jaipur: Rawat Publications, 2008.

Haralambos, M. and R.M. Heald. *Sociology: Themes and Perspectives*. New Delhi: Oxford University Press, 2006.

Lee, David and Howard Newby. *The Problem of Sociology*. London: Routledge, 2000.

Morrison, Ken. *Marx, Durkheim, Weber: Formations of Modern Social Thought*. 2nd Edition. New Delhi: SAGE Publications, 2012.

Ransome, Paul. *Social Theory*. Jaipur: Rawat Publications, 2011.

Ritzer, George and Jeffrey Stepnisky. *Sociological Theory*. 9th Edition. New York: McGraw-Hill Education, 2014.

Royce, Edward. *Classical Social Theory and Modern Society: Marx, Durkheim, Weber*. Jaipur: Rawat Publications, 2015.

Scott, William P. *Dictionary of Sociology*. New Delhi: GOYLSaaB, 1999.

8

MAX WEBER

About Weber

Max Weber (1864–1920) is probably the best known and most influential figure in sociological theory. Weber was born on 21 April 1864 in Erfurt, Germany. He was the eldest of eight children born to Max Weber Sr. and his wife, Helene. His father was a well-known lawyer and a member of the German Parliament. Lewis A. Coser states:

> The young Weber grew up in a cultured bourgeois household. Not only leading politicians but leading academic men were among its frequent house guests. Here Weber met, at an early age, historians Treitschke, Sybel, Dilthey and Mommsen. But his parents' marriage, though at first a seemingly happy one, was soon to show signs of increasing tension, which could hardly be hidden from the children. Weber's mother, with her strong religious commitments and her ingrained Calvinist sense of duty, had little in common with a husband whose personal ethic was hedonistic rather than Protestant.
>
> *(Coser, 2008)*

The clash of personalities and interests of his parents took a severe toll on Weber's physical and mental health. However, following his father, Weber was also trained as a lawyer in Berlin and then took a doctorate in economics in 1889. In 1893, Weber got married to Marianne Schnitger (a cousin from his father's side). Marianne was a sociologist and feminist. She was among the pioneering women who pursued an education and career like any man and was one of the leaders of the liberal feminist movement. In 1918, German women obtained the vote, and in 1919 Marianne Weber became the first women member of the

DOI: 10.4324/9781003291053-10

Baden Parliament (Adams and Sydie, 2016). It is said that the core of their marital relationship was intellectual. They studied together, attended meetings together, but had little or no physical contact. Sexual fulfilment came to Weber only in his late forties, shortly before World War I, in an extramarital affair (Coser, 2008). When Marianne came to know about Weber's extramarital affairs, she was deeply hurt, though they remained bonded to each other as colleagues. Soon after his marriage, Weber received his first academic position at the age of 29. In 1896, he was appointed to a professorship in economics at the University of Freiburg, and then to a more important position at the University of Heidelberg, where he taught political economy and economics. Only 32 years old at the time, Weber was considered one of the youngest scholars to obtain a professorship at a major German university (Morrison, 2012).

However, soon after, Weber suffered the first of a series of serious bouts of psychological illness that forced him to give up his job and abandon academic work for the next six years, between 1897 and 1903. He returned to work in 1903. The period between 1905 and around 1915 was his most productive, beginning with the publication of two extended essays as *The Protestant Ethic and the Spirit of Capitalism* in 1904–1905. In 1909, he accepted the editorship of a sociological publication, as a result of which his academic workload increased substantially. By this time, a large circle of friends, including Georg Simmel, Robert Michels and others, met regularly at the Weber household to discuss the issues of the day. He then worked intermittently on a number of detailed studies in economics, religion, the development of the legal system and other social institutions. By 1909, Weber began writing a large two-volume work entitled *Economy and Society*, which was one of his most ambitious theoretical and historical works.

Weber also carried out extensive research on the history of world's religions, comparing the religions of the Western world with those of China and India. These studies subsequently appeared in print as *The Religion of India* and *The Religion of China* (both published in 1916). *The General Economic History* (1927) was compiled from a series of lectures he gave in Freiburg during 1919–1920, and *On the Methodology of the Social Sciences* was published posthumously in 1922 from a variety of articles and lectures given between 1903 and 1917. In most cases, complete English translations only became available during the 1950s and 1960s. In the June of 1920, Weber died from pneumonia leaving many of his works in unpublished state. It is worth noting that in addition to his academic career, Weber also participated in the German political life and often gave lectures on issues of public interest. However, in many of such talks, Weber tried to reconcile what he thought were conflicting value problems related to the role of the expert in political and scientific life.

While commenting on the contributions of Weber, Paul Ransome states:

> It is difficult not to compare the work of the German social theorist Max Weber (1864–1920) with that of Karl Marx. It could even be suggested that a full appreciation of key aspects of Weber's work only emerges by

making this comparison. There comparisons are inevitable since the writings of Marx, and the political claims of the Marxists who followed him,
provided much of the academic and political context of Weber's own social
theory. It is important to remember, however, that Weber's understanding
of Marx was very limited since many of Marx's most important works (the
Paris Manuscripts, *The German Ideology*, the *Grundrisse*) were not available
during Weber's lifetime. The Marx that Weber did know was mostly based
on his economic writings and *The Communist Manifesto*, and even these as
they were being interpreted, rather simplistically, by the German Social
Democratic Party in the 1890s. For Weber, Marx was the author of an
original, but rigid and one-sidedly materialist, theory of historical development, a point that he tries to prove by offering an alternative explanation
of the emergence of modern capitalism in his famous essay published in
1904/05, *The Protestant Ethic and the Spirit of Capitalism*.

(Ransome, 2011)

Though there exists a vast sociological literature on the comparison of Marx
and Weber, it is worth pointing out that this comparison actually relates to the
fairly specific topic of what social theory has to say about the origins and nature
of modern industrial capitalism. The comparison of Weber with Marx is fair
enough to the extent Weber's political concerns, his worries about the feasi-
bility of socialism and the dominance of economic interests can all be seen in
terms of the rise of capitalism. However, not all of Weber's work should be seen
as a response to Marx. Weber did have other interests as well. For example, as
mentioned earlier, his analysis of German society and politics, his comparative
history of the world religions and the contribution he made to the methodology
of social theory often have very little to do with Marx and Marxism. Let us now
briefly discuss the intellectual influences on the sociological perspective of Max
Weber. The accusation that Weber produced bourgeois social theory as opposed
to the proletarian social theory of Marx is partly based on the fact that Weber
came from a wealthy establishment family, and thus had the benefits of a privileged education and good social and career prospects.

Methodenstreit

The prevalent intellectual and political context had a deep influence on Weber
in shaping his perspective as well as ideas on subject matter of sociology. When
Weber arrived on the academic scene, an intense methodological debate was
going on in Germany between the positivists and anti-positivists with regard to
what methodology should be followed in social sciences. One group was led by
Carl Menger, an economist, who advocated the use of positive science methods
in social sciences as well. He argued that the scientific methodology of natural
sciences should be used to arrive at general theories in social sciences – seeing human motives and social interaction as far too complex to be amenable to

statistical analysis. On the other hand, the anti-positivist scholars (particularly the neo-Kantians) emphasised upon the subjective dimension of social reality, and thus did not see the possibility of any kind of universal generalisations in social sciences. This methodological debate which began in Germany in the latter part of the nineteenth century is popularly referred to as *Methodenstreit*. Whether he liked it or not, however, Weber could not help but become involved in the heated discussions that were taking place in intellectual and academic circles in Germany around 1900 about the role of social-scientific study, the differences between the cognitive aims of social and natural sciences, and the appropriate methodology suitable for respective sciences.

Neo-Kantian scholars, the followers of the great German philosopher, Immanuel Kant (1724–1804), tried to apply philosophical ideas of their master in methodological terms. Thus, taking a cue from Immanuel Kant, neo-Kantian scholars argued that the reality is of two kinds, *natural reality* and *social reality*. What distinguishes social reality from the natural reality is the presence of '*Geist*' (Spirit or Consciousness) and by virtue of the presence of Geist, human beings respond to the external stimuli in a meaningful manner, not mechanically as the physical objects do. Therefore, human behaviour can only be understood in the light of these meanings. Thus, social sciences should try to understand the human behaviour from the actor's point of view keeping in mind the meaning and motives that underlie such behaviour. The neo-Kantians, and other interested parties including Max Weber, thus, turned their attention to some of the major methodological issues. First, they wanted to challenge the idea that the kind of knowledge generated by the natural sciences was *the only* kind of knowledge available. Second, they wanted to show that the two kinds of science had to be different because they were looking at two fundamentally *different kinds* of phenomena. And third, if these points are valid, then it was obvious that two distinct *methodologies* were required to investigate them (Ransome, 2011).

It will be useful to begin by outlining the controversy between those who think of sociology in terms of natural science and those who think of it as being quite different from any natural science and perhaps more like history or philosophy. What are the differences between 'nature' and 'society' which would require radically different methods of enquiry? They were first clearly stated by Wilhelm Dilthey (1833–1911) and were then widely discussed by German historians and philosophers, especially Wilhelm Windelband (1848–1915) and Heinrich Rickert (1863–1936).

Unlike positivists, neo-Kantian scholars believed that there are fundamental differences between the natural world and the social or cultural world. First, the natural or physical world is devoid of consciousness and is relatively static, while the social world consists of conscious beings and hence is highly dynamic as well as diverse. Second, the natural world can only be observed and explained from the outside, while the human behaviour is subjective and guided by unique meanings and motives attributed by the individual. Hence, the subjective dimension of human behaviour cannot be directly observed through empirical observation as asserted by positivists. It can at best be interpreted. Third, the relations between phenomena of the natural world are mechanical relations of causality, whereas the relations between phenomena of the human world are relations of value and purpose. Thus, Dilthey, a German philosopher, argued that the 'human studies' should be concerned not with the establishment of causal connections or the formulation of universal laws, but with the construction of typologies of personality and culture which would serve as the framework for understanding human strivings and purposes in different historical situations. In other words, Dilthey believed that since social or cultural science studied acting individuals with ideas and intentions, a special method of understanding (*Verstehen*) was required, while natural science studied soulless things and, consequently, it did not need to understand its objects.

Windelband, yet another German philosopher and one of the leading neo-Kantians, on the other hand, proposed a logical distinction between natural and social sciences on the basis of their methods. Natural sciences, according to him, use a 'nomothetic' or generalising method, whereas social sciences employ an 'ideographic' or individualising procedure since they are interested in the non-recurring events in reality and the particular or unique aspects of any phenomenon. Windelband further argued:

> The kinds of knowledge generated by the natural and the social sciences were different because they were looking at two different levels of reality. Whereas, the natural scientists were concerned with material objects and with describing the general laws that governed their origins and interactions, social and cultural scientists were concerned with the ethical realm of human action and culture. Although knowledge of natural phenomena could be achieved directly through observation and experimentation, knowledge of human motivation, of norms and patterns of conduct, and of social and cultural values, necessarily had to be based on a more abstract process of theoretical reasoning. You can only infer that somebody is in love; you cannot actually see 'love'.
>
> *(ibid.)*

Another German philosopher, Heinrich Rickert, too emphasised on the association of social phenomena with values. Rickert also strongly influenced Weber's views on the matter. Rickert argued that the natural sciences are 'sciences of fact' and so questions of value were necessarily excluded from the analysis. The social sciences, in contrast, are 'sciences of value' because they are specifically concerned with understanding why social actors choose to act in the ways that they do (ibid.). Hence, Rickert argued that, while it is appropriate to disregard questions of value when studying the physical or chemical properties of things, it is certainly not appropriate to do so when studying human social action and its consequences. For example, it is relatively easy to show what the properties of carbon are, where it comes from and what will happen if you combine it with some other material. What you never need to do is explain how carbon atoms *feel* about any of these things (ibid.).

Weber, thus, analysed the theoretical and methodological arguments of positivists, neo-Kantians and Marxism. Weber partly accepted and partly rejected all the three major theoretical orientations. For example, he accepted positivists' argument for the scientific study of social phenomena and appreciated the need for arriving at generalisations if sociology has to be a social science. But he criticised positivists for not taking into account the unique meanings and motives of the social actors into consideration. Further, he argued that sociology, given the variable nature of the social phenomena, could only aspire for *limited generalisations* (which he called 'thesis'), not universal generalisations as advocated by positivists.

Similarly, Weber appreciated the neo-Kantians for taking cognisance of the subjective meanings and motives of the social actors in order to better understand the social reality, but also stressed the need for building generalisations in social sciences. Weber, agreeing with the neo-Kantians, believed that human beings respond to their environment in a meaningful way and, therefore, human behaviour has to be understood in the context of the underlying meanings. Therefore, Weber argued that to build the strategies of social research on the methods of natural sciences alone would be a serious mistake. The methodology of social sciences should focus on understanding the human behaviour. According to Weber, the cognitive aim of social sciences is to understand the human behaviour. A sociological explanation should therefore be meaningfully as well as causally adequate. Please note that the causal explanations are used in all sciences. Social sciences should also use causal explanations but besides the causal explanation, the explanation in social sciences should be adequate at the level of meanings as well. That is how the cognitive aim of social sciences goes beyond that of the natural sciences.

However, Weber criticised the neo-Kantians' proposition that generalisations are not possible in social sciences. Weber argued that all sciences, whether natural or social, begin with the study of a particular phenomenon and try to arrive at some generalisation. Though Weber admitted that social sciences may not attain as much success in arriving at generalisations as natural sciences because the ability to discover generalisations is dependent upon the degree to which there is a pattern in the reality. So, given the variable nature of the social phenomena, social sciences could only aspire for limited generalisations. He further argued that generalisations arrived in social sciences would not have the same exactitude as of those in natural sciences. Such generalisations would merely be indicative of a trend or tendency. Weber argued that we may call such limited generalisations as 'thesis' rather than the 'theory'.

Weber also partly accepted Marx's views on class conflict (role of economic factors) in society, but argued that there could be other dimensions of the conflict as well, such as status, power, etc. Further, Weber was also sceptical about the inevitability of revolution as forecasted by Marx. Weber accepted the Marxian logic of explaining conflict and change in terms of interplay of economic forces, but at the same time criticised Marxian theory as mono-causal economic determinism. According to Weber, the social phenomenon is far too complex to be explained adequately in terms of a single cause. Hence, Weber argued that the social science methodology should be based on the principle of *causal pluralism*. Please note that Weber was not rejecting the Marxian theory but rather supplementing it. Weber agreed with Marx that economic factors do have a profound influence on social life. But he considered economic factor as only one of the factors that influence social life.

To summarise, Weber is regarded to have been influenced by 'neo-Kantian' ideas in his perception of the nature of social life. According to him, the behaviour of man in society is qualitatively different from that of physical objects and biological organisms. What accounts for these differences is the presence of meanings and motives which underlie the social behaviour of man. Thus, any study of human behaviour in society must take cognisance of these meanings to understand this behaviour. The cognitive aims or objectives of sociological studies are, therefore, different from those of positive sciences. While positive sciences seek to discover the underlying patterns of interactions between various aspects of physical and natural phenomena, the social sciences seek to understand the meanings and motives to explain the social phenomena. Hence, positive science methods alone would prove inadequate to study the social behaviour. Weber, however, was not opposed to building generalisation in social sciences, but he pointed out that given the variable nature of social phenomena, only limited generalisation can be made.

Commenting upon the theoretical and methodological contributions of Weber, Paul Ransome states:

> Weber tended to deal with the more conceptual challenges of social theory on a need-to-know basis. In this sense, Weber was more interested in getting on with studying actual things than in devoting time either to establishing an entire account of historical development, as Marx had done, or to developing a set of principles for turning the study of social phenomena into a proper science, in the manner of Auguste Comte and Emile Durkheim. This approach accounts for why there is no unifying theme in Weber's work, no overall framework into which each of his concepts and ideas can be fitted.
>
> *(ibid.)*

Social Action

Weber conceived of sociology as a comprehensive science of 'social action' which constitutes the basic unit of social life. In consonance with his general perception of the nature of social reality, he defined social action as '*the meaningful behaviour oriented towards other individuals*'. The presence of meaning as well as other individuals is equally important for any behaviour to qualify as social action. For

Weber, the combined qualities of 'action' and 'meaning' were the 'central facts' for sociology's scientific analysis. Weber defined sociology as 'a science which attempts the interpretive understanding of social action in order thereby to arrive at a causal explanation of its course and effects'. The technical category of 'action' described in Weber's work is all human behaviour to which an actor attaches subjective meaning. 'Action is social', explains Weber, 'in so far as, by virtue of the subjective meaning attached to it by the acting individual, it takes account of the behaviour of others and is thereby oriented in its course'. However, an isolated social act does not exist in real social life. Only at the analytical level can one conceptualise an isolated social act. What exists in reality is an ongoing chain of reciprocal social actions, which we call social interaction.

Thus, according to Weber, sociology is a science concerning itself with the interpretive understanding of social action. For Weber, social action is the basic unit of social life and hence the subject matter of sociology. This logically follows from his basic assumption that individuals are cultural beings but have an ability to take a deliberate stand of their own. Therefore, individuals are capable of attributing a subjective meaning to their behaviour. Thus, as a sociologist, one must look at human behaviour as social action. As stated earlier, there are two elements of social action: *presence of meaning* and *orientation towards others*. In the absence of assigned 'meanings' by the individuals, the actions are meaningless and thus outside the purview of sociology. Similarly, the actions which are not oriented towards others are also outside the purview of sociology.

Social action, for Weber, is a meaningful action. Since such meanings attributed by actors to their respective actions could be infinite, this leads us to deduce that social reality is infinitely complex. Now, since meanings are the fundamental character of social action, if the nature of meanings changes, the type of social action also undergoes change. Thus, based on the nature of meanings, Weber constructed a classificatory typology of social action. However, he cautioned that this classificatory typology is only for the purpose of analysis. Though it is rooted in reality, it does not mirror the reality. He based his classification of social action on the pure types of meanings, although such pure types of meanings are never found in reality. Weber argued that since social reality is infinitely complex, there is an infinite variety of meanings that can exist in social life. However, according to Weber, all these meanings can be analytically reduced to four pure types of meanings, though these four pure types of meanings are not found in reality. In other words, in reality, any given social action reflects a combination of two or more pure types of meanings.

Thus, based on these four pure types of meanings, there are four pure types of social actions. Weber classified social action into the following four major types on the basis of the nature of meaning involved:

1. **Goal-Rational Action (Zweckrational Action)**: The actor determines the practical goal (rational, specific and quantifiable) and chooses his means purely in terms of their efficiency to attain the goal. Please note that in

reality there is no pure goal-rational action. But the meaning involved in action tends to be predominantly goal-rational.

2. **Value-Rational Action (Wertrational Action)**: Value-rational action is the one where the means are chosen for their efficiency but the goals are determined by value. The action of a captain who goes down with the sinking ship or that of a soldier who allows himself to be killed rather than yield in a war are examples of such action.

3. **Affective or Emotional Action**: In certain situations, the sole meaning involved in people's behaviour is to give expression to their emotional state. Here emotion or impulse determines the ends and means of action. Such an action is termed as affective or emotional action. For example, the case of a mother who hugs her child or a punch by a bike rider to another motorist in an act of road rage, etc.

4. **Traditional Action**: Traditional actions are those where both ends and means are determined by custom. Here, the meaning involved is that of maintaining a continuity of the tradition. Rituals, ceremonies and practices of tradition fall in this category (Abraham and Morgan, 2010).

Verstehen

After having discussed Weber's perspective and subject matter, let us now move on to his methodology. As stated earlier, the aim of sociology, according to Weber, is different from those of natural sciences. Natural sciences are primarily interested in search for the underlying patterns or laws governing the physical matter. Sociology, on the other hand, seeks to understand social behaviour in terms of meanings and motives, though sociology also attempts to arrive at limited generalisations. Therefore, social sciences cannot rely on positive science methods alone. According to Weber, since the cognitive aim of sociology is to understand human behaviour, a sociological explanation should be adequate both at the level of meanings and at the level of causality. Therefore, Weber suggests *Verstehen* method for sociological enquiry. This expression is taken from Dilthey, but Weber used it in a somewhat different sense. The *Verstehen* approach is usually translated as 'interpretive understanding'.

According to Weber, the *Verstehen* method involves the interpretive understanding of social action through empathetic liaison in order to build a sequence of motives to trace the course and effect of social action. In other words, the researcher adopting this method seeks to understand social action at the 'level of meanings' and then tries to build a sequence of motives which underlie the social action. Thus, a sociological explanation becomes adequate both at the level of meanings and at the level of causality.

According to Weber, the *Verstehen* method involves two steps:

1. direct observational understanding
2. explanatory understanding

The first step involved in the *Verstehen* method is 'direct observational under-standing' of the obvious subjective meanings of actor's behaviour. At this stage, the social scientist looks at the social phenomenon from outside and attributes natural meanings to what he observes. Observational understanding is obtained directly, either because one knows the rules for a certain behaviour (in church, for example) or by empathy when someone expresses his feelings. We under-stand most every day events in this intuitive manner. For example, from facial expressions and gestures we can often have direct observational understanding of an angry outburst. Explanatory understanding is achieved when we understand what prompted the outburst at that precise time and place (Adams and Sydie, 2016). Similarly, through direct observation, we can know the meanings of an obviously hungry man or a man aiming a gun at an animal. We can grasp these meanings because we are aware of the subjective intentions which we attach to our like actions.

The second step involves establishing an empathetic liaison with the actor. Here, the observer identifies himself with the actor by imaginatively placing himself in the actor's situation and then tries to interpret the likely meanings which the actor might have had given to the situation and the consequent motives which would have given rise to the action. We gain an explanatory understanding when we know the motives behind a person's actions. In this case, the action is explained precisely by the intent behind it: what the person wanted to achieve with the action. It is this type of explanatory understand-ing that science should work with, according to Weber. In order to trace the course and effect of social action, the sociologists should try to build a sequence of motives linking one with the other and finally linking them to the effect or consequences of social action. Weber wanted the interpretation of social action to be adequate, both at the level of meanings and at the level of causality. An interpretation of a sequence of events is causally adequate, if careful observa-tions lead to the generalisation that it is probable that the sequence will always occur in the same way. Such a generalisation should be derived statistically, as far as possible.

For example, when we observe a person riding a bicycle, how can we under-stand this behaviour? Paul Ransome has illustrated this process beautifully in the following manner:

> Adopting the techniques of a natural scientist, we can measure how fast he is going, in what direction, how often he changed gear. We can say how tall or heavy he is, what the conditions are like and what kinds of materi-als the bike is made from. What we cannot determine just by looking at the cyclist, however, is *why* he is cycling. For this we need to adopt the approach of the social scientist, going beyond bare description in order to develop theories of action and motivation. Is the cyclist peddling quickly because he is late for a lecture in social theory or because he is trying to improve his fitness? Is he getting pleasure from cycling voluntarily, or is

he having to do so because somebody has stolen his car? The full picture of cycling requires more than observation; it also requires interpretation.

(Ransome, 2011)

However, according to some sociologists, it is not clear as to what Weber really meant when he wished to reconcile the interpretation of action by the *Verstehen* with the causal explanation. Interpreters of Weber have variously suggested that *Verstehen* merely generates causal hypotheses of meanings that can function as causes. The use of *Verstehen* has been criticised severely on the ground that there is no way of validating *Verstehen* interpretations. However, the advantage of *Verstehen* lies in the fact that it can be applied with equal ease to study contemporary social phenomena as well as to study the past historical phenomena. As Weber states, 'One does not have to be a Caesar to know Caesar'. According to some scholars, Weber's approach to the study of the social world represented an attempt to reconcile the differences between those who advocated large-scale research at the macro level and those who advocated small-scale research at the micro level. Weber believed that it was possible to make use of both general principles and individual enquiry. He saw this combination as working best when general concepts were developed and used to enhance the understanding of individual empirical events (Churton and Brown, 2017). However, as Thomas Burger argued, Weber was neither very sophisticated not very consistent in his methodological pronouncements because he felt that he was simply repeating ideas that were well known in his day among German historians (*hermeneutic* tradition). Hermeneutics was a special approach to the understanding and interpretation of published writings. The primary objective of this approach was to understand the thinking of the author as well as the basic structure of the text. Weber and others (for example, Wilhelm Dilthey) sought to extend this idea from the understanding of texts to the understanding of social life (Ritzer and Stepnisky, 2014).

Though *Verstehen* is probably the most widely known concept of Weber, it also happens to be the most misinterpreted one. As mentioned earlier, the *Verstehen* approach is usually translated as 'interpretive understanding'. This approach was used by Weber to refer to the sociologist's ability to understand the social phenomena under study. However, Weber's application of the concept has led to some confusion. Some scholars argue that it is uncertain that whether *Verstehen* is aimed at the individual level (that is, understanding the meanings individuals give to social phenomena and the influence of these meanings on their actions) or whether it is a technique to understand culture, particularly 'the socially constructed rules which define the meaning of action in a given society'. The application of *Verstehen* at the individual level, that is, to understand the unique meanings and motives of individuals in a given social interaction situation, would be similar to social action approaches, particularly micro-sociological approaches like symbolic interactionism. On the other hand, the application of *Verstehen* to understand cultural meanings in a given society would be akin to structural approaches. It is now considered that both interpretations of the term *Verstehen* could be equally valid (Churton and Brown, 2017).

It is worth mentioning here that Weber's perspective towards social reality, his definition of subject matter of sociology and the methodology that he advocated for sociological research were fundamentally different from those of positivists. While positivism was based on the basic premise of 'methodological dualism', Weberianism is based on 'methodological individualism'. Despite the usefulness of general concepts, Weber argued, social theory should also remain sensitive to variations at the micro level of analysis. Weber emphasised on the study of subjective and voluntaristic aspect of the social action. In other words, according to Weber, the sociologist must try to include in his analysis an account of social phenomena as they appear to social actors themselves (Ransome, 2011). Yet another common misconception about *Verstehen* is that it is simply the use of 'intuition' by the researcher. As a result, many critics see it as a 'soft', irrational, subjective research methodology. Weber, however, categorically rejected the idea that *Verstehen* involved simply intuition or empathy. Rather, to Weber, *Verstehen* involved doing systematic and rigorous research. In other words, for Weber, *Verstehen* was a rational procedure of sociological research (Ritzer and Stepnisky, 2014).

Value Neutrality

Fact and value have been at the centre of methodological debates in sociology right from the time of its origin. The word fact derives from the Latin *factum*. A fact is something that has really occurred or is actually the case. The usual test for a statement of fact is its verifiability, that is, whether it can be proven to correspond to experience. Scientific facts are verified by repeatable experiments. Thus, a fact is regarded as an empirically verifiable observation. Values, on the other hand, are socially accepted standards of desirability. In other words, a value is a belief that something is good and desirable. It defines what is important and worthwhile. Values are subjective and hence differ from society to society and culture to culture. This, however, is the general or literal meaning of values.

In sociological literature, the role of values has largely been discussed and debated in terms of their influence on objectivity of social science research. Thus, on the one hand, we have those sociologists who emphasised on the study of only facts in sociological enquiry in order to make it scientific. These sociologists outrightly eliminated the study of subjective values from the subject matter of sociology because of their apprehension that it might compromise the scientific character of their discipline. Such scholars, like the early founding fathers of sociology, be it Comte, Spencer or Durkheim, advocated a positivist approach to study society. That is, they emphasised on the study of only those aspects of social reality which could be empirically observed and hence quantified. Anti-positivist scholars, on the other hand, argued that the subject matter of sociology is the study of human behaviour in society and all human behaviour is guided by values. Hence, these scholars, such as Weber, Mead, etc. suggested social action approach to study society. Social action theorists emphasised on the subjective interpretation of social action and hence argued that positivist methods alone would be inadequate to comprehensively understand social reality. Thus, they emphasised on the use of qualitative methods along with the use of quantitative methods in social science research. Thus, for Weber, social science is value-relevant.

According to some scholars, Weber's stance on the place of values in social research is ambiguous. Weber did believe in the ability to separate fact from value. Weber stated that 'Investigator and teacher should keep unconditionally separate the establishment of empirical facts ... and *his* own personal evaluations, i.e. his evaluation of these facts as satisfactory or unsatisfactory' (Ritzer and Stepnisky, 2014). Weber often differentiated between 'existential knowledge', that is, knowledge of what 'is', and 'normative knowledge', that is, what 'should be'. Every person has his values and the choice of these values is always subjective. Consequently, science can never state an opinion on 'true' values, but must rather limit itself to analysing the effects of various actions. But it can never say what action should be chosen. Science can speak only of facts, never of values.

Since social scientist is a cultural being, Weber cautions the social scientist from using his prestige and knowledge to assert his own values at the expense of others during the course of his research. In other words, Weber implies that since social action is a meaningful action guided by subjective meanings and values of social actors, the social scientist must attempt to understand social action from the subjective point of view of social actors. That is, their social behaviour should be understood in terms of their subjective meanings and values. Doing so, however, Weber argues that the researcher must ensure that his own personal biases, prejudices or cultural values do not contaminate his findings. This view of Weber is also sometimes referred to as *value freedom* in social research. Stated simply, value freedom in social research refers to the ability of the researcher to keep his or her own values (personal, political and religious) from interfering with the research process. Thus, in order to maintain objectivity in social research, Weber insisted on exclusion of values from the actual collection of data and suggested the employment of regular procedures of scientific investigation, such as accurate observation and systematic comparison. Hence, according to Weber, while social science is value-relevant, it must also be value-neutral.

Weber's ideas on the role of values prior to the commencement of social research are captured in his concept of *value relevance*. According to Weber, social and historical reality consists of manifold actions and interests. Given the meaningfulness of social action, the assumption of Weber that social reality is infinitely complex was natural. So, Weber argued that when the investigator studies this 'chaos of facts', he does so from certain points of view. Weber admits that the statement of the problem and the selection of facts the researcher makes are always related, consciously or unconsciously, to 'cultural values'. He studies what is important for him to study. In historical research, this would mean that the choice of objects to study would be made on the basis of what is considered important in the particular society in which researchers live. Thus, according to Weber, there can never be any objective scientific analysis of cultural life, since the investigator always ascribes cultural significance to the phenomena he studies. Weber goes on to state that even the so-called attempts to write an objective history are also based on certain cultural values. The problem, then, is that this also opens the door for various other kinds of value judgements. It is worth mentioning here that although Weber was opposed to confusing fact and value, he did not believe that values should be excised from social sciences. Weber stated that the researchers should be value-frank. In other words, when expressing value positions, the researchers must always keep themselves and their audiences aware of those positions.

According to some scholars, there is a gap between what Weber said and what he actually did. Weber was not afraid to express a value judgement, even in the midst of the analysis of historical data. For example, Gary Abraham has stated that though Weber did believe in the possibility of separating fact from value in social science research, his own work *The Protestant Ethic and the Spirit of Capitalism*, especially his views on Judaism as a world religion, was distorted by his values. Abraham argues:

> In his sociology of religion, Weber termed the Jews 'pariah people'. Weber traced this position of outsider more to the desire of Jews to segregate themselves than to their exclusion by the rest of society. Thus Weber, accepting the general view of the day, argued that Jews would need to sur-render Judaism in order to be assimilated into German society. Abraham argues that this sort of bias affected not only Weber's ideas on Judaism, but his work in general. This casts further doubt on Weber as a 'value-free' sociologist, as well as on the conventional view of Weber as a lib-eral thinker. ... Max Weber was probably as close to tolerant liberalism as majority Germany could offer at the time.
>
> *(ibid.)*

Another scholar, G. Roth, also argued that Weber was more of a nationalist supporting the assimilation of minority groups than he was a classical liberal favouring pluralism, and those values had a profound effect on his work. These views indicate the degree of difficulty in separating fact from value in social sci-ence research.

To summarise, according to Weber, while social science is value-relevant, it must also be value-neutral. Weber admitted that at the level of techni-cal competence, values are unavoidable. For example, the very choice of the topic of research is influenced by the values of the researcher. However still, the researcher must try to check his ideological assumptions from influencing his research. Further, the researcher should not pass any value judgements on the finding of his research. In other words, the researcher should remain indifferent to the moral implications of his research. Further, in order to ensure objectivity and value neutrality in sociological research, Weber suggested that the researcher should make his value preference clear in the research monograph. In other words, the researcher should be value-frank.

Ideal Type

To solve the problem of the relationship of science to values and the value neutrality of science, Weber developed his *ideal-type* methodology. An ideal type, at its most basic level, is a concept constructed by a social scientist on the basis of his interests and theoretical orientation to capture the essential features of some social phenomenon. Weber states that social reality by its very nature is infinitely complex and cannot be comprehended in its totality by the human mind. Therefore, selectivity is unavoidable and in order to exercise selectivity, sociologists should build ideal type of a given social phenomenon. This also implies that *Verstehen* cannot be applied directly to social reality. The social scientist must first build the ideal type and then apply *Verstehen* method to the ideal type. According to Weber:

> An ideal type is formed by the one-sided *accentuation* of one or more points of view and by the synthesis of a great many diffuse, discrete, more or less present and occasionally absent *concrete individual* phenomena, which are arranged according to those one-sidedly emphasized viewpoints into a unified *analytical* construct. ... In its conceptual purity, this mental construct ... cannot be found empirically anywhere in reality.
>
> *(Ritzer and Stepnisky, 2014)*

According to Weber, the most important thing about ideal types is that they are heuristic devices or conceptual tools. They are useful and helpful in doing empirical research and in understanding a specific aspect of the social world. Weber states that the function of ideal type is that it facilitates comparison with empirical reality in order to establish its divergences or similarities. Further, it enables an understanding of these divergences or similarities and helps explain them causally.

> Although social theorists are always faced with the dilemma that there is a reality gap between the ideas and concepts they use and the really real world 'out there', which they hope to explain by using them, Weber suggested that this could sometimes be turned into an advantage. Given that we are free to make up whatever concepts we like, it might be useful for social theorists to develop concepts that represent the purest form, or 'ideal type', of a particular phenomenon. Although there is no expectation that any particular instance of that phenomenon can match the ideal type, it nonetheless provides a useful intellectual tool for thinking about what the most essential or typical characteristics of a particular event or action might

be. For example, in making sociological comparisons between different types of family in a particular society it can be useful to refer to different general types of family rather than attempting the impossible task of describing each and every family individually. Sociologists have developed the ideal-typical descriptions of 'nuclear family' and 'extended family' as part of their methodology. Ideal types provide a way of conceptualising differences even if the ideal type is never observed in its pure form. Weber uses the technique of ideal type in his own analysis of social action, religious ideology, and authority, in particular, bureaucracy.

(Ransome, 2011)

In simpler words, an ideal type is a mental construct – a mental picture – that the investigator uses to approach the complex reality. An ideal type is an analytical construct that serves the investigator as 'a measuring rod' or 'yardstick' to ascertain similarities as well as deviations in concrete cases. It is neither a statistical average nor a hypothesis; rather it is a mental construct, an organization of intelligible relations within a historical entity, formed by exaggerating certain essential features of a given phenomenon so that no one case of that phenomenon corresponds exactly to the constructed type, but every case of that phenomenon falls within the definitional framework. Thus, an ideal type is never an accurate representation of the real thing. For example, as constructed by Weber, the ideal type of capitalism did not fully describe any of the various types of capitalism – mercantile capitalism, entrepreneurial capitalism (characteristic of the eighteenth and nineteenth centuries), matured industrial capitalism, etc. From the point of view of his study, only some of the features of early entrepreneurial capitalism were relevant which depicted the spirit of capitalism. Therefore, Weber isolated these elements and ideally represented these elements alone. Now these elements were not necessarily present in the later forms of capitalism, especially in mature industrial capitalism and finance capitalism. Thus, ideal types do not and cannot mirror the reality faithfully.

The ideal type, as Weber understood, had nothing to do with moral ideal, for the type of perfection implied in the ideal is purely a logical one and not to be found in pure form in any socio-historical situation. Any social phenomenon has an ideal type, be it a brothel, a house of worship or a marketplace. For Weber, an ideal type is strictly a 'methodological device'. The ideal type is a rational grid for logical observation and analysis. In other words, an ideal type is a rational construction for the purpose of research.

Weber uses his ideal-type methodology in part to reject the idea that science can capture reality 'as it is objectively'. As a neo-Kantian, Weber believed that concepts (ideal types) are always creations of human reason that never have a counterpart in reality. This also applies to the 'laws' investigators believe they find in social reality. For example, when Weber discusses Marx, he says the laws Marx and the Marxists thought they had found in history and in bourgeois society were actually nothing but ideal types. As ideal types, they have a very important significance if they are used in a comparison with reality, but according to

Weber they are actually dangerous if we believe they are empirically valid or express actual forces in reality.

Some of the important characteristics and uses of the ideal type are as follows:

1. Ideal type is a one-sided view of social reality which takes into account certain aspects of social life while ignoring others. Which aspects are to be given importance to, and which are to be ignored depends upon the object of study. Thus, an ideal type is a way of exercising selectivity.
2. Ideal-type formulation also helps in the developing the classificatory typology of the social phenomenon, thus facilitating a comprehensive understanding of the infinite social reality. For example, Weber developed classificatory typologies of social action, religious ideology and authority.
3. Ideal type can also help in establishing logical interconnections between different social constellations. For example, Weber in his work, *The Protestant Ethic and the Spirit of Capitalism*, builds ideal types of *the protestant ethic* and *the spirit of capitalism* and establishes the relationship between the two.
4. Ideal type also serves the investigator as a measuring rod to ascertain similarities as well as deviations in concrete cases, thus being helpful in comparison with reality.
5. Ideal type also has a limited utility as a source of prediction. As discussed earlier, Weber argues that the laws Marx and the Marxists thought they had found in history and in bourgeois society were actually nothing but ideal types. As ideal types, they have a very important significance if they are used in a comparison with reality.
6. Further, although ideal type is rooted in reality, it does not represent reality in totality. It is a mental construct. Weber claims that ideal type is a social science equivalent of experimentation in physical and natural sciences. Experimentation is an essential element of scientific method to check the validity and reliability of the research findings in natural sciences. Since due to moral and ethical reasons, experimentation is not possible in social sciences which are involved in the study of human behaviour, the ideal type can serve as an equivalent of experimentation in social sciences. As experimentation is conducted under controlled conditions, likewise an ideal type is also a rational construction based on selectivity.

Thus, according to Weber, the methodology of sociology consists in building ideal types of social behaviour and applying *Verstehen* method to explain this. Weber's thesis in *The Protestant Ethic and the Spirit of Capitalism* is a very good example of the application of this methodology.

Another important element of Weber's methodology is *causal pluralism*. According to Weber, the social reality is extremely complex and, therefore, no social phenomena can be explained adequately in terms of a single cause. An adequate sociological explanation must, therefore, be based on the principle of causal pluralism.

Rationalisation

In sociological literature, it has become standard procedure to compare Weber's explanation of the emergence of modern industrial capitalist society with Marx's account. It is worth noting that Weber was only familiar with a portion of Marx's work. Weber was, however, unhappy about the historical-materialist account for a number of reasons. First, Weber argued that it was highly unlikely that history develops according to any kind of grand plan, let alone the one that Marx describes. Second, Weber disagreed with Marx's historical-materialist perspective which gave too much attention to the economic realm, and thus, underestimated what goes on in other aspects of social life. Weber believed that in trying to understand the origins of modern capitalism, it is necessary to look at developments in the political, legal and religious sphere as well as in the economic sphere. Though Weber accepts the very great significance and influence of the economic sphere, he does not see this as causative of all other phenomena in the way that Marx does (Ransome, 2011).

While Weber agreed with Marx that modern capitalism had become the dominant characteristic of modern industrial society, he disagreed with Marx over the explanation of the emergence of capitalism. For Weber, the originating cause, the fundamental root of this development, was not 'men making history' or 'the class struggle' but the emergence of a new approach to life based around a new kind of rational outlook. Weber believed that this new rationality had its roots in the various intellectual currents that emerged during the European Enlightenment.

> The main intention of the new rationality was to replace vagueness and speculation with precision and calculation. This was a profoundly practical kind of rationality in which social actors no longer behaved spontaneously or emotionally but only after making a careful consideration of the various alternatives available to them. The new rationality took the Enlightenment idea that people could control their own destiny and turned it into a strategy for action. It was all about controlling the outcomes of action, of eliminating fate and chance, through the application of reason. Weber called the new outlook instrumental rationality because it took the degree to which it enabled social actors to achieve the ends they had identified as its main criteria for judging whether an action was or was not rational. A characteristic of modern society is that actions are defined as rational as long as they are effective in achieving particular ends. The new instrumental rationality was also a 'universal rationality' in the sense that it affected the way in which decisions to act were made, not just in economic affairs, but across the full spectrum of activity. Weber argued that instrumental rationality had become a foundation for a new and highly rationalistic way of life or world view.
>
> *(ibid.)*

For Weber, modern society is modern because it has undergone this process of rationalisation. Although Weber partly agreed with Marx about the role of economic factors in the overall social change, he argued that the development of capitalism was itself a consequence and not a cause of the spread of the new instrumental rationality. Weber further argued that instrumental rationality was not confined to the economic sphere alone but also affected the social, political, legal and bureaucratic systems of modern society, for example, the development of democratic systems for electing governments, the rationalisation of government into different departments and the increasing use of bureaucracy as the most instrumentally rational way of organising complex organisations. The legal and medical professions, universities and research institutions and so on are all similarly drawn under the influence of instrumental rationality. According to Weber, the uptake of instrumental rationality through rationalisation can be seen to be a driving force behind all forms of modernisation in modern society. In Durkheim's terms, one might say that the instrumental rationality identified by Weber provides an important source of collective consciousness in modern society. Rationalisation and its consequences regulate the behaviour of social actor and thus contribute to a new social order (ibid.).

Rationalisation is the process whereby an increasing number of social actions and social relationships become based on considerations of efficiency or calculation. It is the process of replacing traditional and emotional thought with reason. It refers to the process by which modern society has increasingly become concerned with efficiency, predictability and calculability. For Weber, modern society is modern because it has undergone this process of rationalisation. Rationality implies the quality of being reasonable, based on facts or reason. According to Weber, instrumental rationality is the characteristic feature of modern society. In this context, an action is said to be rational when the means are chosen purely in terms of their efficiency in achieving the desired goal. There is a tendency to assume that in describing the new instrumental rationality, Weber somehow approves of it and of its effects on social life. This is partly unavoidable, precisely because Weber goes to great lengths not to offer his own opinion (he would regard this as a serious transgression of the principle of value neutrality discussed earlier). Nor does he wish to offer any suggestions about how things could be organised differently (although he is generally critical of the socialist alternative as he thinks the mode of bureaucratised social organisation it envisages would restrict individual freedom).

While discussing about instrumental rationality, Weber highlights the qualitative dimensions of instrumental rationality. This concerns the distinction between formal rationality and substantive rationality. In simpler terms, formal rationality is based on the efficiency of means in achieving the goals. It is based on technical orientation. It eliminates an orientation to values because they are non-technical. It is rule-centric, and rules are based on their efficiency in achieving the organisational goals. It is universal in its orientation because it affects all aspects of social life be it economic, political, legal, bureaucratic, etc. Substantive rationality, on the other hand, is based on making choices between right and wrong on the basis of subjective values of a given society. Actions are selectively chosen in the light of such values or morality. Thus, substantive rationality is not universal, instead it is contextual. The socio-economic and political context varies from society to society and so varies the priorities of different social systems. Further, it is relational and thus, it is people-centric. In other words, basic human values such as freedom, liberty, social justice, etc. constitute the core of substantive rationality.

In other words, Weber makes an important distinction between the rationality of something in terms of *how useful it is in a purely practical sense* (its formal rationality) and *how rational it is in terms of the ends it serves* (its substantive rationality). For example, mechanised farming is a more technically efficient, a more rational way of agricultural production than feudal agriculture. But what is less clear is that whether such farming, particularly in the Third World societies which have a very high proportion of population dependent on agriculture, would be an appropriate choice. There are chances that along with increase in agricultural production, unemployment rate in agricultural sector would also increase with the application of mechanised farming in Third World societies. For the improvement in the general quality of life of people in such societies, there is need for a mix of both mechanised or capital-intensive technology and labour-intensive technology for agricultural production. Just because social actors make sensible choices between the various techniques for doing something, this does not necessarily help us decide if the ends they want to achieve are, in a more substantive sense, also rational. For example, the atomic bomb is the most effective means of mass destruction, but mass destruction is hardly a rational objective.

In general, Weber regrets the loss of high ideals and of meaning in existence that resulted from rationalisation. The paradox and tragedy of our time is that rationalisation has taught people to master nature, to develop technology for producing the means of survival at mass scale and to create administrative bureaucratic systems for regulating social life, while the existential basis of life – the choice of values and ideals and the search for meaning beyond soulless calculation of effective means for achieving a certain goal – is disappearing more and more. According to Weber, modern man is trapped in a rational 'iron cage of commodities and regulations' and he has lost his humanity. At the same time, modern man believes he has achieved the highest stage of development.

The Protestant Ethic and the Spirit of Capitalism

Weber, along with his influential contributions to the theoretical and methodological issues in the social sciences, is also well known for his analysis of rationality and social action. However, Weber's reputation as a major social theorist rests heavily on the two extended essays he published under this title in 1904 and 1905. In these essays, later published as a book, Weber sought to demonstrate that economic factors do not represent a constant and independent variable to which all others stand in dependence. In Weber's view, treating the economic factor as the most important and determining factor was Marx's major weakness and ultimate failure. Weber spent his best and most critical years demonstrating with careful precision that essentially the economic factor, though an important one, is only one of the variables responsible for shaping social structure and triggering social change. Weber instead argued that there exists a two-way relationship between the economic infrastructure and the superstructure. Thus, certain aspects of the superstructure such as religious beliefs, charismatic leadership, education, law, etc. can also influence and change the economic infrastructure.

For instance, Max Weber in his study *The Protestant Ethic and the Spirit of Capitalism* argued that religious beliefs provided the ethics, attitudes and motivations for the development of capitalism. Since ascetic Protestantism preceded the advent of capitalism, Weber maintained that at certain times and places, aspects of the superstructure can play a primary role in directing change. Weber believed that one potential weakness of the Marxist approach is its tendency to underplay the role of ideas, values and beliefs as a motivator of social action. According to Weber, capitalism in Northern Europe evolved when the Protestant (particularly Calvinist) ethic influenced large numbers of people to engage in work in the secular world, developing their own enterprises and engaging in trade and accumulation of wealth for investment. In other words, the Protestant work ethic was an important force behind the unplanned and uncoordinated emergence of modern capitalism. In 1998, the *International Sociological Association* listed *The Protestant Ethic and the Spirit of Capitalism* as the fourth most important sociological book of the twentieth century.

As mentioned earlier, while Weber agreed with Marx that modern capitalism had become the dominant characteristic of modern industrial society, he disagreed with Marx over the explanation of the emergence of capitalism. According to Weber, the originating cause, the fundamental root of this development, was not 'men making history' or 'the class struggle' but the emergence of a new approach to life based around a new kind of rational outlook.

> In the last analysis, the factor which produces capitalism is the rational permanent enterprise with its rational accounting, rational technology and rational law, [complemented by] the rational spirit, the rationalization of the conduct of life in general and a rationalistic economic ethic.
>
> *(Max Weber,* The Protestant Ethic and the Spirit of Capitalism, *1904–1905)*

Weber also rejected Engel's view that Protestantism rose in Europe as a legitimising ideology to nascent capitalism which had already come into existence. Instead, he emphasised the role of ideas as an independent source of change. Refuting Engel's argument, he further states that capitalism existed in an embryo in Babylon, Roman, Chinese and Indian societies, and in China and India other material conditions propitious for the development of capitalism also existed at certain stages in their history. But nowhere did it lead to the development of modern capitalism. This phenomenon is peculiar to Western society alone. The question arises as to why these embryos developed into the modern form of capitalism only in the West and nowhere else. An explanation in terms of the internal dynamics of economic forces alone is unable to account for this peculiarity. It is necessary to take into account specific ethos of the early European capitalistic entrepreneurs and realise that this was precisely what was absent in other civilisations.

In his sociology of religion, Weber used his ideal types to try to answer his fundamental question: Why was it in Europe that capitalism had its breakthrough and later became a dominant force in the world? This question cannot be answered as the Marxists did, simply by pointing to the initial accumulation of capital and the creation of a 'free' class of wage labourers. Even though these institutional factors were important to the origin of capitalism, they do not explain why certain people in history began to act in a capitalist manner. According to Weber, Marxian view on the development of capitalism can at best be regarded as an ideal type construction highlighting the role of economic factor which contributed to the rise of capitalism. After all, according to Weber, any explanation of a historical phenomenon must be traced back to human social action and, thus, the investigator must try to gain an explanatory understanding of why certain people acted as they did, based on those people's own conditions. It was this that Weber attempted to do in his famous study on the connection between the Protestant ethic and the spirit of capitalism.

According to Weber, early capitalism emerged in a part of Europe that had also undergone a religious reformation. What meaningful link was there between Protestantism and the appearance of capitalism? Weber created two ideal types, the Protestant ethic and the spirit of capitalism, to examine this question. In his ideal type on the Protestant ethic, Weber dwells on the values and beliefs that arose within a particularly vigorous and ascetic variety of the Protestant faith, which developed in Northern Europe, and later in North America, during the sixteenth and seventeenth centuries. 'Asceticism' is an attitude of self-restraint, even self-denial, which imposes strict limits on the kind of enjoyment a person may take in the products of his or her work. For Weber, it was the historically fortunate coming together of this religious code of conduct or 'ethic', and the 'spirit' of the newly emerging and instrumentally oriented variety of capitalism, that launched rational capitalism into the modern world.

Weber argues that central to the Protestant faith is the idea that it is the individual and not the Church who carries responsibility for spiritual destiny (individual responsibility). The concept of individual conscience and individual responsibility was built around the idea of 'the calling' developed by the initiator of the Protestant faith, the German theologian Martin Luther (1483–1546). As Weber interprets it: 'The only way of living acceptably to God was through the fulfilment of the obligations imposed upon the individual by his position in the world. That was his calling'. However, this key principle was supplemented soon after by the idea of 'predestination', put forward in the teaching of another Protestant theologian John Calvin (1509–1564). Calvin in his doctrine of predestination argued that God has determined the fate of every man long before that man is born. In other words, in Calvin's view, God has already decided which people will gain salvation and which are condemned to eternal damnation. Those who had not been chosen were destined never to achieve spiritual salvation (Ransome, 2011).

> At first sight this position seems paradoxical. If spiritual salvation has been settled in advance then what is to be gained from pursuing earthly toil in a godly manner, why not simply lead a life of pleasure and idleness? Calvin, however, emphasized that precisely since there can be no certainty of salvation, individuals must prove their spiritual salvation by leading an exemplary life on earth. Moreover, this proof could not simply be demonstrated abstractly by believing in the possibility of salvation hereafter, but through concrete action in the present. Intense worldly activity, thus, became indispensable 'as a sign of election': '[It is] the technical means, not of purchasing salvation, but of getting rid of the fear of damnation'. Through frenetic devotion to one's calling, the individual is provided with a means of demonstrating how certain they are about being saved. Conveniently, 'the earning of money within the modern economic order is, so long as it is done legally, the result and the expression of virtue and proficiency in a calling'. Ascetic Protestantism, thus, unequivocally ties spiritual destiny to profoundly practical and energetic ethic of hard work.
>
> *(ibid.)*

Weber constructs the other ideal type, the spirit of capitalism, on the book *Advice to a Young Tradesman* written in 1748 by Benjamin Franklin (1706–1790). In this book, Franklin offers advice to those who would like to succeed in business. He believes they must remember that time is money, that credit is money and that money, with hard work, can produce more money. This focus on the multiplication of money is also linked to a call for a moral and ascetic life in which those who have provided credit would rather hear the sound of a hammer at five o'clock in the morning and then see the borrower at the pool table (Abrahamson, 2010).

According to Weber, irrespective of whether salvation is actually achieved through hard work, the practical outcome of the idea is that it might give rise to a work-obsessed class of entrepreneurs and business people whose earthly desire for commercial success runs parallel with their religious desire for spiritual salvation. Since the leisurely pursuit and wasteful expenditure of wealth is considered sinful, the only legitimate use for the increasing revenue is to reinvest it in the business itself. The pragmatic saving of capital is justified by the higher substantive aim of the saving of souls. For Weber, it is this coincidence within the Protestant ethic between obsessive hard work and an ascetic attitude towards the wealth it generates that lies at the heart of the causal relationship between Protestantism and capitalism (Ransome, 2011).

In his Protestant ethic thesis, Weber tries to provide a multidimensional explanation for the emergence of modern capitalism. Unlike Marx's historical–materialist account, which relies on the dialectical developments in the means and relations of production to predict the emergence of capitalism from feudalism, Weber's thesis gives the whole event a real sense of historical actuality. According to Weber, modern rational capitalism emerged because of the collision at a particular time and place of a particular set of real but unpredictable circumstances. Some of these circumstances were material ones (technical innovation, new commercial opportunities), but others came from the realm of ideas (Figure 8.1). Weber's explanation can be much more precise about the timing of the whole modern capitalist adventure (Northern Europe in the period 1650–1750), because the release of spare capital is tied to a specific coming together of commercial attitudes and the religious teaching of Luther and Calvin (ibid.).

Weber believes that even though the content of the two cultures, the Protestant ethic and the spirit of capitalism, were different and based on different assumptions, they lead to similar actions. Protestant action was value-rational action, that is, it attempted to live up to the value of being saved and to find signs of salvation. Capitalist action is purposive rational action, that is, it attempts to find effective means of achieving an end, the multiplication of money. To the Protestant, the ascetic life and diligence were part of a life lived in the glory of God and were not directed towards the multiplication of money. Despite this, however, it broke with what Weber calls the 'feudal spirit', which contained an irrational use of wealth in the form of a life of luxury. In order for capitalism to rise, this form of the luxurious use of wealth had to give way to an accumulation and reinvestment of accumulated money. The Protestant ethic played a key role in this transition. According to Weber, early modern capitalism was characterised by the institutionalisation of 'gain spirit' where the ethical and religious ideas regulated and provided legitimisation and justification of the pursuit of economic goals.

Asceticism, according to Weber, contributed to a rational moulding of every aspect of life. Constant control through a systematic effort resulted in a rationalisation of individual conduct even in the conduct of business. Thus, the adherents

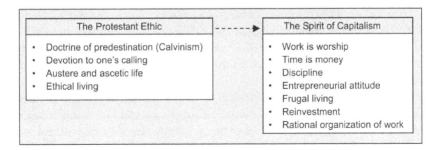

FIGURE 8.1 Ideal Type of the Protestant Ethic and the Spirit of Capitalism

to the Protestant ideology became adept in rationalising economic action while leading an austere and ascetic life. This entrepreneurial attitude, hard work, rational organisation of conduct and frugal living together constituted the spirit of capitalism, which according to Weber was fostered through the Protestant ethic. To avoid misunderstanding, Weber specified that the causal relation-ship between Protestantism and capitalism should not be taken in the sense of a mechanical relationship. Due to his belief in causal pluralism, Weber states that the Protestant ethos was some of the sources of rationalisation of life which helped to create what is known as the *spirit of capitalism*. It was not the sole cause, not even a sufficient cause of capitalism. Raymond Aron makes Weber's posi-tion clear when he writes, 'Protestantism is not the cause but one of the causes of capitalism or rather it is one of the causes of certain aspects of capitalism'.

Thus, Weber has clearly stated that only the spirit of capitalism was created by the Protestant ethos, while there were a number of other contributory fac-tors which along with the spirit of capitalism helped in the growth of capital-ism. Further, Weber made a comparative study of world religions in terms of their beliefs and practices and their repercussions on social life. Weber analysed Confucianism and Taoism in China, Hinduism and Buddhism in India and finally ancient Judaism. He also planned, but was unable to complete, studies on Islam, Talmudic Judaism, early Christianity and various religious sects within the Reformation. The studies Weber carried out deal with the various social conditions in which the different religions operated, the social stratification, the links of various groups to different religions and the importance of various reli-gious leaders.

With the help of comparative study, Weber built a typology of religions. He pointed out that religious activity can be classified into two categories:

1. asceticism
2. mysticism

Asceticism consists of the belief that God direct religious activity, so that the believer sees himself to be the instrument of the divine will. Therefore, the purpose of this life is not to waste it in luxuries and pleasures of flesh, rather one should lead a disciplined life to realise the glory of God.

Mysticism, on the other hand, consists of a consciousness not so much of being an instrument of God but of what Weber calls a *vassal* of God. Religious activ-ity, in this case, is a question of achieving a condition akin to the divine. This is accomplished by contemplation on truths than those which can be demonstrated in this world.

Next, according to Weber, asceticism can manifest itself in two forms – *inner worldly asceticism* and *other worldly asceticism*. Inner worldly asceticism is where individuals not only feel themselves to be the instrument of God's will, but seek to glorify God's name through performing good work in the world. Here success in this world itself becomes a sign of divine approval. Other worldly asceticism, on the other hand, is where the individuals renounce the world so that they may be of service to God alone, as in the case of monastic orders.

Here, Weber pointed out that only inner-worldly ascetic types of religious beliefs which make the believer treat day-to-day working as the calling of God will foster the spirit of capitalism. The other-worldly asceticism and mysticism will not be conducive to the growth of the spirit of capitalism. Certain sets of Protestantism alone were the inner-worldly ascetic type, and hence contributed to the rise of modern capitalism. On the other hand, other religions like Hinduism, Confucianism, Buddhism, etc. were either other-worldly ascetic or had a preponderance of the mysticism and therefore failed to foster the spirit of capitalism, although material conditions propitious for the development of capitalism were present in Indian and Chinese societies.

Weber did not believe that Protestantism 'caused' capitalism or that the early Protestants were cynical money-worshippers (although there were isolated examples of this). Instead, using his fundamental methodology, he attempted to understand acting people so that, on the basis of this knowledge, he could explain historical events. Once capitalism had become established, it no longer needed this value-based foundation as a criterion for action. It was sufficient that purposive rational action had become institutionalised, as it was in the modern capitalist company. But in the transition from pre-capitalist to capitalist action, some justification was needed for the first capitalist to begin acting in an ascetic and world-oriented manner. According to Weber, the Protestant ethic contributed just this kind of strong force that could make people begin acting differently and not simply on the basis of tradition.

As stated earlier, in addition to analysing the role of Protestantism in the rise of early capitalism, Weber also worked on a major comparative study of world religions. This study did not deal with the metaphysical 'essence' of the various religions, rather Weber analysed the importance religion had for the 'the conditions and effects of a particular type of social action'. Weber was particularly interested in how various religions hindered or promoted a special sort of economic rationality and, in this sense, the study of world religions was part of Weber's overall investigation of what specific factors led to the rational capitalism of the Western world. Thus, according to Weber, the basis of this unique Western development is not to be found in the economy, but in its unique rationalisation process. Weber believed inner worldly asceticism to be a crucial factor in the rationalisation of social life. Capitalism is simply an expression of this rationalisation, just as the modern state is with its administration and armies, bureaucracy, legitimatisation of power, science and art. It is the discovery of this rationalisation process that is perhaps Weber's most important contribution to social science. This argument of Weber implies that any religious (or secular) ideology which emphasises on the inner worldly ascetic attitude towards life would lead to rationalisation of social life.

Balwant Nevaskar, in his book, *Capitalist without Capitalism: Jains of India and the Quakers of the West* (1971), states that Max Weber was the first sociologist to have sociologically studied the major religions of India. These studies are contained in his book *The Religion of India* (by Max Weber, the original edition was in German and was published in 1916). Max Weber maintains that the Jains are an exclusive merchant sect and that there is apparently 'a positive relationship between Jainism and economic motivation which is otherwise quite foreign in Hinduism'. Weber seems to suggest that although Jainism is spiritualised in the direction of world renunciation, some features of inner worldly asceticism are also present in it. To begin with, it can be observed that the twin doctrines of 'predestination' and the 'calling' implied in Protestantism are only indirectly present in Jainism but they must be understood in the light of Karma, and not in relation to God. Many aspects of rational conduct promoting savings such as thriftiness, self-discipline, frugality and abstention as part of this worldly asceticism, however, are directly present in Jainism.

In *The Protestant Ethic and the Parsis*, Robert Kennedy does just this and suggests that Zoroastrianism – an ancestral monotheism – set the stage for modernity, which encompasses not only capitalism but also science. Kennedy identifies five abstract values associated with modernity: (1) an underlying order in nature, (2) sensory standard of verification, (3) material work is intrinsically good, (4) maximisation of material prosperity and (5) accumulation rather than consumption of material goods. Using historical data on the Parsis or Zoroastrian Persians who fled from Iran to India after the Islamic conquest in the eighth century AD, Kennedy examines their beliefs, culture and society for correspondences. Finding many, Kennedy suggests that modern economy and science may have their roots in Zoroastrian religion.

Similarly, Clifford Geertz carried out his study in East Java, Indonesia, in the early 1950s with an intention to find a local variant of the Protestant ethic in Muslim societies – inspired by Weber's famous *The Protestant Ethic and the Spirit of Capitalism*. Please note that the dominance of the Weberian perspective among US scholars in general at the time was one factor. Geertz was a student of Talcott Parsons, and Parsons was the one who introduced Weber to American academia by translating *The Protestant Ethic and the Spirit of Capitalism* into English. But of course, Geertz's choice to use the Weberian perspective was not simply because of this teacher–student relation. The most important reason was because he tried to find the relation between religious ideas and human conduct, politics and economic development – between religion and social change. For this analytical endeavour, Weber provided very useful tools.

Weber's *The Protestant Ethic and the Spirit of Capitalism* opened up new vistas of research on the factors contributing to the rise of modern industrial capitalist society in Europe and elsewhere. Please note that Weber emphasised on the role of ideas in shaping the motivations and lifestyles of future capitalists. For him, it was an independent factor responsible of the rise of capitalism. He did not totally reject Marxian theory of rise of capitalism which sought to explain capitalist development in terms of economic forces. He regarded the Marxist view as an ideal-type model highlighting the role of one set of factors, i.e. economic factors.

Weber advocated that the rise of modern capitalism can be explained only by taking into account the multiplicity of factors at work.

After Weber, a number of scholars have attempted to explain the development of capitalism and in the process have highlighted some new factors which contributed to the growth of modern capitalism. These latter-day theories of capitalism should be treated as complementary to those of Marx and Weber. For example, Neil Joseph Smelser, an American sociologist, in his study of Third World countries, found that the state played an important role in the rise of capitalism. He argued that nationalistic ideology (secular inner worldly asceticism) in the Third World societies has played the same role which Protestant ethos did in the case of Europe in the rise of capitalism.

Werner Sombart, a German economist and sociologist, was deeply influenced by the ideas of Marx and Weber. According to Sombart, the development of capitalism can be divided into three stages:

1. *early capitalism*, ending before the industrial revolution
2. *high capitalism*, beginning about 1760
3. *late capitalism*, beginning with World War I

The moving force during the first stage of capitalism was a small number of enterprising businessmen, emerging from all groups of population – noble men, adventurers, merchants and artisans. Here he also highlighted the importance of the flow of *precious metal* (gold, silver, etc.) into Europe from South America. Sombart, in his book *The Jews and Modern Capitalism*, also highlighted the role of Jews in the development of modern capitalism. In addition, he accepted Weber's views that Protestant ethic emphasised values of hard work while deferring gratification and such an attitude favoured creation of capital and its productive reinvestment rather than consumption.

Another scholar, Andre Gunder Frank (1929–2005), a German-American economic historian and sociologist, who promoted dependency theory after the 1970s, has emphasised the role of colonial rule or imperial domination in the development of capitalism among imperial powers. The colonial expansion divided the world into two major zones and created an international division of labour. In such a division, the colonies supplied cheap raw materials to the European imperial powers to feed their manufacturing industries. The manufactured goods were exported back to the colonies which also served as markets. This colonial relationship helped in the rapid capitalist development in the European countries while destroying the handicraft industries of the colonies and suppressing economic growth there.

Weber's thesis on Protestant ethic and the rise of spirit of capitalism has also been criticised on various accounts. Famous English historian R.H. Tawney has pointed out that the empirical evidence on which Weber's interpretation of Protestantism was based was too narrow. According to him, England was the first country to develop capitalism. However, the English Puritans did not believe in the doctrine of predestination. However, sympathisers of Weber argue that this criticism is based on the narrow interpretation of his work. They argue that it was only an ideal-type construction which sought to establish a connection between certain aspects of Protestantism with only some aspects of early entrepreneurial type of capitalism. All that Weber was trying to say was that Protestant ethic contributed to the rationalisation which preceded modern capitalism. At no stage did Weber claim it to be the sole cause. In fact, Weber did admit to the possibility of building other ideal types linking other contributory factors to capitalism. Thus, Weber's thesis should not be treated as a general theory of capitalism development. It is more ideographic in nature. Further, Weber clearly states that the spirit of capitalism was only one component, albeit an important one. There are other components too which together with the spirit constituted the modern capitalism. These components are private ownership of the means of production, technological development such as mechanisation or automation, formally free labour, organisation of capitalist producers into joint stock companies and a universalistic legal system which applies to everyone and is administered equitably, etc. All these elements together form the basis of the ideal type of modern capitalism.

Critics also point out that modern capitalism is no longer guided by inner worldly asceticism but hedonism. In this regard, it can be stated that Weber in his work was only concerned with one dimension of capitalism, that is, the emergence of early capitalism and its link to the protest ethos. Weber had stated in his methodology that since social reality is infinite, we can study social reality scientifically only with the help of ideal types. Further, he stressed on the fact given the infinite and dynamic nature of social reality, the researcher should only aim at limited generalisations. As far as the challenges of late capitalism are concerned, Weber did express his concern for the predomination of formal or instrumental rationality at the expense of substantive rationality.

Authority

Max Weber has defined power as

> The chance of a man or a number of men to realize their own will in a communal action even against the resistance of others who are participating in the action.
>
> *(Haralambos and Heald, 2006)*

Weber, thus, implies that power is simply the degree to which an individual or a group can get its own way in a social relationship. Power, therefore, is an aspect of social relationships. An individual or a group does not hold power in isolation, they hold it in relation to others. Power is, therefore, power over others.

Depending on the circumstances surrounding its use, sociologists classify power into two categories. When power is used in a way that is generally recognised as socially right and necessary, it is called legitimate power. Power used to control others without the support of social approval is referred to as illegitimate power. Thus, from legal point of view, power has been classified into legitimate and illegitimate power. *Authority* is that form of power which is accepted as legitimate, that is as right and just, and, therefore, obeyed on that basis. In other words, when the power is legitimised, it becomes authority and only then it is accepted by people voluntarily. *Coercion* is that form of power which is not regarded as legitimate by those subject to it. For example, government agents demanding and receiving sales tax from a shopkeeper are using legitimate power; gangsters demanding and receiving protection money from the same shopkeeper by threat of violence are using illegitimate power.

Thus, when power gets institutionalised and comes to be accepted as legitimate by those on whom it is being exercised, it is termed authority. Weber's study of authority has to be understood in the context of his general typology of social action. As discussed earlier, Weber built various ideal types of social action which are distinguished by the meanings on which they are based. These include traditional action, affective action and rational action (both goal-rational and value-rational).

Max Weber further argues that the nature of authority is shaped by the manner in which the legitimacy is acquired. Thus, Weber identifies three ideal types of authority systems: the traditional authority, the charismatic authority and the legal-rational authority.

The traditional authority is the characteristic of those societies where the 'traditional action' is predominant. Traditional action is based on established custom. An individual acts in a certain way because of an ingrained habit, because things have always been done that way. In those societies where traditional action is a predominant mode of behaviour, exercise of power is seen legitimate when it is in consonance with the tradition and conforms to the customary rules. Such type of authority was termed by Weber as traditional authority. Weber identified two forms of traditional authority: patriarchalism and patrimonialism. In patriarchalism, authority is distributed on the basis of gerentocratic principles. Thus, the right to exercise authority is vested in the eldest male member. This type of authority is to be found in case of very small-scale societies like the Bushmen of Kalahari Desert or in case of extended kin groups in agrarian societies like lineage or joint families in India.

When the patriarchal domination has developed by having certain subordinate sons of the patriarch or other dependents take over land and authority from the ruler, Weber calls this patrimonial domination and a patrimonial state can develop from it. In the patrimonial state, such as Egypt under the Pharaohs, ancient China, the Inca state, the Jesuit state in Paraguay, or Russia under the czars, the ruler controls his country like a giant princely estate. The master exercises unlimited power over his subjects, the military force and the legal system. Patrimonial dominance is a typical example of the traditional exercise of power in which the legitimacy of the ruler and the relationships between him and his subjects are derived from tradition. Patrimonialism is characterised by the existence of hereditary office of a king or a chief and an administrative staff consisting of courtiers and favourites who together form a nascent bureaucracy. The king or the chief exercises absolute and arbitrary power, subject only to customary rules (Wallace and Wolf, 2012).

The second type of authority is charismatic authority which corresponds to affective action. Charisma refers to a certain quality of an individual's personality by virtue of which he is set apart from ordinary men and treated as endowed with the supernatural, superhuman or at least specifically exceptional power or qualities. These qualities are not accessible to an ordinary person but are regarded as of divine origin and on the basis of them the individual concerned is treated as a leader and is revered. Charismatic type of authority can exist in all types of societies. Charismatic authority gains prominence in the times of crisis where other forms of authority prove inadequate to deal with the situation. Thus, heroes who help to win the war or people with the reputation for therapeutic wisdom who come to be regarded as saviours in times of epidemics and prophets in times of general moral crisis come to acquire charismatic authority.

> Compared to that of the ideal-typical bureaucracy, the staff of the charismatic leader is lacking on virtually all counts. The staff members are not technically trained but are chosen instead for their possession of charismatic qualities or, at least, of qualities similar to those possessed by the charismatic leader. The offices they occupy form no clear hierarchy. Their work does not constitute a career, and there are no promotions, clear appointments, or dismissals. The charismatic leader is free to intervene whenever he or she feels that the staff cannot handle a situation. The organization has no formal rules, no established administrative organs, and no precedents to guide new judgements. In these and other ways, Weber found the staff of the charismatic leader to be 'greatly inferior' to be staff in a bureaucratic form of organization.
>
> *(Ritzer and Stepnisky, 2014)*

Charismatic authority lies outside the realism of everyday routine and the profane sphere. In this respect, it is sharply opposed, both to rational or bureaucratic authority and to traditional authority. Both bureaucratic and traditional authorities are bound by certain type of rules, while charismatic authority is foreign to all rules. Due to this freedom from established rules, charismatic authority can act as a great revolutionary force.

The charismatic movement, with its charismatic authority, differs on several important points from both traditional organisations and bureaucracies. Charisma is a force that is fundamentally outside everyday life and, whether it be religious or political charisma, it is a revolutionary force in history that is capable of breaking down both traditional and rational patterns of living; but charismatic domination is unstable in nature. The authority of the charismatic leader stems from the supernatural, superhuman or perhaps specifically exceptional powers he possesses, at least in the eyes of his followers. This force lies outside the routines of everyday life, and the problem arises when this extraordinary force is to be incorporated into a routine everyday life. Weber calls this process the 'routinisation of charisma', which means that the leader (or if he is dead, his successor) and the followers want to make 'it possible to participate in normal family relations or at least to enjoy a secure social position'. When this happens, the charismatic message is changed into dogma, doctrine, regulations, law or rigid tradition. The charismatic movement develops into either a traditional or a bureaucratic organisation, 'or a combination of both'.

As stated earlier, charismatic authority is inherently unstable. This is on account of several reasons. First, charismatic authority is the product of a crisis situation and, therefore, lasts so long as the crisis lasts. Once the crisis is over, the charismatic authority has to be adapted to everyday matters. This is called the process of routinisation of charisma. Thus, charismatic authority may be transformed into either traditional or legal-rational authority. Second, one of the decisive motives underlying all cases of routinisation of charisma is naturally the striving for security. This means legitimising on one hand the position of authority and, on the other hand, the economic advantages enjoyed by the followers of the leader. Third, another important motive, however, lies in the objective necessity of adaptation of the patterns of order, of the organisation and of the administrative staff to the normal, everyday needs and conditions of carrying on the administration. Finally, there is the problem of succession which renders charismatic authority unstable since the basis of authority is the personal charisma of the leader. It is not easy to find a successor who also possesses those charismatic qualities. Thus, in charismatic authority, discontinuity is inevitable. One of the solutions to the problem of discontinuity is to transform the charisma of the individual into the charisma of the office which can be translated to every incumbent of the office by ritual means. Most important example is the transmission of the charisma of a royal authority by anointing and by coronation. This ideal type of charismatic authority is extremely helpful in the study of radical transformation of traditional societies like Russia, China, India, Egypt and the other Third World countries. All these societies had charismatic leaders to meet the crisis of transition. Thus, you can understand the significance and nature of the authority exercised by Gandhi in India, Lenin in Russia, Mao in China and Nasser in Egypt.

The third ideal type of authority, which corresponds to rational action, is legal-rational authority or bureaucracy. Having begun to define modern society in terms of the spread of instrumental rationality, Weber goes on to argue that as society becomes more and more complex (in terms of both its economics arrangements and its increasing institutional sophistication), the quest for an appropriately rational means of organisation also becomes increasingly urgent. Weber believed that the most rational means of organisation is bureaucratic organisation and hence he felt it was inevitable that bureaucracy would become an ever more dominant feature of modern society. Bureaucracy, for Weber, provides a fine example of formal rationality that is to be found in all spheres of social life in modern society.

In other words, according to Weber, all societies are gradually moving away from the traditional type of authority towards the legal-rational type of authority. Europe was the first to experience this transformation. But Weber regarded those processes as inevitable in all societies advancing towards industrial civilization. In industrial societies, rational action becomes the most predominant form of social behaviour. Weber has termed this process of increasing preponderance of rational action as rationalisation. With increasing rationalisation, legal-rational authority becomes the most common form of authority system.

Legal-rational authority differs sharply from its charismatic and traditional counterparts. The legitimacy of the legal-rational authority stems neither from the perceived personal qualities of the leader nor from a commitment to traditional wisdom. Instead, legal-rational authority is based on the acceptance of a set of impersonal rules. Those who possess authority are able to issue commands and have them obeyed because others accept the legal framework which supports their authority. For example, a police inspector, an income tax office, a judge or a military commander are obeyed not on the basis of any 'tradition' or 'charisma' but because of the acceptance of legal statuses and rules which grant them authority and define the limits of that authority. These rules are rational in the sense that they are consciously constructed for the attainment of a particular goal and they specify the means by which that goal is to be attained. As Weber's view of rational action suggested, precise calculation and systematic assessment of the various means of attaining a goal are involved in the construction of rules which form the basis of legal-rational authority (Haralambos and Heald, 2006).

Weber further argued that like other forms of authority, legal-rational authority produces a particular kind of organisational structure – the bureaucracy. Weber defined bureaucracy as

> a hierarchical organization designed rationally to coordinate work of many individuals in the pursuit of large-scale administrative tasks and organizational goals.
>
> *(ibid.)*

Weber constructed an ideal type of rational-legal bureaucratic organization. He argued that bureaucracies in modern industrial societies are steadily moving towards his 'pure' type. The main characteristics of the ideal-type bureaucracy as envisaged by Weber can be summarised as follows:

1. Bureaucracy is an expert system of administration based on detailed *documentation* and *record-keeping*.
2. Bureaucracy is governed by a *legalistic framework* of formal rules and regulations.

3. Regular activities in bureaucratic organisations are distributed in a fixed way as *official duties* where each administrative official has a clearly defined area of competence and responsibility.
4. Officials are appointed on the basis of their *technical knowledge* and *expertise*.
5. Bureaucracies have a rigidly *hierarchical organisational structure* with clear lines of communication and responsibility.
6. Decisions are made through the application of specific procedures designed to *eliminate subjective judgements*. The ideal official performs his duties in a spirit of formalistic impersonality, without hatred or passion. The activities of a bureaucrat are governed by the rules, not by personal feelings. His actions are, therefore, rational rather than affective.
7. Authority is a characteristic of the post, not of the post holder.
8. Bureaucracy involves *a strict separation between private and official income.* That is, the official does not own any part of the organisation for which he works nor can he use his position for private gain. In Weber's words, 'bureaucracy segregates official activity as something distinct from the sphere of private life' (ibid.).

This ideal type of bureaucracy is most closely approximated in capitalist industrial society where it becomes the major form of organisation control. The development of bureaucracy is due to its 'technical superiority' compared to organisations based on charismatic and traditional authority. Weber believed that primacy of the organisational goals, rational rules and regulations, and the formalistic impersonality of officials make this ideal type of bureaucracy technically superior to any other form of organisation. He also believed that compared to other forms of organisations, tasks in a bureaucracy are performed with greater precision and speed, with less friction and lower costs.

Although Weber appreciated the technical advantages of his ideal type of bureaucracy, he was also aware of its disadvantages. For example, Weber realised that too much emphasis on the achievement of quantitative organisational goals and rational procedures could prevent spontaneity, creativity and individual initiative. The formalistic impersonal attitude of officials tends to produce specialists without spirit. Further, sometimes rule-governed procedures can become rule-bound in the sense that too much red tape prevents decisions being made quickly. Even more seriously, to the extent that the personal career interests of bureaucrats depend on the status of the bureaucracy itself, they have a vested interest in putting the particular aim of increasing the power and authority of the bureaucracy ahead of the universal ends that were supposed to be served by the bureaucracy. In other words, civil servants might become more concerned with protecting the status of the civil service, even of one government department against another, than with delivering a decent service to the public.

In terms of its political and cultural impact, Weber was also very much concerned that bureaucracy has irrational tendencies in the sense that it might override individual freedom and integrity. Based on his own analysis of what was happening in German society during the 1890s, he feared that as more and more aspects of the decision-making process became gathered into fewer and fewer hands, bureaucracies, and the bureaucrats who ran them, would smother personal freedoms resulting in the emergence of what he famously called 'a new iron cage of serfdom'. In the political sphere, the turn towards democracy also meant the spread of detailed procedures for conducting democratic elections, which in turn entailed greater reliance on the electoral process and electoral officials. Consequently, democratisation of a state also means bureaucratisation, particularly because the modern political parties themselves are developing more and more into bureaucratic organisations (Ransome, 2011).

In other words, Weber was apprehensive about the tension that may emerge in modern society between the wider purposes (substantive rationality) of the political process, i.e. democratic participation, and the narrow functional priorities (formal rationality) of bureaucracy, i.e. bureaucratic procedures. This is a good example of value conflict between substantive rationality and formal rationality. Weber also expressed his concern about the increasing centralisation of authority. He argued that a new class of professional bureaucrats might be tempted to subvert bureaucratic authority for their own ends. His major reservations about the prospects of a socialist Germany were less to do with the values of the socialist belief system than with the practical problems it would create through the yet further bureaucratisation of society. Weber's fears came true in the form of communist society that emerged as the Soviet Union in the twentieth century. The Soviet Union was profoundly criticised for not only the concentration of authority in the state but also for depriving its citizens of representation, right and liberty.

However, despite apprehensions about his ideal type of bureaucracy, Weber still believed that bureaucracy was essential to the operation of large-scale industrial societies. In particular, he believed that the state and economic enterprise could not function effectively without bureaucratic control. Weber saw two main dangers if this control was left in the hands of bureaucrats themselves. First, since bureaucrats are trained only to follow orders and conduct routine operations, in times of crisis, bureaucratic leadership may prove to be ineffective. In other words, crisis situations call for spontaneous and creative thinking and dynamic leadership, which bureaucrats are not trained for. Second, in capitalist society, bureaucrats may be swayed by the pressure of capitalist interests and tailor their administrative practices to fit the demands of capital (Haralambos and Heald, 2006).

According to Weber, these dangers could be avoided by the strong parliamentary control of the state bureaucracy. He suggested that professional politicians must hold the top positions in various departments of the state. This will encourage strong and effective leadership since politicians are trained to take decisions. Further, since politicians are public figures, they are accountable for their actions. This would subject bureaucracy to the scrutiny of public as well as opposition parties and hence make it more transparent. However, Weber believed that even with politicians at the head of state bureaucracies, problems would remain. Since the professional politician lacks the technical knowledge controlled by the bureaucracy, he may have little awareness of its inner working and procedures. As a result, he is largely dependent on information supplied to him by bureaucrats. In other words, he may well end up being directed by the bureaucrats. Seymour M. Lipset, in his study of the Cooperative Commonwealth Federation (CCF), a socialist government, in the Canadian province of Saskatchewan, found that it is possible for government bureaucracy to exercise considerable control over its 'political masters'. Lipset found that the entrenched bureaucracy was successfully able to scuttle the reformist policies of this new socialist government. People's representatives appointed as ministers to control the bureaucracy proved ineffective.

Lipset's study illustrates Weber's fears of the power of bureaucrats to act independently from their 'political masters'. Weber believed that only strong parliamentary government could control state bureaucracy. He suggested that state bureaucrats should be made directly and regularly accountable to parliament for their action. The procedure for doing this is the parliamentary committee which would systematically cross-examine top civil servants. In Weber's view, 'This alone guarantees public supervision and a through inquiry' (ibid.).

Thus, Weber's views of bureaucracy appear to be ambivalent. On the one hand, he recognised the 'technical superiority' of bureaucracy over all other forms of organisation. He believed that it was essential for the effective operation of large-scale industrial society. On the other hand, he also saw it as a threat to responsible government. To counter this threat, Weber suggested stronger political control over bureaucracy. However, he remained pessimistic about the consequences of bureaucracy for human freedom and happiness.

Much of the later research on organisations can be seen as a debate with Weber. Students of organisations have refined, elaborated and criticised his views. In particular, they question the proposition that bureaucracy organised on the lines of the Weber's ideal type is the most efficient way of realising organisational goals. It has been argued that certain aspects of the ideal-type bureaucracy may, in practice, reduce organisational efficiency. The critical remarks of some of the important scholars have been discussed below.

In contrast to Weber's ideal type of bureaucracy and his stress on formal and contractual relationships, Robert E. Cole in his study *Japanese Blue Collar: The Changing Tradition* states that Japan has been able to achieve high industrial growth by harmonically synthesising the traditional familial structures, loyalty and paternalistic attitude of the management with the demands of the industry.

Robert K. Merton, an American sociologist, also highlighted some dysfunctional aspects of bureaucracy. He argues that at times certain bureaucratic procedures tend to encourage behaviour which inhibits the realisation of organisational goals. First, since bureaucrats are trained to follow orders and comply strictly with the rules, they are unable to think out of the box in crisis situations. Even the demands of a successful career discourage a bureaucrat to innovate since his career incentives such as promotions are designed to reward conformity. Thus, he may not be inclined to bend the rules even when such actions might further the realisation of organisational goals. Second, too much emphasis on conformity to official regulations may lead to a displacement of goals. It involves the risk of conformity to rules becoming an end in itself rather than the means to an end. This could give rise to the problem of red-tapism. Third, the emphasis on impersonality in bureaucratic procedures may lead to friction between officials and the public. For example, patients in a hospital or an unemployed youth in an employment exchange may expect concern and sympathy for their particular problems. The businesslike and impartial treatment they might receive can lead to bureaucrats being seen as cold, unsympathetic, abrupt and even arrogant. As a result, clients sometimes feel that they have been badly served by bureaucracies. While agreeing that the various elements of bureaucracy outlined in Weber's ideal type serve to further organizational efficiency, Merton maintains that they inevitably produce dysfunctional consequences (ibid.).

As stated earlier, according to Weber, all societies are gradually moving away from the traditional type of authority to legal-rational type of authority. Weber presented an ideal-type bureaucracy and believed that despite its limitations, organisations in modern industrial society were increasingly moving towards that model. Critics often argue that Weber didn't elaborate on the fact that why actual organisations varied in terms of their approximation of the ideal type. They even suggested that Weber's ideal type of bureaucracy was particularly suited to the administration of routine tasks. It is in this context that Alvin W. Gouldner conducted a study of gypsum plant in the United States to explore this dimension. It is concerned to 'clarify some of the social processes leading to different *degrees of bureaucratisation*'.

Alvin Ward Gouldner (1920–1980), an American sociologist, carried out an intensive analysis of one plant owned and operated by the General Gypsum Company. The plant consisted of two parts, a gypsum mine and a factory making wallboards for which gypsum is a major ingredient. Gouldner found that there was a significant difference in the degree of bureaucratisation between the mine and the factory. For example, in the mine, the hierarchy of authority was less developed, the division of labour and spheres of competence were less explicit, there was less emphasis on official rules and procedures and less impersonality in relationships both between workers and between them and the supervisors.

On the basis of his study, Gouldner identified the following reasons for the difference in degrees of bureaucratisation between mine and surface:

First, the nature of the work. Work in the mine was less predictable. For example, the miners had no control over the amount of gypsum available and could not predict various dangers such as cave-ins. Thus, given the uncertainty involved at the workplace, any kind of official procedure would be of little use. Miners often had to make their own decisions on matters which could not be strictly governed by official rules, for example, strategies for digging out the gypsum and propping up the roof. Since the problems they encountered did not follow a standard pattern, a predetermined set of rules was not suitable for their solution. On the other hand, the work was of routine nature in the factory producing wallboards. The machine production of wallboard in the factory followed a standard routine and could therefore be 'rationalised' in terms of a bureaucratic system. Fixed rules and a clearly defined division of labour are more suited to predictable operations.

Second, the degree of solidarity among workers. Given the ever-present danger in the mine, there was a stronger sense of solidarity among workers and between them and the supervisors. Gouldner argued that strong work group solidarity tends to encourage informal work culture within the organisation. Miners depended on their workmates to warn them of loose rocks and to dig them out in the event of a cave-in. In the words of one old miner, 'Friends or no friends, you *got* all to be friends'. A cohesive work group will tend to resist control from above and to institute its own informal work norms.

On the basis of his detailed study of the gypsum plant, Gouldner arrived at the following conclusions:

First, bureaucratic administration is more suited to some tasks than others. In particular, it is not well suited to non-routine, unpredictable operations. Second, the advance of bureaucracy is not inevitable as Weber and others have implied. As the case of the gypsum miners indicates, it can be successfully resisted. Third, Gouldner suggests that sociologists who are concerned with a utopian vision which involves the abolition of bureaucracy would be more fruitfully employed in identifying 'these social processes creating variations in the amount and types of bureaucracy. For these variations do make a vital difference in the lives of men'. By directing their research to this area, sociologists may be able to give direction to those who wish to create organisations with greater democracy and freedom (ibid.).

In his major work *Patterns of Industrial Bureaucracy* (1954), Gouldner, on the basis of his study of gypsum plant, identified three patterns of bureaucracy and bureaucratisation:

1. mock bureaucracy
2. representative bureaucracy
3. punishment-centred bureaucracy

Mock bureaucracy: Mock bureaucracy refers to a pattern of bureaucracy in which official rules and bureaucratic procedures are imposed at the workplace by some 'outside' agency. Neither workers nor management, neither superiors nor subordinates, identify themselves with or participate in the establishment of the rules or view them as their own. For example, Gouldner found in his study that the 'no-smoking' rule at the gypsum plant was initiated by the insurance company, an outside agency. Since neither the management nor the workers were in favour of 'no-smoking' rule, it remained only on paper. Both the management and the workers considered smoking as a natural desire and thus inevitable. The 'no-smoking rule' is an example of mock bureaucracy.

Representative bureaucracy: Representative bureaucracy refers to a pattern of bureaucracy in which both management and workers participate in the formulation as well as the implementation of certain rules. For example, in his study, Gouldner found that the 'safety programme' was designed and enforced with the participation of both sides. It was considered to be a win–win situation for both. While the management was interested in the safety program as it would help to achieve its production targets by minimising the number of accidents in the factory, workers, on the other hand, linked the safety programme to their personal and bodily welfare, maintenance of income and cleanliness. The safety programme, thus, is an example of representative bureaucracy.

Punishment-centred bureaucracy: In the punishment-centred bureaucracy, rules are formulated by one party and imposed on the other as a punishment. In his study, Gouldner found that the 'no-absenteeism' rule was initiated by management and generated many tensions. Management viewed workers as deliberately willing to be absent. Therefore, punishment was installed in order to force the workers not to be absent. The 'no-absenteeism' rule is an example of the punishment-centred bureaucracy (Gouldner, 1954).

This completes our discussion on Gouldner's contributions in facilitating our understanding of the various patterns of industrial bureaucracy. In response to Weber's ideal type of bureaucracy, Gouldner argued that bureaucracy may manifest different patterns under different contexts.

Gouldner's conclusions are supported by the findings of research by Tom Burns and G.M. Stalker. On the basis of their study of 20 Scottish and English firms, mainly in the electronics industry, Burns and Stalker concluded that bureaucratic organisations are best suited to dealing with predictable, familiar and routine situations. They are not well suited to the rapidly changing technical and commercial situation of many sectors of modern industry such as the electronics industry. Since change is the hallmark of modern society, Burns and Stalker suggest that bureaucratic organisations may well be untypical of the future.

Burns and Stalker constructed two ideal types of organisations: 'mechanistic' and 'organic'. The mechanistic organisation comes very close to Weber's model of bureaucracy. It is characterised by rigid hierarchy of authority, rational procedures, specialised division of labour and formalistic impersonality. Communication in such organisations is mainly vertical: instructions flow downwards through a chain of command, information flows upwards and is processed by various levels in the hierarchy before it reaches the top. Each individual in the organisation is responsible for discharging his particular responsibility and no more. By comparison, there is greater flexibility and freedom in organic organisations. Although a hierarchy exists, it tends to become blurred as communication travels in all directions. Communication consists of consultation rather than command, of 'information and advice rather than instructions and decisions'. Organic organisations are marked by informal channels of communication and greater emphasis on human relation approach. Burns and Stalker argue that mechanistic systems are best suited to stable conditions, organic systems to changing conditions (Haralambos and Heald, 2006).

Various scholars have also criticised Weber for focusing exclusively on the formal structure of bureaucracy, that is, the official rules and procedures, the authorised hierarchy of offices and the official duties attached to them. They criticised Weber for ignoring the significance of unofficial practices within an organisation. For example, Peter Blau, on the basis of his study of the functioning of a federal law enforcement agency in Washington, DC, claims that Weber's approach 'implies that any deviation from the formal structure is detrimental to administrative efficiency'. But it may not be so always. Peter Blau argues that the presence of both *formal* and *informal* structures in the organisation may together enhance the efficiency of the organisation. He further suggests that the presence of formal structures alone, may act as a hindrance towards the attainment of organisational goals (ibid.).

Weber: An Assessment

Weber's importance as a classical sociologist did not begin until Talcott Parsons introduced him to the American public. Parsons himself studied and defended a dissertation in Heidelberg during the latter half of the 1920s. And in 1930 he translated *The Protestant Ethic and the Spirit of Capitalism* into English. Parsons later based much of his book *The Structure of Social Action* (1937) on Weber, and as Parsons's influence grew in American and later in international sociology, Weber also gained more and more status as a classic.

Weber's contribution to modern sociology is multidimensional so much so that he can be legitimately considered as one of the founding fathers of modern sociology. He contributed a new perspective on the nature of subject matter of sociology and laid down the foundations of interpretative sociology. In addition, he carried out penetrating analysis of some of the crucial features of Western society like social stratification, bureaucracy, rationality and growth of capitalism. Weber's impact on the development of sociology is captured best by the prominent social theorist, Raymond Aron, who described Weber as 'the greatest of the sociologists'. Aron further stated that 'I would even say that he is *the* sociologist. I shall not attempt to argue the truth of this opinion, which is affirmed today by the majority of sociologists the world over' (Abraham and Morgan, 2010).

First, by viewing the subject matter of sociology in terms of social action, he highlighted the significance of subjective meanings and motives in understanding social behaviour. This view of Weber presented an alternative and a corrective to the positivist approach in sociology. The positivists like Durkheim, by assuming a deterministic perspective, had almost totally ignored the role of the individual's subjectivity in shaping social behaviour. They had restricted the study of social behaviour to externally observable aspects only. Thus, Weber's emphasis on exploring the subjective dimension provided a corrective to overly social determinist perspective of the positivist school.

Second, in terms of methodology, Weber advocates a non-positivist (also sometimes called anti-positivist) approach. Weber draws attention to the uniqueness and subjective nature of social phenomena. Acknowledging the infinitely complex nature of social reality, on account of subjective meanings involved, Weber suggested building the ideal type of the social phenomenon under investigation and then applying *Verstehen* to it. Causal pluralism and value neutrality are other integral aspects of Weber's methodology.

Third, Weber offers a more plausible and comprehensive analysis of social development in comparison to Marx. In addition to material economic factors, Weber also highlights the role of ideas in bringing about social change. This was best demonstrated in his work *The Protestant Ethic and the Spirit of Capitalism* where Weber argued that it is the struggle over ideas that fuels social development, not just technological innovation.

Further, Weber's methodological individualism also sets him apart from Durkheim and Marx. Weber emphasises on the subjective interpretation of the social action of the actor. Durkheim and Marx, on the other hand, tend to adopt a strongly collectivist interpretation of social action. They adopt a structural approach towards social action and look at it as being largely shaped by the socio-cultural institutions. Although Weber argues that as cultural beings social actors share certain cultural values and ideas to some degree and often act together, he resists the idea that individuals are drawn towards particular ways of acting by the pull of collective forces. Thus, Weber's social theory is more *voluntaristic* in the sense that social actors choose how to act rather than being compelled to do so by social forces beyond their control. For much the same reason, Weber concentrates on a theory of social action and not on a theory of society (Ransome, 2011).

Finally, in his analysis of modern society, Weber identifies the crucial significance of the process of rationalisation. His concept of instrumental rationality is widely accepted as one of the most important characteristics of modern society. One of the major preoccupations of critical social theory and the Frankfurt School is to explore the negative impact on modern society of the idea of instrumental rationality described by Max Weber (ibid.).

During the past decade, in particular, with its debate over 'postmodernism', Weber's critique of blind faith in science and rationality seems to have appealed to many. Thus, he is not just an early predecessor of modern sociology and social science, but he is also definitely present, participating in the debate over the problems of modern society.

LET'S THINK

- Dear Learner, in this chapter we have learned about Weber's ideas on the subject matter of sociology and its methodology. Weber also reoriented the objective of social science research. Try to compare Weber's ideas with other classical thinkers like Karl Marx and Emile Durkheim. In what respects do you think Weber's conception of sociology differs from that of Marx and Durkheim? Which one is more satisfactory according to you?

- Think about the ideal types put forward by Weber on authority. Can you relate these ideal types with contemporary social reality in India?

For Practice

Q1. What is the subject matter of sociology according to Max Weber? Which major methods did he suggest for social science research? Illustrate your answer with his sociological contributions.

Q2. Examine Max Weber's method of maintaining objectivity in social research.

Q3. State the meaning and characteristics of an ideal type. What, according to Max Weber, is the use and significance of the 'ideal type' in social science research?

Q4. Distinguish between fact and value in Weber's Protestant ethic and the spirit of capitalism.

Q5. Critically examine Max Weber's theory of the Protestant ethics and the spirit of capitalism. Could it be the otherwise possibility that the tenets of capitalism must also have effected the emergence of the Protestant ethics? Comment with suitable examples.

Model Answers

Q. State the meaning and characteristics of an ideal type. What, according to Max Weber, is the use and significance of the 'ideal type' in social science research?

A. Social action, according to Weber, is the subject matter of sociology. For Weber, social action is a meaningful action. Since such meanings attributed by actors to their respective actions could be infinite, this implies that social reality by its very nature is infinitely complex. Such an infinitely complex social reality cannot be comprehended in its totality by the human mind at a given point of time; therefore, selectivity is unavoidable. In order to exercise selectivity, Weber suggests that sociologists should build ideal type of a given social phenomenon.

According to Weber, an ideal type is formed by the one-sided *accentuation* of one or more points of view and by the synthesis of a great many diffuse, discrete, more or less present and occasionally absent *concrete individual* phenomena, which are arranged according to those one-sidedly emphasised viewpoints into a unified *analytical* construct. In simpler words, an ideal type is a mental construct – a mental picture – that the investigator uses to approach the complex reality. For example, as constructed by Weber, the ideal type of capitalism did not fully describe any of the various types of capitalism – mercantile capitalism, entrepreneurial capitalism (characteristic of the eighteenth and nineteenth centuries), matured industrial capitalism, etc. From the point of view of his study, only some of the features of early entrepreneurial capitalism were relevant which depicted the spirit of capitalism. Therefore, Weber isolated these elements and ideally represented these elements alone.

Some of the important characteristics and uses of the ideal type are as follows:

(i) Ideal type is a one-sided view of social reality which takes into account certain aspects of social life while ignoring others. Which aspects are to be given importance to, and which are to be ignored depends upon the object of study. Thus, an ideal type is a way of exercising selectivity.

(ii) Ideal-type formulation also helps in developing the classificatory typology of the social phenomenon, thus facilitating a comprehensive understanding of the infinite social reality. For example, Weber developed classificatory typologies of social action, religious ideology and authority.

(iii) Ideal type can also help in establishing logical interconnections between different social constellations. For example, Weber in his work *The Protestant Ethic and the Spirit of Capitalism* builds ideal types of *the Protestant ethic* and *the spirit of capitalism* and establishes the relationship between the two.

(iv) Ideal type also serves the investigator as a measuring rod to ascertain similarities as well as deviations in concrete cases, thus being helpful in comparison with reality.

Ideal type also has a limited utility as a source of prediction. As discussed earlier, Weber argues that the laws Marx and the Marxists thought they had found in history and in bourgeois society were actually nothing but ideal types. As ideal types, they have a very important significance if they are used in a comparison with reality.

(v) Further, although ideal type is rooted in reality, it does not represent reality in totality. It is a mental construct. Weber claims that ideal type is a social science equivalent of experimentation in physical and natural sciences. Experimentation is an essential element of scientific method to check the validity and reliability of the research findings in natural sciences. Since due to moral and ethical reasons, experimentation is not possible in social sciences which are involved in the study of human behaviour, ideal type can serve as an equivalent of experimentation in social sciences. As experimentation is conducted under the controlled conditions, likewise an ideal type is also a rational construction based on selectivity.

Thus, according to Weber, the methodology of sociology consists in building ideal types of social behaviour and applying *Verstehen* method to explain this. Weber's thesis on *The Protestant Ethic and the Spirit of Capitalism* is a very good example of the application of this methodology. Another important element of Weber's methodology is *causal pluralism*. According to Weber, the social reality is extremely complex and, therefore, no social phenomena can be explained adequately in terms of a single cause. An adequate sociological explanation must, therefore, be based on the principle of causal pluralism.

Q. Distinguish between fact and value in Weber's Protestant ethic and the spirit of capitalism.

A. Fact and value have been at the centre of methodological debates in sociology right from the time of its origin. A fact is something that has really occurred or is actually the case. The usual test for a statement of fact is its verifiability, that is, whether it can be proven to correspond to experience. Values, on the other hand, are socially accepted standards of desirability. In other words, values are subjective and hence differ from society to society and culture to culture.

In sociological literature, the role of values has largely been discussed and debated in terms of their influence on objectivity of social science research. Early founding fathers of sociology, be it Comte, Spencer or Durkheim, advocated a positivist approach to study society. That is, they emphasised on the study of only those aspects of social reality which could be empirically observed and hence quantified. Anti-positivist scholars, on the other hand, argued that the subject matter of sociology is the study of human behaviour in society and all human behaviour is guided by values. Hence, these scholars, such as Weber, Mead, etc., suggested the social action approach to study society.

For Weber, social science is value-relevant. In other words, Weber implies that since social action is a meaningful action guided by subjective meanings and values of social actors, the social scientist must attempt to understand social action from the subjective point of view of social actors. That is, their social behaviour should be understood in terms of their subjective meanings and values. Doing so, however, Weber argues that the researcher must ensure that his own personal biases, prejudices or cultural values do not contaminate his findings. Hence, according to Weber, while social science is value-relevant, it must also be value-neutral.

In his study *The Protestant Ethic and the Spirit of Capitalism*, Weber largely relied on the historical data and made a comparative study of world religions in terms of their beliefs and practices and their repercussions on social life. Weber analysed Confucianism and Taoism in China, Hinduism and Buddhism in India and finally ancient Judaism. The studies Weber carried out deal with the various social conditions in which the different religions operated, the social stratification, the links of various groups to different religions and the importance of various religious leaders. In this study, Weber has clearly stated that only the spirit of capitalism was created by the Protestant ethos. However, there were a number of other contributory factors which along with the spirit of capitalism helped in the growth of capitalism.

According to some scholars, there is a gap between what Weber said and what he actually did. Weber was not afraid to express a value judgement, even in the midst of the analysis of historical data. For example, Gary Abraham has stated that though Weber did believe in the possibility of separating fact from value in social science research but his own work *The Protestant Ethic and the Spirit of Capitalism*, especially his views on Judaism as a world religion, was distorted by his values. Abraham argues that in his sociology of religion, Weber termed the Jews 'pariah people'. Weber traced this position of outsider more to the desire of Jews to segregate themselves than to their exclusion by the rest of society. Thus Weber, accepting the general view of the day, argued that Jews would need to surrender Judaism in order to be assimilated into German society. Abraham argues that this sort of bias affected not only Weber's ideas on Judaism, but his work in general. This casts further doubt on Weber as a 'value-free' sociologist, as well as on the conventional view of Weber as a liberal thinker.

Another scholar G. Roth also argued that Weber was more of a nationalist supporting the assimilation of minority groups than he was a classical liberal favouring pluralism, and those values had a profound effect on his work. These views indicate the degree of difficulty in separating fact from value in social science research.

References

Abraham, Francis and John Henry Morgan. *Sociological Thought*. New Delhi: Macmillan Publishers India, 2010.

Adams, Bert N. and R.A. Sydie. *Sociological Theory*. New Delhi: SAGE Publications, 2016.

Coser, Lewis A. *Masters of Sociological Thought*. 2nd Edition. Jaipur: Rawat Publications, 2008.

Churton, Mel and Anne Brown. *Theory & Method*. 2nd Edition. Hampshire: Palgrave Macmillan, 2017.

Gouldner, A.W. *Patterns of Industrial Bureaucracy*. New York: The Free Press, 1954.

Haralambos, M. and R.M. Heald. *Sociology: Themes and Perspectives*. New Delhi: Oxford University Press, 2006.

Morrison, Ken. *Marx, Durkheim, Weber: Formations of Modern Social Thought*. 2nd Edition. New Delhi: SAGE Publications, 2012.

Ransome, Paul. *Social Theory*. Jaipur: Rawat Publications, 2011.

Ritzer, George and Jeffrey Stepnisky. *Sociological Theory*. 9th Edition. New York: McGraw-Hill Education, 2014.

Wallace, Ruth A. and Alison Wolf. *Contemporary Sociological Theory: Expanding the Classical Tradition*. 6th Edition. New Delhi: PHI Learning, 2012.

INDEX

Note: Page numbers in *Italics* refer to figures and tables.

Abraham, Gary 339, 370
Abrahamson, Mark 178, 210, 253, 294, 311
absolute monarchy 31
absolute power 252
absolutism 28, 29
abstract theorising 283
acculturation 69, 143, 144
Advice to a Young Tradesman (Franklin) 348
affective action 334, 355–356, 359
Agar, M. 182
aggregation 61, 282
Agrarian Revolution 8, 19; capitalists and the workers, contractual relationships 20; displacement of serfs, consequences 20–21; enclosure movement 20; eviction of the poor peasants 20; first Enclosure Bill, 1710 20; mechanised cultivation 19
agrarian sociology 73
alienation 128, 135, 152, 173, 220, 226, 255–265, 271, 299, 323–324; Blauner's model of alienation *265*; East European communism 270–271; economic factors 261; estrangement 256; human Geist or 'Spirit' 256; industrial capitalism 260–261; lack of sublation 256; manifestation in four ways 260; market forces 261; nature of work and leisure 263; non-manual (white-collar) workers 262; owner-worker-consumer syndrome 261; personality market 262;

production process 259; productive labour 258; religion 258; technology and alienation 264; *see also* capitalism
Alienation and Freedom (Blauner) 264
Allan Williams, Jr. J. 169, 170
altruism 201, 225, 226, 256
altruistic suicide 308–309
Ambedkar, B.R. 320
American Revolution 196
analytical surveys 163, 164
ancestral monotheism 352
Ancient mode of production 246, 254
animism 312–314
anomic suicide 306, 308, 309
anomie, concept of 151, 294, 323
anthropologists 41, 65, 68, 76–78, 81, 132, 141, 143, 152, 317
anthropology and sociology: anthropological linguistics 75; comparative sociology 78; convergence between 77–78; differences in subject matter 76; divergence between 75–76; division of labour 76; field-view of Indian society 77; philosophy of history 75; social anthropology 76–78; sociological enquiry, research 77; study of modern society 77
anti-positivists scholars 127, 130, 131, 145, 208, 299, 328, 329, 369
anti-Semitism 279
anti-thesis 46–47, 224–225, 240–243